HOW TO GET RED WINE OUT OF A WHITE CARPET

HOW TO GET RED WINE OUT OF A WHITE CARPET

And 2000 Other Household Hints, Tips and Formulas for Cleaning, Repairing and Organizing Your Home and Simplifying Your Life

BY ERIK BRUUN

Black Dog & Leventhal
Paperbacks

Published by
Black Dog & Leventhal Publishers, Inc.
151 West 19th Street
New York, NY 10011

Distributed by
Workman Publishing Company
708 Broadway
New York, NY 10003

Cover design by Scott Citron
Book design: Martin Lubin Graphic Design

This book was originally published under the title Household Hints
 and Formulas

Manufactured in the USA

Library of Congress Cataloging-in-Publication Data

Bruun, Erik.
    How to get red wine out of a white carpet / by Erik Bruun.
        p. cm.
    Reprint. Originally published: 1994.
    ISBN 1-57912-214-0
        1. House cleaning. 2. Home economics. I. Title.

TX324 .B78 2001
640–dc21
                                                2001037354

This book is dedicated to Lelia Bruun, a great purveyor of common sense in any household.

This book would not have been possible without the assistance of many people who offered their insights into the smooth running of a household. John Townes and Patti Barrett made mighty contributions to the book in several sections. Their timely and substantial aid made a major difference in the publication of this book. Several other associates, friends and family made significant contributions in numerous areas of expertise. Among those who helped research and review the household tips presented here were Bobbi Crosby, Connie Cameron, Connell McGrath, David May, Cathy Kulick, Janis Leventhal, Dick McWhinnie, Marge Currie, Dr. Bertel Bruun, Marianne Swan, Rachel Fletcher, June Spragg, and, finally, my wife Lelia Bruun. I am indebted to all of these people for their kindness and intelligence. All of the strengths of this book come from them. The shortcomings are mine.

CONTENTS

IV. Safety and Environment

V. Daily Living

Introduction

When Dorothy told the residents of Oz in the 1939 movie *The Wizard of Oz* that no matter how humble, there was no place like home, most of the people sitting in the audience did indeed live in humble homes.

More than 50 years after Dorothy reaffirmed the importance of home, the number of households in the United States has nearly tripled to well over 100 million, with close to two-thirds of our homes being single-family houses.

The post-World War II economic boom spurred the housing construction boom and opened the doors to home ownership to vast numbers of families.

In 1939, less than half of the households in the United States owned the homes they lived in compared to close to two-thirds today. What is more, most of our nation's homes are less crowded, far better equipped, and larger than they were 50 years ago, according the U.S. Census. Two-thirds of American homes have better than two rooms per person as compared to one-third in 1940.

With larger homes, more than triple the number of houses in the country, and the responsibility of home ownership being carried by more than 65 million households, the need for simple advice on how to run a household is more important than ever.

The men and women who ran the households of 1940 had something that we often neglect when running our homes today: common sense.

Modernity does not change the fact that you still have to wash the dishes after eating, prepare three meals a day, and seek out ways to cut down on the electric bill. If anything, it has gotten more complicated to run a household despite the convenience of modern appliances like dishwashers, microwave ovens, and home computers.

This book applies the common sense of yesteryear to the conditions of today's homes. We explore ways to make life easier in the kitchen and seek out tips to simplify the never-ending job of cleaning a house. With the dramatic growth in suburban homes and household gardens, we discuss ways to tend to the outdoors. The need for environmental sensitivity is more important than ever as are the unseen dangers of the modern house.

Not every tip in this book will apply to you, but many will. Use this book and the advice it offers wisely. It can help you find ways to spend less time working on your house and more time enjoying your home and family.

KITCHEN HINTS

Eating smart and cheap
Food, glorious food
The intelligent kitchen

Eating smart and cheap

Balance. That is the key to shopping and eating intelligently. We all want to eat food that is good for us but not too hard on the family budget. Temptation and the desire for easy convenience, however, often get the best of us. By knowing what you want and planning for it in advance, you can successfully get your money's worth from food and devise a healthy eating pattern for life.

The National Cancer Institute and National Heart, Lung and Blood Institute have confirmed that by making the right food choices, you may reduce your risk of developing cardiovascular disease and cancer—which combined account for nearly 75 percent of all deaths.

The seven basic guidelines for a healthy diet are:

- Eat a variety of foods.

- Maintain a desirable weight.

- Avoid too much fat, saturated fat, and cholesterol.

- Eat food with adequate starch and fiber.

- Avoid too much sugar.

- Avoid too much salt.

- If you drink alcoholic beverages, do so in moderation.

At the same time, one has to watch one's budget. By being careful and shopping intelligently, it is possible to eat both smart and cheap. Generally speaking, the more convenient the meal, the more expensive it is. Frozen dinners are more expensive than the same meals made from scratch. Eating out costs twice as much on average as eating at home. And remember, no food is a bargain if it is not eaten. Foods that your family will eat and enjoy should be the basis of the meals you serve.

EATING HEALTHY

THE BASIC GOOD STUFF. A good balanced diet includes a selection of vegetables, fruits, whole-grain breads and cereals, low-fat dairy products, poultry, fish, lean meat, dry beans, and peas. By eating a variety of these products, you assure yourself of a healthy diet that avoids too much fat, saturated fat, cholesterol, and salt, and is high in fiber, starch, and protein. To achieve the above goals, you should think about eating more of the following foods:

- **Low-fat meat, poultry, and fish.** Lean cuts of meat trimmed of fat (round tip roast, pork tenderloin, loin lamb chop), poultry without skin, and fish cooked without breading or fat added.

- **Low-fat dairy products.** One percent or skim milk, buttermilk, low-fat or nonfat yogurt, lower fat cheeses (part-skim ricotta, pot and farmer), ice milk, sherbet.

- **Dry beans and peas.** All beans, peas, and lentils—the dry forms are higher in protein.

- **Whole-grain products.** Breads, bagels, and English muffins made from whole wheat, rye, bran, and corn flour or meal; whole grain or bran cereals; whole wheat pasta; brown rice; and bulgur.

- **Fats and oils high in unsaturates.** Unsaturated vegetable oils (such as canola oil, corn oil, cottonseed oil, olive oil, and soybean oil) and margarine; reduced-calorie mayonnaise and salad dressings.

USE SMALL AMOUNTS OF FAT AND FATTY FOODS. There are numerous ways to cut down on fat. Decrease portions of high-fat foods such as rich desserts, untrimmed and fatty types of meat, fried foods, and especially, breaded foods. When you use margarine, mayonnaise, or salad dressing, use half as much as usual. When you sauté or stir-fry, use only 1/2 teaspoon of fat per serving.

USE LESS SATURATED FAT. While reducing the total consumption of fat, substitute unsaturated fats and oils for saturated fat. Instead of butter, use margarine or vegetable oil. One teaspoon of butter can be replaced with equal portions of margarine or 3/4 teaspoon of vegetable oil in many recipes without affecting quality. Use poultry without skin and fish as a main meal as they are usually lower in fat and saturated fat than most meats.

USE LOW-FAT COOKING METHODS. Bake, steam, broil, microwave, or boil foods rather than fry. Skim fat from soups and gravies.

USE HERBS, SPICES, AND OTHER FLAVORINGS. For a different way to add flavor to meals, use lemon juice, basil, chives, allspice, onion, and garlic in place of fats and sodium.

READ THE FOOD LABEL. The federally mandated food labels are a major boon to consumers. They spell out the basic information that serves as a guide to what you're eating. Pay attention to the label if you really want to watch what you eat. Some tips on what to look for on labels:

- **CALORIES.** The average 5'4", 138-pound active woman needs about 2,200 calories a day. The average 5'10", 174-pound active man needs about 2,900 calories. The new labels let you count your calories with greater accuracy so you can figure out how your intake measures up.

- **CARBOHYDRATES.** When you cut down on fat, you can eat more carbohydrates found in foods such as vegetables, fruit, potatoes and bread. You should choose these over the sometimes more tempting sugars in candy and soda.

- **DIETARY FIBER.** We call it fiber; our ancestors called it roughage. Whatever you call it, you want to eat it. Fruits, vegetables, wholegrain foods, beans, and peas are all good sources.

- **PROTEIN.** According to the American Heart Association, most Americans get more protein than they need. Eat small servings of lean meat, fish, and poultry; use skim or low-fat milk, yogurt, and cheese; and get vegetable proteins from beans, grains, and cereals.

- **VITAMINS AND MINERALS.** You want to reach the goal of 100 percent a day. Try not to get all 100 percent from one food source. Instead, eat a variety of foods that add up to the daily recommended allowance.

- **SODIUM AND CHOLESTEROL.** Sodium, or salt, may contribute to high blood pressure for some people. Try to keep your daily sodium intake less than 2,400 to 3,000 mg. Also, watch the amount of cholesterol you consume: it can contribute to heart disease. Try to consume less than 300 mg of cholesterol a day.

GETTING YOUR MONEY'S WORTH

HOMEMADE FROZEN MEALS. By making your own frozen food you can save time and money. When you have time, prepare extra food and freeze in portion sizes you'll need later. Pancakes, waffles, dinner rolls, plate dinners, chicken pie, spaghetti sauce, and lasagna are examples of some of the convenience foods you can make yourself.

FOOD ADS AND COUPONS. Advertised specials may not be good buys compared to other foods you might buy. Collect and use coupons for foods you usually purchase, and are good buys compared to other brands of food. But beware: Specials and coupon offers invite you to buy on

3

impulse, and impulse buying can upset your budget.

COMPLETE SHOPPING LISTS. Most people write partial shopping lists and then seek inspiration as they amble through the aisles. Although this is a perfectly fine way to shop, it tends to divert one from proper planning. A complete shopping list, based on planned menus and including all the foods you need, will limit impulse buying and keep trips to the store to a minimum.

WAREHOUSE STORES. No-frills stores and large supermarkets generally offer better prices. Try to go when the store is not too busy so you do not feel rushed and can shop carefully.

UNIT PRICING. Large container or small-which one? Food in large containers usually costs less than food in smaller containers, but not always. Check it out yourself by comparing unit prices that are displayed in supermarkets.

GENERIC PRODUCTS. Foods with no brand names or advertising may not be as attractive, but they are just as nutritious as brand name foods, and they are usually less expensive. Some of the generic products available include canned fruits and vegetables, breakfast cereals, pasta, rice, and peanut butter.

FATS, SWEETS, AND ALCOHOL. Fats, sweets, and alcohol account for 20 cents of every food dollar spent in the United States, but offer an infinitesimal amount of nutritional value. This group of foods is a good place to start cutting food dollars for the budget- and health-conscious family. They are also a good place to cut calories. Foods such as candies, soft drinks, and alcoholic beverages are not integral parts of a healthy diet and should be eliminated from most people's diets—or at least consumed with moderation. Money spent for diet soft drinks, coffee, and tea provides almost no nutritional return—even in calories

FOOD RECYCLING. Soups, omelets, and casseroles are wonderful ways to recycle leftovers. Think about ways to reuse your food. One pound of leftover meat bones and trimmings—which you can freeze—combined with one quart of water with chopped onions, carrots, celery, and seasoning can be simmered into an interesting soup. You can even add vegetable skins.

WASTE REDUCTION. Millions of dollars of once-edible food is thrown away each day. By carefully planning what you buy and thinking about how you prepare, use, and serve the food, you can save a lot of money. By avoiding buying too much perishable food and preparing meals that can be used as leftovers, you can save on your food budget. (For more information on this, see the chapter on energy and food savings in the kitchen.)

SPICY TIP. You can save more than 50 percent of your costs on store herbs and spices if you buy them in bulk and store them in your own containers.

FRUITS AND VEGETABLES

BUY IN SEASON Supply and season influence prices of fresh vegetables and fruits. Prices of canned, frozen, and dried vegetables and fruits vary widely by item, brand grade, type of process, and seasoning. Cost studies have shown that in-season vegetables and fruits cost only half as much as out-of-season items. Also, foods in season will be at their peak in quality. Keep in mind, however, that some vegetables and fruits, even in season, may not be within your budget.

COMPARE COSTS. Check different forms of a food—fresh, canned, dried, frozen—to see which is the best buy.

LIMIT PERISHABLE PURCHASES. Even at bargain prices, do not be tempted to get more fresh produce than you or your family can consume. There's no point in spending money on food you may be throwing into the trash or the compost pile.

STOCK UP. As opposed to fresh produce, stock up on canned and frozen products your family likes when you discover a bargain.

SEASON YOURSELF. Season and prepare sauces for frozen vegetables yourself. Frozen vegetables with sauce or butter added or boil-in-the-bag vegetables often cost about twice as much as plain frozen vegetables.

DRESSING OVER. When your salad dressing is reaching the end, you can give it new life by adding two teaspoons of vinegar or lemon juice, shaking it, and then slowly whipping in half a cup of sour cream or mayonnaise.

COMPARING PRICES. Although prices are often dictated by season, supply, and locale, some fruits and vegetables are generally more expensive than others. The following is a rough guideline on the least and most costly fruits and vegetables:

- **Fresh fruits:** Least costly: apples, bananas, grapefruit, oranges, pears, and watermelon. Most costly: grapes and honeydew melon.

- **Fresh vegetables:** Least costly: cabbage, carrots, cucumbers, eggplant, green beans, lettuce, onions, potatoes, sweet potatoes, and turnips. Most costly: asparagus, cauliflower, peas, spinach, and winter squash.

- **Canned fruits and juices:** Least costly: apple sauce, apple juice, apricot juice, citrus juices, pineapple juices, and prune juices. Most costly: apricots, berries, cherries, citrus selections, fruit cocktails, peaches, pears, and plums.

- **Canned vegetables:** Least costly: beets, collard greens, corn, green beans, kale, mixed vegetable juices, mixed vegetables, mustard greens, peas, potatoes, tomato juice, and turnip greens. Most costly: asparagus and mushrooms.

■ **Frozen fruits and juices:** Least costly: concentrated citrus juices and other juices. Most costly: berries, cherries, melon balls, and peaches.

■ **Frozen vegetables:** Least costly: carrots and potatoes. Most costly: asparagus, cauliflower, corn on the cob, sweet potatoes, vegetables in pouch or in cheese and other sauces.

BREADS AND CEREALS

EAT MORE BREADS AND CEREALS. A national survey revealed that about 12 cents of every food dollar goes into flour, cereals, and bakery products. But these same products provide 20 percent or more of thiamin, iron, riboflavin, calcium, and protein in the national diet. Given these numbers and the fact that most breads and cereals are relatively cheap, it makes sense to add more bread and cereal into your diets.

ENRICHED BREADS ARE BETTER. Whole-grain or enriched products are much more nutritious than unenriched products. At comparable prices, enriched bread provides three to four times as much thiamin, niacin, riboflavin, and iron as unenriched bread.

DOMESTIC BREADS ARE CHEAPER. Specialty enriched breads such as French and Italian typically cost much more than enriched white bread with similar nutritional value.

BIGGER DOESN'T MEAN BETTER. A large loaf of bread does not always weigh more or contain more food value than a small loaf. Compare prices of equal weights of bread to determine the better buy.

REGULAR RICE RATES LOWER. Converted, precooked, or instant rice usually costs much more than regular rice. Seasoned rice mixes are much more expensive than regular rice you season at home.

BEWARE HIGH-POWERED CEREALS. Cereals may have nutrients added unnecessarily. Many cereals are fortified to provide between 25 and 100 percent of the U.S. Recommended Daily Allowance of some vitamins and minerals. Cereals with 100 percent are often more expensive. If you are coming reasonably close to following a good diet pattern, these highly fortified cereals may be an unnecessary expense.

CEREAL SELECTION. Instant hot cereals in individual packages and ready-to-serve cereals are almost always more expensive than cereals you cook yourself from large cereal boxes.

HOT CEREALS. Prepare hot cereals for breakfast. They're more filling and less expensive than cold cereals.

DAY-OLD ITEMS. Ask or watch for day-old bread and baked goods in stores and bakeries. You can save a lot of money by taking the store's leftovers.

PIZZA COMBINATIONS. Have some fun with different types of bread by making your own pizza from just about anything. Cheddar, Swiss, or Monterey Jack can be used instead of mozzarella. Use peppers, olives, onions, spices, mushrooms, or canned tomatoes to spice up the dish.

DAIRY PRODUCTS AND MEATS

CHEAPER MILK. Buy fresh milk at a supermarket or retail dairy store and not at convenience stores, where it is usually more expensive. Also, milk sold in larger half-gallon and gallon containers is lower in unit cost than milk sold by the quart or pint. If you can use that much milk without waste, you will save money.

NONFAT DRY MILK. Nonfat dry milk has as much calcium, riboflavin, and protein as whole milk, but has no fat and about half as many calories as whole milk. In some areas, nonfat dry milk is also cheaper. Try nonfat dry milk in cooking and as a beverage. Some families mix equal amounts of fresh whole milk and reconstituted nonfat dry milk for drinking.

MILK PRESERVATION. You can use water instead of milk for scrambled eggs or omelets. Water makes the eggs fluffy, milk makes them watery.

GRATING CHEESE. Grated cheese costs more than equal amounts of the same cheese in wedges or sticks.

CHEESE IN BULK. Cheeses in large boxes and jars and cottage cheese in large cartons cost less per pound than the same products in smaller containers.

KEEP IT SIMPLE. Flavored yogurts and cottage cheeses cost more than plain yogurts and cottage cheeses.

ICE CREAM. Ice cream, which costs about three times more than milk for the equivalent amount of calcium, also costs more than ice milk.

CHEAPER MEAT DOESN'T MEAN BEST DEAL. Keep in mind that the economy of a cut of meat depends on the amount of cooked lean meat it provides as well as its price per pound. Often the cut with a low price per pound is not the best buy in food value or in servings of meat provided. It is the amount of cooked lean meat, or the number of servings for the price, that matters. If average amounts of waste are assumed and you count 3 ounces of cooked lean meat as a serving, you will get the following returns on your meat purchase:

- Three to four servings per pound from items with little or no fat such as flank steak, ground meat, round steak, lean stew meat, boneless roast with little fat, liver, a center cut of ham, veal cutlet and fish steaks and fillets.

- Two to three servings per pound from items with a medium amount of bone, gristle, or fat such as most roasts, some chops and steaks, ham, poultry, and dressed fish.

- One to two servings per pound from items with much bone, gristle, or fat such as rib chops of lamb, pork, or veal, plate and breast of lamb or veal, porterhouse steaks, T-bone steaks, club steaks, spareribs, shanks, short ribs, and chicken wings and backs.

POULTRY IS GOOD BUY. One of the least costly main dishes, poultry is also one of the most popular. The form in which poultry is purchased often determines whether it is a bargain. A whole chicken, for example, is usually a better buy than chicken pieces.

SOME FISH ARE BETTER THAN OTHERS. Compared with many cuts of meat, certain kinds of fish are lower in cost. Canned tuna is an economical main dish; light flaked or chunk tuna is less expensive than solid white tuna. Frozen fish fillets are often moderate in cost all year. Canned sardines, mackerel, and herring are usually thrifty purchases but are high in sodium.

MEAT ALTERNATES. Dry beans, dry peas, peanut butter and eggs provide the same protein and many of the same nutrients found in meat. To vary meals at low costs, try these alternatives, which are usually as good or better buys than the less expensive cuts and kinds of meat.

LIGHT ON THE MEAT, HEAVY ON THE FILLER. Use small servings of meat, poultry, and fish and rely on more economical foods—potatoes, rice, macaroni products, and breads—to fill in meals.

SHOPPING CAREFULLY. Before selecting your meat, look over the entire counter. You may find the same type of meat in different packaging that is better in quality and less expensive.

STRETCHING YOUR MEAT DOLLAR Get all the flavor and value from a piece of meat by using leftover meat in casseroles, salads, sandwiches, and as flavoring for cooked vegetables. Cook meat bones with beans or soup. Use broth to moisten meat.

LONG-LASTING MEALS. Plan up to a week's worth of meals around a large single piece of meat. For example, you can cook a leg of lamb on the first day, have a sliced hot lamb sandwich the next day, shepherd's pie on day 3 and a barley and vegetable soup with stock from the bone on the fourth day.

HEALTHY SNACKS

STOCKING UP. Fill your kitchen with plain or spiced popcorn (don't use microwave popcorn with added fat), whole-grain crackers, unsweetened fruit juices, fresh fruits and vegetables, plain low-fat yogurt, and low-fat, low-sodium cheeses.

PORTABLE FRUIT. Carry a naturally sweet fresh fruit (such as a pear, orange or grapes) for a snack rather than buying candy.

SNACKS ARE SNACKS. Snacks should not supplant meals. Make sure you don't spoil dinner by eating too much of a good snack.

DIETARY FIBER. What you want out of snacks besides good taste is good fiber. Fresh fruits with edible seeds such as berries or skins (apples, peaches), dried fruits, raw vegetables, and whole-grain crackers and bread are all good sources of fiber.

BRUSH THOSE TEETH. If you choose a sticky food such as dried fruit, plan to brush your teeth soon afterwards; otherwise: tooth decay.

FRUIT POPS. Blend different types of fruit together in a processor and then freeze the concoction for a healthy snack.

YOGURT SAUCES. Make sauces and dips with nonfat plain yogurt as the base.

CHIP ALTERNATIVES. Instead of chips, try toasted shredded wheat squares sprinkled with a small amount of grated Parmesan cheese, whole-grain English muffins, or toasted plain corn tortillas.

EATING OUT WITH AN EYE TOWARD HEALTH

CHOOSING THE RIGHT PLACE. Depending on where you go, you can determine the health qualities of your meals. Generally you exercise more control over your dietary destiny in full-service restaurants, cafeterias, steakhouses and pizza parlors. You become more subject to the whims of others in fast-food restaurants, convenience stores, and other people's homes.

TRY ETHNIC CUISINES. Italian and Asian restaurants often feature low-fat dishes, but you have to be selective and aware of portion sizes. Chinese (stay away from the fried foods), Japanese, and Thai (beware the coconut milk) restaurants offer many vegetable-based meals, steamed rice, steamed noodles, and vegetarian meals. A small serving of pasta and a salad at an Italian restaurant is a good healthy choice. Some Latin American restaurants offer a variety of fish and chicken dishes that are low in fat.

HEALTHY APPETIZERS. Enjoy steamed seafood, raw vegetables, or fruit. Go easy on rich sauces, dips, and batter-fried foods such as cheese sticks, vegetables, and chicken pieces. If you want a soup, order a cup and not a bowl. Most soups are heavy on the sodium.

WATCH THOSE CONDIMENTS. Butter and other spreads can make the plainest bread high in fat and calories. Limit your use of soy sauce, steak sauce, ketchup, mustard, pickles, and other condiments that are high in sodium. Ask for pepper or an herb blend instead of salt.

BREAD IS BETTER THAN CRACKERS. Whole-grain types of bread such as wheat, bran, oat, and rye are particularly good, but so are other types of simple breads. They are much preferable to croissants, biscuits, hush puppies, and sweet rolls, which tend to have much higher fat and sugar levels.

VEGETABLES. Look for vegetables seasoned with lemon, herbs, or spices rather than butter and salt. Ask for a tossed salad or baked potato instead of French fries or chips.

DELI DELICACIES. Choose lean deli meats such as turkey or ham over high-fat cold cuts such as salami and bologna. Go heavy on lettuce and tomato for sandwich fillers and light on the mayonnaise, pickles, and oil.

DESSERT. Fruits are the best desserts. If there are none listed under the dessert section, check out the appetizer section. Or order a light dessert such as sherbet, sorbet, or fruit ice, all of which are much lower in calories and fat than ice cream. If you want a rich dessert, split it with a companion.

TELLTALE TERMS. Certain terms on the menu just reek of sodium and fat, offering valuable clues to what you may be getting yourself into dietwise. Some terms that signal higher fat are: buttered or butter; fried; breaded; creamed, creamy, or in a cream sauce; in its own gravy, with gravy, or pan gravy; hollandaise; au gratin or in cheese sauce; scalloped or escalloped; rich; or pastry. Menu descriptions that tip off high sodium content include: smoked, pickled, barbecued, in broth, in cocktail sauce, in a tomato base, with soy sauce, teriyaki, Creole sauce, mustard sauce, marinated, and Parmesan.

DON'T BE AFRAID TO ASK. Restaurants can't always meet every one of your needs, but they often can accommodate you. Besides, it never hurts to ask. After studying the menu—or even better, calling ahead to ask about a restaurant's culinary flexibility—feel free to discuss sizes, how the meals are prepared, the availability of food items not on the menu, and whether they can alter their cooking methods for your special request.

NAVIGATE FAST FOOD. Although fast-food restaurants have increasingly steered away from serving junk food by offering healthful options, much of the food you can find there is high in sodium, which you want to avoid. Nevertheless, you can eat a relatively healthy meal in a fast-food restaurant by loading up on salads (but go easy on the dressings), skipping dessert, choosing milk, juice, or water instead of soda or a milk shake, and skipping French fries if you order a sandwich that is deep-fat fried or served with sauce or cheese. For the main meal, you may want to order roast beef over a hamburger. And one last little-known fact: Breaded and deep-fat fried fish and chicken sandwiches have more fat and calories than plain burgers.

Food, glorious food

GENERAL COOKING TIPS

FRYING PAN TIPS. Heat the frying pan before adding butter or oil when frying. If you sprinkle salt onto the pan it will prevent spattering. To prevent food from sticking to the pan, boil a little bit of vinegar in the pan when it is new. Combine butter with oil to reduce the chances of burning.

BROILED WATER. Pour a cup of water into the bottom portion of a broiling pan before using it in the oven. The water will absorb grease and smoke.

KNIFE SHARPENING. Make a habit of sharpening your knife each time you use it. When it comes time for a professional sharpening, ask your butcher who he or she uses.

ODOR OVERRIDERS. Slowly cook a few teaspoons of cinnamon and sugar on top of the stove to enhance the smell of your kitchen and cover up unpleasant smells.

THE RIGHT TEMPERATURE. If you are going to fry or sauté food, make sure the food is at room temperature for best results.

EXTRA COUNTER SPACE. You can add extra counter space to your kitchen through a couple of nifty tricks. Pull out the drawers and place cookie pans or trays on top, place a wooden board over the sink, or set up the ironing board.

FROZEN FRESHNESS. Whenever you cook something that has been frozen, add something fresh like parsley, dill, or lemon juice to give the dish some extra life.

WAXED ICE TRAYS. Place wax paper underneath ice cube trays to prevent them from sticking to the freezer shelf.

OIL SPRAY. Keep a spray bottle with a small amount of oil in it by the stove. When you want the oil for pans, meats, fish, and other uses, you will have easy access to the oil.

THAWING. If you have time, the best way to thaw frozen food is to let it sit in the refrigerator. This is especially true for meat and poultry for reasons of both safety and taste.

CARDBOARD CARTON CHARCOAL. Pack pieces of charcoal in cardboard egg cartons for cookouts to prevent making a mess on the way. Also, you can light the charcoal by igniting the carton.

ALPHABET SPICES. If you have trouble remembering where your spices are, put them in a rack in alphabetic order.

CONDIMENTS AND BEVERAGES

Sugar and honey

HONEY SLIDES. Before plunging a spoon into a honey jar, run hot water over the spoon; the honey will easily slide off the spoon. The same holds true for pouring honey into a measuring cup.

DECRYSTALLIZED HONEY. Place crystallized honey into a microwave for up to a minute—depending on the amount of crystallization—to restore the honey's freshness and usefulness.

CRACKERS AND SUGAR. To prevent sugar from caking, put a couple of crackers in the sugar canister.

Coffee and tea

TASTY TEA. Hard mint candy or lemon drops plopped into your tea is a tasty alternative to sugar, giving the beverage a tangy flavor. Or you can add leftover orange, apple, or lemon rind.

ENHANCED FLAVORS. Dry an old orange peel and stick in a tin of tea to add flavor to the tea leaves.

COFFEE CONDIMENT. Rather than buying gourmet coffees, add almond extract or vanilla to your coffee as it brews.

PURE WATER = BETTER COFFEE. Coffee will often taste better if you use purified water. It also helps extend the life of your coffee maker.

COFFEE STORAGE. Store coffee in a tight container in your refrigerator or, even better, the freezer. It will keep the flavor better.

LEFTOVER COFFEE CUBES. Wondering to do with that leftover dose of coffee? Pour it in an ice tray and freeze it. The cubes can be used in eggnog, milk, or for cooling off the next batch of piping hot coffee.

NO-SPILL FUNNELS. Avoid spilling by using a funnel to fill your thermos bottle.

Salt, pepper and more

SALT SAVER. Add a few grains of rice to the salt shaker to prevent moisture from clumping up the salt.

SHAKER HOLE PLUGGERS. Use colorless fingernail polish to plug holes in salt shakers. Be sure to clean the shaker top thoroughly prior to applying the polish.

STRAW SOLUTION. Instead of waiting impatiently for ketchup to seep out of a new bottle, insert a straw or butter knife to the bottom of the bottle. When you remove the straw the ketchup will flow more rapidly.

BLACK RINGS. Don't worry if there is a black ring along the top of a ketchup or mustard jar. It is safe. Just wipe it off.

OIL AND VINEGAR COAGULATOR. To keep oil and vinegar from parting ways, add a little bit of egg white and shake up the dressing.

OIL THEN VINEGAR. When mixing oil and vinegar into a salad, put the oil in first. If you put the vinegar in first, the oil tends to slip off the lettuce.

CURRY ENHANCER. Make your curry powder more pungent by heating it up in the oven for five minutes or less and then adding the powder to the dish.

OLD SPICE JARS. Put old spice jars to use as salad dressing containers for picnics and box lunches. When you let the dressing sit in a salad, it tends to wilt. This way will keep the salad crisp.

KEEPING SANDWICHES DRY. For picnics and box lunches, instead of applying mayonnaise or other wet condiments to the bread in a sandwich, spread it between the meats and lettuce. This will prevent the bread from getting soggy.

DAIRY PRODUCTS

Butter

BIGGER BUTTER. You can make butter spread more easily and put it to greater use by whipping it up with an electric beater. Be sure to let the butter warm to room temperature first. This can increase the butter to almost twice its normal volume.

BUTTER CUTTER. A heated knife is the easiest way to cut cold butter.

BUTTER DEBURNING TACTIC. Add a dab of vegetable oil or olive oil to butter to help prevent it from burning while sautéing.

SOFTENED-UP BUTTER. Cover hard butter with an upside-down heated cooking dish (similar to a dome) to soften it.

REVIVING OLD BUTTER. Knead cold water and a bit of carbonated water into stale or tainted butter and let it sit for a couple of hours.

ICED BUTTER CUBES. Add herbs to melted butter, pour the concoction into an ice tray, and freeze it. Next time you want to make a vegetable sauce you will have the basic ingredients at hand.

Cheese

FROZEN CHEESES. Some cheeses you can freeze and some you can't. You can freeze Swiss, cheddar, Edam, Gouda, Muenster, provolone, and other natural cheeses from Greece, Italy, and France.

CHEESE FRESHENER. To keep cheese fresh and free of mold, wrap it in a vinegar-soaked cloth. When you cut cheese, butter the edge of the left-over piece to prevent the cheese from drying out.

CHEESE STORAGE. Store cheese in its original wrapper whenever possible, but be sure to give it air by opening it occasionally to keep it fresh.

MOLDY CHEESE PREVENTION. Add a couple of lumps of sugar to the container that is holding your cheese, to help keep the cheese moist.

CHEESY TEMPERATURE. Serve cheese at room temperature. Think ahead by removing the cheese from the refrigerator about an hour before you intend to serve it.

GREAT CHEESE GRATING. Dab a bit of vegetable oil on the grater before you grate the cheese. This will make the grating go more smoothly and will ease things when it comes time for washing.

COTTAGE CHEESE STORAGE. To make your cottage cheese last longer, store it upside down in the refrigerator.

Eggs

EGG-CRACKING PREVENTION. Generally speaking, fresh eggs tend to crack more easily than older eggs. Add a teaspoon of vinegar to water when you are boiling eggs to lessen the chances of cracking. If an egg does crack during boiling, add a touch of vinegar to seal the crack. Rub wet salt over the shell of a cracked egg before boiling it. This will keep the white from leaking out. Do not despair if you have cracked an egg. Wrap it with aluminum foil and you can soft- or hard-boil it.

POKED EGGS. Stick a sharp needle into the broad end of an egg before putting it in boiling water to prevent the egg from cracking.

GAUGING EGGS. Old eggs are smooth and shiny. Fresh eggs look rough and dull. Bad eggs float to the surface of cool, salted water. Fresh eggs sink. You can determine whether an egg is raw by spinning it. If it wobbles, it is raw. If it spins easily, it has been boiled.

OPENED EGGS. If you crack open an egg and discover that the white is very watery, the egg is not fresh.

CENTERED YOLKS. Gently stir the water while you are hard-boiling eggs to keep the yolk in the center of the egg.

MEDIUM EGGS. Don't use extra large eggs for baking cakes. They may cause the cakes to fall.

SLICING EGGS. Wet the knife before you slice hard-boiled eggs to prevent the yolk from falling apart.

CONTAINED POACHED EGGS. Add a tablespoon of vinegar to the water before poaching eggs. This will help contain the egg whites in the water.

FUNNELED EGGS. Here's a clever way to separate the yolk from the egg white. Crack a raw egg into a funnel. The white will slip through the funnel and the yolk will stay on top. Don't forget to accumulate the egg whites in a pan or bowl below.

EGG DABBING. If part of an egg yolk leaks into the white while separating, you can pick up the yolk by touching it with a damp cloth or with half of an egg shell.

SHELL REMOVAL. The quicker you rinse hard-boiled eggs after boiling the easier it will be to remove the shells. To remove the shell easily, bang the egg on the side of the sink until the surface is thoroughly cracked. This will make for relatively easy picking.

TWO WHITES IN ONE. To double the volume of egg whites, add a teaspoon of water for each egg white before beating.

EXTRA EGG WHITES. If you have lots of extra egg whites, you can use them to make a face mask. Leave the mixture on until there's a slick surface; then wash it off with water.

FROZEN EGG WHITES. Put leftover egg whites in ice-tray cubes. When they are frozen, pop them out and store them in the freezer in a plastic bag for future use.

Milks and creams

BOILING MILK. Two tips. (1) Sprinkle a teaspoon of sugar into milk before boiling it to help prevent the milk from burning. Don't stir the sugar. (2) To avoid boiling-over the milk, first rinse the pan with very cold water. This will also limit the amount of milk sticking to the pan.

HOMEMADE CONDENSED MILK. Here's how to make sweetened condensed milk at home: mix 1/2 cup of hot water with 1 1/2 cups granulated sugar. Then slowly add 2 1/2 cups of dry skim milk powder. Put it in a refrigerator for a full day.

FROZEN CREAM. Freeze leftover heavy cream for later use. Remember that once frozen, heavy cream can never be whipped again.

ACCELERATED CREAM WHIPPING. You can cut in half the amount of time it takes to whip cream by adding three to four drops of lemon juice for each cup of cream prior to whipping. Chilling the cream, bowl, and beater also hastens the whipping the process.

STUBBORN WHIPPING CREAM? If your cream refuses to cooperate in the whipping, add one egg white and try again.

HONEY AND WHIPPED CREAM. When you add honey instead of sugar to whipped cream, the cream will stay firm longer and will have an extra special sweetness.

CLEAN-UP REDUCTION. You can prevent splatter when whipping cream by either setting the bowl in the sink, thus making it easier to clean up afterwards, or by placing a cover or towel between the beaters and the machine.

SPLATTER PROTECTION. If you are using a hand-held beater, use a paper plate to protect yourself from splatters by punching two holes in the plate, inserting the blade posts through it and then connecting it to the beater. The plate will serve as a shield while you batter.

WHIPPED CREAM CUBES. If you have leftover whipped cream, put dabs of it on waxed paper and freeze them. Once they are frozen, collect them in a bag. The frozen cream is great for future uses such as dessert toppings or dual-purpose coolants for hot chocolate or coffee.

FRUITY YOGURT. Experiment with your own yogurt flavors by mixing plain yogurt and fresh fruit in a blender. The fruit gives the yogurt a freshness you won't find in stores.

SOUR CREAM SOLUTION. Make your own sour cream by mixing three or four drops of lemon juice with 3/4 cup whipping cream and leaving the concoction at room temperature for 30 minutes.

VEGETABLES

General tips

VEGETABLE FRESHENER. To make wilted vegetables crisp and fresh again, add a splash of vinegar to the water in which you are soaking the vegetables.

UNFREEZING FROZEN VEGETABLES. Pour boiling water over frozen vegetables and then cook the vegetables as you would if they were fresh.

VEGETABLE LINER. Place a wet towel in the bottom of the vegetable compartment of your refrigerator and/or place a dry sponge in the compartment to absorb moisture, thus preventing mildew and keeping the fruit and vegetables fresher longer.

THE ADVANTAGES OF STEAMING. Steam vegetables rather than boil them to keep them crisp. Steaming also preserves more of the vegetable's nutrients than does boiling.

WILTED VEGGIES? If fresh vegetables are looking tired and are browning, tear off the brown edges, sprinkle the vegetable with cool water, wrap it in a paper towel, and place it in the refrigerator for about an hour.

VEGETABLE STORAGE GUIDELINES. Potatoes, onions, and squash should be stored in cool, dark places. Root vegetables will remain fresh for about two weeks in the refrigerator. When you store the root vegetables be sure to tear or cut off the green tops, which will extract nutrients in storage.

VEGETABLE WATER. Save the water from boiled vegetables for later use in stews, soups, or casseroles. The water is flavorful and rich in minerals and vitamins.

FROZEN HERBS. Herbs are excellent candidates for freezing. Wash the herb and put it in a plastic container. When you need the herb, cut off the amount you need.

Celery

HOMEMADE CELERY SALT. Dry celery leaves thoroughly and then crush them to a powder and mix with salt to make your own celery salt.

CELERY STORAGE. Soak celery in lemon juice and water before storing in the refrigerator to prevent it from turning brown.

CELERY PEELING. Rid your celery of strings by peeling it with a potato peeler.

Corn

AN EYE FOR THE RIGHT EAR. Do not buy husked corn. The flavor has escaped. You can tell if an ear is reasonably fresh by whether the butt of the ear is dry or brown, or if the leaves at the top are shriveled. All are sure signs of old corn.

CORN SILK REMOVAL. Brush downward on a cob of corn with a damp paper towel or terry cloth to remove strands of corn silk. Another technique is to rub the cob with a vegetable brush under running water.

CORN STORAGE. The fresher the corn, the better. But if you have to store it, stick the butt end in water when you refrigerate it.

SHOE-HORNED CORN. Use a shoe horn to shear off kernels of corn from the cob. The shape is perfect.

COLD CORN. If you have leftover ears of corn, cover them in cellophane and keep the plastic wrap in the refrigerator. Cold corn is a tasty and healthy treat for snacking.

Garlic

GARLIC BUSTING AND STORAGE. Using a broad chef's knife, smash down on the garlic with the knife's broad side. The garlic will break open and is ready for peeling. Once peeled, store the garlic in cooking oil. The garlic will stay moist and you can use the garlic-tainted oil for cooking.

PEELING GARLIC. Drop garlic in boiling water for a few seconds to loosen its skin for peeling.

GARLIC PASTING. Work a little bit of salt into the garlic with a butter knife until you have a puree of garlic that you can use as a substitute for regular garlic. This has the added advantage of not having nasty little pieces of garlic floating around your meals that can get stuck in your mouth.

THE IMPLICATIONS OF FINE GARLIC. The darker you let your garlic become and the finer you chop it, the more pungent the flavor when it comes time to cook it.

GARLIC DEODORIZER. Rub your hands with fresh ginger to remove the smell of garlic and onions.

BITTER GARLIC. Don't overcook garlic when sautéing. It will turn bitter.

Herbs and spices

HERBAL STORAGE. Fresh basil, dill, parsley, and watercress can be kept fresh for a week or more by washing them and putting them upright in a glass with a bit of water at the bottom. Put a plastic bag over the glass and refrigerate.

FRESH HERBS VS. DRY HERBS. The rule of thumb with herbs is to use three times the amount of fresh herbs as dried herbs for the same impact. With dried herbs, crunch the herbs with your hands to release the flavor.

FROZEN HERBS. Freeze fresh herbs by placing them in the cubes of ice trays and pouring water into the tray. Once the trays have been frozen, remove the cubes and place them in a plastic bag in the freezer. When it comes time to use the herbs, just plop the frozen cubes into whatever you are cooking.

GINGER STORAGE. Preserve ginger by putting it in a plastic bag in the freezer. Every time you need fresh ginger, grate the desired amount and put the rest back in the freezer.

MICROWAVE HERBS. For instant-drying herbs, place them in a paper towel in the microwave oven and turn the oven on high for a minute.

Lettuce and cabbage

CORING ICEBERG LETTUCE. Smash the lettuce head on the counter and twist the core out to prevent the lettuce from going rusty. Always tear lettuce as cutting causes the edges to turn brown. Lettuce stays fresh longer if it is stored in a brown paper bag.

PAPER BAG PRESERVATION. Lettuce, celery, and some other vegetables last longer if you keep them in paper rather than plastic bags.

CABBAGE DEODORIZERS. Ways to stifle the stink from boiling cabbage include: (1) plopping a walnut in the boiling water; (2) adding a bit of baking soda—which also keeps the vegetable green; or (3) simmering a pan of vinegar on top of the stove to neutralize the smell.

Onions and peppers

SWEET ONIONS. By sprinkling sugar on onions, they will sauté more evenly.

MILDER ONIONS. Let onion rings sit in cold water for about an hour before serving with salads to make the taste more mild.

NO MORE ONION TEARS. For this most vexing of kitchen complaints, try the following tactics:

- Soak the onions in cold water for 5 to 10 minutes before peeling them under a running tap.
- Peel the onions while holding them under water.
- Place the onions in the freezer for a short time—about five minutes—before peeling or cutting them.
- Chew gum when you're peeling onions.
- Cut the root end of the onion last. If you keep the root attached, the leftover onion will last longer.

PEPPER COATING. Cover peppers with olive oil before stuffing and baking them to keep the vegetable's original color

BUTTERED ONIONS. Rub the cut edges of onions with butter before putting them in the refrigerator.

Potatoes

POTATO STORAGE. To keep potatoes from sprouting, add a few apples to the pile.

PEELED POTATOES. To extend the life of peeled potatoes, store them in a refrigerator in water with a dash of vinegar added.

PARTIAL POTATO PEELING. If you are boiling potatoes with the skin still on them, peel a band around the center of the potato to prevent the skin from bursting. Also, the potatoes will look more appealing.

SPEED POTATO BAKING. To speed up the baking process, boil the potato in salt water for about 10 minutes before putting it in a hot oven. Another way to hasten the baking is to cut a thin slice from each end of the potato before putting it in the oven.

DESKINNING. Do yourself a favor and wait to skin vegetables and fruits like potatoes, tomatoes, and pears until after you have boiled them. The skins come off much more easily and cooking with the skins on helps to retain their flavor and nutrients. Be sure not to overcook.

WHITE POTATOES. Add a dash of lemon juice to the water when you boil peeled potatoes to keep them white.

REHEATED POTATOES. Leftover baked potatoes can be used later by dipping them in water and baking them at 350 degrees Fahrenheit until they are heated through.

GOUGE THOSE POTATO EYES. Remove potato eyes; they are poisonous.

REVIVED POTATOES. For dried-out and apparently spent old potatoes, soak them in cold water and put them in the refrigerator to add new life.

Tomatoes

TOMATO RIPENERS. If you store apples with green tomatoes, the tomatoes will ripen faster than normal. If you put them all in a paper bag and poke a hole in the bag and place it in a dark and cool place, the ripening process will be even quicker. Ethylene gas emitted from the apple causes the tomato to ripen. The same can be done with peaches and pears.

DIRECT SUNLIGHT BAD. Never put tomatoes in direct sunlight; it will make them mushy.

LIFESPAN OF TOMATO. Tomatoes will remain fresh for three days if left uncovered in a refrigerator. On the other hand, if you pick tomatoes and cherry tomatoes late in the season, store them in a dark place and they will remain tasty.

TOMATO PEELING. Stick a fork in the tomato and hold it over the gas burner until the skin starts to blister and get dark. Remove the tomato from the burner and the fork and you will be able to peel its skin off easily. Or you can submerge the tomato in boiling water for 30 seconds and then peel.

FROZEN TOMATOES. Leftover tomatoes can be frozen and later used for stews.

Miscellaneous vegetables

ASPARAGUS STORAGE. Trim the stem ends of the asparagus and then wrap the vegetables in wet paper towels or stand them up in a container with a small amount of water to keep them fresh for a day or two.

ASPARAGUS CORES. There is no reason to throw away the tough lower portions of asparagus stalks. Use a potato peeler to peel the stalks until you get to the tender interior and add the core to the asparagus tips when you cook them.

AVOCADO RIPENING. Put avocados in a bowl of flour to hasten the ripening process. Or place the avocado in a brown bag for a couple of days.

CRUSHING AN AVOCADO. Turn your avocado into mush by putting it through a potato ricer. This is the quickest way to achieve an even consistency for dips and guacamole. Add lemon juice to prevent the avocado from turning brown.

BRUSSELS SPROUT CROSSES. For quicker and more consistent cooking, cut a cross into the stem of Brussels sprouts.

CARROTS AND APPLES DON'T MIX. Never store apples with carrots. The apples emit a gas that gives the carrots a bitter taste.

FADING MUSHROOMS. Resurrect fading mushrooms into a tasty appetizer by marinating the in a vinaigrette dressing.

PEELED SQUASH. Save yourself the trouble of peeling acorn and butternut squash by cutting the vegetable in sections, removing the seeds, and cooking. Once you are done cooking, scoop out the pulp.

FRUIT

General tips

SPEEDY RIPENING. Ripen green fruits by placing them in a perforated plastic bag. The bag retains the odorless gas that fruits produce to promote ripening and the holes allow air movement.

LIME JUICE AND FRUIT CUPS. For a delicious snack or dessert, slice up whatever fruit is in season, mix it all up, and squeeze a lime over the mix.

MOLDY FRUIT. Moldy fruit is safe to eat; just cut out the icky bits.

PEACHES AND PLUMS. The best peaches are the freshest peaches. Once picked, a peach does not get any sweeter, just mushier. So pick the firmest peaches you can find. With plums, however, the soft ones are the sweetest. But not too soft—those are rotting.

Bananas

BANANA RIPENER. Wrap green bananas in a wet towel and put them in a brown paper bag to speed the ripening process. Ripe bananas are more fattening than green ones.

APPLES AND BANANAS DON'T MIX. If you place apples and bananas in the same dish, the ethylene from the apples will rapidly brown the bananas.

SHAPELY APPLE SLICES. Stop your apple slices from getting too mushy when cooked by adding sugar to the slices prior to cooking.

APPLE CRACK PREVENTION. Stop apple skins from cracking when baked by carving a thin band out of the skin around the center of the apple.

BANANA SAVING TACTIC. Peel and mash leftover bananas and sprinkle lemon juice on them before putting the mixture in an airtight container in the freezer. Use one lemon for every six bananas. You can use the frozen banana mix later for recipes that need ripe bananas.

PICKING BANANAS. The best bananas to buy are the bright yellow ones with a touch of green at the stem and no bruises. Although these bananas are underripe, you will have time to let them ripen at home.

Berries

BRIGHT BERRIES BEST. The brighter the berry, the better the berry. Cherries are at their sweetest when they are dark red and still firm.

BERRY STORAGE. Store berries unwashed in a perforated container or colander in the refrigerator. They will last several days.

BERRY FREEZING. Freeze berries by putting them on a cookie sheet first and, once frozen, pack them into an airtight container. Put them back in the freezer. This will prevent berries from turning into mush.

Lemons, oranges, and citrus fruits

LEMON PRESERVER. Cover the cut surface of a lemon with egg white to help preserve the lemon's freshness.

CITRUS REFRIGERATION. Citrus fruits will stay reasonably fresh in a refrigerator for three to four weeks.

LEMON AND LIME CUTS. If you have one of those households where you only need bits and pieces of lemons and limes at a time, take note. Cut a lemon or lime into quarters and freeze the section pieces in a plastic bag. Next time you need a lemon or lime quarter, you will have a fresh one available.

JUICY FRUITS. Use the following tactics to get more juice out of your citrus fruit:

- Zap lemons in a microwave before squeezing or let the lemons sit in a heated oven for a few minutes.

- Place the citrus fruit in hot water for 15 minutes and roll it on a hard surface before squeezing.

- Store oranges at room temperature.

EASY PEELING. Soak oranges in very hot water for a few minutes to soften up the rind for peeling. Or pour boiling water over the fruit for the same results.

TANGERINE PEELS. Next time a recipe calls for an orange peel, you'll be glad you followed this tip. Dry out old tangerine peels and then pulverize the peel into small pieces by throwing it in a blender. Store the pieces in a dry place.

ORANGE PICKING. Good oranges are firm and heavy with nicely textured skins. The sweetest oranges are Kings, Temples, and Valencias.

CITRUS SMELL KILLERS. Make a pomander out of an old lemon or orange by sticking cloves into the fruit. Hang the pomander in the kitchen, bathroom, or anywhere else that you would like to smell nice. The pomander will last for years.

SWEET GRAPEFRUITS. Grapefruits have reached their sweetness peak when their skins turn greenish yellow.

Melons

SMELLY MELONS. Generally speaking, sweet smell is a sign of ripeness in a melon.

GAUGING WATERMELONS. Watermelons that are firm and smooth and with creamy undersides are good picks. Knock the outside of the melon with your fist. If it is ripe, you should hear a hollow thumping sound. The deeper the red in the melon, the juicier the melon. White streaks indicate a lack of sweetness.

CANTALOUPE COVER. When storing cantaloupes in a refrigerator be sure to remember to cover them to prevent the melon's odor from contaminating other food and the refrigerator.

HONEYDEW TIPS. Honeydew melons that are greenish white and feel very hard will most likely never ripen properly. The best honeydew melons have smooth skin and are creamy or yellowish white.

SOUPS, GRAVIES, SNACKS, AND OTHER TIDBITS

Soups

SALTY SOUP. If there's too much salt in your soup, plop in a cut raw potato. The potato will absorb the salt. Once the soup is finished, remove the potato. Or add a teaspoon of cider vinegar and a teaspoon of sugar.

BROTH ENHANCEMENT. Add chopped onions, carrots, and celery—and maybe even a dash of red wine—to chicken or beef broth to enhance the flavor. Let it simmer for 20 minutes or so.

FATTY SOUP REMOVAL. Drop a couple of ice cubes into soup to attract fat on the top of the brew. The fat will stick to the ice cubes and you can remove them. Plan B calls for removing fats by running a lettuce leaf slowly through the soup. The leaf absorbs the grease.

THE BEST FAT REMOVER. If you have the time, the best way to remove fat from soup is to put the soup in the refrigerator and allow the fat to harden. Then place a piece of wax paper over the top of the soup, let it sit for a while, and then peel it off with the coagulated fat.

SOUP POTATO THICKENER. Try thickening your soup with powdered mashed potatoes instead of flour. It makes for a tastier thickener than flour.

ICED SOUP CUBES. Leftover soup can be turned into a handy and healthy snack by pouring the remains into an ice cube tray and placing it in the freezer. Simply thaw the cubes when you are ready for soup again. Or you can pour the soup in a round bowl, freeze the whole thing and then dump the frozen soup into a plastic bag to store in the freezer. When it comes time to eat the soup, you will have exact portions ready to thaw.

Sauces and gravy

SAUCY TIP. Stir 1 teaspoon of flour into sour cream before adding it to a sauce that will boil. In this way the sauce can boil but the sour cream won't curdle because of the flour.

PINCH OF SALT. By adding a pinch of salt to the flour before mixing it into the gravy you will add some zest to the gravy and cut down on lumps.

BAKING SODA AND GREASE. A pinch of baking soda added to gravy will absorb excess grease.

EXCESSIVE FAT. Get rid of the extra fat in the gravy by letting it float to the top and then skimming the top with a very dry piece of bread to absorb it.

WINE AND GRAVY. When you add wine to gravy you might want to consider cooking it for 10 or 15 minutes extra. The alcohol will be boiled off but the flavor will remain.

GRAVY GROWTH. Stretch your gravy by adding a teaspoon of beef or chicken bouillon, some water and flour or cornstarch, and mixing it all up.

GRAVY THICKENER. The best way to thicken gravy is to blend flour and butter together and add to it to the gravy by beating it in a little bit at a time, or by adding water and cornstarch.

COFFEE'S ROLE. By adding a bit of instant coffee you can turn pale gravy brown without adding any bitter taste.

SMOOTH GRAVY. Get the lumps out of your gravy by running it through a sieve or beating the gravy with a whisk.

DARK GRAVY. Make your gravy dark and brown by browning the flour in a pan prior to mixing it into the gravy.

Rice and pasta

RICE WHITENER. While the rice is boiling, add lemon juice to keep the grains whole and the rice white.

REHEATED RICE. Place cooked rice in a coffee filter and place the filter in a vegetable steamer over boiling water. The steam reheats the rice without making it mushy.

FLAVORED RICE. Instead of using water to boil rice, try chicken or beef broth or even pure tomato juice.

LIMITED BOILING WATER. Add a lump of butter or a couple of spoonfuls of cooking oil to water when boiling pasta or rice to prevent the water from boiling over.

DAY-OLD PASTA. Reheat old pasta that has been put in a refrigerator by sautéing it in butter. Add garlic powder for extra flavor.

Oils

WOK CLEANSER. Prevent your wok from rusting by spraying vegetable oil in the wok after cleaning and drying it.

OIL DISPENSER. Thoroughly clean out an old detergent bottle to hold cooking oil. When it comes time to use the oil you can simply squirt the oil into the pan.

SLITTED OIL. Instead of removing the seal and cap from your bottle of oil, slit a hole in the cap. This will allow you to be more precise when you measure the oil for recipes.

Popcorn, nuts, and other snacks

FROZEN NUTS. You will find it much easier to crack open most nuts if you keep them in the freezer. This is especially true for Brazil nuts.

NUT CHOPPING MADE EASY. You'll find chopping and cutting nuts much easier if you first put the shelled nuts in the oven at 350 degrees for about five minutes.

BAD NUTS. Nuts that smell or look moldy produce cancer-causing agents known as aflatoxins, so don't eat them.

ALMOND SKINNING. Make life simple for yourself when it comes time to skin almonds by dropping the almonds in boiling water and then letting them cool off for a couple of minutes. All you have to do now is pinch the almonds to pop the nut out of its skin.

POPCORN ON ICE. Frozen popcorn kernels will provide puffier and larger popcorn and fewer kernels will fail to pop. Running ice cold water over the kernels before popping will also eliminate duds.

PREHEATED POPPER. Preheat the hot-air popper and you will increase the percentage of popped kernels and your yield of popcorn will be fluffier.

CRISPY SANDWICHES. Instead of sticking the lettuce in a sandwich for picnics or brown bag lunches, wrap the lettuce in a wet towel and put it to the side. When it comes time to eat, place the lettuce in the sandwich. This will prevent the sandwiches from getting soggy while they sit.

ALTERNATIVE BABY FOOD. Purée frozen vegetables in a food processor and pour the results into an ice cube tray. Freeze the mix and then wrap them into individual servings for future use. You can do the same thing with leftovers.

SEAFOOD

FISHY SELECTIONS. Fish fillets should not smell fishy. When buying whole fish, the gills should be red, the eyes clear, and the scales moist on a firm flesh.

FISH THAW. Thaw fish in milk. The milk provides new freshness to the fish and draws out the frozen taste.

GILL REMOVAL. Improve the taste of your fish by removing its gills prior to baking or poaching.

FROZEN FISH. The best way to freeze freshly caught fish is in a clean milk carton filled with water. When you eat the fish, pour the melted water—which will now be packed with nutrients—into your house plants.

CLAM SAND REMOVAL. Here's a neat trick for getting the sand out of clams. Sprinkle cornmeal over the clams about three hours before serving and cover them with cold water. When the time comes to eat the clams, the clams will have discharged the sand to consume the cornmeal.

FISH SKIN. Like cats, there's more than one way to skin a fish. But the easiest way is to freeze the fish first.

CRACKERED FISH. Crushed crackers can be used as crumbs for coating fish and other meats.

FISH COOKING. The rule of thumb in determining how long to cook a fish is to measure the thickness of the fish at its thickest part and let the fish cook 10 minutes for each inch of thickness.

LEMON FISH FRYING. Cut down on the smoke and smell when frying fish by adding lemon juice to the shortening.

DEODORIZING FISH. To eliminate the fishy odor in your pan, wash it with vinegar after cooking the fish.

SAUTÉING FISH GINGERLY. Add some zest to the fish by placing a few slices of fresh ginger in the oil when sautéing fish.

FISH DEODORIZING. Either rub your hands with lemon slices or wash your hands with water and vinegar to rid your hands of the smell of fish.

EASY-OPENING CLAMS AND OYSTER. Here's a simple way to open clams and oysters without inadvertently smashing a thumb. Wash the shellfish with water and then put them in the freezer. Within an hour, the shells will open.

MEATS

General tips

SAFETY CLUES. Brown beef that has been in the refrigerator for a day or two is safe, but if it smells or is in the refrigerator and brown for more than two days, throw it out. You have a week to eat hot dogs once you've opened the package; unopened they will stay preserved for as much as a month or longer.

MEAT STORAGE RULES OF THUMB. You can refrigerate the following meats for the following amounts of time:

- Bacon: 1 week

- Leftover beef stew or roast: 3 or 4 days

- Any kind of chicken or turkey: 1 or 2 days

- Leftover fish: 2 or 3 days

- Leftover fresh ham or pork: 3 or 4 days

- Meat loaf: 2 or 3 days

- Meat sauce: 3 or 4 days

- Cooked pork or lamb: 3 or 4 days

- Tuna salad: 1 or 2 days

DOMED SKILLETS. Stop grease from splattering you and the stove by placing a colander upside down over a pan or skillet when you are sautéing. Because the air can escape through the holes, the meat will still brown.

FRESHER MEAT. Do like the butcher and loosely wrap your meat and poultry in wax paper. If you keep the original wrapping on, the air will not circulate around the flesh. Don't forget to cut the label from the original wrapping and place it on the meat. Otherwise you may forget its weight and expiration date.

MEAT TENDERIZERS. There are all sorts of ways to tenderize tough meats. Some of them include:

- Drench the meat in vinegar water for a few minutes.

- Pour some lime juice over steak two to three hours before cooking.

- A dash of strong tea in a roast or stew acts as a tenderizer and speeds up the cooking time.

- Rub steak with oil and vinegar about two hours before cooking.

- The acids in tomatoes will tenderize the toughest of pot roasts.

PATTED DOWN MEAT Use paper towels to wipe off meats before sautéing them. Soaking up some of the moisture makes it easier to brown the meat.

EAT GROUND MEAT FAST Meat that has been ground up should be eaten as soon as possible; the same is true of organ meat.

MEATLOAF FACILITATOR Place a slice of bacon on the bottom of the meatloaf to prevent the meatloaf from sticking to the pan.

MEATLOAF MUFFINS. Cut the amount of cooking time in half for meatloaf by putting the meat in muffin tins.

MOIST MEATBALLS. You can guarantee moist meatballs by inserting a small chunk of ice into the center of the meatballs before cooking them.

FASTER HAMBURGER COOKING. Speed up the time it takes to cook a hamburger by making holes in the center of the patties.

USING A LIGHT HAMBURGER TOUCH. The less you shape your hamburgers the juicier the hamburgers will be.

STEAK DIVETS. Cut the edges of fat on chops and steaks in regular intervals to stop the meat from curling when it's cooked.

CASSEROLE CASING. If you are going to freeze a casserole, line the pan with aluminum foil first and then fill it with the casserole and cook it. When you are done, take the casserole out in the foil and store it in the freezer. You now have the casserole dish for other uses.

SALTING ROASTS. If you are adding salt to roasts, don't do it until just before the meat is finished cooking. Salt absorbs the juices from the meat, so too much salt too early will lead to a dry roast.

EASIER SLICING. It is easier to cut meat thinly if the meat is partially frozen.

HAM THAWING. Hams should be thawed in the refrigerator and not outside; ham is vulnerable to bacteria, even if it is salted or smoked.

HAM SKINNING. The longer you wait to remove skin from baked ham, the tougher it is to accomplish the task. Aim for taking off the skin as soon as it is cool enough to handle.

HOT HAM. Run hot water over a canned ham before opening it to melt the gelatin. When you open the can, the ham will slide right out.

HAM AND LAMB CARVING. First cut a few slices lengthwise from the bottom. Flip the meat over on a steady surface and then cut perpendicular to the bone. Finally cut along the bone and remove the slices.

TRIMMING LAMB. Cut the excess fat off lamb before roasting, broiling, or sautéing to cut down on the smell and make the taste milder. Sprinkled cinnamon on the lamb will have the same effect.

Poultry

PRE-SEASONED CHICKEN. Add flavor to your chicken by seasoning it with salt, pepper, and other spices the day before roasting.

DENTAL FLOSS. Dental floss is better than string for tying up poultry for roasting or baking.

MICROWAVE THAWING. Allow eight to 10 minutes per pound for thawing poultry.

LEFTOVER GIZZARDS. Save the gizzards, backs, necks, and other leftover bits of chicken and turkey in the freezer to use to make broths, soups, and stews.

STUFFED CHEESECLOTH. Before stuffing your turkey, line it with a cheesecloth and then stuff it. When the turkey is cooked, pull out the cheesecloth to remove the stuffing.

CHEESECLOTH COVER. Dunk the cheesecloth in melted butter until it is saturated and then lay it on top of the turkey while cooking. This will keep the bird's breasts moist. When the cooking is almost done, remove the cheesecloth and let the skin brown for 30 minutes.

TESTING FOR DONENESS. You can tell if your fowl in the oven is ready for eating by poking its thigh with a fork. If the juice runs clear, your bird is sufficiently cooked.

TURKEY BASTE. A mixture of 1/4 cup honey and two cups of water is good for basting turkey.

EXTRA CRISPY. For crispier fried chicken add 3 or 4 teaspoons of cornstarch for each cup of flour. You can spice up the mix by adding salt, pepper, and other spices.

CARVING TACTICS. First remove the drumsticks, then the wings, and lastly the breast meat. For big, fat drumsticks, slice meat from the leg by going parallel to the bone of the leg and thigh bones.

STALKED TURKEYS. Lay out a bed of celery stalks in the pan and place your turkey on top. The celery will elevate the bird, keeping the turkey from sticking to the dish and allowing the gravy to form. When you are done cooking, there is no reason to keep the celery.

DE-SKINNING A BIRD. By removing the skin from a whole chicken you will drastically cut back on its fattiness. The best way to remove the skin is to dislocate the wings and cut the chicken down to the breastbone. Flatten the chicken with its back up and simply pull off the skin.

RED BONES? Red bones in poultry means you're eating a fowl that was once frozen.

BREAKFASTS

Meats and eggs

PUFFIER OMELETS. Add a dash of cornstarch before beating an omelet to make it fluffier.

PERFORATED SAUSAGE. Pierce sausages with a fork before and during cooking to prevent the sausage from erupting out of its skin and spattering all over the stove.

DECURLED BACON. Dip bacon into cold water before frying it to keep it from curling up.

BACON SLICE SEPARATION. Zapping bacon in the microwave for about 30 seconds separates bacon slices. Or even more clever, if less gainly, roll the package of bacon into the shape of a tube and secure it with rubber bands: The bacon will be loose when you open the package.

FROZEN BACON SEPARATION. For frozen bacon, slide a warmed spatula under each slice of bacon to separate the pieces.

The rest of breakfast

LIGHTENED PANCAKES AND WAFFLES. To make for a lighter breakfast treat, use club soda for the liquid in the batter for pancakes and waffles. The only problem is that you can't store the batter.

UNSTUCK WAFFLES. If you do not have a nonstick waffle iron, make sure to brush the iron with vegetable oil every time you make a waffle.

LEFTOVER PANCAKES. There is no reason to throw away leftover pancakes. Just line them with wax paper to prevent sticking and put them in the freezer. When you want to reheat them, put them in the toaster.

OVERNIGHT PORRIDGE. To avoid buying instant hot cereal mixes but still enjoy the convenience, pour boiling water at night into a thermos filled with porridge oats. By the time morning arrives, the cereal is hot and ready for consumption.

LEFTOVER EGGNOG. Substitute leftover eggnog for milk in pancakes and muffin recipes.

BAKED GOODS

General tips

WET BUT STEADY PAPER. To keep wax paper or aluminum foil in place when it comes time to roll the dough, wipe the counter with a wet sponge or towel. In the same way, a damp towel under a bowl will keep the latter in place.

STOP THE STICKIES. Before measuring sticky liquids with your measuring cup or spoons, rinse them with oil and then hot water. You will find it much easier to pour the liquids.

DELUMPED SUGAR. You can take the lumps out of a sack of sugar by putting the sack in the refrigerator for a day or two.

MIXING DRY INGREDIENTS. Save yourself the headache of cleaning an extra dish by mixing the dry ingredients for cakes in a paper or plastic bag. Not only is there one less bowl to clean, you can mix up the ingredients by simply shaking the bag.

Breads

HOT CUTS. Use a hot knife to cut fresh bread more easily.

STALE REVIVALS. Several alternatives can be used to breathe freshness back into stale breads. They include:

- Putting the bread in a covered casserole and placing the casserole in a pan of hot water in a heated oven.
- Placing stale rolls and buns in a wet paper bag and putting the bag in an oven at 350 degrees Fahrenheit for less than 10 minutes.
- Spraying the bread with cold water, wrapping it in foil, and putting it in the oven at 375 degrees Fahrenheit for about 10 minutes.

FROZEN DOUGH. Bread dough can easily be set aside in the freezer for future baking. Just mix the dough and wrap it. Or you can let the dough rise, punch it down, and wrap it. When it comes time to bake the bread, let the dough thaw before baking.

POTATO WATER. Leftover water from boiling potatoes is an excellent substitute for regular water when making bread dough. The potato water adds flavor and offers food for the yeast.

RECYCLED BREAD. Recycle old bread by freezing it and then later crushing it into crumbs or slicing, dicing, and seasoning it to use as croutons.

SLICED CRUST. Prevent bread crusts from cracking by taking a razor and slashing cuts into the unbaked loaf immediately before you put it in the oven.

CRUMBY CARTONS. Use empty salt cartons with spout for bread crumb containers. The spout makes it easy to pour. Use a funnel to get the crumbs in the container.

CEREALS AS CRUMBS. You can use cereals in place of crumbs by running the cereal through a processor or blender. The cereals add an interesting taste.

Cakes, cookies, and muffins

FINER CAKES. Whenever you make a cake, add a tablespoon or two of boiling water to the butter and sugar mix to create a more finely textured cake.

HONEY SWEETENER. Moisten and sweeten your pancakes, cakes, and muffins by adding a tablespoon or two of honey to the batter.

ICING RUNNETH OVER. Douse the cake with powdered sugar to prevent the icing from running off the cake.

ADHESIVE RAISINS. Keep raisins and other dried fruits from sinking to the bottom of the batter by rolling them in flour prior to putting them in the batter.

EASY SLIDING CAKE. To keep your cake from sticking to its plate when you are serving, sprinkle granulated sugar on the cake plate prior to serving.

ALTERNATIVE FROSTING. Instead of frosting the top of the cupcakes, cut the cupcakes in half and put the frosting in the middle. When you stick the center back together you still get the tasty icing, but you no longer have to worry about the mess if you pack them into sandwich bags.

CRUNCHY MUFFIN CRUST. For a crunchy crust, sprinkle white or brown sugar over muffin batter when it is in the pan.

EASY ENGLISH MUFFIN SPLITTING. Thaw frozen English muffins by putting them in the microwave oven for 30 seconds on high. The muffins will be primed for splitting evenly.

PRESERVED CAKES. Here's a tip you might find on an IQ test. What's the best way to cut a cake if you're only going to use a couple of slices but want to save the rest for later? Answer: Cut the cake in half and take a portion from the middle. When you are done slicing the cake, you can press the two halves back together and keep it moist.

SCOOPS OF BATTER. An ice cream scoop will help you portion out dabs of batter for muffins and cupcakes.

THE TOWEL SOLUTION. By placing a wet towel underneath a hot pan of muffins you will help loosen the muffins and make it easier to extract them from the pan.

CAKE REVIVAL. Brush some milk or cold water over the sides of stale cake and put the cake in the oven for 20 minutes to restore freshness.

CAKE ATTACHMENTS. Stick a slice of bread onto the open edge of a used cake with toothpicks to keep the cut edge fresh.

LEFTOVER CAKES. Slice leftover birthday cake into several wedges and put them in the freezer. They will make for a great treat down the road.

CHILLED DOUGH. It is easier to handle chilled cookie dough than dough at room temperature. If you have the time, you may find it worthwhile to put the dough in the refrigerator or freezer for a few minutes before rolling it.

DENTAL CHEESECAKE CUTS. Use tightly held unflavored dental floss to cut through cheesecake. When you are finished with the slice, pull the floss out from under.

MERINGUE CUTS. Use a knife coated with butter to cut meringue smoothly.

WET HANDS FOR COOKIES. Wet your hands with cold water before shaping cookie dough. This will help prevent the dough from sticking to your hands, especially if the dough contains a lot of shortening.

Pies

PIE CRUST CRISPNESS. Keep your pie crust from becoming soggy by greasing the pie plate with butter before putting on the dough.

CREASED PAPER. Make cleanups simpler by putting a crease down the center of the wax paper before placing it on the counter for mixing dry baking ingredients or manipulating batters. When it comes time to clean up, you already have a spout for pouring the leftovers out.

POSITIONING PIES. Two-crust pies should be placed in the bottom shelf of the oven to make sure the bottom is thoroughly baked and top is lightly browned.

COLD CRUST INGREDIENTS. The chillier you make the ingredients, the better the pie crust will turn out. To make the crust flaky, sprinkle or brush the top crust with water prior to baking.

PIE CUTS. The easiest way to slice soft pies is with a buttered knife.

ASSEMBLY LINE BAKING. Speed up the baking process by cutting sheets of aluminum foil to fit the cookie sheets and then placing the dough on the foil while other cookie sheets are in the oven. When the first batch is done, you will have the second batch ready to go in right away.

Sugar, flour, and other ingredients

BAKING SODA TEST. To determine whether your baking soda has passed its usefulness, pour several tablespoons of hot water over half a teaspoon of baking soda. If the baking soda is still good, the mixture should bubble over. If it does not bubble actively, it's time to get new baking soda.

UNSALTED BUTTER. Always use unsalted butter when baking.

FLOUR STORAGE. To maintain moisture, store flour in an opened bag in a plastic bag or air-tight container. Whole-grain flour should be kept in a cool, dry place such as the refrigerator.

CAKE FLOUR. Make cake flour by sifting in one tablespoon of cornstarch for every cup of flour.

TOASTED OATS. Toast the oats before adding them to oatmeal cookies by putting them in a pan and baking them in an oven for about 10 minutes at 300 degrees.

NO-MESS CHOCOLATE. Save yourself the headache of cleaning up melted chocolate from the pan by inserting chocolate chips or squares into a boil-able plastic bag, tying it up, and placing it in boiling water. When the chocolate is melted, cut off a corner and squeeze the melted chocolate out.

INSTANT CONFECTIONARY SUGAR. You can quickly make confectionary sugar by grinding regular sugar in a food processor.

SIFTED SUGAR. Before using confectionary sugar for icing, sift the sugar. This will prevent lumping.

BROWN SUGAR SOFTENERS. To prevent brown sugar from hardening, keep it in freezer. If the brown sugar has hardened, place either apple slices, a piece of bread, or a couple of marshmallows in a bag or container of brown sugar and let it sit for a day or so. If all else fails, grate the block of sugar on a cheese-grater.

BROWN SUGAR SUBSTITUTES. Mix two tablespoons of molasses with one cup of white sugar to make a cup of brown sugar. Or mix a cup of white sugar with a teaspoon of maple flavoring and a teaspoon of molasses.

SUGAR COLORING. Here's how to make colored sugar for decorating cookies, cakes, and muffins. Mix a drop of food coloring for every teaspoon of sugar in a plastic bag. Rub the mixture together with your fingers until the sugar acquires the desired coloring.

HOMEMADE PASTRY BAGS. Take a heavy plastic bag and cut a hole in the corner to make your own homemade pastry bag.

Desserts

UNMOLDING GELATIN. There are two ways to get gelatin desserts and salads out of the molds. Either dip the mold in hot water or wrap the mold in a towel drenched in hot water for 15 to 30 seconds. Either way, when you are done use both hands to release the gelatin with a quick downward snap of the hands.

GELATIN SLIDING. Having released the gelatin from the mold onto the plate, make sure you have already sprinkled some water on the plate. You can then slide the gelatin about until it is centered. Otherwise, the gelatin might stick to where it landed.

CUSTARD WRAPPING. Ever notice how restaurants rest plastic wrap on custards and puddings? This is to prevent skin from forming on the top. You can use this same trick at home with your desserts.

The intelligent kitchen

So what makes a kitchen intelligent? Good question. Convenience. Comfort. Easy access. Good equipment. Energy efficiency. Fresh produce. These are some of the elements that distinguish the well-run kitchen.

If you have the luxury of being able to design your own kitchen, there are several factors you should consider before going with some of the standard kitchen designs. For example, counter heights are typically designed to meet the comfort needs of the slightly taller than average woman. Your height may differ from the average, and you may not be the only one who uses the counter.

Some people are naturally organized. An undiscovered gene tells them exactly where things should go and compels them always to put everything back where it belongs. Not all of us are so lucky. We need to think ahead about how to structure a kitchen and buy the right kinds of appliances.

The kitchen in almost any home is the prime candidate for clutter central. Food, flatware, appliances, dishes, pots and pans, cookbooks, and seemingly hundreds of knick-knacks all need their place. Finding logical places to keep everything in a convenient manner is hard enough; remembering to maintain a clutter-free kitchen is a constant battle.

Smart kitchens are also energy efficient. Although a few hints are offered in this section on ways to keep down energy use, the chapter on energy conservation offers many more tips on how to save energy in the kitchen and throughout the house.

The smartest kitchens have their own food growing on the premises. There are limits, of course, to how much food one can harvest in a kitchen, but more and more people are finding ways to raise vegetable gardens in their kitchens. It is not as difficult as you may think and it adds to the appearance of the kitchen—especially to the freshness and flavor of your meals. What better way to guarantee good, wholesome food than to grow it yourself?

THE PRACTICAL KITCHEN

THE MAGIC KITCHEN TRIANGLE. Professional kitchen designers say that well-designed kitchens consist of work triangles with the three points being the sink, the range, and refrigerator. The theory calls for the three centers to be about equal distances from each other, with distances being no less than 4 feet and no more than 7 feet. The total of the three sides should be less than 22 feet. The basic counter shapes that allow for this arrangement are the U, L, and galley shapes. This theory has withstood the test of time, so do not ignore it if you choose to design your own kitchen.

WORK CENTERS. A well-organized kitchen consists of a series of work centers where the bulk of the equipment, utensils, food, and other items needed for the center are within easy access. For example, the food preparation center should have small appliances, non-perishables, and standard kitchen utensils such as knives and rolling pins. Work centers in the typical kitchen can be divided into the following categories: the sink, refrigerator, range/oven, food preparation, pantry, and waste/compost centers.

MULTIPLE COUNTER HEIGHTS. If you are able, try to find a way to create counters of varying heights. The ideal counter height is determined by measuring the distance from your elbow to the floor. Not only do our heights vary, but so does the ideal height for different tasks. Some tasks such as chopping, rolling pie crust, and kneading bread are most comfortably done 6 inches lower than the standard counter height (36 inches), and the ideal sink height is 2 inches higher than the standard counter height. If you cannot make different counter heights, you may be able to install an adjustable counter that can be raised and lowered to meet your needs.

UPLIFTING TIP. If you cannot adjust the counter's height, you can elevate yourself from the floor by standing on a floor skid or low stool. If you happen to be too tall for the task at hand, you can raise the counter space by placing a large cutting board on the counter or stacking several cutting boards.

FOOTSTOOL CONVENIENCE. If you are under 5 feet 5 inches, then most kitchens were not designed for you. Solve the problem of having to stand on your toes to reach into cabinets by investing in a footstool or making one.

CABINET SHELVES. The best material for shelves is plastic laminate. They are low maintenance, easily cleaned, and often quite attractive. Companies are coming out with increasingly more varied and interesting patterns. Shelves should be thick, adjustable, well made, and removable.

NIX ON THE FORMALDEHYDE. Formaldehyde is often used in the fabrication of paneling, hardwood plywood, particleboard, and fiberboard. It also has been linked to cancer. Try to use construction materials in your kitchen, and the rest of the house, that are not made with formaldehyde.

PANTRY INSPIRATIONS. Convenience often dictates how you eat. Provide a readily accessible stock of whole-foods snacks by installing a shallow bookshelf-like unit in the pantry. Stock it with popcorn, nuts, dried fruits, pretzels, and other goodies for the sake of your health and your children's health. You will all be more likely to snack on healthful foods with this type of convenient shelving and supplies.

TWO SINKS BETTER THAN ONE. Two sinks in a kitchen instead of one both allows for more than one person at a time to use the sink and makes life much easier by having one sink devoted to food preparation and the other to cleaning up dishes and pots.

SINK SEATS. One of the more uncomfortable tasks in the kitchen is leaning over a sink to wash. You can alter the space under the sink to allow you to bring up a chair or stool for a more comfortable way of completing the task.

WINDOW PLACEMENT. Try to put a window behind the sink. It makes the job of washing much more pleasant. Avoid putting windows near or over a stove. It will pose a serious fire hazard if you install curtains. Place windows for maximum ventilation.

SKYLIGHT DELIGHT. A skylight can transform a dark, box-like kitchen into a sun-drenched oasis of a kitchen. Although there is sometimes a net energy loss from a skylight, the added light often outweighs the downside. Skylights are an excellent way to improve ventilation in a kitchen and make it easier to grow plants and indoor vegetable gardens.

LET THERE BE LIGHT. Studies have shown that there is a direct correlation between light and health. Since the kitchen is where people get most of their sustenance, it makes sense that light be a part of that equation. A liberal use of properly placed windows and skylights ensures adequate natural light. Artificial light is also key to a well-designed kitchen. Professionals recommend the following amounts of wattage for incandescent lights:

- 80 square feet: 182–308 watts for low ceilings; 224–392 watts for high ceilings;

- 140 square feet: 280–462 watts for low ceilings; 322–546 watts for high ceilings;

- 250 square feet: 420–700 watts for low ceilings; 508–840 watts for high ceilings.

For fluorescent lights, subtract the total wattage by about 30 percent for the equivalent amount. Low ceilings are defined as being 7 feet. High ceilings are 10 feet.

MIRROR ENHANCERS. In China, mirrors are often used in kitchens to create a more peaceful atmosphere. You may want to import this idea and use mirrors to brighten the kitchen and make the room appear larger. The only drawback is that kitchen mirrors have a tendency to steam up.

FLOOR CHOICES. Conventional wisdom says that tile and stone floors are the way to go, but they are also cold on the feet and very hard surfaces. Vinyl and linoleum floors are relatively easy to maintain. Carpets absorb sound and are soft, but maintenance can be very difficult with spills and all. Wood offers the best of all the options, a happy medium of attractiveness, easy maintenance, and comfort. Oak, maple, birch, cherry, and pecan are all suitable for wood floors. Dark woods hide the grime and dirt the best.

KITCHEN APPLIANCE MUSTS. The food processor, toaster oven and mini-vacuum are all wonderful utensils for any kitchen. Food processors save enormous amounts of time with their capacity for slicing, dicing, whipping, chopping, shredding, pureeing and more. Toaster ovens can do many of the jobs of a full-fledged oven but with a fraction of the energy. Mini-vacuums are a big plus in any kitchen for easy cleanup tasks on dry messes. There are some new mini-vacuums designed for wet messes as well, but they are more expensive. Computers are another important tool for the kitchen. See the chapter on computers for kitchen uses.

FIRE SAFETY. More than 130,000 kitchen fires are reported every year—there are certainly many times more that are not reported—and about 16 percent of fatal fires in this country are caused by kitchen fires. So fire safety should be an important element in any kitchen, both in how the kitchen is designed and equipped. All kitchens should have usable fire extinguishers that are rated ABC for paper, wood, cloth, and plastics (A), grease (B), and electric (C) fires. Unfortunately, smoke detectors are often triggered by the routine smoke that kitchens produce thus it is usually not recommended to use them in the kitchen.

FIRE BLANKETS. In Europe, fire blankets are routinely kept in kitchens. You can smother all types of fires by placing blankets over the blaze. You should have a fire blanket in your kitchen.

BAKING SODA. Baking soda is an excellent extinguisher of grease fires. Keep a marked container of it near the stove for rapid use.

COST-EFFECTIVE REFRIGERATION. Refrigerators are major energy consumers, so pick the right size carefully. You want to find the size that balances the concern of not getting too big a refrigerator that cools more space than you need over not getting one that is so small that packed food infringes on circulation. The rule of thumb here is 8–10 cubic feet for a family of two plus 1 cubic foot for each additional person in the family. The freezer space should be 2 cubic feet per person.

BLACKBOARD REFRIGERATOR. Put a blackboard on the refrigerator to post notices on what is coming for dinner and what leftovers and goodies are available for snacks. This will stop everyone in the house from holding the door open and staring at the food for a snack while the refrigeration escapes; it will head off any family members from eating the dinner ingredients.

DISHWASHERS. A good buy. If you are wondering about the cost effectiveness of buying a dishwasher, think no more. Two reasons: One is that the average dishwasher uses less than 10 gallons of water to wash the equivalent amount of dishes in the sink (more than 15 gallons). The second reason is that washing dishes by hand is a guaranteed inducement to want to eat out. It is much cheaper to eat home. This is usually a hidden financial benefit of owning a dishwasher.

SPLIT COOKING DECISION. Although it is more expensive, you may want to consider not getting an oven and stove burners as one appliance. Instead, separate the tasks with a gas range and an electric oven. Gas stove tops are much more flexible and precise than electric burners, and electric ovens beat gas stoves hands down because they generate a much more uniform heat and do not dry the food.

MICROWAVE OVENS. There is no question that microwave ovens are extremely convenient, but the debate continues over whether they may prove to be unhealthful appliances. If you get a microwave oven be sure to read the instructions. They are very finicky about what they can cook and what they can't. In general, use containers that allow the microwave to penetrate the food that needs to be heated. If you are unsure, place water in the container and put it on high for a minute. The water should be heated but the container remain cool. Do not put metal containers in microwave ovens.

VENTILATION KEY. Kitchens generate a tremendous amount of airborne grease, odors, and other elements. It is important to install a good ventilation system and use a range hood to keep the air moving. Well-placed windows, skylights, and plants are good natural ventilators and air cleansers.

OUT-OF-SIGHT GARBAGE AND COMPOST. With the heightened awareness of recycling, more and more commercial recycling disposal units have been put on the market. In general, you want to hide garbage cans behind a cupboard door and keep recyclables near the garbage. Composting is an excellent way to reuse organic wastes that might otherwise stink up the garbage can. But the sights and smells of kitchen compost are not pleasant. To lessen the downsides of composting, place the compost bin in a corner and under cover. Do not add meats to the compost pile.

ORGANIZING TIPS

ALPHABETICAL SPICES. Supermarkets make it easier for customers to find spices quickly by arranging the spices in alphabetical order. If you have a dozen or more spice jars, you should employ this trick.

SPICE RACKS. Spice racks are an ingenious anti-clutter tool. Either place a spice rack at eye level inside a cupboard, pantry, or on the wall or door for easy convenience. An alternative to spice racks is a lazy Susan. Keep spices that you rarely use in a dark space to preserve them longer.

CUPBOARD TIERS. Install tiered shelves similar to miniature bleachers in the cupboard to elevate items in the back of the cupboard for easy visibility. You can either buy or make the tiered shelves. Either way, they will help a crowded cupboard. If you do not get a tiered shelf, organize the cupboard so that the tallest and largest items are in the back of the shelf.

FOLD-DOWN RACKS. Fold-down racks that can be attached to the bottom of your cabinets to hold spices, cookbooks, and other items are available in many hardware and houseware stores.

CUPBOARD AND CABINET AIRSPACE. If you have a cupboard and cabinet with relatively high shelves, use the extra air space to hang items such as cups or light food items.

CUPBOARD DOORS. Install shallow shelves or wall mounts on the inside of cupboard doors to create extra space for holding items such as spices, aluminum foil boxes, dishwasher detergent, and other items for cleaning. Very good wire containers are made commercially for exactly this purpose.

CANNED STORAGE. Install narrow shelves in the cabinet or along inconspicuous walls to store cans, small boxes, and jars in single rows.

LAZY SUSAN. For tough-to-reach corners in the cupboard, a lazy Susan may be just the solution. Get as large a lazy Susan as you can that will still fit in the cupboard. If there is room, get one with more than one level for extra storage. The great joy of this contraption is that you do not have to pull out half the cupboard to find an item; just spin the wheel until you find what you are seeking.

ORGANIZED DRAWERS. Get a commercially made drawer organizer to suit the needs of whatever it is that you are storing in the drawers. By their very nature, drawers are clutter makers. Each time you open and close a drawer the items shift about. An organizer will cut down on the movements.

UTENSILS FACE FORWARD. Kitchen utensils kept in a kitchen drawer should be placed with their handles to the back of the drawer. You will than have no trouble identifying the utensil as its user end is out in the open and not under cover.

LOUD TIMERS. No matter how hard you try, it is inevitable that every once in a while you lose track of time and forget about the dish in the oven or on the stove. Avoid burning the food by getting a timer, preferably a loud one. Set the timer a few minutes before the desired time if you have some extra preparations to do.

SEE-THROUGH PRODUCE. Use glass or see-through plastic containers to hold grains, sugars, rice, flour, and other items. The food is often an attractive addition to the kitchen, but, more importantly, you will be able to find what you are looking for very easily.

FUNCTION OVER FORM. The kitchen is perhaps the most well-stocked room in the house, so make sure that everything in the kitchen has a practical purpose. With some exceptions, mere decorations will only clutter things further. If you want something pretty in the kitchen, try to make sure it serves an ulterior, practical purpose.

WALL GRIDS. Those wall grids that look like giant tic-tac-toe boards offer an excellent way to organize your utensils, dishes, and pots and pans without cluttering up the cupboard. They use space that might otherwise be unused.

MOUNTED DISH RACKS. Mounting a wire dish rack above the sink serves a double purpose. (1) It is within easy reach for placing dishes after washing them. And (2) it reduces moisture problems by draining dishes directly into the sink.

KNIFE STORAGE. Knife racks are definitely the best way to store knives. They protect the knife blades from chipping by stopping them from banging into each other and provide the safest storage. You can use wooden blocks, specially designed knife racks, or wall hangers with heavy magnets to hold the knives in place.

SIMPLE SETTINGS. Here's a time saver. When it comes time to unload the flatware from the dishwasher, rather than organize the utensils into knives, spoons, and forks, place one of each in a napkin and set aside in the drawer. At meal time, all you have to do is lift the package out for an instant place setting.

BAGGED GARBAGE. Store plastic garbage bags on the bottom of the garbage pails. When you remove the old plastic bag full of trash all you have to do is reach down for the next fresh garbage bag. What could be simpler?

TWO IN ONE. Even the best of planners sometimes end up with two bottles of the same item. If you have two partially used containers of the same spices, ketchup, mayonnaise, or whatever, you can mix them together and throw out or recycle the empty jar.

HANG IN THERE. Why not hang baskets from the ceiling or wall for extra storage space? Some stores have used ingenious methods to convert tacky-looking ceilings into both handsome and practical storage space by hanging hand-woven baskets with goodies inside. You can hang fruits, herbs, teas, and all sorts of other things.

DIVIDE AND STORE. Make a home-made divider with plywood to keep flat baking pans, platters and trays. Place the new storage compartment above the refrigerator, an often overlooked storage space for the kitchen.

HOOKED VALUABLES. Place an attractive hook on the wall next to the sink for hanging jewelry and watches. When you get into some heavy duty washing or cooking you may want to take these off. With the hook you will always have a place to keep them and won't forget where they are.

CANNED CASH. Save time in the morning by keeping a collection of coins in a glass container. In this way bus money and spare change will be readily available for the family when you are in a rush out the door.

WINE STORAGE. Wine racks are the only way to go when it comes to storing wine. Wine bottles have to be kept on their side to keep the cork wet.

SINK SPACE. Don't forget the space underneath the kitchen sink. It is not an ideal location to store lots of items because you want to maintain easy access to the plumbing, but there is no reason why you can't store things there. Use the floor space for equipment and install mounts to hold lighter items on the walls and door.

ICE COLD ADVICE. Label frozen goods in the freezer with information about the contents and the date placed in the freezer. For easy reference, keep a freezer storage guide listing how long you can freeze items in the freezer.

LOGICAL GROUPINGS. There are two logical ways to group kitchen foods. One is foods that fit in the same category. Canned goods and soups, basic items such as sugar, flour, and pastas could all be logically stored in the same area because they have something in common. The other grouping is foods that you might use together. Mexican food items and hot sauces could be kept in the same area under this category, as could coffee, tea, sugar, and cups or pasta, spaghetti sauce, and associated ingredients. The most important thing when grouping items, however, is to do it in a way that makes sense to you. After all, it's your kitchen.

CONVENIENCE COUNTS I. Be sure to store the foods, utensils, dishes, and equipment you use most in the most convenient spots in the kitchen, generally the counters, shelves at eye level, and the top drawers.

CONVENIENCE COUNTS II. Store kitchen equipment and food items near their point of use. Blenders, toasters, and other small appliances are best stored near their designated electric plugs. Spatulas, cooking spoons, and other cooking utensils should be kept near the stove. And so on.

COUPON STORAGE. Get an index card box to store coupons.

EASY EATING OUT. The easiest way to keep your kitchen organized is to order food out. For those evenings when you cannot bear the thought of cooking but can afford the luxury of eating out, be sure to keep a file with the take-out menus from local restaurants.

COLOR-CODED CORDS. Pasta isn't always the only spaghetti in the kitchen. If your kitchen has lots of utensils with cords that get all mixed up, mark them with different colored twist-ties to more easily keep track of which one is which.

Kitchen cleaning

The fun of the kitchen is in the cooking. Nobody ever really looks forward to cleaning up the mess afterwards. Unfortunately, short of luring someone else to do the job, there are few ways of getting around this unpleasant task.

Nevertheless, there are ways to ease the burden of kitchen cleaning. The most important rules of thumb are regular maintenance, regular maintenance, and regular maintenance. Let the messes pile up in the kitchen and you are in for trouble down the road. Besides being decidedly unpleasant, it is also unsanitary. The rug has not been invented yet for you to sweep the pots and pans under.

Some things can be done to limit the mess. In the section on foods, some tips are offered on how to keep down the mess. For example, why not melt chocolate in plastic bags submerged in boiling water? A brilliant way to avoid an annoying cleanup task. In other cases, a heavy dose of prevention can eliminate some major cleansing headaches. The best way to clean ovens is to buy a self-cleaning oven. They really work. If only solutions such as this could be found for every kitchen problem!

The Shakers had the right idea when it came to keeping their kitchens and homes clean. Most people know about how beautiful Shaker cabinets and furniture are with their simple lines. What is not so well known is that one of the reasons their cupboards and kitchen furniture were so simple was to make cleaning easier. By keeping handles and accessories to a minimum, all they had to do was wipe up with a cloth without having to worry about foods and stains getting stuck in hard-to-reach crevices.

The other thing to think about when cleaning kitchens is non-hazardous and environmentally-friendly ways to accomplish the task. The temptation may be to apply the most powerful chemical solution to problems. Nuke it, you may want to say. But often there is a better and ecologically cleaner way to accomplish the task.

So with that in mind, here are some tips as you make your way through the kitchen mess.

CUPBOARDS AND COUNTERS

TOOTHBRUSH SOLUTION. Use a toothbrush to reach the nooks and crannies around drawer and cabinet handles. A toothbrush also comes in handy for cleaning the grout around ceramic tiles. Spray tile cleaner and rub.

UPLIFTING CANISTERS. Stop rust stains from forming around metal canisters by placing them on plastic containers lids.

WEB BUSTERS. Look for spider webs as you clean the cupboards. Dust them with a long-handled brush or feather duster.

WOODEN SURFACES. Rub salad oil or boiled linseed oil into wooden surfaces to protect them. Deodorize wood by mixing 1/2 cup of baking soda with a quart of water and rubbing it into the wood. When it is dry, restore the wood by applying the salad oil or boiled linseed oil with a fine steel wool pad.

PLASTIC LAMINATE CLEANING. Baking soda is the wonder cleanser here. Use a two-sided sponge with fiber on one side and sponge on the other. The fiber side will get out the stains. Use the sponge side to wipe. For tough spots, instead of using bleach (which may discolor the top), apply liquid dish detergent and let it sit for 5 to 10 minutes before wiping with the fiber-side of the sponge.

MARBLE STAINS. You should use vinegar or lemon juice to clean stains on marble, but do so with great care. The acid can affect the marble. Never let the juice or vinegar sit for more than a minute on the marble.

NO-HANDLE CUPBOARDS. When you buy your next cupboard, get one without handles or decorative hardware. This will make it easier to clean.

HANDLE CLEANING. Use a sponge soaked in water and liquid detergent to clean the oil slicks around handle grips. Let the soapy water sit for a minute or two and then dry.

CUPBOARD CLEANSER. Mix one part ammonia to five parts water for the perfect cleansing solution to remove grease from cupboards.

EASY CABINET CLEANING. Make cleaning cabinets easy by lining the shelves with clear plastic wrap. When it comes time to clean, just lift the plastic off and replace it with a new sheet.

WOODEN CABINET GREASE CLEANING. For wooden cabinets, remove grease by putting a very thin coat of car wax on the appropriate places. After it has dried, buff.

SINKS

NATURAL DRAIN CLEARING. Clear the sink drain by pouring a 1/2 cup of baking soda down the drain followed by a cup of vinegar. Let it sit for a few minutes and then run the hot water. This will also help keep the sink from smelling.

UNPLUGGING GREASE. If grease is getting in the way of easy drainage from the sink, pour a cup of baking soda, then a cup of salt, and finally a quart of boiling water down the drain.

CLOGGED DRAIN-PREVENTION TACTICS. Apply the following rules and you will cut down drastically on having to worry about unplugging drains:

- Place a strainer over the drain to stop big bits of food from descending into the pipes.

- Never, ever pour coffee grounds or grease down the drain.

- Pour boiling water down the drain on a weekly basis.

METAL RETRIEVER. If you have dropped a metal object or cutlery down the drain, you may be able to lure it out by attaching a magnet to a strong piece of string and dropping the line into the drain. When the metal is attracted to the magnet, slowly pull it out.

STAIN PREVENTION. Try not to leave acidic foods such as fruit juices, salad dressing, and vinegar in a porcelain sink; they will stain it.

WATER SPOT REMOVAL. Apply rubbing alcohol or white vinegar to a damp cloth and rub to remove rust and water spots from stainless steel sinks. Use a cloth soaked in vinegar to remove rust stains caused by leaking faucets.

PORCELAIN STAIN REMOVAL. For porcelain sinks, remove stains by filling the sink with warm water and adding a few tablespoons of chlorine bleach. Let the bleach solution sit for an hour or more before draining and rinsing. If the spots don't want to go, drench some paper towels in the bleach and cover the spots overnight.

SHINY STEEL. Give a stainless steel sink a shine by applying club soda or white vinegar. Baking soda works well for cleaning stainless steel sinks. Never use bleach on stainless steel sinks because it leaves stains.

STAINLESS STEEL SCRATCHES. Cover up scratches in stainless steel sinks by rubbing fine steel wool over the scratch and then buffing with a soft cloth.

RUST REMOVAL. Get rid of rust spots in stainless steel sinks by rubbing them with lighter fluid. When the job is done, wipe with liquid cleaner.

For light stains, you may be able to use a cut lemon to rub the rust out.

SPOTLESS TAPS. Polish kitchen taps with a coat of liquid wax to keep them clean of water spots.

WITHDRAWING MINERAL DEPOSITS. Remove mineral deposits on a faucet by rubbing the cut surface of a lemon on the spout and moving it around. Or apply a non-abrasive cleaner to a toothbrush and rub. One last option is to soak a paper towel in white vinegar, leave it on the stain, and later rub it out.

THE FLOOR

AMMONIA SOLUTION. A mixture of ammonia and lots of water can be used to clean floors that are no-wax vinyl, hardwood covered with poly-urethane, or tile. Just mop the floor with the solution. When the bucket gets too dirty, refill the bucket.

SCRAPERS. For stubborn spots, you may have to get on your hands and knees and use a scraper if regular cleaners applied with a mop do not do the trick.

EGG-VAPORATION. If you drop a raw egg on the floor, save yourself some elbow grease by applying a heavy dose of salt to the mess. Wait about five minutes and sweep up the dried-up egg.

FAST ABSORBER. For fast absorption, use the inside of a disposable diaper to clean up spills.

VINEGAR SHINE. You can save yourself the trouble of waxing a linoleum floor but still get the shine by using a damp mop to clean the floor and then mopping it a second time with a cup of white vinegar in the water.

OLD-FASHIONED MOPS. String mops have their advantages over sponge mops. With a string mop it is easier to reach tights spots, clean under counters, and you can remove the stringy head and clean it in the washer and dryer.

TIDBIT TIPS. Use toothpaste to clean crayon marks on the floor and erasers to rub out heel marks.

BIG APPLIANCES

Dishwasher

OUNCE OF PREVENTION. Make your life and the life of your dishwasher simpler by always being sure to rinse all dishes before putting them in the dishwasher. Even the best dishwashers cannot handle more than a little bit of stray food.

REGULAR MAINTENANCE. Clean dishwasher regularly, especially the door seal and filter, to prevent food from recirculating between washes.

SILVER AND STEEL DON'T MIX. Place silver or silver-plated flatware and stainless steel in separate baskets. If washed together, the steel may stain the silver.

BAKING SODA SOLUTIONS. Use a damp rag with baking soda sprinkled on it to clean the inside and outside of the dishwasher. If the inside smells, pour some baking soda on the bottom of the dishwasher and let it sit overnight before wiping up. Some people use equal parts baking soda and dishwasher soap for the dishwasher. They say it leaves the dishes, silver, and machine cleaner.

DE-LIMING THE DISHWASHER. Stop lime from building up in the dish-washer by putting 1/2 to 1 cup of bleach into an empty dishwasher and letting it go through the first wash cycle. When it drains, add two cups of vinegar for the rinse cycle. Do not run the dry cycle. Instead, run the dishwasher through a full cycle using regular detergent.

FILM REMOVAL. To banish film from your dishes and dishwasher, try the following technique. Pour a cup of bleach into a bowl at the bottom of the washer and let the machine go through the washing cycle. Do not let it go through the dry cycle. Then pour out the bleach and replace it with a cup of vinegar. Now let the dishwasher go through the entire cycle.

SOME NEVER, EVERS. Never put hand-painted dishes or antique glassware in an automatic dishwasher.

GLASS-CLEANING SOLUTION. To remove crud from glasses, add 1/2 cup bleach to the wash cycle and 1/2 cup of vinegar to the rinse.

WHY A DRY CYCLE? Save on your electric bill by opening the dishwasher door and turning off the machine when it has completed the wash cycle. Let the air dry dishes the old-fashioned way.

Ovens, stoves, and grills

SALTED SPILLS. If the juice from pies, casseroles, or other dishes spills into the oven, shake some salt onto the spill. Next time you turn the oven on, the juice will burn to crisp, making it easy to scrape off with a spatula.

BAKING SODA. Use baking soda to clean the chrome and glass doors of ovens. Baking soda is a good cleaner for any chrome appliance.

HELPING SELF-CLEANING OVENS. Self-cleaning ovens can't do everything, so if you spill something in the oven wipe it up to prevent staining.

BOTTOM-CLEANING. Keep the bottom of the oven clean by applying automatic dishwasher soap and covering it with wet towels. Let it sit for two to three hours and then wipe. You can use the same method with baking soda instead of dishwasher soap.

AMMONIA SOFTENER. Soften the really tough dirt and mess in the oven before cleaning by placing a saucer full of ammonia in the oven the night before you clean it. Although you must be careful of the ammonia vapors yourself, they will erode the residue, making it easier to wipe later.

GREASE REMOVAL. Apply baking soda to spots of splattered grease. Rub the soda with a damp cloth, rinse the spot with clear water, and dry.

FLOUR AND SODA EXTINGUISHERS. To put out grease fires, dump flour or baking soda on the flames. It is a much more effective way to douse the fire than water, which may spread the burning grease and not extinguish it. Store your baking soda and flour within easy reach of the stove.

HIGHLY HEATED COIL CLEANING. You do not need to do anything special to clean spills on heating coils other then wiping off as much as you can with a cloth and then turning the heat on to high to burn what is left over.

CHROME BURNER CLEANING. To remove grease marks from chrome burner rings and other detachable parts, soak them in ammonia overnight and rinse thoroughly the next day.

CHROME RUST REMOVAL. Remove rust from chrome on all kitchen appliances by rubbing aluminum foil around your finger (shiny side out) and rubbing the rust until it disappears. When the rust is gone, rub with a damp cloth. To give chrome a shiny look, add rubbing alcohol to a soft cloth and wipe the chrome.

GRILL CLEANING. Use a bathtub filled with water and detergent or water and ammonia to clean grills from the oven or barbecue.

OILED GRILLS. Keep your barbecue grill cleaner by rubbing it with vegetable oil.

MICROWAVE CLEANING. Clean a spill in a microwave oven by covering it with a wet paper towel or cloth and zapping it on high for 10 seconds. Then simply wipe. For regular cleanings, just dab a little bit of baking soda on a damp cloth and wipe. Clean the glass door by first rubbing ashes from the fireplace on it and then wiping it clean with newspaper.

LEMON-FRESH CLEAN. Add a slice of lemon to a bowl of hot water in a microwave oven for a natural clean. Turn the microwave on high to boil the water. Wipe the interior with a damp cloth after the water generates plenty of steam.

FISH AROMA KILLER. Kill the smell of fish in a microwave oven by pouring vanilla into a bowl and turning the oven on high for a minute or more.

Refrigerator

THE PROPER TIME. The best time to do a major cleaning of a refrigerator is when there is only a little bit of food in it. Turn off the refrigerator early to allow enough time for it to defrost. As a rule of thumb, do not let the frost in the freezer get more then 1/4-inch thick before defrosting.

BAKING SODA ROLES. Baking soda should play a major role in keeping your refrigerator clean. First, always keep an open box of baking soda to absorb smells. (A bowl of vanilla also helps keep the refrigerator smelling nice.) Then, when it is time to clean, you can use that same box of baking soda to mix with water to clean the inside and outside of the refrigerator. Use a solution of one tablespoon of baking soda for each quart of water. Replace the box of baking soda in the refrigerator every couple of months.

ICKY REFRIGERATOR TOP? If you have let the top of the refrigerator go without cleaning and it is now graced by a slimy, dirty layer of grease, attack this problem with a solution of one part ammonia to 10 parts water. Allow the solution to set in the grease and then wipe it off with paper towels. Apply a layer of appliance wax for easier cleaning the next time.

REFRIGERATOR PARTS REMOVAL. It is easier to clean the shelves and drawers from a refrigerator by taking them out of the appliance and washing them in the sink.

NO POWER. Don't panic. If there is a power outage, frozen food will last about 48 hours provided you do not open the freezer.

GASKET TEST. Determine whether the gasket needs to be cleaned (or even replaced) by sticking a sheet of newspaper in the door. If the paper rips when you try to pull it out, the seal is fine. If it slides out, clean the gasket.

REFRIGERATOR ART. To remove magic marker drawings and marks on the refrigerator door, apply lighter fluid and then wash with soap and water. Rinse thoroughly to prevent any residual fuel from igniting.

Trash compactor

GOOD-SMELLING GARBAGE. Cover up the bad odors from a garbage disposal by grinding up half a lemon or orange rinds. You can apply this method for the trash compactor or to a simple garbage can as well.

CLEAN COMPACTOR. The best way to stop a trash compactor from smelling bad is to put only dry trash in it. Put peelings and other leftover organic materials in a compost pile. Dispose of meat, fish, and diapers elsewhere.

LITTLE APPLIANCES

BLENDER CLEANSING. Rather than reaching for every nook and cranny in the blender, fill it partially with hot water, add a bit of detergent, and turn it on for about 10 seconds. Rinse it with clean water and then let it dry.

SEDIMENT DESTRUCTION. If your blender is having trouble reaching its full capacity, sediment may be obstructing the blade. Fill the blender with warm water and liquid detergent and then let it sit overnight.

CAN OPENER CLEANSING. Clean the blade of your electric can opener by running a paper towel through the cutting process. Loosen the grime in the blade and the rest of the appliance by brushing it with a toothbrush.

COFFEE MAKER CLEANING. Make a solution of baking soda and water and run it through the coffee maker, followed by at least one brew of regular water. Or mix a solution of equal parts vinegar and water and brew it through the coffee maker. Follow this with two brews of regular clean water. If you make a habit of doing either of these techniques, your home- or office-brewed coffee is sure to taste better. Use a toothpick to clean residue from the machine's tubes and notches.

PENNY-WISE COFFEE CLEANER. For glass coffee makers, drop a few pennies to the bottom and pour a little vinegar on top. Let the mix sit for about 15 minutes, shake it up, pour it out, and rinse. This will help keep it clean and prevent sediment from building up.

COFFEE MINERAL CUTBACKS. Reduce mineral buildup in a drip coffee maker by putting a piece of loofah sponge or a marble inside the water tank. They will attract the mineral deposits away from the coffee maker's parts.

IMPORTANT TOASTER TIP. It may seem obvious, but don't forget to unplug toasters and toaster ovens before you clean them. Also, never immerse toasters (or any appliance) in water. Use a brush to get crumbs out of toasters and/or shake out toasters that do not have a crumb tray.

SHINY TOASTERS. Wipe toasters with baking soda to give them a good shine.

PLASTIC REMOVER. If plastic has melted into the toaster, apply nail polish remover.

RAZOR-SHARP TIP. Take off the really stubborn bits from the inside of a toaster oven glass with a razor blade.

GRINDING CLEANER. Run a piece of bread through a meat grinder before washing it.

DISHES

DETERGENT STRETCHER. Extend the life of your liquid dish detergent by adding a small amount of water to it when it is close to being empty. You will be able to eke out a few more washes with it.

MAKE SURE IT'S HOT. Use very hot water to wash dishes to both kill off the bacteria and let the dishes dry faster.

SUPPLEMENTAL BLEACH. Adding a tablespoon of bleach to a sink full of dishwater will help keep the dish cloth clean and will kill the germs on the dishes.

GREASE CUTTER. Add vinegar to dishwater to cut the grease.

DISHWASHING MASTER PLAN. The most efficient way to wash dishes in a sink full of water is to first wash the glasses, then plates, and finally the pots and pans. Why? Because by following this path of attack, you will cut down on the amount of grease polluting the sink, especially for the glassware.

CHINA SAFETY NET. Before you clean valuable china, crystal, or other fragile wares, lay a towel at the bottom of the sink to cushion anything that slips. To prevent china from chipping, place cloth napkins between the dishes and be sure to hang the cups and not stack them.

CRACKED CHINA CLEANER. Apply baking powder to cracks in china, let sit for a couple of hours, and then wash normally.

CHINA TIP. Egg and milk should be rinsed promptly from china dishes with cold water before washing.

CRYSTAL CLEAN. If your cut glassware gets really thick with white film, apply vinegar to dissolve it. For regular cleaning use a solution of one part vinegar to three parts water.

CIGARETTE, COFFEE OR TEA STAINS. Use a damp cloth dipped in baking soda to clean coffee and tea stains and cigarette burns from china. To remove tea stains from cups and teapots add a dash of bleach to lukewarm water.

PLASTIC COFFEE AND TEA STAINS. Scour coffee and tea stains from plastic cups and dishes with baking soda.

CORNING DISHES. Apply baking soda to clean Corning dishes.

CRUMPLED NEWSPAPERS. Get rid of bad smells from plastic dishes by crumpling wads of newspaper, stuffing them in the containers, covering them tightly and letting sit overnight.

STAINLESS STEEL SEGREGATION. Do not let stainless steel cutlery come into contact with salt in hot water, vinegar, rhubarb or lemon juice. These will all corrode the steel.

STAINLESS STEEL SPOTS. Abolish spots from stainless steel cutlery by soaking it in undiluted vinegar.

UTENSIL RUST REMOVAL. Get rid of the rust on a knife or other silverware by sticking it into an onion and letting it sit for a while. Move the knife back and forth a few times to let the onion juices work their magic. When you are done, wash the silverware with soap and water.

SILVER SPOONS. Rub egg stains on silver spoons with salt before washing.

SPONGE WASHING. Put your sponges in the dishwasher for easy cleaning.

CASSEROLE CLEANSING. Food firmly lodged into the side of the casserole dish? Fill it with boiling water and a couple of tablespoons of baking soda. Let it sit for a while and then scour vigorously.

GLAZED POTTERY. Wash glazed pottery with a mild detergent in warm water to avoid damaging the glaze.

PAINT SPOT REMOVER. Use hot vinegar to remove paint spots from glass.

SAFETY GLASS CLEANING. Stop good glass from expanding and possibly bursting when placed in hot water by putting the glass in sideways.

GLASS CUSHION. When washing glassware in the sink, line the bottom with a rubber mat to protect the glass from breaking.

SILVER CLEANING. Clean silver relatively easily by adding a tablespoon of baking soda for every quart of water. Put the solution in a pot and add the silverware. Let the water boil for three minutes. When it has cooled off, polish the silver. For tough stains, scrub white toothpaste into it with a toothbrush.

THE BEST DRYING TOWELS. To make the absolutely best drying towels, place them in the laundry for numerous washings so they will develop a soft—and lint-free—surface for maximum drying capacity.

FROZEN STEEL WOOLS. When you are done scouring with steel wool, put it in the freezer to prevent it from rusting.

POTS, PANS, AND OTHER KITCHEN UTENSILS

SCORCHED PANS. If you badly burn a pan, fill it with some water and add several tablespoons of baking soda. Boil the mix until the scorched parts loosen and float to the surface. Or pour some vinegar on the bottom and cover the burned bits with Comet, and let it sit overnight.

STREAKED OUT. Rub streaks on stainless steel with baby oil to remove the marks.

BROILER PAN CLEANING. Remove scorched food from a broiler pan by sprinkling dry laundry detergent on while the pan is still hot. Dampen a paper towel with water and cover the spot with it. Leave it on for 10 to 20 minutes and the food will come off easily.

RUST REMOVAL. Remove rust from baking pans by applying cleaning powder to a raw potato and scouring the rust with it.

MARBLE WARNINGS. To prevent burning the bottom pot in a double boiler, place a couple of marbles in it. They will start to rattle when the water gets low, so you can add some water before it is too late.

HANDY TOOTHBRUSH. For reaching small areas on graters, beaters, and other cooking items, keep a toothbrush nearby for precise scouring. Never, ever use that toothbrush again for your teeth, especially if you have used it to clean silver.

LIME DEPOSIT PREVENTION. Stop the formation of lime deposits in your tea kettle early on by pouring an equal amount of water and vinegar in the kettle, bringing it to a boil, and then letting it stand for 12 to 24 hours.

COPPER CLEANSING. Add three tablespoons of salt to a spray bottle filled with vinegar. Drench the copper pot with the solution, let the cleanser sit for a while, and then rub it clean with a cloth. You can also clean copper with salt and half a lemon.

HOMEMADE COPPER POLISH. Mix equal parts of flour, white vinegar, and salt for your own homemade copper polish. Use the mixture by rubbing copper with it and then washing it off with hot water.

POLISHED COPPER POTS. Use toothpaste or Worcestershire sauce to polish copper pots. Rub it in and the tarnish will disappear.

RUSTPROOF TIN PANS. Wipe buttered paper throughout a tin pan and leave it in an oven at 350 degrees for 15 minutes to make the pan rustproof.

ENAMEL UNSTUCKER. For enamel saucepans that have food stuck on them, pour a strong solution of salty water into the pot and let it sit for three or more hours. Then place the pot in the stove and bring it to a slow boil.

STICKY BAKING DISHES. For baking dishes with gobs of sticky brown stuff, spray with oven cleaner and let soak for about 10 minutes; then wash off with warm water.

GREAT GRATER CLEANING. Think ahead when using a grater. Dab some salad oil on it before using to simplify cleaning later. Use a toothbrush to get the tough-to-reach parts of the grater when it comes time to clean it.

DEODORIZED CUTTING BOARDS. Get rid of the odor of onions and garlic on your cutting board by rubbing lime or lemon juice into the wood.

CUTTING BOARD CLEANING. Clean a stained bread board by coating it lightly with some salt and rubbing it with a juicy lemon slice.

CUTTING BOARD PRESERVATION. Make your wooden cutting board last forever by covering it with vegetable oil about every six months and letting it sit overnight.

CUTTING BOARD JUST LIKE NEW. For cutting boards that are too far gone with cuts and grime, get a scraper with a replaceable blade and scrape the board down. When the job is done, brush the board with vegetable oil.

CAST-IRON CLEANING. Clean the outside of cast-iron pans with stove polish or commercial oven cleaner. Allow the cleaner to sit for two to three hours and remove it with a solution of water and vinegar. To clean the inside, rub the inside of the pan while it is still warm with waxed paper to prevent rusting and then apply a little bit of oil to keep the pan seasoned. Never clean the inside with soap. If the pan is giving food a funny taste, try scrubbing it with salt.

THOROUGH THERMOS CLEANING. Simply add a few tablespoons of baking soda to warm water to clean a thermos bottle. For coffee stains, pour in a tablespoon of raw rice with a cup of warm water. Shake it up and rinse.

ICE CUBE TRAY CLEANSING. Drench plastic ice-cube trays with white vinegar for several hours to remove tough stains.

PRESERVED SALAD BOWLS. Wipe wooden salad bowls with paper towels soaked in cooking oil to prevent them from drying and cracking. Do not dunk salad bowls in water for more than a few seconds. The wood will dry and possibly split.

Floors, carpets, and rugs

Floors are the worst. They are always there underfoot and are difficult to hide when dirty. You can't push them in the closet or cover them with a tablecloth. And if you try covering them, they just look messier than they did at first.

Of all the things in the house, floors (next to counters) have to be cleaned most often. In addition to picking up all the baby toys and the clothing and the dog bones, you have to deal with actually cleaning them as well. Not an easy task. Maybe one day we will have houses where the floors have automatic vacuum systems that suck up any dust or debris that touch their shiny surfaces. But, for now, we have floors—beautiful in many cases—that need to be cleaned.

We can blame the necessity of keeping our floors really clean on the invention of the vacuum cleaner. Once upon a time, before electricity and the vacuum, when people only had brooms to keep a place tidy, you can be assured that the homes of the average citizen weren't quite as clean as they are today. And, another advantage of no electricity, it was darker. You couldn't see the dirt!

But we aren't suggesting going back to those times. Instead here are a few ideas on how to live in these times.

HARD-SURFACE FLOORS

VACUUM FIRST. Vacuuming hard-surface floors before you wash them saves you time when you wash or polish them because dirt doesn't get around to grind into the floor covering.

ONCE A WEEK. It is recommended that you vacuum your wood and other hard-surface floors once a week and more often in areas of heavy traffic.

KNOW THE SURFACE. It may sound obvious, but know what your floor is made of. The cleaning method that works for one surface can ruin another.

TWO VACUUMS. If you can, it is a good idea to have two vacuums: a big canister-type vacuum for carpets and rugs and a smaller one for hardwood floors, kitchen floors, etc.

ASPHALT TILE. Use plastic casters on furniture legs to minimize scratches and indentations. Remove heel marks by dipping fine-grade steel wool in liquid floor wax and rubbing spot gently. Wipe with damp cloth.

The best way to clean is to mix 1/4 cup low-sudsing all-purpose cleaner, 1 cup ammonia and 1/2 gallon water. Use rubber gloves and work in ventilated area. Apply with sponge mop and rinse with cool water. Apply two coats of self-polishing floor finish and allow to dry between coats.

BRICK FLOOR. Keep floor sealed and waxed because it is very porous and stains easily. Damp mop with a solution of water and a cup of vinegar. Floor will glisten without being polished.

GLAZED CERAMIC TILE. Damp mop with all-purpose cleaner, using synthetic scouring pad and nonabrasive cleaner for stubborn spots. Dry with soft cloth to avoid streaks. If floor dries with luster-dulling film, mop again with water containing a cup of white vinegar.

UNGLAZED CERAMIC TILE. Unglazed tile is porous; you might want to seal it to resist stains. Damp mopping with sponge mop after you vacuum will let you put off washing and rewaxing floor until it is really dirty. Try a cup of vinegar in mop water to make floor shine.

CONCRETE. The floor-cleaning task most likely to be avoided and, as a result, the floor that gets really dirty. Get rid of loose surface dirt and then try this mixture: mix 1/4 cup all-purpose cleaner with 1 cup clear ammonia and 1/2 gallon cool water. Apply to area with sponge mop and rinse with clear water. (Make sure the area is well ventilated. Wear rubber gloves.)

KITTY LITTER HELPS. Spread kitty litter on garage floor to absorb oil and grease.

CORK. A cork floor recovers quickly from the pressure of chair legs, but water will do it in every time. You must use solvent-based cleaners and polishes.

FLAGSTONE AND SLATE. Needs to be sealed if inside. To keep ahead of dirt, damp mop with sponge mop using clear water and all-purpose cleaning solution in warm water to which fabric softener has been added. Apply in slow, even strokes with just enough pressure to loosen and pick up dirt.

LINOLEUM. Needs to be waxed to shine and stand up to foot traffic. But once waxed, it just needs vacuuming and wiping with damp mop.

MARBLE. Damp mop with sponge mop, using clear water, an all-purpose cleaning solution in warm water, or a mix of 1/2 gallon water and 1 cup fabric softener.

VINYL. These no-wax floors are great and easy to maintain. Damp mop and vacuum. Clean heel marks with scouring pad. Use all-purpose cleaning solution to wash when you need to. If floor loses shine, use a gloss-renewing product available from floor manufacturer. Never throw just anything on the floor—you might damage the surface.

WOOD. Product used to seal wood floors determines how you take care of them. The popular polyurethane finish requires no waxing. There are special non-water-based wood floor cleaners on the market that can be found at flooring distributors. Avoid putting water on wood floors, though you can lightly damp mop one that has been polyurethaned.

REMOVING HEEL MARKS. To remove greasy heel marks from vinyl or linoleum floors, try silver polish or white appliance wax.

RUB SCUFF MARKS. Rub scuff marks from floors and fingerprints from woodwork by using a rubber or art-gum eraser.

WAX REMOVER. Before waxing a very dirty resilient floor, remove the old polish with a solution of 1 cup ammonia in 1 gallon water.

PROTECTING FLOOR. Attach strips of weatherstripping to the bottoms of rockers, chair legs, and sofa feet to prevent marking the floor.

END OF PILE. To pick up those final floor sweepings that are too fine for the lip of the dust pan, wet a piece of paper and whisk it over the pile.

TWO PASSES PLEASE. You mop a floor faster when you make two passes. First, take a quick trip over it to spread the solution and wait a few minutes for it to dissolve soil. Then wring your mop dry and mop again more carefully to remove dirt.

USE YOUR FINGER. When you strip a floor, scrape it with your fingernail to tell if old wax is softened and off or not. If nothing gathers under your nail, the floor is wax free.

TWO COATS. When applying wax or finish, give the area one coat, then apply second coat in the traffic areas only and under things. This prevents wax from building up in areas where it won't have a chance to be worn off.

RINSE, RINSE. Your floor won't shine if soap residue remains after mopping. Try adding white vinegar in rinse water to neutralize alkalinity.

BUFFING HELPS. Buffing smoothes the surface of anything, so that light is absorbed instead of reflected. The new white nylon pads on floor

67

machines beat the old lambswool.

AVOID HIGH HEELS. Spiked heels can really damage floors. Take your heels off at home. You will feel better, too.

CARPETS

STAINS. Use plain club soda on fresh stains. Pour some on the spot and let it set for a few seconds, then sponge up. Older stains may need more work: try combining 2 tablespoons of detergent, 3 tablespoons of vinegar and 1 quart of water. Work this into stain and blot dry. Or make a mixture of powdered laundry detergent and warm water and brush into stain with soft brush. Blot up. Repeat if needed.

BURN IN CARPET. Remove some fuzz from an inconspicuous place in the carpet, either by shaving or pulling with pliers or tweezers. Roll it into the shape of the burn. Apply a good glue to the backing of the rug and press down into the burned place. Cover with a piece of tissue and place a book on top. This lets glue dry slowly.

To repair a small area burned down to the carpet backing, snip off the charred fibers and put white glue in the opening. Then snip fibers from a scrap of carpet or an inconspicuous part of the carpet. When glue gets tacky, poke fibers into place. If burn isn't all the way down to the backing, snip off charred tips of the fibers with scissors. The slightly shorter length of a few carpet fibers will never be noticed.

FLATTENED CARPET. Raise pile with steam iron. Build up good steam and hold iron over damaged spot. Do not touch the carpet with iron. Brush.

FIXING BRAIDED RUG. Use clean fabric glue to fix these instead of sewing. It's easy.

INDOOR/OUTDOOR SPOT. Spray with commercial prewash spray and let sit a few minutes, then hose down.

REMOVING WAX. You can use an iron to lift candle wax from carpet. Place a brown paper bag over the spot and put a hot iron over it. The wax will be absorbed into the bag.

MAKE CARPET BRIGHTER. Sprinkle salt on the carpet and let stand for an hour before you vacuum; the carpet will be brighter. Salt is also good to use on muddy footprints.

REMOVING GUM. Press ice cubes against gum on the carpet until it becomes brittle and breaks off. Then use a spot remover to get rid of all of it.

USE DOOR MATS. Place small area mats at the entrances to your home. This really helps cut down on the grime that comes in the house.

REMOVE SHOES. The cleanest houses are the ones where you take your shoes off at the door. Have a big pile of slippers at the door for your guests. Or socks. This works except if you have animals.

COFFEE STAINS. Blot spilled coffee immediately! Then mix 1 tsp. mild detergent, 1 tsp. white vinegar, and 1 quart warm water. Apply solution to the spot. Let carpet dry. Apply dry-cleaning fluid and let carpet dry again. Vacuum gently.

TOUCH UP WORK. If the spot remover you used on the carpet alters the color, try touching up small places with acrylic artist paint. If that doesn't work, try a felt-tipped marker or a permanent ink marker of the appropriate color. Go slowly and blend color into fibers.

RAISE DEPRESSIONS IN CARPET. To raise depressions left in carpet by heavy furniture, try steaming. Hold a steam iron close for steam to reach carpet, but don't let the iron touch the carpet. Lift fibers by scraping them with edge of a coin or spoon.

LOOSE THREADS. If carpet thread is loose, snip it level with the pile. If you try to pull out the thread, you risk unraveling part of the carpet.

NATURAL FIBER RUGS. After vacuuming surface and underneath fiber, sisal, and grass rugs, remove dirt and restore moisture to rugs with a damp cloth.

VACUUM ONCE A WEEK. It has been proven by all who know about these things that carpets really do need to be vacuumed at least once a week. This keeps them in good shape longer and prevents surface dirt from being ground into the fibers.

PAY ATTENTION TO CERTAIN AREAS. Areas of heavy traffic need more vacuuming as do places in front of chairs and couches. People tend to move their feet around while sitting; this can cause dirt from shoes to be ground into carpeting.

BLOCKING. After cleaning, or in any way dampening carpets, never set furniture directly on wet carpet. That may rust or cause the wood to stain it. Instead, place a small piece of cardboard about two inches square under each leg. Make sure there's no printing on the cardboard.

DRYING CARPET. Carpet pile will dry the way it's left when you finish shampooing. If you are not careful about how you leave it, it will reflect light differently and look streaky. Before it dries you should "rake" the pile with a carpet rake or a bamboo leaf rake. Be sure the nap is all standing or lying the same way, then let it dry.

69

TAKE YOUR TIME. When vacuuming, one leisurely stroke will beat four short strokes any day. Let vacuum work for you; it needs time for the beater bar to loosen the dirt and for the air flow to suck it up.

VACUUMING STAIRS. Vacuum center traffic areas of carpeted stairs with your beater bar vacuum to get out that ground-in and embedded dirt. You can wipe the sides, which are hardly ever stepped on, with damp cloth or dust them with a broom.

FRINGE ON RUGS. The fringe found on area rugs will always collect dust and dirt. They are a nightmare to vacuum because they get stuck. Instead, brush them with a counter brush using a down and away stroke. This will whisk out the soil so that you can just sweep or vacuum it, and not the fringes, up.

LOSING SUCTION? If your vacuum seems to be losing suction, the culprit is most likely a plugged vacuum hose. Items such as toothpicks and broomstraws can lodge crosswise in the hose and cut the flow of air. Try reversing the hose for a minute to see if you can push out the clog. If that doesn't do the trick, a mop handle or small garden hose can work to dislodge the obstruction.

MUDDY CARPETS. To remove mud from carpet, allow it to dry, then scrape or brush off as much as possible. Apply dish detergent solution of 20 parts water to 1 part dish detergent to whatever stain remains. Blot, rinse, and blot dry. If the stain remains, apply a dry cleaning solvent; blot dry.

PAINT ON CARPET. To remove fresh latex paint from carpet: Soak with dish detergent diluted with 20 parts water; agitate; blot; rinse; blot. If paint has dried, a little lacquer thinner will soften and remove it. A Q-tip with a bit of paint remover touched on a hard drop of paint will also soften it back to its original liquid state so that it can be blotted and rinsed out.

REARRANGE FURNITURE. To even out carpet wear, rearrange your furniture occasionally. Use scatter rugs in front of favorite pieces of furniture. Turn throw rugs and area rugs frequently.

CORNSTARCH CLEANS. Cornstarch acts as a rug cleaner. Sprinkle it on. Let stand for 5 to 30 minutes, then vacuum.

DEODORIZE WITH BAKING SODA. To deodorize a carpet, liberally apply baking soda (4 pounds for a 9- x 12-foot rug). Let stand for at least 15 minutes, then vacuum.

REMOVING EXCREMENT. To remove excrement, vomit, or urine: After scraping off solids, apply a detergent solution (1/2 tsp. mild detergent per pint of water) and blot. Then use an ammonia solution (1 Tbsp. per cup of water) and blot. Follow with a solution of equal parts white vinegar and water. Blot, flush with water, and blot again.

RED WINE STAINS. If red wine is spilled on the carpet, sponge with club soda. Or cover the stain with salt and let it absorb the wine. Vacuum the residue. If a stain remains, wipe gently with a solution of detergent, water, and a few drops of white vinegar.

Bedrooms/ dining rooms/ living rooms

After the hard-to-clean rooms like the kitchen and bathroom, the rest of the house seems like a breeze. What is it to pick up and vacuum a bedroom or living room? Pick up that clutter and put it away. Dust with that rag. Polish that table. Sweep the floor. You've got it. Sometimes a family room takes harder use and is, therefore, a bit harder to keep looking good. But maybe your family room has big doors that can close; you can then pretend it doesn't exist, except for the family.

Bedrooms will be easier to clean if everything that belongs there can be stored away. Under-the-bed storage is a great help for this. Baskets help catch odds and ends, everything from sweaters to Q-tips. Some headboards have built-in bookcases and shelves where you can store things, and a bedside table usually holds those treasures you can't bear to give away.

If you are to have any hope of keeping children's rooms clean, it's vital that you organize the room so that it's easy for them to put things away. The room usually has to change as the child grows and interests change. A two-year-old may need a low shelf on which to put blocks while a six-year-old may need lots of bright plastic boxes in which to put all her Legos.

Closets need to fit your children, too. Provide lots of hooks when they are little. A basket or hamper near the closet is a good idea, too.

KEEP IT SIMPLE. The greatest invention for the bed has to be the duvet, that comforter that simply slips over everything and gets thrown on top of the bed in the morning. No more fussing and tucking and folding back with spreads and blankets and all. The comforter serves all purposes, and it looks good. This is a simple way for children to keep their beds neat, too.

VACUUM THE BED. Spreads and blankets collect dust just like anything else. The next time you are collecting the dust bunnies under the bed, vacuum the top of the bed, too. Strange but true.

STORE EXTRA MATTRESSES. Store extra mattresses under the beds in your child's room to use for instant beds when a friend sleeps over.

NO HEADBOARD? Make your own. You can make your own headboard and hang it on the wall behind your bed. Cut a piece of hardwood to size; paint or stain, then hang with heavy-duty picture wire or mount it with screws or toggles. To make a padded headboard, start with a base of plywood and cover with polyester batting. Cover with fabric; overlap to back of plywood. Mount with picture hangers or bolts.

MATTRESS CLEANING. If your mattress has a mildew attack, try to get it outside and brush off the mildew. Or vacuum it and throw away the vacuum bag when you are done. Lay outside in sun until dry, or dry with a fan indoors.

PILLOW TALK. Know what your pillow is filled with so you know how to clean it. Some polyester-filled pillows are washable, others are not. The label should tell you. Refresh pillows by airing near an open window or hanging on a clothesline outside.

INSTANT PILLOW. Stuff rectangular sheets of bubble pack into a pillowcase.

CURB CORNERS. Soften the corners of a sharp bed frame with carpet scraps to prevent scraping of legs or gouging of walls.

ROLLING STORAGE. Add casters to old drawers and slide under the bed for extra storage.

SPREAD HANGER. Attach a sturdy towel rack to the back of a bedroom door to store the bedspread neatly overnight.

CLEAN THE CEILING. Clean once every other week with brush of vacuum cleaner. Get cobwebs off with feather duster. Don't crush them into the ceiling; they will leave black smudge marks. Use a sponge mop on a dirty ceiling.

CLEANING RADIATORS. First, thoroughly vacuum the radiator. Do this often so the heating unit doesn't recirculate all the dirt and grime into the air. After vacuuming, clean the unit with a solution of 1/2 cup vinegar, 1 cup ammonia, and 1/4 cup baking soda mixed in a gallon of warm water. Do wear rubber gloves and work in a well-ventilated area. Rinse with clear water.

WALLS

CLEANING WALLS. Walls get what we call "passive dirty" versus "active dirty." Dirt just sort of floats over and lands there. Of course, children tend to put sticky hands on walls, too, and crayons and whatever. Anyway, they do need to get tended to on a regular basis.

Clean walls regularly with your vacuum brush attachment. Test any product you may want to use on your wall in an inconspicuous place before using. Wash walls from the bottom to the top, overlapping cleaned areas to prevent streaks.

REMOVING TAPE FROM WALLS. Take transparent tape off walls without marring the paint or wallpaper by using a warm iron. Through a protective cloth, press the tape with the iron to soften and loosen its adhesive backing.

GET SMUDGES WHILE FRESH. Remove finger smudges while they are fresh. Do not scrub with excessive pressure, or use synthetic scouring pads or abrasive cleaners.

SMOKE STAINS CAN COME OFF. Slight smoke stains on brick above a fireplace can be removed with an abrasive cleanser. Scrub the cleanser into moistened brick and then rinse with clear water, making sure no white residue remains.

GETTING THOSE CRAYON MARKS OFF. You can lift crayon marks off a painted wall by rubbing them carefully with a cloth or sponge dampened with mineral spirits or lighter fluid. Remove any shine by sponging lightly with hot water.

DEALING WITH WALLPAPER. Wallpaper is not always washable. Some is, so you can carefully wash with a light cleaning solution. With unwashable paper you can try these ideas:

- Smudges can be removed gently from wallpaper with an art-gum eraser.

- Soil can come off with a piece of rye bread, wadded up and used like an eraser.

- To clean a grease spot, blot with paper towels and sprinkle cornstarch on stain. After cornstarch absorbs grease, rub it off gently and vacuum.

- To remove crayon from wallpaper, rub with a dry soap-filled, fine-grade steel wool pad. Or use a wad of white paper toweling that has been moistened lightly with dry cleaning solvent.

KEEP ARMS DRY. To keep your arms dry while washing walls, wrap a strip of cotton batting around your wrists and secure it with rubber bands.

CERAMIC TILE. Clean both glazed and unglazed ceramic tile regularly with an all-purpose cleaning solution or spray tile-and-grout cleaner. Scrub dirt from the grout with a toothbrush, taking care not to scratch the tile. It is a good idea to rinse after cleaning. Then buff dry with a soft cloth to bring out the shine.

MIRROR TILE. You can use a glass cleaner on mirror tile; never use soap. Try mixing 1/3 cup clear ammonia with 1 gallon warm water. Apply with a squeegee or pour into spray container and spray it on tiles. Buff with lint-free cloth or paper towels.

A PAINTED WALL CLEANER. Mix 1/2 cup vinegar, 1 cup clear ammonia, 1/4 cup baking soda, and 1 gallon warm water.

FIREPLACES

ROUTINE CARE. Give your fireplace and its accessories routine cleanings throughout the woodburning season so you don't end up with an accumulation of soot, ashes, and creosote.

VACUUM OFTEN. Vacuum often to prevent dust and soot from building up on the hearth. But be sure to vacuum only when all the embers have been out for at least 12 hours.

BURN SEASONED WOOD. Be sure to burn only well-dried wood to minimize dangerous creosote buildup.

INSPECT OFTEN. Inspect the flue, firebox, and chimney yearly for any creosote accumulation.

DON'T USE ABRASIVE CLEANERS. Avoid abrasive cleaners inside the fireplace. Many leave a flammable residue, and they can wear away the firebrick.

ANDIRON CARE. Try cleaning brass andirons with fine-grade steel wool dipped in cooking oil and rubbed gently.

GLASS ENCLOSURES. Remove smoke stains on glass enclosures with a solution of 1/2 cup vinegar in 1 gallon warm water. Add 1 Tbsp. clear ammonia. Spray on the glass or wipe it on with a cloth. Rinse with warm water and dry with clean cloth.

BAKED-ON CREOSOTE. If sap and creosote have baked onto your fireplace grate, you will need to use a commercial oven cleaner. Work outdoors, wear rubber gloves, and observe all precautions. Allow to sit overnight.

VARIOUS STUFF AROUND THE HOUSE

BOOK CARE. Arrange books at the front of the shelves so air can circulate and prevent mustiness. Try to protect from direct sunlight, which will fade the bindings. Vacuum once a year with small brush attachment. Remove dust from binding and edges. To remove grease stains from books, rub with soft white-bread crumbs.

VACUUM STEREO AND CDS. Vacuum your compact disc collection and your stereo equipment often to keep them dust free.

REMOVING HARDENED WAX. A big problem with any kind of candlestick is the dripping wax. Remove the hardened wax drip by pushing it off candlestick with the ball of your finger or fingernail covered with a thin cloth. If the wax resists these methods, dip the candlestick in warm water to soften the wax for removal; if the candlestick is not immersible, soften the wax with warm air from a hair dryer. Silver candlesticks can be placed in the freezer first. After wax freezes, it will peel off.

WIDE VACUUM. If you have a large house and lots of carpeting, invest in a wide-track vacuum. It covers a 16-inch width of carpet at a time, instead of the usual 10–12 inches.

CARPET SWEEPERS. Carpet sweepers are fine for surface litter but they don't get at the embedded dirt. The carpet may look clean, but it will soon be filled with dirt.

ODOR REMOVAL. Air fresheners don't really kill the odor, they just mask it. The only way to get rid of an odor is to find and get rid of the source. As long as the source of the problem remains, there will always be the odor.

DOORKNOBS GET DIRTY. Spray doorknobs and a 10-inch area around them with an all-purpose cleaner solution. Let sit for a minute to dissolve the dirt, and then wipe off with a terrycloth towel.

SCUFF MARKS ON DOORS. Black marks on the bottom of doors can be worked on with a green nylon scrub sponge and a cleaning solution. Get the sponge wet and scrub with care. Dry with a clean cloth.

DUST FIRST! Always dust first before you vacuum. This knocks stuff onto the floor so the vacuum will get it.

TREATING DUST MOPS. Dust mops are more efficient on hard-surface floors than bristle brooms. To treat a dust mop, spray with Endust or a dust mop oil. Roll it up like a sock and place in a plastic bag for 12 hours. This will help it do the job better.

FURNITURE

USE LESS POLISH. One big problem with furniture is that it accumulates too much polish. Use less, and use it less often.

MOVING FURNITURE. To move furniture without scratching the floor, tilt the unit to lift each leg and lay a towel under it, then pull towel as you move the unit.

WHITE FURNITURE CLEANER. To spruce up white painted furniture, wash with a solution of 1 Tbsp. baking soda in 1 quart warm water.

FURNITURE CLEANER. Cover a water mark on finished wooden furniture with mayonnaise, then sprinkle with salt. With a clean cloth, rub the mixture until stain disappears, then buff until dry. Rewax if needed.

TURN BARE OAK GRAY. You can turn bare oak from brown to a driftwood gray by rubbing with ammonia. This is permanent, though, so take care.

DISGUISE SCRATCHES. You can disguise a scratch on furniture by rubbing bits of pecans or Brazil nuts into the wood. Or by using furniture crayons to match the stain more exactly.

REMOVING WHITE RINGS. Wait before you attack. Sometimes they disappear of their own free will. You can try cigarette ashes (ugh) moistened with cooking oil and applied with finger. If it doesn't work, you can try table salt and a drop of water; or silver polish or car polish. Be careful.

WICKER CARE. Remove dust from wicker with a vacuum. Grime can be removed by washing with a solution of 2 Tbsp. ammonia per gallon of water. Use a toothbrush to get at those hard-to-reach spots. Rinse well and dry in shade.

WET WICKER ONCE A YEAR. To prevent wicker from drying out, wet it down at least once a year. Don't leave outside when not in use. Sunshine dehydrates it and water rots it.

USE MIRRORS. Place mirrors behind and on the bottom of the china cabinet to make your glassware sparkle.

ACID BATHS. Never use an acid bath to strip furniture because it weakens the glue and removes all the natural oils in the wood.

BLEACHING. To bleach wood, scrub the surface with 1 part chlorine bleach to 10 parts water to remove color, then rinse with water and dry quickly with soft rag. The wood must be sealed after this process. Mix up a thin solution of Plaster of Paris and water and apply it to the whole surface and let dry. Then wipe off the excess with damp cloth. The Plaster of Paris will sink into the wood and seal it below the surface. Select an alcohol-based wood stain and brush it onto the surface evenly. Then brush on a coat of white oil and polish frequently and thoroughly with beeswax polish.

DECK CHAIRS. Remove the canvas and wash it in soapy water with a little ammonia. Scrub if needed. Rinse well and dry in air, then press with iron. Scrub frame and replace canvas.

DENTS. Cover dents in wood with wet blotting paper and press with hot iron, repeating if necessary. The compressed wood fibers will swell to original size. Polish as usual.

DUST PUMP. Use an old bicycle pump or a hair dryer to blow dust away on bedsprings or any intricate object.

PICTURE FRAMES. To clean gilt frames, mix 1 egg white with 1 teaspoon bicarbonate of soda and sponge surface with mixture. Or wipe with liquid detergent, then polish with clean cloth.

POLISHING HINT. To make large flat surfaces easier to polish, heat a brick or an old-fashioned flat iron in oven until hot. Wrap the hot brick in several pieces of old blanket and apply the polish to the flat side of the blanket. Then iron the surface in the direction of the grain until area is covered with polish. The heat melts the wax and allows it to sink into wood easily and the weight of the brick eliminates arm ache.

RUSH. To clean rush, sponge with warm salt water then rinse with hot water and dry in the sun. If it has yellowed, sponge with lemon juice and salt, then rinse and dry. If it has sagged, clean it, then saturate with hot water and dry outside.

WOODWORM HOLES. Place the point of a penknife into the dead wormholes with the blade in the same direction as the wood grain, and push the blade in a little way to destroy the perfect circular shape of the hole. Fill the hole well with beeswax polish mixed with a wood stain to match the color of the wood.

TO CLEAN OAK. To clean and feed oak, rub the surface with boiled linseed oil on a soft cloth, then polish off excess with soft dry chamois cloth.

CHILL MARKS. Cloudy "chill" marks appear on French polished furniture when exposed to extremes of temperature. To remove these marks, gently wave a lighted taper from side to side over the marks until they disappear, taking care not to scorch varnish! Then rub over area with a warm cloth and polish well. Keep article at a constant temperature.

PERFUME STAINS. To remove perfume stains from polished wood, rub the stain lightly and quickly with denatured alcohol followed by plenty of boiled linseed oil. (Do not use denatured alcohol on varnished surfaces because it will dissolve varnish.)

WATER STAINS. Rub water stains on polished wood with petroleum jelly or boiled linseed oil and repeat frequently.

Bathrooms

I t's much easier to live with some dirty rooms than with others. You can easily go to sleep at night knowing there are lots of weird dust bunnies under your bed, but in the morning when you brush your teeth you really do want to face a clean sink.

Bathrooms tend to get messy quickly. Used towels, makeup bottles, and toothpaste tubes get thrown around and need to be picked up daily. Clothing gets tossed before you take a shower and needs to be remembered. Having storage areas or hampers in the bathroom helps with these simple tasks. But even if you have a place for everything, you still can end up with soap scum!

TEACH EVERYONE TO HELP. Teach your kids and your spouse to rinse out the tub or shower stall after each use. Rinse it while you are still wet. Spray water on all surfaces, get some soap on a sponge, and wipe around the tub or shower and rinse. The sink should also get this treatment at least once a day.

KEEP TILE CLEAN. If you keep the tile and porcelain surfaces clean, you won't have to use abrasives (which scratch surfaces) to get at built-up gunk.

CLEAN TOILET AND FLOOR ONCE A WEEK. Vacuum floor first to get up all hair and loose dirt. Be sure it's completely dry before you vacuum.

CLEAN SHOWER STALLS FIRST. Use a tile cleaner and a tile brush. Tile cleaner needs to sit a while before it works, because it is mainly a chemical action that gets things clean. Once it has set, you can scrub area around where first applied. A brush works well because it gets into grout between tiles.

MOVE TO SHOWER DOOR. If you have a shower door, scrub that too. If the door has a runner (the worst!) clean it with a toothbrush and a cleaning formula. If this doesn't work, use a paint scraper; move it back and forth inside the runner. This can be disgusting, but gets easier and more tolerable each time you do it. Don't rinse anything till you have finished the job.

USE THAT TOOTHBRUSH AROUND TUB. Start at the end opposite the faucet and use the toothbrush at the top of the tub where it meets the tile. The brush can get out much of the gook, but you may have to use bleach on bad areas.

CLEAN DISCOLORED PORCELAIN. Try a mix of lemon juice and borax on discolored porcelain. Scrub the paste into the stain and rinse well.

GET THE YELLOW OUT. If your tub is yellowed, try rubbing with a small amount of salt and turpentine, mixed to a paste. Rinse well.

GROSS GROUT. Use a toothbrush or nailbrush to clean grout. Dip brush in bleach to get out difficult spots and mildew.

GROUT CLEANER. Mix 3 cups of baking soda with 1 cup warm water to form a paste. Scrub on grout and rinse well.

GET HAIR OUT FIRST. Dampen a piece of tissue or toilet paper and quickly pick up hair that is in sink or tub before cleaning.

CLEAN SINK DRAIN. Bad job, but if the water isn't going out it is time to check sink drain for hair. Twist the stopper and pull. Clean hair and slime off, and replace. A world of difference.

CLEAN FIXTURES WITH RUBBING ALCOHOL. Use a cotton ball and rub rubbing alcohol on fixtures such as the faucet, drain to the tub, and toilet handle after cleaning for a real shine.

CLEAN CAREFULLY. All the new fiberglass and plastic tubs need to be treated carefully using mild bathroom and non-abrasive cleansers. Spray these on, let sit, and then (when still wet) scrub the surface lightly with a white nylon-faced sponge.

KEEP SQUEEGEE IN SHOWER. For the clean types, keep the squeegee in the shower and then while you are showering you can use it on walls to remove soap scum just before you are done. Saves lots of work later.

WAX THAT WALL. If your fiberglass shower enclosure seems to collect dirt, it may be because of too much cleaning with abrasives. Try applying a coat of car wax and see how a glossy finish will help repel soap deposits.

TOILET RINGS. If you have a ring in your toilet, rub it gently with a pumice stone to remove it. Make sure the pumice stone is wet so you won't scratch the surface. Don't use abrasives.

BRUSH BOWL DAILY. Brush the toilet bowl daily to prevent hard-water buildup. It will help prevent rings, too, which are caused by hard-water deposits.

SAVE THAT CLEANER. Don't pour liquid toilet bowl cleaner directly into toilet because it will become very diluted. First, use toilet brush to force water out of bowl, then apply cleaner to brush and swish around bowl and under rim.

SAVE THAT SODA. Put that flat cola drink in your toilet. Let sit for an hour or so then swish around and flush. A clean toilet!

VINEGAR FOR HARD WATER. Use a solution of white vinegar and water to remove hard-water deposits on shower enclosures.

GROUT COVERUPS. Use white shoe polish to cover up spots on white grout.

TRY LEMON OIL. Lemon oil will remove water spots on metal shower frames of shower doors.

CLOGGED HEAD. If your shower head is clogged with lime and mineral deposits, try boiling it in 1/2 cup white vinegar mixed with 1 quart of water for 15 minutes. Plastic shower heads can be soaked in a hot vinegar and water solution of same ratio.

HAIR SPRAY ON MIRROR. If there is a cloud of hair spray on mirror, wipe with rubbing alcohol.

USE WINDOW CLEANER ON MIRRORS. Spray mirror lightly and evenly and wipe with dry cloth till dry.

EMPTY MEDICINE CABINET REGULARLY. Attack medicine cabinets often and throw out old medicine. Wipe and clean shelves. Keep medicine away from children and locked.

AVOID BATHTUB RINGS. To avoid bathtub rings, don't use oily bath preparation. Use a water softener if you live in a hard-water area. Rinse the tub immediately after bathing.

GETTING RID OF RINGS. Wipe off with undiluted ammonia or a wet sponge generously sprinkled with baking soda; rinse clean and wipe dry. For a stubborn stain, scour with automatic dishwashing detergent or rub with cloth dipped in vinegar.

CLEAN SHOWER CURTAIN. If you have mildew on your shower curtain, soak it in tub of water mixed with water softener.

USE A LEMON. Rub stained enamel fixtures with a cut lemon; for stubborn stains, use a paste of lemon juice and borax.

DEFOGGER FOR MIRROR. To prevent bathroom mirror from fogging up during cold weather, spread a little shaving cream on the mirror and wipe it off with a tissue.

Windows/ draperies

Most homes have windows and we are happy that they do. Some people make it a point to never clean their windows. They tend to have curtains and think that no one can see the windows anyway; so they focus on the curtains if they focus on anything. But a clean window can really make a difference in a house and is a big part of anyone's spring cleaning ritual. When you feel the urge to be outdoors, clean a window and you'll feel as if you are bringing some of that clear spring air inside.

Like anything else, it's not hard once you get started. It's the idea of window cleaning that is the worst part. If you really have a thing about it, and want to avoid it at all costs, then hire a professional window-cleaning service to help. They know what they are doing and, if you can afford it, can make this once-a-year job easy on you.

WINDOWS

GET THE WHOLE FAMILY INVOLVED. If you have children, this is one time they might want to help with housework. Even the youngest child can have a task to do if the window isn't too high. Or if the children are older, put a time limit on it and make it into a game with a prize at the end for everyone!

USE DIFFERENT STROKES. Use vertical strokes when washing outside and horizontal strokes when washing inside (or vice versa). This way you will know which side those streaks are on.

WASH WINDOWS FROM TOP TO BOTTOM. This way you won't have drips messing up what you have already done.

SQUEEGEES ARE GREAT. Use a long-handled squeegee on big windows. These are easy to use and don't leave many streaks.

ERASE FOR SHINE. Use a clean blackboard eraser over a just-washed window if you really want it to shine.

AVOID STEEL WOOL. Never use steel wool on glass and avoid getting window cleaner on woodwork.

WASH ON A CLOUDY DAY. Try not to wash windows in the sun because the glass may streak.

WHAT TO USE? Some say use newspaper and others say never use newspaper. Others swear by paper towels. One tip is to use newspaper that has been crumbled up and dipped into a bowl of vinegar. Dip in the paper, wipe glass, and then wipe till almost dry with same paper. Then shine with cloth or more newspaper.

TRY SOME COLA. Use leftover cola drink on grease spots.

WINDOW SOLUTIONS. Mix 1/3 cup of ammonia in 1 gallon of warm water. Apply with a sponge or pour into spray bottle. Or try mixing 1/2 cup ammonia, 1 cup white vinegar and 2 Tbsp. of cornstarch to a bucket of warm water.

PROTECT HANDS. Wear rubber gloves when washing with strong solutions.

SPOTTED SILLS. Pour diluted rubbing alcohol on a cloth and rub the entire sill. It will look freshly painted.

SCREEN WINDOWS. Rub a brush-type roller over the screen to pick up dust.

LOOSEN STICKY WINDOWS. To loosen sticky windows, lubricate the channels with silicone spray, a bar of soap, or a candle.

BREAK THAT SEAL. To break a paint seal, force the blade of a putty knife between the sash and the frame; slide the blade up and down the length of the window and across the top and bottom as needed.

CLEAN SCREENS. Screens become embedded with bugs, dirt, and what have you. To clean, take them down and bring them outside. Lay them flat on an old dropcloth so they won't be scratched while cleaning. Scrub them with a brush and some all-purpose cleaning solution. Rinse with a garden hose. Shake them gently to get water off and dry in the sun.

AVOID TOO MUCH SOAP. Too much soap in a washing solution will cause streaking.

WIPE THE SQUEEGEE. Always wipe the squeegee blade between strokes with a damp cloth, not a dry one. The dampness will remove excess water, yet leave the blade lubricated so that it won't twitch when it hits a dry piece on the glass.

CLEANING JALOUSIES. To clean slatted windows, a 6-inch tweezers-like squeegee is on the market. Wipe dish detergent solution on the slats and then squeegee it off one slat at a time and wipe with a dry cloth.

GET LABELS OFF. Labels, stickers, etc., that stay behind on glass can be taken off with either a razor or blade scraper or a heavy-duty solvent. Always wet the window first if you are going to use a scraper and work carefully so you don't scratch the glass.

BUGS IN THE TRACK. For window tracks that are filled with bugs, loosen the debris with an old toothbrush and vacuum with the crevice attachment. If track is wet, spray on cleaning solution and let it sit for 5 minutes. Then wrap a screwdriver with a piece of toweling and run blade down track. Most of the gook sticks to the towel. Repeat again if needed.

DRAPERIES/CURTAINS

CURTAINS AND THE LIKE. Bedspreads, tablecloths, sheets, and quilts can make good curtains and may be cheaper than fabric. Look at some of the new rods on market; they may be decorative statement themselves. You just have to drape the sheet over the rod. No sewing involved!

DRAPERY WEIGHTS. To keep draperies hanging evenly, slip old keys in the hems.

PROTECT DRAPES. A coat hanger will protect drapes from damage during carpet cleaning or other jobs in the vicinity. Fold the drapes in half (like pants) over the hanger, and place the hanger on the curtain rod.

CLEAN BLINDS. Clean blinds often and they will be much easier to deal with. If the dust is left on, it blends with sticky airborne oils and becomes a stubborn sticky coating that requires much more cleaning. Dust often, using a puff duster on closed blinds.

REALLY CLEAN BLINDS. If you have let the blinds go and they are a mess, then take them down and put in closed position on old tarp. Scrub the blinds with a soft brush and ammonia solution, then turn them over and do the other side. Rinse with a hose and then shake to reduce water spots.

WEIGHING A SHADE. If a shade tends to curl up at the bottom, you can usually weight it with matched pairs of refrigerator magnets.

RESURFACE WORN SHADES. You can resurface worn shades with new fabric attached with rubber cement. Bed sheets, cut to fit, work well this way. Be careful to smooth out the fabric so there are no air bubbles, or the shade will wrinkle when it rolls up.

CLEAN WINDOW SHADE. To remove stains and smudges from a window shade, lay it on a flat surface and clean the blemishes with an art-gum eraser or a dough-type wallpaper cleaner.

IF SHADE ALWAYS GOES UP. If a shade won't stay down, easing the tension can help. Roll the shade up, remove it from its brackets, and unroll it by hand; then replace it in the brackets and roll it up again.

Cleaning/
miscellaneous

Cleaning can always be put off until tomorrow. But tricks along the way certainly do help. Some of these may strike a note and you may always remember them. Others you will read and dismiss and promptly forget. But someday they may prove handy. You just never know when you will need to know how to make life easier. And that's what tips are all about, after all.

CLEANING THE CHARCOAL GRILL. Mix 1/2 cup of liquid cleaner with 1 gallon of water and pour it into a heavy-duty plastic garbage bag (or plastic garbage can). Immerse the grill in the bag, secure with a twist tie, and leave soaking overnight. The next day, brush off the burnt-on soil, rinse, and you are ready to barbecue.

TO PREVENT WALLS FROM BEING MARKED with nail holes from false starts when hanging a picture, make a paper pattern of the picture frame. After you have found the correct position for a hanger, perforate the paper with a sharp pencil to mark the wall.

TO REMOVE LIME FROM A TEA KETTLE: Boil a strong vinegar solution (1/2 cup vinegar to 1 pint water) in the kettle.

IF TWO DRINKING GLASSES STICK TOGETHER, fill the top glass with cold water and set the bottom one in hot water to separate them.

FREEZE CANDLES. Put candles in freezer before you burn them; they won't drip as much.

TELEPHONE. Clean with rubbing alcohol.

OLDIE BUT GOODIE. Clean pewter with cabbage leaves!

STORE OUT-OF-SEASON CLOTHES in a large, new, plastic, lidded trash can. The clothes will stay mothproof and dry, even in a damp basement.

IF A PICTURE WON'T HANG STRAIGHT, wrap masking tape around the wire on both sides of the hook so the wire won't slip. Or install nails or hooks a short distance apart horizontally; two hooks are better than one for keeping pictures in place.

HANGING FROM A MOLDING? If you are hanging a picture from molding, try using nylon fishing line rather than picture wire. It won't show as much.

FILL DENTS IN FLOOR. Try filling dents in a wood floor with clear nail polish or shellac. Because the floor's color shows through, the dents will not be apparent.

PEGBOARD IS VERSATILE. Pegboard is most often used on walls. But it can be used as a room divider or to make the inside of a closet or cabinet door more functional.

SAVE COFFEE CANS and nail them to the wall to make bins for clips, pins, nails, or other small items.

DRAWER HELP. To increase the capacity of a drawer, outfit it with a lift-out tray. Fill tray with items you often use and use space around tray for items you rarely use.

EXTRA CLOSET SPACE. For extra closet space, see if your closets can hold a second shelf above the one that is there. If you install a main clothes rod high enough, you may be able to install another rod beneath it on which to hang slacks, shirts, and skirts.

EXTRA CORNER. The corner of a room or large closet can become a closet for hard-to-store items like golf bags, skis, and the like. Simply angle a decorative folding screen across the little-used corner.

CONVERT TO CEDAR CLOSET. Change an ordinary closet into a cedar closet by installing thin cedar sheets over inside surfaces. Then weather-strip to keep the scent in.

LINE MEDICINE CABINET shelves with blotting paper to absorb any spills.

HANG A BASKET NEAR THE FRONT DOOR and always keep your keys in it. You will always know where they are. Also use this for outgoing mail.

THERMOS BOTTLE. Fill a thermos bottle with warm water and add 1 teaspoon bicarbonate of soda. Replace the stopper and shake, then rinse well and dry. This removes musty smell.

CLOUDY GLASS. When glass clouds, and ordinary washing doesn't help clean it, cover the glass with wet potato peelings and leave for 24 hours. Then rinse in cold water and dry.

DECANTERS. To clean decanters, fill with warm water and 1 tablespoon of baking powder and some crushed eggshells. Leave for 12 hours then rinse with warm water.

CLEANING OILY BOTTLES. To clean oily bottles, fill them with fine ashes and place in a pan of cold water. Gradually heat the water till it boils, then simmer for 30 minutes. When cool, wash out the ashes with cold water and wash the bottle in hot soapy water; rinse and dry.

SAVE CRYSTAL. Cover the shelves used for storing crystal with felt or thick paper to prevent glass from chipping.

PHOTOGRAPHS. Clean old photographs by rubbing gently with stale bread.

PLAYING CARDS. To clean playing cards, rub the surface with a soft cloth dipped in a weak solution of camphor oil and warm water.

ENVELOPES. Envelopes sealed with egg whites cannot be steamed open.

LEATHER BOOK BINDINGS. Clean leather-bound books with Goddard's Saddler's Wax and cheesecloth.

SILVER POLISHING CLOTHS. Mix 1 cup water with silver paste and soak old towels in the mixture. When saturated, hang the cloths up to dry without squeezing. Use these cloths to dry silver after washing.

CLEANING GOLD. Wash plain gold articles in lukewarm soapy water and dry with a cotton cloth, then polish with a chamois cloth. Wash filigree gold in lukewarm water with a little ammonia added, then dry and polish with chamois cloth.

BRASS. To clean very dirty brass, boil the article in a pan of water with 1 tablespoon of salt and 1 cup white vinegar for several hours. Never scour lacquered or varnished brass. Apply a paste made of lemon juice and cream of tartar, and leave on for five minutes. Then wash in warm water and dry with soft cloth. To remove lacquer, sponge article with denatured alcohol. Lemon juice mixed with metal polish will help to keep article clean longer.

DOOR PLATES. When cleaning door plates, cut the exact shape and size of the door plates out of thick cardboard. Place template around the plate while cleaning to protect the surrounding surface.

COPPER. Wash in hot, soapy water and rub dry with soft, chamois cloth; then air thoroughly. To clean very dirty copper, boil in a pan of water with salt and white vinegar for several hours. If tarnished, rub with mix of salt and white vinegar or half a lemon dipped in salt. Rinse and wash in hot soapy water. Rinse again and dry well.

WINDOWSILL CLEANER. If your wooden windowsills are rain spotted, refresh them by wiping with a little diluted rubbing alcohol on a soft cloth.

BATHROOM CLEANER. Keep a bottle of rubbing alcohol handy to shine chrome fixtures and to remove hair spray from mirrors.

AMMONIA USES. Before waxing a very dirty resilient floor, remove old polish with a solution of 1 cup ammonia in 1 gallon water. Combine ammonia with silver paste polish and apply with soft cloth to clean silver-plated and stainless steel cutlery. When laundering sheets, towels, and clothes, remove absorbed body oil by adding 1 cup ammonia to the usual amount of granular detergent.

USE MUFFIN TIN. Keep those tacks and nails assorted in an old muffin tin.

BEAUTIFUL BAKING SODA:

- Deodorize dishwasher: toss a handful of baking soda into bottom between washes.
- Remove grease from grill by soaking in 1/4 cup baking soda per quart warm water.
- Spruce up white painted furniture by washing with solution of 1 Tbsp. baking soda in 1 quart warm water.
- Remove wallpaper smudges with thick baking soda paste.

ADD BORAX. Add 1/2 cup borax to soap or detergent when doing laundry to eliminate diaper odors and stains and make diapers more absorbent.

USE BORAX FOR SHINE. For an especially brilliant shine, rinse your fine china in a sinkful of warm water with 1/2 cup borax added; rinse again in clear water.

MUD SCRAPER. Make a killer doormat that will scrub off the worst mud by gluing or nailing bottle caps side by side, smooth side down, on a piece of plywood.

VACUUM ATTACHMENT. Instead of removing all the contents of a drawer to dust it, cover the nozzle of the vacuum with cheesecloth so that small objects aren't sucked up into hose.

FIREPLACE FRESHENER. Add some dried citrus rinds to the fire for a spicy fragrance.

CORD HOLDER. To keep vacuum cleaner cord from retracting while in use, clip a clothespin to it after pulling it to desired length.

USE COTTON SWABS for cleaning between blender and phone buttons, in sewing machine and camera crevices, in shower-door runners, and other small spots.

SCREEN CLEANER. Save used sheets of fabric softener to remove dust and static from TV and computer screens.

USE GLOVES ON BLINDS. Wearing soft cotton gloves sprayed with furniture polish, wipe each slat of Venetian blinds with one long stroke.

SALVAGE A SPONGE. To save a soured sponge, saturate it with lemon juice, then rinse thoroughly.

USE A MAGNET. Use a small magnet to pick up spilled pins, needles, tacks, and staples.

FLUSH ENHANCER. Check under the rim of your toilet bowl with a mirror to see if openings appear clogged. If they are, clean them with a wire hanger.

RENEW CHAMOIS. To renew an old piece of chamois, soak it for 15 minutes in a bucket of warm water mixed with 1 teaspoon of olive oil.

PEANUT BUTTER REMOVES TAGS. Use a dab of peanut butter to remove remains of price tags on pots, pans and other metal or plastic items.

PROTECT FROM RUST. Use petroleum jelly to protect the metal parts on tools, fishing rods, cooking utensils, etc. by rubbing lightly.

USE A PIPE CLEANER to remove the dirt from the wheel of a can opener or clean the bobbin area of a sewing machine. You can also use pipe cleaners to open ports in gas ranges, steam irons, and aerosol containers.

FLOWER CLEANER. Clean artificial flowers by shaking them in a large paper bag filled with 1/2 cup salt.

SILLY PUTTY CLEANS, TOO. Use Silly Putty to remove lint from clothes, erase pencil marks and clean computer keys.

USE TOOTHPASTE ON SCRATCHES. Cover a stain or scratch on acrylic or plastic with toothpaste, let dry, then rub with soft cloth.

BRUSH SOFTENER. Revive old paint brushes in a solution of white vinegar and water, then wash in heavy-duty detergent.

WAX PAPER WORKS ON FLOORS. Clean and shine a floor between waxings by putting wax paper over the mop head and running it over the floor.

USE WAX PAPER FOR SHINE. For a quick shine, rub appliance exteriors and other surfaces with wax paper.

Laundry/ ironing

L aundry is one of those necessities of life that you really cannot get away from. It is always there, unless you happen to send all your clothing to the dry cleaners or are a member of a nudist colony. Since laundry is part of our lives we have to accept it and approach it from a rational point of view. Some people even like doing laundry. So it goes.

Laundry is one thing that has to be done regularly. If you don't have a washer and dryer, you probably spend time at a laundromat; but these tips can help you there, too. Don't let it scare you, even though some of the new fabric labels can be a bit intimidating. Take a deep breath and realize that people have been dealing with cleaning their clothing for years and years. And be thankful we have advanced beyond the stage of scrubbing on rocks to get out spots. We really have come a long way.

GENERAL TIPS

ORGANIZE THE EFFORT. Some like to have a fixed day as "laundry day": one day a week when they wash all their clothes. Others throw wash in the machine in the morning before leaving for work and take it out later in the day. Whichever works for you is fine. Some families prefer that each member do his or her own laundry. That's a good idea, but only works in ideal situations with people who care about wearing clean clothes.

ANYONE CAN DO IT. It is important to remember that anyone can do laundry. Divvy up the tasks according to time and plan it.

ORGANIZE THE ROOM. If you are lucky enough to have a laundry room, put baskets in it to hold different types of laundry. It can be as simple as a white basket for whites and a colored one for colored clothing. This will eliminate a sorting step.

NAME TAGS. If you have little children around the same size you can sew name tags in their clothing or use colored laundry markers and give each item a different colored dot on the label. This enables your children to help sort the clothes after they have been washed.

LAUNDROMAT TOTE. Get a tote of some kind to hold all your supplies so once you get to the laundromat you don't have to buy something you forgot. Take lots of change, too. Read and follow instructions on the wall. Find a good laundromat: a clean one with an attendant on duty. One with a coffee bar is always nice.

SORTING CLOTHES

IMPORTANCE OF SORTING. The first step is to sort clothes into different categories. You will save time and energy and end up with laundry loads that look clean and smell fresh.

EMPTY ALL POCKETS. As you start to sort, remember to empty all pockets and close zippers to prevent sagging.

CHECK FOR STAINS. Check for heavy or troublesome stains, which could become set by the washing process. Many stains won't respond well to a presoak and require special treatment before washing. (See Stain tips.)

SEPARATE BY DEGREE OF SOIL. Try to separate heavily soiled clothes from lightly soiled ones. Heavy soils have a tendency to become transferred, and can makes whites dingy.

SEPARATE BY COLOR. It is easiest to sort by color. Put all the whites in one pile, all the light colors in another, and the bright and dark colors in a third. Then separate the dark pile into colorfast and noncolorfast items.

COMBINE THE PILES. The trick is, once you have sorted, to combine the different piles into like groups: put whites and light-colored articles with similar amounts of soil into one group; separate white synthetics and wash them with other whites; separate permanent press, blends, and synthetics from cottons and other natural-fiber garments.

WATCH FOR LINT. Keep fabrics that produce lint (like towels) separate from fabrics that attract lint (like knits and corduroy).

AVOID TOO-SMALL LOADS. Try to avoid sorting into loads that are too small. A washing machine is more efficient in its use of water and electricity at its recommended full capacity, reducing the total number of loads you will need to do.

FINAL CHECKS. As part of sorting process, close all zippers, hooks, and buttons. Turn pockets inside out. Remove non-washable decorative items such as buckles or pins.

READ THE LABEL

IMPORTANCE OF LABELS. Labels on clothing tell you what the fabric is made of and how to care for it. Anything labeled hand wash should not go into the washer. Believe the label even if you don't want to. The fabric will last longer.

CARE OF BLENDS. Blends of fibers should be cared for according to the fiber with the highest percentage of the blend. A blend of 60 percent cotton and 40 percent polyester should be cleaned as if it were all cotton.

What the labels mean:

- **Block to dry:** Shape the garment to its correct size and shape it while drying.

- **Cold wash—cold rinse.** Use cold water from a faucet or the cold temperature setting on the washing machine.

- **Cool iron.** Iron item at the lowest setting.

- **Damp wipe.** Just wipe with a damp cloth or sponge and add a little bit of a mild detergent. Surface clean only.

- **Gentle cycle.** Can be washed in a machine that has a delicate or gentle setting; otherwise, wash by hand.

- **Do not iron.** Don't iron this or press with any heat.

- **Dry clean only.** Can be dry cleaned professionally or you can clean it yourself in a dry-cleaning machine.

- **Dry flat.** Lay garment on a flat surface to dry; do not place in dryer.

- **Permanent press cycle.** Use appropriate machine setting. Or use a warm wash, cold rinse, and short spin cycle.

- **Hand wash.** Launder by hand only with mild detergent; usually can be dry cleaned.

- **Hand wash only.** Launder by hand only in mild detergent in lukewarm water. Machine washing and dry cleaning are not advisable.

- **Hot iron.** Iron at a hot setting.

- **Iron damp.** Dampen article before ironing.

- **Line dry.** Hand damp and allow to dry on line.

- **Machine wash.** Wash and dry as usual.

- **Machine wash separately**. Machine wash alone or with same colors only to avoid color bleeding.

- **No bleach.** Do not use any type of bleach.

- **Professionally dry clean only.** Do not use a self-service machine; have garment cleaned by a professional dry cleaner.

- **Steam iron.** Use an iron with steam.

- **Tumble dry.** Can be tumbled in a dryer at heat recommended on label.

- **Tumble dry, remove promptly.** Can be tumbled dry in a dryer at recommended heat, but if your machine does not have a cooldown, remove the garment when tumbling stops.

PRODUCTS

KNOW WHAT YOU NEED. There are lots of different laundry products on the market today, many of which are designed to make your life easier. Study the labels.

FOLLOW INSTRUCTIONS. Read the label on your detergent bottle and use the amount of detergent indicated. If you have an average load of wash that is moderately soiled, don't overcompensate. If the label says to add a capful or scoop, then do just that, especially with the concentrates. You may need to add more detergent if you have a large load of wash that is heavily soiled.

DETERGENTS. Whether you use a powder or liquid, there are a variety of detergents to handle laundry needs. There are the new concentrated detergents, some with bleach or fabric softener added and others free of dyes and perfumes. Some have no enzymes (enzymes are useful because they digest protein or oil-based stains).

CONCENTRATED DETERGENTS. Concentrated detergents generally offer more cleaning power ounce-per-ounce than conventional detergents, so you use less to get the whole wash clean. Products sold this way feature smaller packages, making it easier to carry and store. This makes less waste environmentally speaking, too.

PRICES. You don't have to pay extra for performance. You pay for the convenience of liquids or premeasured packets. Detergents containing fabric softener don't cost any more than the detergent products alone but, according to Consumer Reports, they don't work very well, either as cleaners or softeners.

IF YOU ARE SENSITIVE. If you have allergies or sensitive skin, consider a detergent without enzymes or perfumes, the most likely sources of irritation.

PHOSPHORUS CONTENT. Phosphates (compounds including the element phosphorus) enhance cleaning but can spur the growth of algae in waterways. Again, read the labels.

USING CHLORINE BLEACH. Chlorine bleach is that old standby that makes whites whiter and acts as a mild disinfectant. But it can also cause faded colors and white spots when used incorrectly. Use with these guidelines:

- Bleach only when necessary.

- Before you bleach, read the garment's care label.

- Don't use chlorine bleach on wool, silk, mohair, or non-colorfast fabrics.

- Test fabrics before using bleach by mixing 1 tablespoon of chlorine bleach in 1/4 cup water. Apply to a spot that won't be noticed and see if there is a color change. If it does not bleed, use according to directions.

- If your washer has a bleach dispenser, use according to directions. If not, follow directions on the bleach bottle.

- *Never* use chlorine bleach with ammonia or toilet bowl cleaners. The combination can produce deadly fumes.

NON-CHLORINE BLEACH. This is the "all-fabric" bleach that promises the benefits of chlorine bleach without the risk. These don't whiten as well as chlorine bleach, but they are safer on fabrics. They are more expensive to use than chlorine bleaches and will brighten colors without fading.

USING FABRIC SOFTENERS. Fabric softeners are waxy materials distantly related to soap. Three basic types: rinse liquids are added to wash during rinse cycle; dryer sheets are thrown into dryer along with laundry; detergent softeners contain both products. Rated most effective are the liquids you add to rinse cycle. Some people are very sensitive to these products, so be careful of ones that are scented.

THE MACHINES

DON'T OVERLOAD. It is important not to overload the washing machine. Mix small and large items in each load for good circulation and distribute the load evenly around the wash basket.

SELECT CYCLES. Select the cycle and the length of washing time according to the kind of load you are washing. Follow the guidelines that come with the washer.

SHAKE IT OUT. Shake out each item before putting it into the dryer to minimize wrinkling and speed up drying time. Don't overload the dryer and try to take items out of the dryer as soon as it stops.

USING A CLOTHESLINE. If you sometimes prefer hanging clothes outside to dry (a romantic image these days), make sure you use clean clothespins. Attach items to the clothesline by their sturdiest edges. Dry white and light items in the sun, bright-colored items in the shade.

SELECT WATER TEMPERATURE. Use the right water temperature for what you are washing. Hot water is most effective for getting clothes clean because it removes soil and stains better.

Follow this guide:

- *Hot water* is best for whites, items that retain their dyes (colorfast), heavily soiled clothes, or greasy stains.

- *Warm water* should be used for permanent press and other 100 percent man-made fibers, blends of natural and man-made fibers, and moderately-soiled items.

- *Cold water* will help keep most dyes in dark or bright-colored clothing from running and minimize shrinking of washable woolens. Cold water is also good for lightly soiled clothing and clothes stained with blood, wine, or coffee.

DRYER SETTINGS. You can choose different heat levels for different fabrics. Typically, you select high heat for regular fabrics such as cotton, medium for permanent-press items, and low heat for delicate fabrics and knits.

AVOID OVERDRYING. You can avoid overdrying by experimenting with the cycle control. It is possible for many dryers to deliver dried laundry quicker and more efficiently by beginning the automatic cycles not at the marked starting point but at a point closer on the dial to the "less dry" position. Overdrying can wrinkle or shrink fabrics.

DEALING WITH STAINS

A BUNCH OF STAINS. When you think about it, what is laundry but a collection of stains? Dealing with the run-of-the-mill type of stains is what we do every time we do a load of wash. It is the trickier stains that need more attention to detail.

SPONGE PROMPTLY. Always sponge stains promptly with cool water to prevent setting.

TEST PRODUCT. Always test your stain-removal agent on a hidden part of the garment first to check articles for colorfastness and bleachability.

PRETREAT FABRIC. Before laundering, pretreat or presoak stained article with a stain- removal product or a detergent with dual-enzyme action.

AIR-DRY STAIN. Air-dry treated and washed items since some stains are not visible when wet and heat from a dryer could set them.

Tackling the different types of stains:

ALCOHOL. Rinse in clear, warm water until the stain is gone, then wash as usual. Nonwashable items can be rinsed with water and dried well.

BLOOD. If stain is fresh, soak in cold water. If dry, soak in warm water with detergent or an enzyme presoak product and wash. If persistent, use bleach safe for fabric.

CHOCOLATE. Sponge stain with cold water; don't use hot water. Then add 2 tablespoons of borax to 2 cups of warm water and sponge the stain with solution. Rinse well and wash as usual. Or soak in a detergent containing enzymes and water for 30 minutes. If stain remains, soak overnight. Then wash in the hottest temperature safe for fabric. If stain persists, rewash using bleach safe for fabric.

COFFEE. Sponge or soak stain promptly in cool water. Then, while still wet, rub detergent directly into any remaining stain. Wash in hottest temperature for fabric using bleach safe for fabric. For older stains, presoak in enzyme detergent.

GREASE (BUTTER, COOKING OIL, OR SALAD DRESSING). Dampen stain. Rub with dual-enzyme detergent or stain remover and wash in hottest temperature safe for fabric. Make sure stain is completely removed before drying in dryer or ironing.

INK. Sponge the area around the stain with rubbing alcohol before applying detergent directly on the stain. Place the stain face down on clean paper towels. Apply the same detergent to back of stain. Replace paper towels under the stain often. Rinse thoroughly. Launder with detergent in hottest water safe for fabric.

You can also try saturating with hairspray and rubbing with a clean cloth. Repeat if stain stays. On polyesters, rub with alcohol.

MOTOR OILS, CAR GREASE. For very heavy stains, place face down on clean paper towels. Apply a dual-enzyme detergent on the back of stain. Replace towels frequently. When detergent dries, pretreat stain again with a detergent, then wash in hottest water temperature safe for fabric.

PERSPIRATION. If perspiration has changed the color of fabric, apply ammonia to fresh stains, white vinegar to old stains. Rinse. While fabric is still damp, rub with a dual-enzyme detergent (or stain remover) and wash in hottest temperature safe for fabric. Stubborn stains may respond to washing in bleach and hottest temperature safe for fabric.

PERFUME. Immediately sponge stain with cold water. Rub detergent into remaining stain and wash in hottest water safe for fabric.

RED WINE. Sprinkle spill immediately with lots of salt. Dunk it in cold water and rub stain out before washing. Or you can sponge or soak in cold water, and while still wet, rub detergent into remaining stain. Wash in hottest water safe for fabric. For older stains, presoak in enzyme detergent or stain removal product.

MILDEW. Wash new stains in hot, soapy water as soon as possible. For bad stains on whites, soak in solution of one part chlorine bleach to eight parts cold water for 10 minutes. Wring out the water and place in a weak solution of cold water and white vinegar to neutralize the bleaching action. Rinse well and wash.

EGG. Soak fabric in warm solution of biodegradable laundry detergent and water. Wash.

MAKEUP. Rub dual-enzyme detergent directly into dampened stain until outline is gone. Wash in water temperature recommended for fabric. Oil-based beige makeup contains iron oxide, a very stubborn stain. Detergents with phosphorous are most effective overall, but good nonphosphorous products can do well, too.

GRASS. You can try sponging with denatured alcohol before washing. Also, soak in a detergent containing enzymes and water for 30 minutes. Then wash in hottest temperature safe for fabric. If stain persists, rewash using bleach safe for fabric.

WINE. Sponge or soak stain promptly in cool water. Then, while still wet, rub detergent directly into any remaining stain. Launder in hottest temperature safe for fabric using bleach safe for fabric. For older stains, presoak in enzyme detergent.

GRAVY. If there is any solid material on the surface, gently scrape up as much as possible. Presoak the fabric in an enzyme detergent for 30 minutes before washing in hottest water safe for fabric. Remember to test for colorfastness.

GENERAL LAUNDRY TIPS

STUCK CHEWING GUM. To remove chewing gum, apply ice to harden the gum and scrape it off. Soften with egg white before laundering. Or place the garment in a plastic bag and put it in the freezer; scrape off. Or sponge with a dry-cleaning solvent.

REMOVE KNOTS. Remove knots from a sweater with a fine piece of sandpaper. Or shave the sweater with a razor.

STIFF SHIRT. If your chamois shirt is stiff, soak it in warm water to which a spoonful of olive oil has been added.

SCORCHED WHITES? Sponge with a piece of cotton soaked in peroxide. Or bleach with water and lay it in the sun to dry.

CLEANING COMFORTERS. Wash down comforters individually in the washing machine with hot water and soap. Rinse well and tumble dry. When dry, shake vigorously to fluff out the feathers.

HARD-WATER BUILDUP. To rid your clothes washer of hard-water buildup, fill it with water, add 1 cup white vinegar, and let it run (without laundry) through a complete cycle.

PREVENTING WRINKLES. To prevent wrinkles on permanent press fabrics, wash in warm water and rinse in cold water. Place a dry towel with the wet clothes in the half-filled dryer. Hang or fold the clothes as soon as they are dry.

YELLOWED WHITES. If white wash-and-wear items turn yellow, make a solution of 2 gallons hot water, 1/2 cup automatic dishwasher detergent, and 1/4 cup liquid bleach; soak clothing for 1/2 hour. Launder and rinse in water to which you have added 1/2 cup white vinegar.

FOLDING LAUNDRY. Remove clothes from dryer as soon as possible. Fold towels lengthwise first so you don't have to refold them when you hang on rack in bathroom.

FOLDING CONTOUR SHEETS. Fold in half, bringing contoured ends together; at each corner align the contoured edges and invert one into the other; Fold in half again, bringing one matched set of corners to the other; invert one set into the other set. Then fold as usual, smoothing edges as you go.

USE A BELT. Sort the laundry and bundle each load with a belt for carrying to the laundromat.

WASHING DELICATES. Put small hand-washables in a large jar and add detergent and water. Shake the jar for 1 minute; let soak for 3 minutes; then shake again. Rinse and air dry.

LINGERIE BAG. Place delicate clothing in a mesh bag so that it doesn't tangle with other clothes in washing machine.

PREVENT PILLING. To help prevent pilling when washing sweaters, put them inside a pillowcase and tie with string before placing in washing machine.

CONTROL SUDS. If suds are overflowing washer, sprinkle salt on the excess suds to tame them.

GENTLE DETERGENT. If you have run out of a gentle soap for hand-washables, use shampoo instead.

LAUNDRY CART. Keep a basket on a skateboard directly below the laundry chute. When you are ready to do laundry, simply roll the load to the washer.

IRONING

START AT LOW SETTING. When ironing a variety of fabrics, start with iron at the lowest setting and work up to the highest. Go with the weave of the cloth so that you don't stretch the fabric.

PREVENT SHINE. To prevent a shine, iron dark fabrics, rayons, and acetates on the wrong side.

EASY IRON WHEN TRAVELING. If you are traveling and don't have an iron, hang your just-unpacked clothes in the bathroom and run hot water in the shower. Close the door and let the steam smooth out wrinkles. Works well with wool and silk.

NO IRONING BOARD. If you have an iron but no board, cover a counter with newspaper and then a towel. Or use newspapers put into a pillow-case. Or place a towel on the floor or over the corner of a bed.

HOLDING THE CLOTHES. Throw sprinkled clothing into a plastic bag and put it in the refrigerator or freezer. The bags holds the moisture in and the low temperature prevents mildew.

PESKY CREASES. You may not have to iron creases caused by sitting. Go over the wrinkles in your pants or skirt with a washcloth or sponge moistened in warm water, then hang to dry.

USE THAT MICROWAVE. You can sprinkle clothes lightly with water, place in a plastic bag, and microwave on High for 1 minute or until warm to the touch; iron at once. (Make sure there's no metal parts on clothing!)

CLOTHES DAMPENER. Fill a trigger spray bottle with water and keep with ironing supplies.

CLEAN THOSE PORTS. Use a pipe cleaner to clean and open the ports in a steam iron.

REMOVE SCORCH MARKS. Remove scorch marks left by an iron by saturating them with hydrogen peroxide.

DO SOMETHING ELSE. Iron while you listen to the opera or catch up on the news on TV or anything else. Some people like to iron; they find it peaceful. It can be once you set up a rhythm.

CLEANING THE IRON. Pour household ammonia on a damp washcloth and iron across it—don't breathe the fumes! Repeat until surface is clean.

CLEAN HOT IRON. You can clean the iron while it is hot by sprinkling salt over a piece of paper, running the iron over it and continuing ironing.

IRON LENGTHWISE. Always iron clothes lengthwise; circular strokes will stretch material.

IRON CLEAN CLOTHES. Never iron dirty clothes. The heat will set the stains more firmly into the fabric.

IRONING EMBROIDERY. Iron on top of embroidery on top of a fluffy towel.

IRONING SHIRTS. To iron a shirt, iron the back first, then move to the arms, the front of the shirt and do the collars, cuffs, and top of the front last.

MAKE IT SHARP. Make a sharp crease by rubbing a piece of damp soap inside the crease. Then iron on the outside with a damp cloth. Or dampen crease with gum arabic.

REMOVING A CREASE. To get a crease out, soak the creased garment in a solution of 5 cups water with 5 Tbsp. vinegar for 4 hours and then dry until damp and steam iron.

Indoor plants

I f you have a green thumb, indoor plants can be a delight. A bright, sun-filled room with lots of green plants around adds a touch of summer year-round. It's only when the plants get buggy and filled with disease and the leaves turn brown that it can all become a nuisance instead of a joy. If you know plants and are willing to give them the care they need, by all means indulge yourself and put them around the house. If you aren't willing to take the time to care for them, then buy a few silk plants and pretend. They stay in bloom longer and simply need dusting.

GROW YOUR LEFTOVERS. Your kids will love it if you turn your dinner into a plant. Cut the top inch or two off a beet, parsnip, or turnip and trim off the greens. Set the flat, cut end of the vegetable in a low container lined with pebbles and filled with water. Keep water clean and watch the green, leafy stalks come from the vegetable. (Don't keep forever.)

AVOCADO STANDBY. The old standby, the slender avocado tree weighted down by a little pom-pom of leaves, usually looks odd if it isn't pinched back enough. Cut that stem back drastically to a 3- or 4-inch stem. New growth will come from the stem to get a bushier plant.

POISONOUS PLANTS TO WATCH OUT FOR. Some houseplants to avoid are: oleander, caladium, dieffenbachias, monsteras, philodendrons, and even English ivy. The plants are okay unless a cat or toddler decides to chew away on the leaves. So keep them up high and train your cats not to nibble.

NITROGEN BOOST. Supplement houseplant fertilizers with an extra dose of nitrogen by adding a little gelatin to the water once a month. Empty an envelope of unflavored gelatin into 1 cup of boiling water, stir until dissolved, and mix with 3 cups cool water. Apply immediately.

PLANT PEST CONTROL. Control spider mites, aphids, and whiteflies with a spray of 2 Tbsp. biodegradable liquid detergent in a gallon of water. Coat the leaves on both sides. One treatment may not kill all the bugs, so spray again in 3 to 5 days. Dip small plants in the solution.

For a stronger solution, purée two hot peppers and two or three garlic cloves and 2 Tbsp. liquid detergent, then strain into a spray bottle.

WHEN TO WATER. The warmer the room, the more often the plants will need water. Plants in sun or bright light need more frequent watering than plants in low light. Small pots dry out faster than large ones, clay faster than plastic. Water runs right through a potbound plant without thoroughly wetting the soil. If the pot is too large, the excess soil will hold too much water and the roots will drown. Repot your plant if this happens.

HOW TO WATER. Always use room-temperature water and apply it thoroughly, until the water seeps through the drainage holes at the bottom of the pot. If this happens almost immediately, it may be because the soil is really porous or because the plant is potbound. In these cases, let the pot sit in a saucer of water for no more than 15 minutes. Never let it remain standing in water.

WATER HANGING BASKETS. Take the hanging basket to the sink or tub where you can immerse the plant. Give it a gentle shower with spray.

DON'T OVERFEED. After overwatering, overfeeding is the largest cause of houseplant death. Dilute the fertilizer to a weaker strength than that recommended by the manufacturer. Wet soil before feeding. Don't feed an ailing plant.

PINCH FOR HEALTH. Pinch plants back to keep them healthy. Soft, new growth can be pinched off between your thumb and first finger to force a stem to branch out. It also keeps vining plants full instead of long and lanky.

GROOM PLANTS OFTEN. Grooming pays off in the end. Take off all yellow and faded leaves; cut or pinch off faded blossoms. Neatly trim brown tips off of leaves. Gently wash off large leaves with a soft, damp cloth. Don't use the commercial leaf shiners or milk or mineral oil on leaves; they only attract dirt.

VACATION CARE. If you have a house full of plants and you will be away for more than a week, you might want to ask a friend or plant sitter to help. Group plants together and leave instructions. For shorter times away, water the plants well before you go. Turn down the heat and put the pots where they won't get direct sun. Or put all your plants in the bathtub or stall shower. Cover with plastic taped to walls and the side of the tub to create a mini-greenhouse. Spray well and water well before covering with plastic.

YELLOW LEAVES. If the leaves are yellow and growth is straggly: Are you overwatering? Is the plant getting enough light? Is the temperature too high? Are you underfeeding? Does the plant need repotting?

IF LEAVES FALL OFF PLANT. Are you overwatering? Is the plant standing in a draft? Is the humidity level too low? Is the temperature too low?

IS PLANT WILTING? Check to see if potting mixture is too dry. Are you overwatering? Is there adequate drainage? Is the location too sunny? Is the temperature too high?

VARIEGATED LEAVES. If variegated leaves get too green, the plant may not be getting enough light. Move to a sunnier spot.

STAND POTS ON PEBBLES. To increase humidity, stand pots on a tray lined with moist pebbles. The water evaporates into the surrounding air.

CLEAN LEAVES. Wipe houseplant leaves clean with a damp paintbrush.

HOUSEPLANT HOE. Bend the tines of an old fork at a right angle and use to aerate the soil of your potted plants.

PLANT SAUCER. If a hanging plant doesn't have an adequate saucer, put a shower cap over the container's bottom while you water it.

USE ICE CUBES. If watering hanging plants always makes a mess and you can't move the plant to a sink, try watering with ice cubes. They melt slowly and will do the job.

INSTANT STAKE. If a houseplant is hanging over, use a pencil for a stake and tie with string or dental floss.

Caring for antiques

I t's a good idea to set priorities for your antiques and other older possessions. They can be a part of your daily life, and still be protected to some degree. But there are trade-offs.

The normal wear and tear of daily life is especially wearing and tearing for old objects. And the conditions that people prefer are not always the same that inanimate objects tolerate well.

You probably don't want to live in the museum-like environment that is best for the preservation of antiques and other old objects. Most people enjoy a bright, cheery, sunny room. But light—especially ultraviolet light—is one of the more significant causes of damage to old wood, paper, textiles, and other materials.

Perhaps you and your family are active, outdoors people who are always tramping dirt and dust into the house. Fine, but a dusty environment is bad for those antiques.

You may want to turn up the thermostat when it gets cold in winter, or occasionally blast the air conditioner to cool off quickly in sweltering heat. But your comfort zone may not be the same as your old possessions—and fluctuations are especially bad for them.

So it's important to ask yourself some basic questions about your older possessions. Why do you own them? What is their role in your life? Did you acquire that old chair because you enjoy sitting in it—or is it a family heirloom that you want to preserve for your children? Is your collection of old postcards primarily an investment or do you enjoy showing the cards off to visitors?

Answering these questions will help you determine how you will use, store, and care for various antiques and collectibles. If enjoyment and use are most important, you may have to sacrifice some longevity and value. If an item is a legacy or investment, then you may want to store it away—or at least keep it under controlled conditions—to preserve its condition and value.

If you want the middle-ground it's especially important to know how to keep the items in the best condition possible. This includes proper cleaning, polishing, storage, use, repair, and refinishing. And it includes knowing what to avoid.

GENERAL HISTORIC PRESERVATION TIPS

KNOW THE VALUE. For a variety of reasons, you should take an inventory of your old possessions and have them appraised. Among other benefits, this will tell you if particular objects are worth the careful effort to preserve them or if their only real value is the enjoyment they give you. The monetary value of antiques and collectibles is extremely variable, and many different factors determine the value of an item and how much it might fetch on the market.

WORTH WHAT YOU THINK? There is always the possibility that an item you're hoarding is worth less than it may seem. An old table may be a valuable example of a rare and important style. However, it may also be very common. And antique dealers and collectors are very picky about the condition and authenticity. If it has been irreparably damaged, or repaired incorrectly, its primary value may be your own use and enjoyment.

DON'T TAKE FOR GRANTED. On the other hand, items that you take for granted may have value you never realized. That humble old dresser may actually be a rare example of an important style. Or if you stashed away your kids' toys in the 1950's and 60's, you may be sitting on a bonanza for avid collectors of toys from that era. (Even empty old toy boxes used for storage can be a valuable item to some collectors.)

BE SPECIFIC. It's a good idea to find trustworthy experts who deal in specific items to help you determine significance and value. Someone who deals in furniture is less likely to be familiar with other objects, and there are often very specific items that are in demand. The majority of old magazines in a stack may be worthless, but one issue may contain a feature about a highly collectible celebrity or an advertisement that's considered a treasure by certain collectors.

REPAIR CAREFULLY. Determining the value of an item will also help you decide how to repair or restore it. If it is a valuable item worth preserving perfectly, find a specialist who will use authentic materials and techniques. It you simply want to make it usable or attractive, a less expensive do-it-yourself repair job may be appropriate.

AN ANTIQUE ROOM? If you want to protect your antiques without putting them into storage—and you have the space—consider consolidating them in one room, where they can be part of the house but are less subject to wear and tear. This also gives you more control over their environment without cramping your comfort or lifestyle.

ON LOAN. Another possibility is lending an important piece to a local historic society or museum. In addition to being more socially useful than locking it away in storage, such institutions are likely to give it the tender loving care it deserves. Obviously, it's important to make sure of the insurance, liability, and other legal aspects of any such agreement.

TEMPERATURE AND HUMIDITY. Relative humidity (the amount of moisture the air can hold at particular temperatures) is among the most important conditions affecting old items. Ideally, they should be in an area where relative humidity is constantly in the middle range. This includes minimizing changes in temperature and avoiding both too much moisture and too much dryness in the air.

CONTROLLING HUMIDITY. For areas where you plan to store or display old items, a humidity gauge is helpful, so you can keep track of conditions. It is also worthwhile to install a humidifier that will keep conditions in the important middle range.

KEEP AWAY FROM MOISTURE. Don't use old prints or photographs to decorate bathrooms, because the moisture will damage them. Don't use a damp basement or a laundry room for storage. Be careful if you store items in the attic to make sure the temperature and humidity don't fluctuate too much.

WATCH THE SUN. Antiques don't like direct sunlight. The most damaging section of the light spectrum is ultraviolet light. Whenever possible, place them away from windows and places where the sun streams into a room. Use blinds, shades, or curtains to keep the sun out on bright days. If possible, artificial lights—and even windows—should have a filter that reduces the ultraviolet rays in the room.

INSIDE WALLS. Walls that are backed by the outside of the house are more subject to condensation and cold, which can damage items. Hang old paintings or place furniture and other items by interior walls that have other rooms or hallways behind them.

PICTURES, SILVERWARE, BOOKS, AND OTHER OLD STUFF

PICTURES. Place small pieces of cork along the back edges of paintings, to keep them from being too snug to the wall and to allow air to circulate behind them.

NOT ABOVE THE FIREPLACE. An old painting above a fireplace is picturesque. However, if you actually use the fireplace, don't use the wall above as a display area, because of the heat and smoke. Be careful about objects that you place on the mantle for the same reason.

Also, keep old valuables away from radiators, heat vents, and other areas where the temperature will fluctuate.

TIE THEM SHUT. If you have to move furniture, remove the drawers first. Not only will this make it lighter, you'll avoid damage if a drawer falls out during moving. Also, tie doors or unremovable drawers shut, so they won't swing open and damage the hinges.

STICKY DRAWERS. If the drawers of old furniture become tight and difficult to open, it may be a temporary result of swelling that will change with the humidity. If not, use some candlewax or a bar of pure soap along the sides and runners to lubricate it safely.

THE DANGERS OF READING. Books were made to be read, photos and drawings were created to look at. However, in addition to the obvious danger of tearing pages and breaking bindings, those uses also cause invisible damage to older paper material. Grease and acid from your fingers and the exposure to light and air add to deterioration. So handle valuable old books and paper items as little as possible.

WEAR GLOVES. Use non-acidic thin cloth gloves or tissue paper if you're handling old books and papers to keep acids, grease, and other material on your hands from damaging the paper.

MAKE DUPLICATES. Make duplicate copies of your older photographs, and use the copies to show off your baby pictures. Lock away the originals in a light-tight container to reduce fading. This is especially important for color photos.

Do the same for old documents, illustrations, or pages of old books you frequently show people.

FRAME THE ORIGINALS. If you do want to display the originals, frame them in glass to protect them.

BACK THEM RIGHT. Use pure, acid-proof cardboard or matting board to mount and frame prints and photos.

DUSTING BOOKS. When you dust a book, keep it closed tightly to prevent the dust from getting into the pages.

REMOVING BOOKS. To protect the spine of a book when you remove it from a shelf, reach over the top of the book and pull it towards you, instead of yanking it out by the binding. Or gently push the books from either side and gently pull the book you want by the side covers.

LET BOOKS BREATHE. It's important to give books breathing room to avoid buildup of moisture and mold. Leave space between books and the back of the bookcase. If possible, also leave a space between the bookcase and the wall, to allow air to flow behind it.

HAPPY MEDIUM. Books lined on a shelf need a happy medium of pressure. They should be firmly packed, without squeezing each other too tightly. Books on a shelf should be next to books of about the same height. Otherwise, the pressure will be uneven.

NO NITRATE. If you have film from the late 19th and early decades of the 20th century, check to see if it is nitrate based. If so, you'd be better off having it copied, because nitrate film is very combustible.

PRESERVE THE PATINA. Make sure to preserve your old items' patina. The term "patina" is used in various ways, but essentially refers to the original qualities of a material's surface, especially those that emerge as it ages. Patina might be called the benevolent side of time's effect on old items. Unlike rust and other destructive effects of aging, it is one of the major qualities that are attractive in antiques.

- Patina may either be the original aged finish, the buildup of preservative methods over time, a natural weathering, or all three. Sometimes a patina is consciously applied to a new or old item to give it an old look and stimulate the patination process.

- The patina of specific materials varies. In wood, it often refers to the way the original finish has been mellowed and positively affected by light and other conditions over time. In brass and bronze, it is a partial dulling. The patina of old pewter can refer to the darkening of sections of the surface.

- When you polish, clean, or restore an old item, make sure that the methods and materials you use will protect and highlight its patina. In many cases, the wrong polishing or cleaning method, or too much elbow-grease, or inappropriate efforts to revive the luster can cover over or wear away the desirable patina. So it's important to know how to maintain and treat the specific material you are working with.

POLISHING PEWTER. Olive oil on a very mild abrasive can be used for polishing pewter. Don't try to shine up old pewter objects too thoroughly.

STORING SILVER. Silver does not like acids. If you are wrapping silver, use acid-proof material, not acidic papers like newspaper. Don't store silver objects in the drawers of oak cabinets, or place them directly on top of oak for prolonged periods. Oak contains acids that silver doesn't like.

SILVER AND FOOD. Silver utensils and containers can obviously be used for eating, but make sure you wash them soon after using. Many foods contain ingredients including salt and acids that lead to tarnish and other damage. It's best to use salt shakers made of other materials instead, and preserve your silver ones for display. Don't store fruit in silver bowls or trays for a long time, and wash the silver afterward.

SILVER POLISHING. Be sure to use the right polish on silver, and don't use gritty abrasive polishing material. Also, don't try too hard to polish away the darker areas around silver patterns; they are part of the design and patina.

IVORY AND LIGHT. Ivory is especially sensitive to light and should not be placed in direct sun—but not in complete darkness either, because it will age more gracefully with some light on it. Ivory becomes yellow as it ages, which is considered part of its patina.

IVORY AND WATER. Despite the affinity of Ivory soap for water, real ivory does not like to take baths. Don't wash it by soaking. Instead, clean gently with a soft cloth or sponge. If you use cloth or sponge damp, make sure the item is completely dry afterward.

GLASS CARE. Glass should be washed regularly. Use lukewarm water. If it has ornamentation, however, have it examined to make sure it won't dissolve if washed. Also, make sure it doesn't have old adhesive repairs that might dissolve in water.

GLASS BOTTLES. You may be able to dissolve dirt from the inside of an old bottle by filling it with a mixture of vinegar and water for a day or two and then rinsing it out.

Indoor repairs

T here will be times when a room or piece of furniture needs more than a good shine. No matter what preventative maintenance you employ or how careful you are around the house, you will have to fix rather than clean something.

If you are a handy person and the repair appears simple, you may want to do the work yourself. At other times, the job may be complicated and you will want to hire a professional or specialist. For repairs on an antique or particularly valuable item, we recommend hiring a specialist. The chapter on the home workshop offers detailed guidelines on when to choose a professional and when to tackle the problem yourself.

There are, however, many simple things you can do to fill in a hole in the wall or loosen a jammed drawer.

SQUEAKY FLOOR. Apply cornstarch between floor boards if the floor is squeaking. It will help lubricate the boards. If this does not work, you may have to try nailing or screwing the board into the joist below.

POLISHED SCREENS. You can repair very small holes in window screens by applying several layers of clear nail polish.

STITCHING SCREENS. For small holes or tears in screens, mend the hole by stitching fine wire or nylon thread with a matching color back and forth until the hole is sealed.

REMOVING BROKEN LIGHT BULBS. Use a raw potato to remove a broken light bulb from its socket by first turning the switch off, then jamming the potato into the base and twisting the bulb out.

SHELF WOOD. If you are making a shelf less than a foot wide, use 1-inch softwood lumber. Place it so that the heart side of the wood—the side closest to the center—is facing the ceiling so that the growth rings are curved upward; the weight of the items on the shelves will help prevent warping. Plywood is also excellent for shelves.

SHELF STRENGTHENER. You can strengthen a shelf by attaching a 1-by-2-inch wood strip along the front or back edge or by adding support from below with a vertical divider.

BRACKET TACTICS. If you are using brackets for shelving, you may want to either camouflage them by painting them the same color as the wall they are attached to or paint them a bold color to add to the design of the room.

SMOOTH CAULKING. When you apply caulk, be sure to overfill each joint a little bit and then remove the excess with a wet rag or your finger. Apply the caulk evenly and firmly.

CAULK PRESERVATION. To prevent caulk from drying out in its tube between projects, stick a screw or nail in the tip of the open caulk tube.

CLOTHESPIN CLAMPS. Use clothespins with springs as lightweight clamps for handyman projects.

HOMEMADE RUSTY NUT LOOSENERS. Apply a small amount of ammonia to rusty nuts or bolts that are stuck. If there is no rust, pour a small amount of cola on the nut or bolt if it refuses to budge.

CIRCUIT BREAKERS. If the power suddenly goes off in a section of your house, a circuit breaker may have blown. Circuit breakers are designed to protect your wiring from overheating. When a fuse blows, it usually means that the metal strip in the fuse has melted and the fuse needs to be replaced. Simply turn off the circuit breaker, replace the fuse, and turn the circuit breaker back on. Always keep spare fuses around the circuit box as well as a flashlight.

NATURALLY RECHARGED BATTERIES. You can temporarily restore some of the power in old batteries by letting them sit in the sunlight for a day.

LUBRICATED WATER VALVES. Valves often become stuck if they are not used. Lubricate and turn them on occasion to keep them in good working order.

Walls

ADHESIVE HANGING. To stop the plaster from cracking when you hammer in a nail to hang a picture, place a small piece of adhesive tape where you plan to drive the nail. Hammer the nail through the tape.

STUD PREFERENCE. Whenever you mount a heavy object onto a wall, be sure to use the studs behind the walls for support. Studs are usually located next to windows and doors, electric boxes, and usually at regular intervals of 16 to 24 inches.

SEARCHING FOR STUDS. You can usually find studs in the wall by looking for nail holes in the baseboard or for wallboard seams. Or you can run a magnetic compass along the wall until the needle is attracted to metal in the studs behind the wall. The last-ditch resort in finding the studs is to drill a tiny hole at a sharp angle and then place a hanger wire into the hole until it reaches the stud. Mark the distance and measure it on the outside portion of the wall.

TRIPLE-COATED WALL REPAIR. Finish plaster cracks and drywall seams with drywall tape and three coats of all-purpose drywall compound. Apply the first coat before applying the tape. Let it dry and then place the dampened tape on top with a second coat of compound on top. The third coat should be very thin to fill out minor imperfections.

KEEP DRYWALL DRY. Always let the drywall compounds dry completely before applying tape or new layers of compound on top. Otherwise, the tape may buckle.

MIX THE PRE-MIX. For pre-mixed drywall compounds, be sure to mix it up well with a clean stick or utensil to get rid of air bubbles. If you do not, the compound may make bubbles on the wall.

ROLLED WALLPAPER. Use a paint roller instead of a sponge to apply a solution for wallpapering. Squeeze the roll before placing it on the wall to avoid dripping.

VARNISHED CLEAN. Be sure to remove grease with clear varnish from a wall that is going to be wallpapered. Otherwise, the grease may soak through the wallpaper.

Fixing doors

SQUEAKY DOOR. You can usually stop a door from squeaking by putting a few drops of oil at the top of each hinge. Move the door back and forth to work the oil into the hinge. If the squeaking does not stop, raise the pin and add some more oil.

SQUEAKY AND STUCK LOCKS. Apply graphite to noisy or squeaking locks for lubrication. You can buy the graphite at a hardware store. If the lock is tight or won't turn at all, you may need to lubricate it with graphite as well.

RATTLING KNOBS. To stop a knob from rattling, loosen the set-screw (the one sticking out of the handle beneath the knob), then remove the knob. Place a small piece of putty or modeling clay in the knob. Put the knob back on. Push it on as far as possible and then tighten the screw.

SCREWY DOORS. If the door is sticking or dragging, there may be a problem with the screws in the hinges. Try tightening the screws. If screws are not holding, replace them one at a time with a longer screw. Or insert a matchstick in the hole and put the old screw back in.

STUCK DOORS. The door may be out of shape if it is dragging or getting stuck. Before doing anything about it, however, consider whether it is hot and humid outside. The problem may just be from heat swells. Otherwise, look for a shiny spot on the door where it sticks. Depending on the scope of the problem, you should either sand the spot down with sandpaper or use a planer. Be careful not to overdo it as you want the door to fit tightly.

SANDING EDGES. Before painting a door, be sure to sand its edges. Buildup of paint may cause the door to stick.

Repairing drawers

STICKY DRAWERS. If your drawer is getting stuck, remove the drawer and look for shiny places on the top or bottom edges or on the sides. Sand down the shiny areas. Try drawer to see if it moves more easily. Repeat sanding if it still sticks.

WAXED DRAWERS. To make the drawer glide more easily, rub the drawer and the frame where they touch with candle wax, paraffin, or soap. This is important if the drawers are usually filled with heavy items.

WORN GLIDERS. If the gliders are badly worn, the drawer may not close all the way. The drawer front strikes the frame, so the drawer needs to be lifted. Remove the drawer and insert two or three smooth-head thumbtacks along the front of each glide to raise the drawer.

DAMP STICKINESS. If the drawers only stick in damp weather, fix the problem when the weather dries by coating the unfinished wood with a penetrating sealer or with wax.

Toilet repairs

NON-STOP RUNNING. If the water won't stop running, the problem may be with the float ball. Check to see if there is water in it by lifting its arm, unscrewing it and shaking it. If there is water, replace it with a new one. Plan B is to then try bending the float arm downward so that the bent arm triggers the water to stop rising when it is slightly less than an inch from the top of the overflow tube.

WATER STOPPER. If neither of the above solutions works, the problem may be in the float arm assembly. Turn off the shutoff valve underneath the toilet and dismantle the float arm assembly. If a piece looks worn, replace it. You may have to replace the entire contraption with a plastic ball-cock assembly purchased at a local hardware store.

PARTIALLY FILLED TANKS. If the toilet gurgles or the tank gets only partially filled, the problem may be with the valve seat (the drain at the bottom of the tank). See if the stopper ball that covers it is properly positioned. If not, turn off the water valve and flush the toilet of its water.

Then loosen the screw that holds the guide arm which controls the stopper ball and reposition the stopper ball. Don't forget to retighten the screw. Also, check for corrosion on the inside of the valve seat. If it feels rough, scour it with wet-dry sandpaper. If neither of these tactics works, you may have to replace the stopper ball with a flapper ball available at hardware stores.

INCOMPLETE FLUSH. If you are only getting a partial flush from your toilet, then the stopper ball may be falling on the valve seat too quickly. To correct this, raise the guide arm that holds the stopper ball by loosening the thumbscrew and lifting the guide arm so that the stopper ball will float longer. Or you can make the same effect by unhooking the lift wire and shortening it, bending it in the new position, and then rehooking it in the same hole or a different hole for even more of an impact.

MINOR PROJECTS

LEAKY FAUCETS. Faucets may look very different from each other from the outside, but the insides are all fairly similar. Before repairing a leaky faucet, first turn off the water at the shut-off valve nearest to the faucet and then turn on the faucet until the waters is drained. Loosen the packing with a wrench (usually by turning it counter-clockwise) and pull out the valve unit. Remove the screw holding the old washer at the bottom of the valve unit and replace both the washer and the screw. Place the valve back on the faucet until the handle is back in the proper position. Tighten the packing unit and turn the water back on at the shut-off valve.

REPLACING ELECTRIC PLUGS. If your electric plug or cord is damaged, you can replace it by cutting the cord at the damaged part or near the base of the plug. Dismantle the plug or get a new plug with a UL label and slip it back on the cord. Clip and separate the cord and tie the two ends into an underwriter's knot. Remove about 1/2 inch of insulation from the end of the wires without cutting any of the small wires. Twist each of the wires clockwise and pull the knot down firmly into the plug. Pull each wire around a corresponding terminal's screw and wrap the wire around the screw clockwise. Tighten the screw so that the insulation comes to the screw but is not under it. Place the insulation cover back on the screw.

FIXING CRACKS AROUND THE BATH OR SHOWER. A crack between the bathtub and the wall can lead to extensive damage to the walls and house frame from water damage. You can use either waterproof grout or plastic seal to make the repair. Grout comes in powder form and needs to be mixed with water. Plastic sealer looks like toothpaste, comes in a tube, and is more expensive than grout.

To repair the crack, remove the old crack filler and wash the surface to remove dirt, grease, and excess soap. Let the surface dry thoroughly before applying either the plastic sealer or grout with a putty knife. If you use the sealer, be sure to work fast. If you use grout, do not pour the excess grout down the drain when you are done. Clean the putty knife before the grout dries.

SETTING FLEXIBLE TILE. Fixing damaged or loose tiles is one of those tedious jobs that needs to be done but is seemingly too minor for you to seek a professional. You can set tile yourself by first removing the loose or damaged tile. Place a warm iron on tiles to soften the adhesive. Scrape off the old adhesive from the floor or wall (and the tile if you plan to use the same tile again). Fit the new tiles in the proper place. Some tiles can be cut with a knife or shears, others with a saw. Tile is less likely to break if it is warm. Spread the appropriate adhesive on the floor or wall with a paint brush or putty knife. Wait until the adhesive begins to set before placing the tile. Press tile on firmly with a rolling pin.

SETTING CERAMIC OR PLASTIC TILE Remove the old tile and scrape the adhesive off the floor and the old tile if you plan to use it again. If you are using new tile and need to fit it, mark it carefully to size and cut it with a saw. You can make straight cuts on tile by scoring it first. It will then snap off if you press it on the edge of a hard surface. Spread the appropriate adhesive on the wall or floor and press the tile firmly into place. Joints on ceramic tile should be filled with grout after the tile has firmly set. After mixing water into the grout to form a paste, press the mixture in with your finger and smooth the surface. Remove excess grout before it dries. Let the grout dry overnight before it gets wet again.

REPAIRING SCREENS. There is virtually no point of having a screen door or window if there is a gaping hole to let the insects into your house. Repair a hole by first trimming the edge of the rip, hole, or tear with a scissors to make smooth edges. Cut a rectangular patch from another screen or get a ready-cut screen patch that is about an inch larger than the hole on all sides. Remove the three outside wires on all four sides of the patch and bend the ends of the wires over a block or the edge of a ruler. Place the hole over the patch from the outside with the patch being held tightly against the screen so that the bent wires go through the screen. From inside, bend down the ends of the wires toward the center of the hole. If necessary, have somebody press the patch in from the outside while your are doing this.

REPLACING A BROKEN WINDOW. Working from the outside of the house, remove the broken glass with pliers to avoid cutting your fingers. Remove the old putty and glazier points with pliers. Place a thin ribbon of putty in the frame and place a fitted piece of glass firmly against the putty. Insert the glazier points by tapping them with a hammer carefully to prevent the glass from breaking. Points should be placed near the corners first and then every 4 to 6 inches along the way. Fill the groove with putty or glazing compound by pressing it in firmly with a putty knife or your fingers. The putty should form a smooth seal around the window.

PATCHING VINYL FLOORS. If you need to replace a piece of vinyl flooring, first cut an oversized replacement patch that corresponds to the area you will replace. Tape the patch to the floor where you plan to place it. If possible, cut along the flooring pattern lines. Use a utility knife to cut through both the replacement patch and the vinyl to be replaced. Use a scraper to remove the vinyl attached to the floor. If needed, use an iron or heat gun to soften the floor's adhesive. Apply new adhesive on the floor and place the patch in the appropriate place. Wipe off any excess glue and cover the patch with a heavy weight for at least a day.

PATCHING HOLES AND CRACKS IN THE WALL. To fix a hole or crack in a plaster wall or wallboard you can use either spackling compound (which is convenient for small jobs) or patching plaster that can be bought in larger packages and costs less. Both substances need to be mixed with water. Remove all loose plaster and then with a knife scrape out plaster from the back of the crack until the back of the crack is wider than the front surface. Dampen the surface of the crack with a wet cloth or paint brush. Prepare the patching compound according to the package's directions.

Fill the small holes with the patching mixture. Be sure to press the mixture until it completely fills the hole. Smooth the surface with a putty knife. After the patch has dried, sand it by wrapping sandpaper around a small block of wood. This makes the surface even. For larger holes, first partly fill the hole and let it dry. This gives a base for the final fill. Add a second batch of compound. Let it dry and sand. If the hole is very large, you may need to use a wadded newspaper for backing when you apply multiple layers of the compound. If the wall is textured, you will want to make the patch match it while the plaster is still wet. Use a sponge or comb to do the texturing.

Tools and the home workshop

Tools, tools, tools. They are an essential part of any household that follows the Boy Scout motto "Be prepared."

Like the rest of your home, your collection of tools is a very personal matter. If your mechanical aptitude is limited to changing light bulbs or hanging pictures, you're likely to be satisfied with the least number of tools you can get by with to handle everyday chores and emergencies. If you are a hands-on type, you'll obviously want to build a more extensive and specialized assortment of implements.

A good rule of thumb is to make sure you have a versatile selection of basic tools to handle the most common carpentry, decorating, plumbing, electrical, and mechanical tasks and repairs you'll encounter. Also consider what you need for outdoor maintenance, and use the same approach.

If possible, of course, the ideal is to bite the bullet and buy a complete set of well-built tools. That includes differing sizes and designs of individual tools to handle specific circumstances. But if that's beyond your means, look for adjustable wrenches and other tools that can handle more than one size job, and can be used in different ways.

Quality is important too, because it will make your work easier and the tool will last longer.

If you're on a tight budget, at least spend what you can to buy the best of the basics, rather than splurge on one area and neglect others. You don't want to have an assortment of hammers but only one screwdriver.

The tools you acquire after that will reflect your own inclinations and needs. If you work more extensively on specific types of projects, your tool collection will eventually reflect that. If car repair is your forte, you'll probably find a set of socket wrenches most useful, while someone who is more inclined to carpentry will probably opt for woodworking tools.

HIRING A PRO

YOU OR THE PRO? In deciding whether to correct a minor repair or major project yourself or hire a professional you should consider several factors. What kind of repair is it and do you have the time, tools, and knowledge to do it? What are the ramifications of doing it wrong? Will it make the problem worse in the long term? Are reputable repairmen available and at what price? How much will you save if you do the work yourself? Think carefully about these elements. If you start and need to call in a professional repairman, you will almost certainly have to pay for the full cost of his doing it from start to finish.

AGREEMENT IN WRITING. Contracting for work, having it done, and getting satisfactory results can be a trying experience even with a reputable repairman. To make matters as simple as possible up front, write an agreement down. Do not rely on a verbal understanding. Instead, either you or the repairman should sign an agreement in advance.

SPECIFIC CONCERNS. The written specification of the project will vary depending on the nature of the repair. It should include the exact location and extent of the repair; an indication of any repairs that need to be done beforehand if the project involves new work (for example, putting new siding on a house); the type, quality, color, and size of material to be used; the number of coats of paint for a painting project; and an agreement that all the work shall conform to local and state codes.

OTHER ISSUES. An agreement between you and the contractor should further describe a time schedule for the job; who cleans up the mess that results from the job; the amount in which the repairman or contractor shall assume responsibility for damage to your or a neighbor's property; that any changes in the contract shall be in writing and agreed to by both parties; that you are freed from all liens that may be placed against the job for failure of the contractor-repairman to pay for materials, labor, or equipment; and a payment schedule.

GO WITH WHO YOU KNOW. Try to select a repairman or contractor whose work you know. Inspect some of his previous work and ask the owners if they were satisfied with the contractor's work. If you need help, consult with an architect, businessman, or the Better Business Bureau in your area.

THREE BIDS. The variety in prices that contractors charge for work can be enormous. Some contractors will give high bids because they have so much other work that the job is only worth it to them if they get a large profit. Other contractors may give a low bid because they desperately need the work. In considering bids, do not forget about the quality of the contractor who submits the bid. The cheapest bid may not be the best.

CASH PRICE. The contract should show the cash price. If you are not paying cash, it should show the cash down payment, the unpaid balance, the amount financed, and the total number of payments. This will show you the amount of work you are paying for financing above the cost of the rest of the work.

CHECKING THE JOB. You may wish to check on the work in progress. However, stay out of the way whenever possible. Interference can cause delays, affect the quality of the work, or cause disagreements and added costs. When the job is done, inspect the project with repairman, referring to the contract when questions arise. Sign off the contract and make final payment after all the work has been completely corrected.

GENERAL TOOL AND WORKSHOP TIPS

AMONG THE BASICS. Tools that will handle a variety of common jobs include a claw hammer, hand saw, screwdriver(s), wrench, pliers, and hand-drill. Other often useful items: a level, a tape measure, straight ruler and T-Square for measuring; a plane, sandpaper and files for smoothing and roughing up surfaces; hacksaw and wire cutter for working with metals; a plumber's helper and a plumber's snake, for the obvious; a flashlight to see with, and an assortment of screws, nails and tacks.

OUTDOORS. For basic gardening and yardwork, it's helpful to have a hose and/or watering can, a shovel for larger holes and a trowel for smaller ones, a lawnmower, yard rake and a garden rake, clippers for shearing, a pruning tool for heavier snipping, an outdoor saw, and a garden cart.

POWER TOOLS. When you're budgeting your money, you should buy good basic hand tools first. When you're ready for power tools, buy those that can be used for different purposes. A power drill not only makes it easier to drill holes, but you can also use it with attachments for sawing, sanding, and other purposes.

ELECTRIC YARD TOOLS. If an extension chord can extend to the edges of your property, and your yardwork is not heavy-duty, consider buying electric chain saws, weed cutters, and lawn mowers. They are often less temperamental than their gas-powered counterparts. Use outdoor extension cords, and don't plug them in on wet days.

SELF- OR FOOT-PROPELLED? Self propelled lawn mowers that you walk behind may be easier to use than a power-mower you have to push if you have an open, straightforward lawn. However, a manually pushed mower is often easier to use and maneuver if you have a lot of nooks and crannies or a very small lawn.

WILL YOU USE IT? If you're working on a project that requires a specialized tool, think twice about whether it's worth buying. Despite the old adage "Neither a borrower or a lender be," it may be more appropriate to borrow a tool from a friend or rent it, rather than spend your hard-earned money on something you'll use once and never again have use for. At other times, a specific repair may be a good excuse to buy a useful tool that you'll need more often.

VERSATILE BUT CAREFUL. While many of the common tools can be used for a variety of purposes, don't stray too far from the use that a tool was made for.

STORAGE AND WORK AREA. Follow the old saying "A place for everything, and everything in its place." The specifics will depend on your home and interest in handiwork. If you have the space, a workshop with your tools and hardware clearly displayed is the ideal. If your quarters are more cramped, you may have to limit yourself to a section of closet and/or a toolbox. In either case, though, make sure you have them in a central location, and organized in a way that will make things easy to find and put back. Some people like to paint an outline of the tool by the corresponding wall hook to remind themselves and others where each tool belongs.

NICHE STORAGE. Build a shelf between the studs of unfinished walls in your work area for a very efficient storage shelf. Simply nail an old board between the studs. If you are really short on shelf space and want to be clever, try nailing the tops of glass containers to the underside of shelves and then placing the containers in the secured tops. Instead of unscrewing the top each time to access the contents, you unscrew the container. Be sure that the containers are either glass so you can see the contents or that they are clearly marked.

SOFT UNDERFOOT. If the floor of the work area is made of concrete, cover it with pieces of carpeting or cardboard. It will be easier on your feet and will prevent tools from breaking if they fall.

WORK AREA. Your work area should be bright so you can see what you're doing. Fluorescents are good illumination. You can add brightness by painting walls white. The height of the work area should be between your waist and your hips, about 34 to 36 inches for most people.

SEPARATE AND GROUP. Sort your tools and hardware into categories, and store them in ways that allow you to find the right item quickly. Keep screwdrivers of different sizes and types together in one area, wrenches in another, etc. Also keep nails separate from screws, electrical parts separate from plumbing, etc. This will become more important as your collection of items grows.

CONDITIONS. Your storage area shouldn't be too damp or too dry. Dampness can speed rusting of metal and also damage wood handles. Too much dryness isn't good for handles either. Also, don't put your tools under basement pipes that may drip in humid weather.

MOISTURE ABSORBERS. Throw a couple of pieces of chalk or charcoal in with the tools of the toolbox to absorb moisture and lessen the chances of rust forming on your tools.

WHAT YOU SEE. Storing nails, screws, and other small items in clear glass jars, rather than cans, allows you to see what they contain at a glance, rather than having to rummage through each one individually.

WIRE ROLLS. Use old cardboard tubes for towels or toilet paper to store electrical cords. Color code the ends of the tubes if you have several.

SHARP TOOLS. In addition to cutting tools that obviously need sharpening such as mower blades, clippers, and axes, many other tools will work better if their edges are sharp. Paint scrapers, shovels, hoes, drills, chisels, planes, pry bars and saws are among the tools that benefit from sharpening.

SHARPENING TOOLS. Sharpening is an art, and different tools require different sharpening techniques and equipment. You can do a lot of sharpening yourself, but a bad job can ruin the tool. If you want to do it yourself, make sure you know the right method for that item. If it's a valuable or sensitive surface, it may be better to take the tool to a professional.

CHECK THE HANDLES. With older, wood-handled tools, pay attention to the condition of the handle. If it is rotting, it may break or lose the tool head while you're using it. This is inconvenient at best, and dangerous at worst, if you're cutting with an ax or hammering. The handles of most tools can be replaced.

BRIGHT IDEA. Buy some brightly colored, thick, ribbons—in any color but green—and tie them around the handle of your shovels, clippers, or other tools. Or else paint all or a portion of the handles in a bright color. This will make them easier to find if you absent-mindedly put them down and forget where.

SPECIFIC TOOLS

Hammers and nails

WHAT SIZE? A good medium weight (12–13 ounces) claw hammer is good for general purposes.

HAMMERING. Hammering isn't as easy as it may seem. For maximum effect with minimal effort, hold a hammer near the end of the handle for more hitting power. To start a nail, hold it in place and tap it in gently a few times until it is firmly set. Hit it straight in.

COMB PROTECTION. Some people place a comb through the nail to hold it steady rather than their fingers to prevent them from being banged by the hammer.

MARKLESS HAMMER STROKES. To avoid hammer marks on the wood, use a nail set or another nail to drive a nail the last fraction of an inch into the wood.

MARKLESS NAIL REMOVAL. To remove a nail without leaving a mark, place a small block of wood under the head of the hammer when you use the claw end of the hammer to pull the nail out.

PROTECTED HAMMERING. If you are hammering nails in molding or other fragile materials that you do not want to scar or damage, use a strip of pegboard to shield the wood. Hammer the nail through one of the holes as far as you can, then finish the job with a nail set.

NAIL SELECTION. Box nails have large heads. Use them for rough work when appearance doesn't matter. Finishing nails have very small heads. You can drive them below the surface with a nail set or other nail, and cover them. Use them where appearance is important, such as putting up paneling or building shelves.

HAMMERING IT IN. Hammers have either slightly rounded faces or flat ones. You're less likely to hit the surrounding wood with a rounded face.

RIP OR CLAW. Carpentry hammers include ripping hammers and claw hammers. The non-hammering end of a claw hammer is slightly curved, for pulling nails. The ripping hammer has a straight claw for prying apart boards and other heavy work. The claw hammer is best to start with, but a ripping hammer is more suited to heavy-duty jobs.

SMOOTH HANDLES, SMOOTH HANDS. If you keep the handles on your tools smooth, your hands will be grateful. Sand a tool's worn wooden handles and then apply linseed oil or furniture polish to reduce friction. Also be sure to smooth out areas of loose wood and remove potential splinters.

Screwdrivers and screws

WHAT KIND? You need two types of screwdrivers for household repairs: straight blade and Phillips (with a crossed tip). Both come in various sizes. The tip of a screwdriver should correspond with the screw slot's length and width as nearly as possible. If the tip is too large, it may scar the wood surface. If it is too narrow it may damage or even strip the screw's slot.

SCREWDRIVER SIZES. Buy a set of screwdrivers of different sizes. If you can't afford a full range, at least buy a small, medium, and large. Using the wrong-sized screwdriver can lead to frustration. It may also ruin the head of the screw so badly it can't be removed, or cause other damage to the object it is attached to. Also buy a similar range of Phillips-head screwdrivers; size is especially important with those, because the "x" notches on the screwhead are particularly vulnerable to being chewed up.

PUSH AND TWIST. When using the screwdriver, push against the head of the screw as you turn it.

NAIL FIRST. It is easier to put a screw into the wood if you make a hole first with a nail or a drill. Rub wax or soap on the screw threads to make the screw go in easier.

Pliers, wrenches, and nuts

MULTIPLE USES FOR PLIERS. Use slip joint pliers to hold a nut while turning a bolt with a screwdriver, bending or cutting wire, straightening a bent nail, or turning nuts.

PLIER PROTECTORS. To prevent the jaws of locking pliers from scarring wood, slit a hole in two old tennis balls and insert each one over each of the jaws.

TURNING NUTS. When using a pliers to turn a nut, wrap tape or cloth around it to avoid scratching it.

REMOVING NAILS. Pull the nail out at the same angle it was driven in. Use small blocks under the pliers if you need leverage.

TOUGH NUTS. An adjustable wrench can be fitted for all different sizes of nuts. If a nut is hard to loosen, apply a few drops of penetrating oil or kerosene. Let it soak a couple of hours or overnight. If the wrench has a tendency to slip off, try turning it over.

SCREW SELECTION. Screws are best where holding strength is important. Use them to install towel bars or curtain rods, repairing drawers, or mounting hinges. If a screw comes loose, you can refill the holes with matchsticks or wood putty and replace them.

MOLLY SCREWS. Molly screws have two parts—a screw and a casing—that make them good for holding heavy items on plastered walls. To install, first make a small hole in the plaster and drive the casing in even with the wall surface. Tighten the screw to make the casing spread in back. Remove the screw and put it through the item you are hanging, into casing, and tighten.

TOGGLE BOLTS. Toggle bolts serve a similar purpose to molly screws. Drill a hole in the plaster large enough for the folded toggle to go through. Remove toggle. Bolt it through whatever you are hanging. Replace the toggle. Push the toggle through the wall and tighten.

PLASTIC ANCHOR SCREWS. Use plastic anchor screws for attaching items to concrete walls. First make a small hole in the wall and drive the casing in even with the wall surface. Put the screw through the item and into the casing, and tighten.

CRESCENT WRENCH. An adjustable wrench is a must for any toolbox. A 10-inch Crescent wrench is good for most purposes. When using the wrench, be sure to position it so that the pressure of turning a bolt is placed on the fixed jaw and not the adjustable one.

Saws

WHAT YOU SAW. While you can get by with one saw for woodwork, you'll have more versatility if you have both a crosscut and a rip saw. The crosscut saw is designed to cut against the grain of wood, while the ripsaw is made for situations where you are cutting in the same direction as the grains and fibers.

SAW POINTS. The number of teeth in each inch of a saw is its point number. A saw with less teeth (and lower point number) cuts quickly, but not as precisely. For a more refined cut, a higher point saw with more teeth is best, although it cuts more slowly. A saw in the range of 7 or 8 is considered a happy medium for an all-purpose saw. Ten points is considered good for most indoor purposes.

SCREWDRIVER ASSISTANCE. If the wood starts to bind as you are cutting it with a handsaw, stick the end of the screwdriver at the end of the gap in the wood to hold the wood apart.

SPECIALIZED SAWS. You can get by with a basic crosscut saw for basic use. If you do more specialized sawing, a wide variety of saws is available: hacksaws, used for cutting metal and other tough material; coping saws, for curves and other careful cutting; pruning saws, for outside cutting; and a miter saw, for cutting at angles.

CUTTING. Mark where you want to cut. Pull the saw back and forth several times to start a groove. Let the weight of the saw do the cutting at first. If you are sawing a board, it will be easier if you support it and hold it firmly when you're cutting.

SAW COVERS. Cover the teeth of a saw with a split piece of garden hose for safe storage.

SMOOTHER SAWING. Rub a handsaw with a bar of dry soap to cut down on the friction. This will make it easier to saw many jobs.

Miscellaneous tools

FILES. Store your files so they are standing up vertically in a rack to keep their surface from rubbing against other objects.

UTILITY KNIFE. Use a utility knife for projects that might ruin an ordinary knife blade such as cutting insulation, vinyl flooring, shingles, or other rough materials. When the blade becomes dull, either flip it to the other side or get a replacement blade.

SCISSOR SHARPENING. You can sharpen scissors by using them to cut folded pieces of aluminum foil.

SHARPENED FLAT BARS. Keep flat bars sharpened to make it easier to place the bar between boards when you have to pry them.

SHOVELS AND TROWELS. Consider the type of dirt you'll be digging when you buy a shovel or trowel. If you're working primarily with light, loose dirt that moves easily, an inexpensive one may fill the bill. But in general, the sturdier the better. This is especially important if your soil is crusty or heavy. A strong well-built shovel can handle the pressure you have to apply. In such conditions, a flimsy shovel is harder to work, and may bend or break more readily.

WEDGES. If you use wedges to split wood, have more than one on hand, preferably of differing sizes. Sometimes they get caught in the log, and you'll need another one to finish the job, and to extricate the other one.

LEVEL TEST. To test whether your level is working place it on a level surface and check the location of the bubble. Flip the level over and see if the bubble is in the identical position. If not, the level may be askew.

Power tools

CLEAN UNDER MOWERS. Regularly clean the grass built up under your lawn mower. This will allow the blade to move more freely, keep it from overtaxing the engine, and reduce the chances of moisture and other materials in the grass contributing to rust and other deterioration.

EMPTY OUT GAS. Empty the gas, and most of the oil, from your mower, chain saw, and other equipment before you put them away for the winter. Also don't use gas next spring that may still be left in the gas can.

SERVICE. Mowers, chain saws, and other outdoor power equipment should be serviced at least once a year. You can do it yourself if you're mechanical, or else take it to a repair shop to have the blade sharpened, the engine cleaned, and the parts lubricated.

SAFE POWER CIRCULAR SAWS. Make sure that the saw you use is equipped with a guard that will automatically adjust in use so that none of the teeth is exposed above the work and that it has an automatic power cut-off button. Always wear goggles or a face mask when using a power saw. Carefully examine the material before cutting to make sure that it is free of nails or other metal.

STICK TO THE PATH. Once you've started using a power saw, do not try to veer from the path you have started in the wood; it will cause the blade to bend.

WATCH WHERE YOU'RE DRILLING. Tape a penlight to the casing of a power drill to better see what you are drilling.

CLEAN DRILLING. When using a power drill, place a spare wooden block behind the hole being drilled and let the drill go into the block. This will help keep the hole clean as the drill bit exits.

LUBRICATED BITS. Apply silicone spray to drill bits for lubrication. It will make the bits stronger and keep them sharper longer.

EXTENSION CORDS. Use heavy-duty, grounded extension cords for power tools that have a 14-gauge or larger. Place a hook over the work area to drape the extension cord over when you are working to avoid potential problems with the cord on the workbench itself.

External house repairs

I f you're tempted to do extensive work on your house's foundation, structure, or roof, it's best to think again. Do-it-yourself projects for some aspects of the home are fine, because mistakes may simply be cosmetic, or so obvious that you'll know they need correcting.

But a well intentioned error in more critical aspects of the house can set the stage for disaster in ways that are not apparent. The foundation holds up your house by distributing pressure and stress in very specific and complex ways.

Improper alterations can undermine the house's structure gradually over time or more dramatically. For instance, patching a crack in a basement wall may seem a simple and obvious repair job. However, it may be better to let it leak than to patch it incorrectly from the inside, because you could be trapping water inside the wall with no way to escape. The same goes for roofing: An incorrect fix-up job can make a minor leak worse.

It's a good idea to regularly examine your house for potential trouble spots. If you see something worrisome, there are things you can do to prevent or correct some problems.

If you are comfortable enough with your skills to undertake major repair jobs, you probably already know more than we can tell you here. If not, consult with an expert before doing anything significant.

CHECK THE SLOPE. Examine the ground around your house to make sure it is angled to carry water away. Water is essential for life, but it can be the enemy of a house's structure.

DEPRESSIONS. Also look for depressions that collect water in pools next to the house. If they're not too drastic, you can probably fill these in yourself.

WATCH THE RAINFALL. Also watch how the rainwater flows during the next heavy rainfall. See if it collects near the house.

PLANT CAREFULLY. If you plan to put in shrubbery, trees, or a garden bed near the foundation, make sure the roots won't grow into the house or that the bed isn't going to create planting and drainage problems.

LADDER CONTROL. The ladder should be at enough of an angle to the wall to provide a solid triangular base, but not so far out that it bounces when you're in the middle of it. The rule of thumb is that the distance of the ladder from the wall is equal to one-fourth the ladder's height.

WHY NOT BINOCULARS? If you plan to climb a ladder just to inspect something on the roof or a high spot on the house, consider using binoculars instead. It is much safer.

ROOF REPAIR OR REPLACEMENT? The number of broken, loose or missing shingles on a roof as well as the number of leaks will determine whether you should repair the roof or replace it. If there are several problems, it is probably a good sign that it is time to replace the roof. If you want to repair a minor leak yourself, remember that most leaks are not located directly above the water spots on the ceilings. Look for the leak on a higher point in the roof.

CRUMBLING ASPHALT. For asphalt roofs, bend one of the shingles to gauge its malleability. If the asphalt crumbles or breaks, it is a clear sign that the roof is a candidate for replacement.

AGAINST THE WALL. Rest the top of the ladder against the wall of the house, and don't lean it against overhanging eaves. This will prevent damage to the roof and gutters and will make the ladder much safer and sturdier. Never let the ladder lean against window panes or glass doors.

LADDER CANS. If you have to place a ladder on a soft piece of ground, stick a large empty can such as a paint can under each leg.

LADDER PULLEY. Raise and lower your materials and tools with a rope and a sling. When climbing up or down the ladder, use both hands and face the ladder.

GUTTERS. Gutters are a major protection against water damage. Not all houses have gutters. Often it is assumed that the roof hangs far enough out to avoid problems. If you don't have gutters, observe where the water does go from the roof in a rainstorm or as snow melts. Gutters may not be necessary—but if it resembles a waterfall that is pounding near the foundation, it may be wise to add them.

CHECKING GUTTER FLOW. To check how well your gutters are working, pour water into them and watch how it runs. Gutters should be slightly slanted towards the downspout to carry water into it. Also watch during a heavy rainstorm. Water shouldn't be overflowing from the gutter.

CORRECTING ANGLE. If the angle of the gutter is wrong, the hangers that hold the gutters can be adjusted to correct the problem.

LOOK FOR BREAKS. Examine the joints where sections of gutter or downspout are joined to make sure they are tight, and are not leaking.

CLEAN OUT DEBRIS. Make sure the gutter and downspout are clear of leaves and other debris, and clear them out. If that is a chronic problem, a covering screen may help. Always clean a gutter from a ladder and not the roof.

CLEAN DOWNSPOUT. If the downspout is clogged, use a plumber's helper or other long, flexible cable to clear it out.

LEAF FLUSHING. If the gutter spout is clogged, try flushing it out by inserting a hose with a high-pressure nozzle from below and spraying the water upwards.

SEND WATER SCURRYING. At its base, the downspout should send water scurrying away from the house, not just forming a puddle at the foundation. Use a splashpan, drain tile, or downspout extension to direct water further into the lawn, or into drainage gullies. An underground drain tile or dry well may be called for in some circumstances.

FENCE POST SUPPORT. To secure the base of a loose fence post, pound a long, strong pipe into the ground immediately next to the post until there is about a foot of pipe sticking out. Attach the post to the pipe with U-straps.

LONG-LASTING FENCE POSTS. To make a fence post that will last, use rot-resistant wood and set the post in gravel. For posts that need especially sturdy bases, use a concrete collar. Always place the post in first and then add the cement, not the other way around.

USE YOUR KNEES. When digging with a shovel or post hole digger, always be sure to bend your knees and use your legs as opposed to your back when lifting. This will help avoid back strain.

MILDEW. Look around the base of the house for the tell-tale green signs that mildew has found itself a home in your home. Low areas on the house that are subjected to splashing rains or seeping moisture are especially susceptible. If you find mildew, clean it off with a chlorine-based cleaning mix. Once it's off, let the wood dry out, and apply a waterproof paint or other treatment.

CEMENT ON WHEELS. A convenient way to mix and move concrete for smaller jobs is to place the dry concrete mix at the upper end of a wheelbarrow and pour a small amount of water on the lower end. Use a trowel, small shovel, or hoe to move the mix into the water and make the concrete.

CEMENT STROKES. Once the water disappears from the top of a freshly laid batch of cement, skim the top of the surface with a wood float to make the surface appear more dense.

WOODPILE NO-NO'S. If you store firewood, make sure it is not piled directly against the house. Firewood can often provide a jumping off point for termites and other wood-chomping insects. Or, worse yet, the logs can contain dry-rot, a fungus that can do untold structural damage once it makes its way into the house. So make a container for firewood near the house, or at least keep a good distance between an open stack of wood and the walls.

VINES. Vines add bucolic beauty and charm when climbing up the side of a house. However, in practical terms, you should be very wary of them. Some cling tenaciously with tiny claws or suction cups that can damage paint and siding, and are murder to remove. They may also trap dampness. If you enjoy the sight of vines, use trellises and limit yourself to the more benevolent varieties such as honeysuckle, which are less likely to cling and tear walls up beneath them.

MARKED STORM AND SCREEN WINDOWS. Keep track of where each storm window or screen goes by drawing a diagram of the house and assigning each window a number. Write the appropriate number in a hidden corner of each storm window or screen so that you can easily match them with their proper places in the fall and spring.

SCREEN PRESERVATION. Clean and lightly spray metal screens with spar varnish each year to preserve metal screens indefinitely.

OUTSIDE PROJECTS

REPAIRING WOOD SHINGLE CRACKS. If a wood shingle is cracked, it is usually better to repair the crack than replace the shingle. If the crack is small (1/4 inch or less), pull out loose splinters so that only the large, solid pieces remain. Check the roofing material under the shingles to determine where the nails should go. Sometimes shingles are nailed to wood slats spaced 4 or 5 inches apart. Sometimes they are nailed to wood sheathing. After the loose splinters are removed, butt the solid pieces tightly together and nail the split shingle together with galvanized roofing nails. Do not drive the heads of the nails into the shingle and damage its surface. Cover the crack with asphalt roofing cement. Apply a dab of cement over the nailheads.

If the crack is wide, add a sheet metal patch. To do this, drive a square piece of sheet metal up under the cracked shingle. Make sure that the top of the sheet metal goes beyond the upper edge of the crack. Now complete the job as described above for the small crack.

REPLACING A WOOD SHINGLE. If the crack is beyond repair, replace the shingle. First remove the damaged shingle. Using a screwdriver or chisel, cut the damaged shingle into smaller pieces that can be removed by pulling with your fingers. Using a hacksaw blade, cut the nails off flush with the wood slats or sheathing. Since shingles overlap, you may have to pry up the shingle above enough to get at all the nails. Take care not to crack the good shingle. Measure the empty space and cut a replacement shingle to fit the space. Using a block of wood and hammer, drive the replacement shingle into place. Nail the new shingle in place with galvanized roofing nails. Apply a dab of asphalt cement to cover the nailheads.

REPAIRING ASPHALT SHINGLES. If an asphalt shingle needs to be repaired, simply raise the damaged or torn shingle and apply an ample amount of asphalt cement to the underside. Now press the shingle firmly into place and nail it down with broad-headed, galvanized roofing nails. Always remember to apply asphalt cement to the nailheads.

REPLACING ASPHALT SHINGLES. If the shingle needs replacing, select a strip the same as the piece to be replaced. Your asphalt roofing will usually come in shingle strips. Some roofing is in single, separate shingles. Raise the shingles above the damaged one. Pull the nails from the damaged shingles with the claw hammer. If the nails cannot be reached with a hammer, cut them off with a hacksaw blade. Remove the damaged shingle, and slip the new shingle into place. Nail the new shingle in with broad-headed, galvanized roofing nails. Place two nails to each tab (six nails would be needed for a full shingle strip). The shingles should be covered by the upper shingles when they are lowered into place. Apply a dab of cement over the nailheads and lower the upper shingles into place.

STRAIGHTENING WARPED WALL BOARDS AND SHINGLES. Use screws, rather than nails, to straighten the warped board back in line. First, drill guide holes for the screws into the thicker portion of the board. Then drill the larger holes to countersink the screws. Now pull the warped board into line by tightening the screw into the sheathing. Cover the head of the screw with putty.

BINDING SPLIT WOOD BOARDS OR SHINGLES. First, cut a piece of building paper to slip underneath the split board or shingle. Make it wide enough to fit between the in-place nails. Butt the two halves of the split shingle tightly together. Then nail both halves into place with galvanized nails. Countersink the nailheads and cover them with putty.

REPLACING DAMAGED WOOD SHINGLES. Using a chisel and hammer, splinter the shingle into small, slender pieces. Carefully remove the splintered pieces so as not to damage the remaining shingles. Pull the exposed nails with a claw hammer. Examine the building paper underneath and patch any tears or cuts with asphalt cement. Slip the new shingle into position. Nail the shingle into place with galvanized shingle nails.

REPAIRING WOOD SIDING. Instead of replacing the entire siding board, it is easier to cut out the damaged portion. Using a square, mark the board for cut lines. Pry up the bottom edge of the board and insert wedges underneath. Using the saw, cut out the damaged portion of the siding. Make the cut carefully. Don't damage siding boards above or below. Splinter the damaged portion into smaller pieces, using the hammer and chisel. Remove the pieces with a pry-bar or chisel. Remove the remaining nails with the claw hammer. Examine the building paper underneath and patch any tears or cuts with asphalt cement. Use asphalt cement sparingly, because too much will prevent the breathing of the exterior. Measure the damaged board opening, mark the saw cut lines, and cut the replacement board to fit the opening. Slip the new board into position and drive it into place with a hammer. Hammer against a small wood block to avoid damaging the board. Nail the board in place with galvanized siding nails using the existing nailing pattern.

REPLACING ASBESTOS SHINGLES. Remove the damaged shingle by shattering it with a hammer. If the shingle is not brittle enough to shatter, splinter it into pieces. Remove the pieces and nails. Drill the nail holes in the new shingle at its lower edge. Position the holes like the old nail holes. Examine the building paper underneath and patch any tears or cuts with asphalt cement. Slip the new shingle into position. Nail the shingle in place with galvanized shingle nails.

FLAT ROOF REPAIR. Before repairing a hole on a flat roof, sweep off nearby dirt and gravel, then cut out a square or rectangular section around the damaged area with a utility knife. Apply roofing cement on the carved out area and lay down a matching section of asphalt shingle in the cutout area. Nail down the patch with galvanized roofing nails spaced 2 inches apart along the edge. Smear the top of the repair patch and the area surrounding it up to 3 inches away from each side with another layer of roofing cement then take a second patch that is about 2 inches longer on each side than the first patch and place it on top. If there is gravel on the roof, put in back in place after the cement has dried.

STORM WINDOW PUTTY REPLACEMENT. Using a chisel, remove the cracked and loose putty from the frame. Apply a coat of linseed oil to the exposed wood frame. Reseal the glass with a bead of putty or plastic glazing with a putty knife. Press the putty firmly in place to assure a tight seal. Allow approximately a week for the putty to dry, then paint it to match the existing trim.

REPLACING GLASS IN WOODEN STORM WINDOWS. Always use safety glass for storm windows. Start the job by measuring the opening to be glazed. Subtract 1/16 to 1/8 inch from each of the two dimensions to allow for irregularities in the frame. The glass may be ordered cut to size or it can be cut using a glass cutter. Remove the damaged glass, old putty, and old glazier's points from the frame with a chisel. Apply a coat of linseed oil to the frame. Using the putty knife, spread a thin layer of putty on all sides of the frame in which the glass is to rest. This back-puttying of the glass will assure a tight joint and will cushion the glass. Place the new glass in the opening and press it firmly against the bed of putty. Now place the glazier's points flat against the glass about every 8 inches and drive the points into the frame with a nail set and hammer. make sure that at least 1/8 inch of the glazier's point is left projecting along the glass to hold the glass in place. Apply putty along the four edges of the glass and the outer edges of the frame or molding. Press the putty down firmly at an angle from the glass to the edge of the frame to provide a tight seal. Allow the putty to dry for at least a week, then paint it to match the existing trim.

CAULKING OUTDOOR CRACKS. Cracks and holes that may need caulking may exist between the window and door frames and the main frame of the house; gaps in sidings and at corners of the house; the joints formed by siding and masonry; the underside of eaves where wall and eave meet; the joints where steps and porches meet the house; and the surface of wood siding, trim, and fascias. Before applying new caulk or putty to a crack or hole, remove the old and wipe the area clean with a cloth soaked with a solvent similar to cleaning fluid. Most joints can be caulked with "rope form" caulking by forcing the material into the crack with your fingers. For large opening or cracks, use "bulk" caulking and apply with a putty knife or small trowel. Clean away the excess as you work. To seal around glass in windows and doors, use putty and apply with a putty knife. Lay a small roll of putty (1/8 to 1/4 inch thick) around the sash or frame so that it fills the groove in which the glass rests. Make sure that the putty is fully applied to both the glass and the sash or frame. Press the putty firmly with the knife to assure a good seal. Trim away excess as you work. For holes in wood surfaces, use putty and apply with a putty knife.

FILLING MASONRY CRACKS. Chip out the loose mortar with a chisel. Mix a batch of mortar according to the directions on the package. Wet the masonry before you begin and keep it wet as you work. Apply the mortar with a small pointing trowel. Press the mortar firmly into the joint, making sure the joint is full. Remove the excess mortar with the edge of the trowel. Now finish the joint to match the existing joints. Hold the trowel at a 45-degree angle to the joint, push the tip into the joint, and then firmly move the trowel along the joint. Fill and finish a joint before you start another. Keep the newly filled joints damp for two or three days by frequently wetting with a fine spray from a water hose or by covering with wet burlap.

PLUGGING GUTTER LEAKS. Once you locate a leak, use a wire brush to clean the area free of loose metal and rust and wipe it clean with a cloth. Use a putty knife to apply asphalt roofing cement over the leak area and spread it. If crack or hole is greater than 1/4 inch, cut a small piece of canvas 1/2 to 3/4 inches larger than the hole. Apply a thin layer of roofing cement over the leak area. Place the canvas patch over the cement and press it firmly. Now apply a second heavy coat of cement, fully covering the patch. Clean the putty knife with solvent or cleaning fluid.

REPAIRING CONCRETE CRACKS. Only repair concrete when the surface is dry. You want to work quickly because concrete mixtures dry fast. Begin the project by chiseling out the hole or crack wider under the surface. Clean the concrete surface thoroughly with a wire brush. Mix a batch of mortar according to the directions on the package. Put the mixture into the crack with a trowel and then smooth it out with a wood float. Clean the tools immediately with paint thinner. For big cracks, spread the mixture over the full width of the crack until the level of mortar is slightly above the concrete surface. Be sure to force the mixture to the bottom of the break.

REPLACING CONCRETE. It is often easier to replace a badly heaved or cracked concrete block than to repair it. First dispose of the misshapen concrete block with a sledge hammer and then place 2-by-4 wood boards along the edge of the former block. Place the concrete in the block. Place slightly more concrete in the space than needed and then skim off the excess concrete.

PAINTING

Painting a house can be as much of an art as painting a picture. While you can get away with simply opening a can of paint and slapping on a coat or two, proper painting requires patience and care.

The preparation is as important as the painting. The amount will depend on the condition of the existing surface to be painted. If it is in fairly good shape, some quick scraping of old paint and sanding will be sufficient. However more pre-painting work is obviously necessary if the paint is more badly worn or cracked or large pieces have peeled. In some cases, the term "painting the house" may seem to be a misnomer because you may end up spending more time scraping than painting.

In cases where the paint is especially thick or "alligatored" you may be better off using a paint burner to remove it completely down to the bare wood rather than trying to do a superficial paint job.

TAKE IT EASY. If you dislike painting, this will come as a relief. It's best not to paint too often, because a buildup of too much paint can be as detrimental as too little. So before you paint, take a close look at your house to see if it really needs it. If the paint is merely dingy, but otherwise in good condition, a quick wash may be a better answer than a paint job.

HOW LONG? The exact length of time will depend on your house, but it is generally recommended to leave between three and five years between paintings.

CHECK IT OUT FIRST. Before sanding, check the wall thoroughly for cracks and other deficiencies that need to be corrected. Repair any damages and caulk any holes you find. Be sure to use paintable caulk. (You may find caulking and other wall repairs will also reduce your heating bill.)

CLEAR SURFACE. Before you start painting make sure the surface is clean and clear. All holes and cracks should be caulked, damaged or decayed wood should be replaced, remove rust in metal areas and on nails with a wire brush and steel wool, and remove all defective paint.

SUBSTITUTE CAULK. You can fill in the holes of old woodwork with a homemade caulk. Make a thick paste out of flour and the paint you are using and apply it to the hole or crack. The plug will exactly match the color of the paint.

ROUGH IT UP. Make sure you rough up painted surfaces with sandpaper or a wire brush before painting. This will make the paint hold better and reduce the chances that it will peel before its time. It's especially vital if you're covering over a glossy paint.

PROTECT OTHER AREAS. While it may be a pain in the neck, removing shutters, taping over trim and window glass, and covering lower roofs, porches, bushes, and gardens will ultimately pay off.

WAIT TO REMOVE. Wait until the paint is dry before removing the coverings; otherwise you may inadvertently do exactly what you were trying to avoid, and spread wet paint where you don't want it.

LAZY PROTECTION. However, if you really don't have the patience to go that whole route, one shortcut is to hold a rigid but thin sheet of cardboard between the area you are painting and any nearby glass or trim as you are painting, to catch wayward drops. When you are taking it away, lift straight to minimize the possibility of streaking.

PETROLEUM PROTECTION. When you paint a door, cover the hinges and knobs with petroleum jelly. In this way you can easily wipe remove any spills on the hardware.

KNOW YOUR PAINT. Write down the information about the paint you're using, including the brand and the specific color mix, and store it some-place safe. When it's time to touch up or paint another section in the future, you won't unintentionally come out with a two-toned house.

PAINT TEST. Before buying huge amounts of stain or blended paints, first test the color on the house by painting a patch in a relatively obscure cor-ner. Display samples do not always demonstrate the subtleties of the color on a house.

USE GOOD BRUSHES. You'll save yourself aggravation by spending a little more to buy a quality brush. The bristles of cheap brushes are not as responsive and you may have to work harder. They also give you less con-trol, and you'll end up with a more uneven distribution of paint on the sur-face. Low-quality brushes also tend to lose their bristles more readily as you paint; these are aggravating to pick out of the wet paint. By adding a few drops of oil and rubbing it into the bristles you will keep the brush soft.

BRUSH CUPS. Stop paint from running off the brush and on to your hand, stick a paper cup, piece of cardboard, or half a rubber ball facing upward throughout brush's handle.

PAINTBRUSH PRESERVATION. If you need to store your paintbrush in the midst of a project, you should ideally clean the brush between painting sessions. However, there is a trick of the trade that you may want to try. Place the brush or roller in a tightly sealed plastic bag and put it in the freezer. The brush or roller will not dry for at least a day or two.

PAINTBRUSH RESTORATION. Before throwing out an old paintbrush with hardened paint in it, stick it in a pot of simmering vinegar and remove the paint with a wire brush.

SCREENED PAINT. The best way to get rid of lumps in the paint is to pour the paint through a screen into another bucket or container.

SPILL CONTROL. If you're going to use the paint right out of the bucket, punch two or three nailholes in the small groove in the top rim of your paint can. As you wipe the paint from your brush on the rim, this will allow the paint to drip back into the can, rather than collecting in the groove and spilling over and dripping down the sides of the can.

MASKING PAINT. Cover the rim of a can of paint with masking tape if you are going to pour paint from the can. When you are done, simply remove the tape to clean the top of the can of paint.

ROLLERS. If the surface you're painting has large, even surfaces, you might choose to use a roller, which is generally faster than painting with a brush. However, it's still a good idea to paint around the periphery with a brush for more even edges.

DRYING BRUSHES. If you soak your brush between painting sessions, be sure to drain out all of the liquid or you'll have a drippy mess when you start painting again.

- Before you're ready to begin painting, stand the brush straight up in an empty can for a few minutes to let the fluid drip out. Or, better yet, suspend it from a wire or stick laid across the top of an empty can that's taller than the brush.

- After it stops draining, you may still need to get the fluid trapped inside the bristles. Lay a newspaper or cloth somewhere out of the way, and snap the paint out onto it with a few quick, downward flicks of your wrist (similar to the casting motion that fly fishermen use).

- Then, to be absolutely sure, take an old towel, wrap it around the brush, and squeeze the bristles from the top downward into a can.

FOLLOW THE SUN. Consider the path of the sunlight on your house when figuring out your painting pattern. Paint should not be applied or dry in the direct sunlight, so plan your painting to keep the new paint in the shade, not the sun.

GOOD PAINTING DAYS. Choose a day for painting when rain or heavy winds are not expected. Don't plan to paint if the temperature is below 50 degrees or higher than 90.

NO NEED TO WAKE UP EARLY. Outdoor painting may give you an excuse to stay in bed a little late. You do not want to start painting until after the dew has evaporated in the morning.

GOING DOWN... It's best to start painting at the top of a wall and work your way down, so paint that drips downward can be smoothed out as you go. The most efficient painting technique is to start with long, horizontal strokes then crossing those strokes with vertical brushes to completely cover the surface with the least amount of paint.

GO OVER IT AGAIN. It may also be necessary to go back from the top when you're done, to even out any paint that has dripped down individual clapboards.

HOW MUCH PAINT? The precise amount of paint will depend on what you're covering, and its condition. If you're painting new wood, apply primer, then two moderate coats. If you're painting an existing paint job in fairly good condition, you needn't apply the primer, and you may be able to get away with just one coat if the colors are the same. However, you should still apply primer to sections that have peeled to bare wood. A good rule to follow is to apply three coats of paint for fresh wood, two coats for old surfaces if painting is done every five years, and one coat if a fresh coat is applied every three years.

THICK CAMOUFLAGE. A thicker application can help camouflage many sins on rough, weathered old walls and paint. But you should not take that easy way out too much, because a moderate coat on a carefully prepared surface will last longer, and look better than a thick coat on a sloppy surface.

PAINTING STAIRS. If you need to use the stairs that you are painting, paint every other step, then let it dry before going back and painting the rest of the steps. In this way you will be able to use the dry, skipped steps on the staircase at the same time as the job is being done.

CIRCULAR PAINTING. When painting circular objects such as downspouts, apply the paint first diagonally. Then cross the diagonal strokes by working downward along the long dimension.

KEEPING IT WHITE. To stop white paint from yellowing, pour several drops of black paint in for every quart of white paint.

BEWARE OF FUMES. Even outside, the fumes from paint can travel up your nose, and make you woozy or worse, especially if you're working in corners or other enclosed spaces. Try to keep your head back slightly. And take a break periodically to air yourself out.

BEE ON THE LOOKOUT. Watch out for bees and wasps, which may have nests in the eaves, or in the house with an entry hole in the wall. Also be careful when removing shutters: Wasps love to build nests behind them.

BUY A CHEAP RADIO. That may seem like it has little to do with painting, but many people find that tunes or talk gives them something to occupy their mind while painting. However, don't bring out your good radio. Despite your best intentions, you're probably going to instinctively change stations to avoid an annoying song or talk-show host, or adjust the volume, with paint-covered fingers. So buy yourself a painting radio.

WINTER

SLIP SLIDING AWAY. Rock salt will melt ice and snow on slippery walks and driveways, but it can harm vegetation and damage floors if trampled into the house. Sand is useful, but can be messy when tracked indoors. A layer of kitty litter provides good traction, and is less messy. If you do use kitty litter, buy a basic brand that doesn't contain deodorizing crystals or other chemicals. You may also have to do a bit of work in spring to remove the compacted layer of litter when the snow melts.

ROOF SNOW. Usually you needn't be too concerned about snow build up on roofs. Most homes can withstand a lot. In fact, snow acts as a natural layer of insulation to keep heat from escaping through the roof.

Nevertheless, you should keep an eye on the roof during snowy winters, especially if it has different levels or flat sections. And watch during warm ups to make sure the snow has a way to flow down off the roof as it melts; trapped water can cause roof damage and leaks.

SNOW REMOVAL. If you can get to your roof safely, it may be helpful to remove some snow if the buildup becomes worrisome or if you want to help it melt faster and drain better.

NOT ALL. You needn't try to remove all snow or get to the entire roof. Merely removing portions of the top layer, or creating drainage valleys, will help to open it up to sun and provide a path for water to flow.

DON'T GOUGE ROOF. Be careful not to dig your shovel down too deeply, because you may tear up roofing by mistake.

CHECK GUTTERS. Also check the gutters and clear them of snow and ice. If they freeze up, a thin layer of rock salt can loosen up the ice. If gutter clogging and damage is a chronic problem because gutters stick out too far from the roof, it may be wise to move them back in closer to the house next spring.

SNOWPLOW DIPLOMACY. Hiring the wrong snowplow service can add to the stress of the season. The plower may show up in the middle of a storm and not come back, or else be so conscientious that you can't afford the number of visits he makes. Careless work can also tear up your driveway and yard.

- Rather than trusting the classifieds or bulletin boards, ask your friends if they know of a reliable snowplow service.

- Make sure you and the plower understand each other. Would you rather call him when you need him or have him show up automatically when the snowfall reaches a certain level?

145

■ Also work out how deeply he'll plow: If it's too low, the surface of your driveway and lawn can be damaged; too high and snow can build up and form ice. And work out in advance where he'll push the snowpiles, and make him aware of low shrubs or areas of your lawn you want to protect. (Mark them with high stakes if necessary.)

EASY SLIDING SHOVELS. Apply candle wax, furniture polish, or vegetable oil to your snow shovel to make the snow fall off easily when you have to shovel it.

WOOD NOTS. Avoid resinous woods like pine in your winter fires. They will eventually build up a sticky (potentially flammable) coating in your chimney. If you use scrap lumber for kindling or firewood, avoid painted or chemically treated wood, because the fumes are toxic.

KEEP WATER RUNNING. During extreme cold spells in the single digits and below, keep a trickle of hot water flowing through your faucets, to avoid freezing, bursting pipes.

UNBLOCKING PIPES. If you turn on the water, and nothing comes out, ice may be blocking the water. If you can get to the pipe, use a heated hair dryer aimed at the pipe to unthaw it. Pipes along outside walls are especially vulnerable to freezing.

TENDING A BURST PIPE. If you have a minor burst pipe, you can mend it temporarily by turning the water off and securing a thick piece of rubber over the hole with a clamp. This will keep the pipe in place in many cases until you can get a plumber to replace the broken pipe.

KEEP AN EYE OUT. When taking a trip, make sure a neighbor keeps a watchful eye on your house, to check for damage and turn on the water during a cold snap.

BENDING BUSHES. After a heavy snowfall, many bushes seem bent and damaged. Often they'll spring right back as the snow melts, and they're best left alone. If one looks particularly troubled, though, it wouldn't hurt to carefully shake off the snow.

Your outdoor home

For some people, keeping up with their yard and garden is a chore. For others it's a labor of love. Fortunately, there are many ways to create and maintain a pleasing exterior environment for your home, whether you're a grudging gardener or an enthusiastic one.

If you'd rather be sailing (or napping, or doing anything but yard-work) you can create an attractive yard that almost takes care of itself. If, on the other hand, you enjoy the creativity and physical satisfactions of gardening and landscaping, there are many opportunities to indulge your green thumb, even on a small lot.

The key is planning and research. Rather than buying a shrub here, a flower there, it's best to start out with a unified master plan that incorporates all of the elements you'll want to develop in the seasons ahead. A bit of time and thought now will make your outdoor work more efficient and enjoyable in the long run, and will spare you from disappointment and the need to correct problems later.

Your landscape is the total effect created by individual features of your property: its size, shape, and terrain; lawns, gardens, trees, and shrubs; the house, walkways, patios and other structures on it; and how your property relates to the neighborhood and region.

A good way to orient yourself is to bone up on the basics of landscaping, gardening, and ecology. Also look into the specific personalities of the plants you are working with or are considering adding. Take some books out of the library, and ask your gardening friends, or experts at the local garden center or extension service, for advice.

One word of warning. It's easy to get confused and intimidated by all of the details and theories involved. Many seem contradictory. For example, there are good insects and bad insects, even within the same family. How to know which is which?

Don't let it scare you off. If you start with the basics, you can usually trust your instincts and learn through experience. Nature, after all, has been working its magic unassisted by human expertise for millions of years. It's likely to forgive you a few mistakes.

PLANNING POINTERS

PACE YOURSELF. Whatever your goals or level of interest, it's best to start out small and simple. It's tempting to underestimate the work involved and create gardens that are too big or numerous to keep up with, which can be worse than doing nothing at all. If you find that your enthusiasm is growing along with your plants, you can always expand and elaborate on your plantings over time.

FANTASIZE. Spend a little time fantasizing about what you'd ultimately like your property to look like, and then break it down into individual steps and stages that will lead to the overall effect you want to achieve.

QUESTION YOURSELF. Ask yourself a lot of questions. Do you prefer bright sunlight or shade? Are you a formal type who prefers a carefully manicured look or are you more casual and enjoy bucolic clutter?

How important is all of this to you? Do you want to spend the time and money to make your property as appealing as possible? Or is your goal simply to keep it neat and presentable?

ANALYZE YOUR PROPERTY. Scrutinize your property and decide what it needs. Do you want to restore a bit of nature to your section of a barren new housing development? Or are you trying to spruce up an overgrown old property? Do you want to make a small yard seem larger or are you trying to enhance a sense of intimacy?

LOOK AROUND. Look carefully at other properties for ideas as you go about your daily round. Also peruse gardening and home books and magazines for ideas. Decide which have an overall effect you like, and look for specific effects you might duplicate.

PLAN ON PAPER. Playing with different possibilities on paper will help you to focus on specifics.

- Draw an overhead diagram of your property as it exists with beds, trees, structures, and other features. If you're methodical, measure the square footage, and draw it out on graph paper to the exact scale, with each block a square foot. However, you can be less exact, simply by estimating.

■ Also sketch ground-level views of the property at present. If you don't trust your artistic ability, take snapshots.

■ Then make several photocopies of each of these present views. Use the copies to draw in various possible plans until you hit on the combination that strikes your fancy.

SET A SCHEDULE. Once you've decided on your ultimate vision, break it down into steps that will lead toward your goals. What can you do now? What should be postponed? You might want to make a schedule of goals to accomplish each year.

BE A MATCHMAKER. Match the characteristics of specific plants with different sites, and think of the overall effect you want to achieve. This includes their requirements for light and soil, their growing habits and ultimate size, when they bloom, and other qualities. That way you can avoid mistakes like putting a sun-loving juniper in a shady spot where a hemlock would be more at home.

TRY IT OUT. Before actually putting a new plant in the ground, keep it in the container and place it in the spot you have chosen; then leave it for a little while before you break out the shovel. Observe it from different angles and move it around a bit. You'll then be less likely to regret your choice or decide after planting that it should be moved three feet to the left.

STAKEOUT. If you haven't bought a plant yet (or if it is too heavy to lug around from place to place) insert stakes in the ground in potential locations to get a sense of how a plant will look there. (Ski poles are handy for this.)

SITE WITH A FRIEND. Stand in the locations where you are likely to be viewing your yard most often. Have someone else go into the general area of the planting. Have them move around and direct them until they are in the spot that is most attractive or hides features that you may be trying to block from view. Also, stand in different areas to get a better idea of how it will look from various angles.

THE ROPE TRICK. When you're deciding where to put garden beds or hedgerows, lay rope or string on the ground and experiment with the location and shape until you find what you like. You can then use that as a guide while digging out the bed too.

KEEP A NOTEBOOK. Unfortunately, the best seasons to do renovation work on plantings are spring and autumn, when plant characteristics are least evident (or the plants themselves are invisible). So keep a notebook during the growing season to remember the ideas that come to you during the summer or problems that you want to correct.

Record the location and characteristics of vegetation, including the color, dates of bloom, size, growing habits, etc. Also include problems or improvements, such as tall plants that need to be moved further back in the garden, or empty spots that need to be filled.

PHOTOGRAPH IT. It's especially helpful to take photographs or videotape the yard and garden every couple of days during the growing season as a companion to the notebook. Be sure to include the date.

REMEMBER THE WINTER. Since much garden work happens in the growing season, it's easy to forget what the property will look like in winter. So it's a good idea to also keep a record of your yard in late fall, winter, and early spring too, so you can factor that into your overall planning.

MARKING PLANT SITES. Place small identification stakes or popsicle sticks by your plants and write their names in pencil or waterproof ink. You can also number them to correspond with the entries in your notebook. When you venture out in the garden in early spring, you'll know which plants are where, even though they can't be seen or recognized.

LANDSCAPING TIPS

GOING NATIVE. Like other fashions, tastes in gardening and landscaping go in cycles from extreme formality to a more natural approach that is supposed to look untended. In recent years the pendulum has been swinging away from formal gardens to a more natural approach that uses native plants and takes advantage of the region's terrain. The most avid natural gardeners believe that even long-established immigrant plants should not be encouraged.

Wherever your own personal taste falls on this spectrum, your life will be easier if you work with the natural qualities of your region. That includes buying native plants, and appreciating and incorporating the wild ones that appear uninvited. If you live in an arid region, you'll waste a lot of time and resources trying to duplicate the landscape of a moist cool climate, and vice versa. By emphasizing the environment of your region, you'll be doing your part to encourage regional diversity over homogenous sprawl.

BE CURVY. The straight lines and angles of formal gardens appeal to many people, and may be most appropriate for a small area. But curves are friendly and create a flowing, natural feeling. If you're laying out a garden bed, curve it around the edges of the yard. If you're creating an island bed, make an oval or other rounded shape rather than square.

FOCUS. Tie your yard together by emphasizing, or adding, focal points, such as trees, rocks, mounds, pools, and other features. If these already are present, figure out ways to lead the eye to them. If your yard is flat and featureless, figure out what you might add to give it a point of interest.

USE ILLUSION. You can use optical illusions in many ways. If you want to make a small yard look larger, you can create an exaggerated sense of depth and distance by placing larger bushes and trees close to the common vantage points and smaller versions of them further away.

A PATH OF FANTASY. Make a path that curves around and behind hedges, rocks, or other large features. It creates the feeling that the path is leading somewhere, even if it stops a couple of feet behind the obstacle. This effect is heightened if you narrow the width of the path as it recedes.

MIRROR, MIRROR. If the angles on your property are right, try placing a mirror unobtrusively in a gap in the vegetation or other location that will reflect in a way that seems to enlarge your property.

FOLIAGE AND FENCES. If you don't have the patience to wait for shrubs to grow enough to offer privacy, erect a fence, and plant bushes in front of it and vines that will cover it. You can also install little shelves or baskets with hanging plants on them.

GREEN POWER. Painting the fence green will add to the illusion of a mass of vegetation. Or if you are facing the back of a garage or other obstacle, paint it green to make it less obtrusive while the shrubbery grows.

COORDINATE COLORS. Consider the hues of the entire landscape, and how they affect your other goals. In addition to flowers, look at the colors and seasonal variations of leaves, stems, grasses, and other forms.

COLOR AND SPACE. Color affects the sense of space in your yard, and you should plan it to fit your landscape goals. The effect will depend on the conditions in your yard, as well as how you use them.

- A brightly-colored flower garden will seem closer than a more muted one. A close-in bright garden may enhance a three-dimensional effect when combined with a more subtle garden further out. However, if it is too close or large, it may overwhelm the background and make the yard seem smaller.

- A bright garden in the distance will visually bring in the boundaries of the property. If you don't care, that may be your choice. But if you are trying to create a sense of distance, use more subtle colors.

- A yard with short wildflowers of differing colors, such as violets, dandelions, and snowdrops, can seem much more expansive when the sun plays across them. But if they are tall and excessive, the yard may seem crowded and cramped.

DON'T NEGLECT YOUR NOSE. Remember the aromatic characteristic of flowers, shrubs, and other plants when you choose and site them. Many plants add fragrance to the sensations of the season, but only within a limited distance. Their aroma will be wasted if placed in a distant corner of the yard that is seldom visited.

CLOSE-IN FRAGRANCE. Fragrant flowers such as bee balm or nicotiana, or shrubs such as lilacs, should be placed close by where you can enjoy their olfactory, as well as their visual, appeal. Herbs can also add to the scents near the house.

INDOOR AROMA. Placing aromatic plants near windows will allow the scent to waft into your house.

UNWANTED SCENTS. It works the other way, too. Not all plants appeal to everyone's nose. So either avoid those you dislike or put them where you can enjoy their visual beauty without offending your nostrils. Some examples:

- Marigolds have a pungent scent that some people consider spicy but others find annoying.

- Boxwoods emit an odor that is nostalgic and attractive to some, but it reminds others of a catbox.

- Cleome is another plant with a debatable scent. Some like it, others would rather see, but not smell, it.

WATCH FOR WETLANDS. If you plan any landscaping that involves extensive work around brooks, ponds, or other wet areas, check to make sure you're not running afoul of wetlands regulations. Also, if you have a spot for dumping leaves or brush, make sure it is not in a protected area.

NEIGHBORLINESS. Be a good neighbor, even when you are planting for privacy. Planting a row of tall trees in the northern corner of your yard will not affect the light in your yard, but it will eventually shade the home on the north. Ask your neighbors how they feel about that and plant accordingly.

POOL YOUR RESOURCES. Consider joining forces with your neighbor for plantings and other landscaping projects that affect both properties. You could pool your resources to buy better, larger, and more shrubs for a mutually beneficial privacy hedge.

ALLEVIATING WINTER BLUES. The use of evergreens, underlying forms of branches, and berries are among the features you can use to make winter seem less bleak. This is more crucial in colder climates. If you are in a warm southern climate or the temperate Northwest, you can also choose vegetation that will brighten up the winter months.

TREES AND SHRUBS

KEEP IT SHORT. When using trees or tall-growing shrubs for privacy or to hide unwanted features from view, figure out the minimum height they need to be to accomplish that. Then prune or top them off annually to keep them at that height. Keeping them short will prevent them from opening up and thinning out as they grow. It also opens up your property to more sky and light.

LOOK SOUTH. Take note of the path of the sun when choosing a location for trees and shrubs, and decide how much sun and shade you ultimately want, and where. A row of white pines along the southern border of your property may be attractive when they're short, but will eventually block out the sunlight for much of the day. Will that bring welcome shade or will it make your yard gloomier and colder?

MESSY TREES. To make your yardwork less taxing, choose trees that make the least amount of mess. Avoid trees that drop an excessive number of fruit, nuts, or other seeds, such as locusts and walnuts.

DON'T BOMB YOUR HOUSE. Keep fruit and nut trees away from the house. A steady bombardment of heavy apples or chestnuts isn't good for the roof. It also makes your house more tempting as a residence for squirrels and other animals attracted by this ready food supply.

PINE PRECAUTIONS. Pines and other needled evergreens will turn your soil more acid over time, because of the dropping needles. They also will push back your lawn as they grow, because the needles build up a layer that smothers grass.

TOO MUCH SHADE. Norway maples are more difficult to grow grass or other plants around than other maples, because their canopy of leaves blocks out more light and rain.

UNAPPRECIATED HEDGES. There are many choices for hedges and screens. Some, such as privet, euonymous, arborvitae, and hemlock are well known. Others are less appreciated. Sometimes they are considered weeds, because they are so prolific or are not as attractive as their more cultivated cousins. However, as long as you work to keep them under control, they can serve your purposes inexpensively.

THE HUMBLE HONEYSUCKLE. Many varieties of honeysuckle bushes make a great screen. They are hardy and prolific and their leaves come out early and stay late. Some varieties should be used at a distance because they are less attractive close up, especially in mid-summer as their leaves tend to wither and their berries get messy. Trim them often to keep growth fresh and the bush under control.

FORSYTHIA FOR PRIVACY. People often grow small forsythia bushes because its bright yellow flowers signal the arrival of spring. But its value for screening is underappreciated. Left alone, forsythias can easily become a thick tangle of leaves that provide great natural screening. Mature forsythia also offer privacy in winter because their branches are tangled so thickly.

- Forsythia on a bank or slope is also effective for erosion control, because its branches droop over and sprout new roots when they touch the ground.

BAMBOO WALLS. While some people consider it a pest, bamboo can be used to create an almost instant privacy screen. It grows very quickly within weeks into a tall mass of leaves and stems. It dies back during the winter, but will return every year. Be prepared to live with bamboo forever, because once it finds a home it's extremely difficult to remove. However, the brittle stalks can easily be cut down by hand to keep them under control.

- For year-round privacy, or to camouflage a fence or wall, plant tall bamboo in front of it. You'll have to look at what's behind it for the barren months, but the bamboo provides quick cover during the growing season.

- Plant a more substantial hedge in front of bamboo for the future. Just make sure to keep the bamboo from overwhelming it while it is growing.

IGNITING THE BURNING BUSH. To bring out the fiery autumn reds of Burning-bush euonymous early in the season, plant them in direct sunlight.

Gardening basics

P lants are like people. They come in all shapes, sizes, and colors, and each has its own individual personality, demands, and quirks. But their lives, too, follow predictable cycles of birth and maturity before they shuffle off their mortal coil.

Understanding the psychology and social life of plants, and their relationship to each other, will add to your appreciation and the effectiveness of outdoor chores.

Like us, their behavior is rooted in the perpetual quest for the basics: nourishment, survival, and growth. And, just as humans do many things in the name of love, plants are also driven by the basic drive to mate and perpetuate their species.

Whether we call a particular plant a fruit, vegetable, flower, or tree, all plants share a basic physical structure and patterns of behavior based on those basic drives.

Their leaves convert sunlight to food. Roots draw moisture and nutrients from the soil. Stems and branches transport water and food through the plant. Buds become flowers and flowers become seeds. The apple or tomato you eat serves the same basic function for the plant as the flowers of the lilac that you enjoy looking at.

BASIC TIPS

KNOW WHAT YOU'RE BUYING. A rose by any other name may not smell as sweet. Many plants have the same basic name, but specific varieties within that family may have very different characteristics. They vary in size, appearance, taste, and many other ways. So look at the labels and ask to make sure you know what to expect, and how you should treat the plant.

GO FOR THE NATURAL. The more you use nature to accomplish your gardening goals the better. There may be situations that call for chemical fertilizers or pesticides, and many are not inherently harmful when used carefully. But as a general rule, try to find solutions that are as natural as possible. Often it's easier and less expensive, and you'll feel better about your effect on the environment.

WAIT. Patience is a virtue. While spring is the busiest season for gardening, give the ground a chance to dry out and warm up after the winter snows melt. Walking on and working the soil when it's still soggy and cold will compact it, making it harder to breathe and drain.

AVOID JACK FROST. No matter how warm and sunny it seems, wait until the likelihood of frost is past before planting annuals and most vegetables. While gardens in warm and temperate regions of the South and Pacific Northwest can get going in early spring, in colder northern climes you may have to wait until around Memorial Day to be safe.

HARDY PERENNIALS. Perennial flowers, and some vegetables, however, can be planted earlier. Perennials are used to winter weather, and so are more likely to withstand frost.

TRANSPLANTING TIME. The best times to transplant are spring and autumn. Generally, you shouldn't transplant flowers, trees, and shrubs during the middle of the growing season, because the plant is busy doing its job and disruptions are traumatic.

MOVING DAYS. It's better to move plants on cool, overcast, or damp days than warm sunny ones.

IF YOU'RE DARING... However, certain plants can be moved whenever the urge strikes you anyway. The plant may not immediately look its best after transplanting during mid-summer, but it may come around soon or revive the following year. Nevertheless, you should only try this if you have an abundance of vegetation and don't mind risking the loss of the plant.

WATER LOW. Water close to the ground. While the upper portion of a plant benefits from a good shower, it's most important to make sure the roots are getting their share of water.

NOT AT MID-DAY. Avoid watering during mid-day, because it evaporates more quickly. The drops on leaves also act as magnifiers for the sun's rays, which can burn the plant.

WATER WEEKLY. Rather than a short daily session with the hose, water deeply once or twice a week. This soaks the soil further down, which allows the deeper roots to enjoy a drink. It also encourages healthy root growth, while superficial watering may encourage the plant to be lazy and keep its roots close to the surface.

HOSE CONTROL. If you have to maneuver a long hose around garden beds, shrubs, small trees, and other obstacles, place stakes about 2 to 3 feet high around them. This will reduce the chances of the hose being dragged over them.

FLEXIBLE FAUCET. A flexible attachment where the hose and faucet join will help to minimize the damage caused by twisting as you move the hose around.

PUTTING THE HOSE AWAY. Being left outside in the sun is not good for a hose, so store it inside when you're not using it.

WINTER CARE. When you put the hose away for the winter, make sure all of the water is drained out of it.

KEEP THAT OLD HOSE. A leaky hose isn't a useless hose. Seal the far end, punch a series of holes and lay it on the ground as a low watering drip and spray hose.

SHARE THE BOUNTY. If you have fruit trees, berry bushes, or a vegetable garden that bears more food than you can eat, call the local food bank, homeless shelter, or other community service agency. They can make use of your excess edibles, and may even send over a crew to gather them up, saving you the time of cleaning up yourself.

IS THERE MONEY IN YOUR YARD? You may make a bit of extra money. Floral shops and other merchants may be willing to buy wild or cultivated flowers, or appealing branches like ripe bittersweet, as material for their dried arrangements or to sell as sprigs and sprays. Ask around.

PLANT SUPPLIES

PROPAGATE YOUR EXISTING PLANTS. Try cultivating the seeds or offspring of your existing plants. You may be able to create an orchard or enlarge your garden or landscaping at no cost.

GIVE SEEDS A HAND. Collect fruits and other seeds that are produced by trees and other plants on your property. Then plant them in desirable locations and see if they sprout the following year. You can plant many, if you want to increase the odds. (Be sure to mark the sites.)

GROW SEEDS IN SEEDLING CONTAINERS. If you do this, check its growing requirements. While some can be grown right away, others need to go through a period of extreme cold before planting, and should either be left outside during the winter or placed in a freezer for awhile.

BABIES IN THE LAWN. Examine your lawn carefully in early spring. You may have an array of tiny tree seedlings. Try cultivating a few to see if they survive to become trees.

SET UP AN EXCHANGE. To increase the diversity of your gardens and plantings, work out an exchange with your friends to coordinate what you buy and grow. Agree to plant and share different types of vegetables, so you can enjoy a more varied harvest. Or make arrangements to buy different types of perennials, bushes, or other ornamental plants and swap them as they spread.

SHOP LATE. To save money on trees, shrubs, and perennial plants, visit your local garden centers in late summer. Often they want to clear out their stocks before winter, and greatly reduce prices.

PRE-GROWN OR SEEDLINGS? The easiest way to purchase plants is to buy them pre-grown in containers. This also will also get your garden going faster because you won't have to wait for late bloomers.

However, starting plants yourself from seedlings offers more personal satisfaction, and allows you to plant a larger quantity than you might be able to afford otherwise. Starting them indoors is also a great way to beat the late winter blues, and remind yourself that spring is indeed around the corner.

- **Starting out.** You can buy seedling starter kits, with specially made growing trays. Or you can use plastic TV dinner trays, the bottom half of milk cartons, or other wide, open containers.

- **Greenhouse effect.** A clear plastic covering over the seedling container will provide a miniature greenhouse effect and seal in moisture. If a container has one, use that. Or you can cut plastic wrap and tie it with a string or rubber band around the top.

- **Spare that water.** Water seedlings regularly but don't overwater. Too much water in the soil can cause the tender stem to rot, and breed other problems.

- **Sterile soil.** It's best to use special growing mix rather than standard soil for seedlings. In the enclosed environment of seedling containers, normal soil can breed fungus and diseases that will kill off the tender babies.

- **Time your seedlings.** Most seedlings should not be planted in the ground until the danger of frost is over in your region. Read the labels carefully and start your seedlings at a time that's right for them. If you plant too soon, they may become too big for their britches before they can be planted outside. Too late and you'll be waiting all season for flowers or crops.

- **Hardening off seedlings.** Just like human children, seedlings need an occasional dose of tough-love to prepare them for the harsh world outside. To get them used to the outdoors, seedlings should be "hardened off" for a week or two before planting. Take them outdoors for several hours during the day in a bright spot (but not direct sunlight) and then bring them indoors at night.

- **Reduce your trips.** If you grow a large quantity of seedlings, consolidate the containers on a roll-cart or large tray that you can move easily. This will reduce the number of trips required to haul them in and out of the house during the hardening phase.

SOIL

Creating good growing soil is like preparing a healthy gourmet meal. You want the right mix of ingredients that plants will find tasty and nourishing. The exact recipe will depend on what you want to grow and the condition of the property.

Soil is a mixture of sand, stones and other inorganic materials, plus air, water, and decomposed vegetation, animal remains, and microscopic life forms. Organisms in the soil break down and release nitrogen and other nutrients, and make them available to the plant. While it's possible to find perfect soil, most can use help to compensate for deficiencies, to replenish the ingredients that have been depleted, or balance characteristics that may be too dominant.

Not all plants take to all kinds of soil, and you'll want to match plants with the soil that suits them best.

Nevertheless, you needn't be intimidated by all of the theories and specifics of soil science. Good soil is good soil for most plants, and you can adjust the qualities at the specific sites of plants to give them an extra boost.

THE NUMBERS. When shopping for fertilizer, pay attention to the three-number code that gives the percentage of nitrogen, phosphorus, and potassium (potash), in that order. These are major mineral nutrients in soil. Nitrogen zaps up leaf and stem growth, phosphorous stimulates the roots and flowers and seeds, and potassium makes the plant healthy and sturdy.

MORE OR LESS. Each of the three ingredients is important and soil should contain all of them. Some fertilizers have a balance, others have more of one ingredient for particular results or conditions.

FERTILIZE FOR THE SEASON. In spring fertilizing, you'll want a mix of ingredients that encourage leaves and other top-growth more. Later fertilizing should emphasize healthy root growth and sturdiness. Avoid nitrogen-rich fertilizers late in the season, so you don't encourage the plant to send tender new growth into a cold cruel world.

MANURE TEA. You wouldn't want to serve it to guests, but manure tea is a concoction your soil will happily slurp up. It is just what it sounds like, a mixture of manure and water. You can make it in small or large amounts. Experiment with a precise mixture that suits your needs.

MANURE. While manure in its raw form, as a powder, or as a tea is a valuable tool for building healthy soil and plants, it should be used sparingly. And try to keep it from directly touching the plants or roots because it can damage them.

- **Consistency.** Soil should have a moist consistency that supports the plant's roots and stems, while being loose enough to breathe and drain excess water. Clay soil is generally heavier and does not drain well, while sandy soil is gritty and drier.

- **Watch it drain.** Dig a hole in your garden. Pour some water into it, and see how quickly it drains. If the water sits there for a long time instead of being absorbed, it is probably clay and needs loosening up. If it shoots away and leaves little moisture behind, it's too sandy.

- **The jar test.** To test the consistency of your soil, partially fill a clear glass jar with water. Then put a smaller amount of soil into it, close the lid, and shake and swirl the jar for about a minute. As it settles, larger gravelly particles will sink to the bottom, then sand and looser silt. Clay and organic material will stay suspended longer (often for several days). When it calms down enough for you to see the amounts of each, you will have an idea of the composition of your soil.

- **Loosen up.** Rich organic materials will benefit both clay and sandy soil. Soil that is too heavy with clay can also be loosened up with sand or other loose, gritty material.

- **Peat moss.** Peat moss will benefit both extremes. It should be mixed thoroughly into the soil.

- **The acid test.** Have your soil tested for acidity and alkalinity, which is measured in pH levels from 0 to 14; the lower the pH level the more acidic the soil. Your local Cooperative Extension Service can tell you who to contact for testing.

- **A litmus test.** You can also get a general idea yourself by inserting damp litmus paper into the soil to see if it comes out red (acidic) or blue (alkaline).

- **Proper pH levels.** Different plants tolerate differing pH levels. Rhododendrons, blueberries, and many evergreen trees, for example, grow best in very acidic soil. Apples, phlox, and dandelions favor alkaline soils. Most prefer something in-between. Additives can balance the soil or create the levels suited to specific plants.

- **Compost.** Never underestimate the value of compost, the catch-all term for decomposing organic materials that enrich soil and give it a better texture and consistency.

- **Many theories.** Beyond the basics there are many theories about the best composting techniques, from highly scientific methods to the more laid-back "just throw it all together and let it rot for a while" approach. The best way is whatever suits your beliefs and temperament. Every little bit helps.

- **Compost bin.** A compost bin can be as simple as a pile in a corner of the yard. Or you can build an enclosure of stakes and wire netting, or a wooden box. If you want to be scientific, special composting equipment is also available.

COMPOST CONTENTS. Compost can include a wide variety of ingredients.

- From your yard, you can use leaves, evergreen needles, bark, twigs, rotting wood, grass clippings, etc.

- Kitchen wastes can include remains of meals, such as vegetables, fruits, coffee grounds, egg shells, etc.

- Many other materials can be added, such as hair, sawdust, and fireplace ash (make sure it has been sitting a long time and is completely dead).

- Adding soil and peat moss to the mix will help the process along too.

...BUT NOT EVERYTHING. The compost pile should be as organic as possible. Avoid putting in meats and very fatty foods. No TV dinners or other highly processed foods. Don't put in painted or chemically treated wood.

Don't throw seedy weeds into the compost or diseased plants or leaves from blighted trees.

BREAK IT UP. Compost will decompose more rapidly if the ingredients are in small pieces, so break up large sticks, crumple up food, and let your lawnmower chew up leaves before adding them to the pile.

GIVE IT AIR. Make sure the compost gets plenty of air circulation but also traps heat. Periodically turn it to stir up the process.

QUICK COMPOSTING. Despite the elaborate techniques often recommended for compost, some people say compost works just as well by working the materials directly in the soil, and letting them decompose on the spot.

MULCH. Mulch is material placed on the surface to hold moisture in the soil, prevent weeds, and protect the plant from winter weather. Like compost, mulch comes in many forms. It can have the neat, uniform look of the processed wood-bark chips seen in the flower beds at fast-food restaurants or it can be a more disheveled collection of decomposing leaves, wood and straw.

COVERING. If your goal for mulch is strictly to control weeds, sheets of dark plastic or other material laid between plants is an effective way to block out light and air.

MULCH AS COMPOST. A layer of organic material such as wood chips or sawdust, straw, or leaves can become compost as it decays.

WAIT FOR WINTER MULCH. Don't apply winter mulch too early. Its purpose is to prevent the soil temperature from fluctuating in freeze-thaw cycles, not to keep the ground warm. It should be put in place when the ground begins to harden around the time of the first frost, not much earlier.

LEAVING LOGS. If it doesn't offend your visual sensibilities, leave stumps and felled tree trunks alone. As they decay, they become a handy source of mulch and soil enricher, which you can shovel or scoop out.

Also, squat logs that are not destined for the fireplace can be stood on end in an unobtrusive location, and will serve the same purpose.

Flower gardens

USING ANNUALS AND PERENNIALS. Apart from their obvious similarities, annual and perennial flowers have different, sometimes contradictory, characteristics. You can use them in combination to serve differing purposes. (However, some flowers can be either annual or perennial, depending on conditions or the specific variety.)

ANNUALS FOR INSTANT COLOR. "Live fast and die young." That's the fate of annuals, which last for one season, but grow rapidly and provide continuous color for most of their short lives. Pansies and Johnny-jump-ups, for example, bloom from early spring into the autumn. Others, like Cosmos, may wait until midsummer to bloom, but once they get going there's no stopping them.

PERENNIALS FOR VARIETY AND STABILITY. Perennials, on the other hand, have distinct periods of bloom, and so they may be in their glory for only a few weeks or even days. However, their core remains alive and they return year after year and add a sense of permanence to a garden. Their leaves and flowers also tend to be more varied and interesting than annuals.

BIENNIALS. Biennials are not long lasting like perennials, but generally last more than one season. Some will mature during their first year, and bloom in the second.

EASY ANNUALS. The most common container-grown annuals, such as marigolds, pansies, impatiens and zinnias are generally easy to care for. They are also easiest to work with because what you see is what you get.

PRE-GROWN ANNUALS. For the longest-lasting bloom, buy pre-grown annuals in containers. Some annuals, such as zinnias, cosmos, and dahlias, take a while to mature before they show their colors. Pre-growns have already gotten this process out of the way, so you won't have to wait for results.

CLIPPING ANNUALS. Most annuals will produce flowers more prolifically if you continually clip the fading flowers throughout the season. The plant will work to produce new blooms to replace those you remove, instead of turning flowers into seeds.

CLIPPING PERENNIALS. You can also clip many perennials, but you have to be careful. Those that create many flowers, such as bee balm and coral bells, will benefit from clipping. But others, including peonies, large delphiniums, and day lilies, are less likely to sprout new blossoms when clipped, and should be enjoyed while they're out instead.

PERENNIAL BLOOM. Know the flowering schedule of different perennials and choose a combination that will provide a flow of color throughout the season. A season-long garden will include:

- Early-blooming plants like daffodils, tulips, and hyacinths

- Later-spring flowerers such as forget-me-nots, bachelor's buttons, and bleeding hearts

- Early summer bloomers like peonies, astilbe, delphinium, and irises

- Mid- and later summer blossoms such as bee balm, day lilies, phlox, and goldenrod

- Late bloomers like asters and chrysanthemums

SIMPLE GARDENS. To add color to your yard with the least fuss, plant a simple annual bed.

- Dig out a bed a couple of feet deep.

- Go to the local garden center and buy bags of enriched soil mix, wood-bark mulch and peat-moss, and any other soil boosters that are appropriate.

- Buy an assortment of container annuals that are long blooming and easy to care for.

- When you get home, thoroughly mix the dirt you removed from the ground with the soil you just bought to create a mound of soil that is loose and easy to work, and has good drainage.

- Scatter the mulch on top, and then place the flowers in the bed in an appealing arrangement.

STRENGTH IN NUMBERS. While variety is the spice of life in a flower garden, plan for the effect you want, rather than arranging different flowers individually and haphazardly. Even if you want an array of different shapes and colors, such as the effect of a cottage garden, it's still a good idea to use groupings and patterns and relationships.

GROUPINGS. Place groupings of flowers of the same variety together instead of spreading them around the garden haphazardly and individually. If you have twelve pansies, you might put all in one section, or have two or three smaller groupings, rather than a pansy here and another there.

EARLY BULBS. Allow the leaves and stems of early-blooming bulbs like tulips and daffodils to die back naturally, so they can receive nourishment. They will generally fade away in time to be replaced by later plants. However, they can be trimmed if necessary to give their successors enough room to grow.

WHAT'S IN A NAME? A rose by any other name may not smell as sweet. It's wise to pay attention to the specific varieties of plants you're buying, to make sure you're getting what you want. Different varieties from the same family can have very different characteristics.

You can emphasize particular colors, or shapes, or differing varieties of one family.

COORDINATING COLORS. Colors are the palette of gardeners. Planning how the colors of individual flowers work together will help you create a more appealing picture.

DON'T OVERWHELM. Unless it's part of a specific color scheme, put some distance between a vivid bright flower and a more muted, subtle one, so the more subtle one is not overwhelmed.

CHEERFUL OR SOOTHING. Bright reds, yellows, and white flowers will cheer up your yard. However, too much can become busy and distracting. Blues and purples and greens have a calm appeal.

QUICK COMBINATIONS. An easy way to diversify is to create a grouping of two or three varieties, and then repeat that pattern in a row.

ONE-COLORED GARDENS. Try a garden comprised of different flowers and shadings based on one basic color. For example, red-hued Dahlias, dianthus, bee balm, peonies, astilbes, zinnias, and phlox can create a vivid corner of the yard. Blue-based ageratums, pansies, larkspur, delphinium, violets, and lobelia can create a dramatic but cool and soothing scene.

TWO-TONED GARDEN. Or create a two-toned garden of complementary colors, such as bright red flowers mixed with yellow marigolds, goldenrod, black-eyed Susans.

TALL TO SHORT. For obvious reasons, you should group plants by height so they are all visible. Taller plants like delphinium, phlox, and hollyhocks should be in the rear, medium-height plants like bachelor's buttons, astilbe, lady's mantle, and cosmos in the center, and short plants like pansies, alysium, sedum, and lobelia in the front. It may not be easy to judge the first few times around, but you'll get a feel for it after you worked with the fully-grown plants.

HORIZONTAL HEIGHT. Also pay attention to the height on the horizontal plane across the garden. Rather than a completely irregular mix of heights from side to side, try for a definite effect, such as a taller grouping in the center or tall plants on the ends flanking shorter plants toward the center.

FERTILIZE FOR FLOWERING. When fertilizing your flowers, make sure to select a brand whose ingredients encourage blossoms. Some fertilizers promote growth, but create large leafy plants with few flowers.

SHADY COLORS. Brighten up the shady areas of your yard with beds of flowers that are happier there, such as primrose, larkspur, and impatiens. You can also include versatile flowers that tolerate partial shade, such as pansies.

THIN AND MOVE PERENNIALS. In the spring or autumn, divide perennials that spread rapidly (such as bee balm, bachelor buttons, and lamb's ears) to keep them from taking over your garden. The clumps that you remove can often be placed elsewhere on your property or given away.

STORING DAHLIAS. Dahlias can be grown from seed or bought as container annuals. However, if you have dahlias whose colors appeal to you, you can dig up the bulbs at the end of the season, wrap them and store in a cool, dark place indoors. Then replant them next year.

NICOTIANA. Many people plant nicotiana for its fragrance, but the aroma has been bred out of some modern varieties, so it's important to make sure you're buying one that will emit the desired scent.

PRESERVING FLOWERS. You can preserve a portion of your garden in the form of dried flowers. These can either be made into wreaths or placed in vases or other simple arrangements.

AIR DRYING. Clip the flowers with stems, tie a string around the stems, and hang upside down in a dark, dry area. They can be hung from nails, or from a rope stretched across the room.

SILICA GEL. Flowers can also be dried by placing them in silica gel or sand. They are usually heated in the powder and then set aside to allow the powder to absorb their moisture.

EVERLASTINGS. Grow flowers that are especially conducive to drying and preservation. They are known as "everlastings" and are generally papery and dry. Statice and celisia (cockscomb) are among the everlastings.

Vegetable gardens

PLACEMENT, PLACEMENT, PLACEMENT. Where you place your garden and how you lay out the different plants within it will have a lot to do with how successful your harvest is. The garden itself should be located where the light, soil, and drainage are most suited for vegetables. And the layout of crops within it can be important. Consider the size of plants and their individual needs for light as well as their demands on the soil.

BALANCING THE NEEDS. It's best to know what factors are most important for individual plants too, because you may have to make tradeoffs. For example, although the light in certain sections of the garden will be best for specific crops, you also want to rotate crops (change their position) over the years to preserve the soil quality.

SEPARATE GARDENS. Consider more than one food garden: a larger plot for the bigger plants and a smaller one close to the house for herbs and the more compact vegetables. Or a shadier garden and a sunnier one, to meet the differing needs of various vegetables.

COMBINATION GARDEN. Your vegetable garden doesn't have to be an elite spot open only to those particular edibles. You can combine vegetables with flowers for example. Not only will this add visual appeal, but nectar-rich flowers in your vegetable garden can attract beneficial insects. Also consider including berries and herbs. (Be careful about berries: Make sure they don't attract unwanted animals or diseases.)

DRAINAGE. It's important to have good drainage in a vegetable garden. A high, slightly sloped site is a good choice. Don't site the garden in low spots where water and frost will collect. If you don't have naturally good drainage, installing drain pipes below the garden can help carry away excess water.

SITE FOR SUNLIGHT. Most vegetables are sun worshippers, so find a spot

167

that gets as much sun as possible during the day. Avoid placing the garden too close to trees to prevent excess shade and damage and soil depletion caused by the trees' roots.

ROOT BARRIER. If you have to put a garden near a tree's root system, you can minimize the intrusion by digging a trench a few feet deep at the edge of the garden, and inserting a thin barrier of sheet metal or other material. Don't disrupt the tree's roots too much while doing this.

PLACE PLANTS FOR LIGHT. For your planting plan within the garden itself, consider the movement and direction of sunlight and place crops where the conditions will be best for them. If you don't have a totally sunny area for your garden, place the plants that need the most sun in places that get the most rays during the day and the shadier plants in the areas that are in shadows.

SHADY CROPS. Lettuce, spinach, and pumpkins are among the plants that are best for shadier areas.

SUNNY CROPS. Tomatoes, corn, peppers, and melons are among the crops that do best with full sunlight.

HEIGHT. Plant taller crops like corn where they will not block the sun from the lower ones as they shoot up. Usually toward the north is best. If there are areas where a tall crop will throw shade, put the plants most shade suited on the other side.

SCHEDULE PLANTING. Know the schedule of the crops you are planting. Some vegetables can stand up to Jack Frost or prefer cool weather, while others are easy victims of frost, and need warmer weather. Vegetables also take differing lengths of time to mature and bear crops.

COLD-TOLERANT PLANTS. Plants that can withstand some cold and the risk of frost after planting include broccoli, peas, spinach, turnips, and onions. Somewhat less rugged, but still cold-tolerant, plants include beets, radishes, and carrots.

VEGGIES TO WAIT WITH. Wait until the frost danger is over before planting beans, squash, tomatoes, sweet corn, and melons.

CROP ROTATION. Instead of growing the same crops in the same spot year after year, shift them around. Different vegetables make different demands on the soil, so rotation keeps a particular nutrient from being depleted too much, and gives the soil a chance to replenish itself. It also helps minimize disease and daunts insects.

LEAF AND ROOTS. Alternate leafy plants that have lots of top growth, like tomatoes, with root crops like carrots.

PLANT COVER CROPS. Plant cover crops, such as winter rye, alfalfa, legumes, or clover, on unused sections of the garden to enhance the soil's ability to release nitrogen and other nutrients to plants. You can plant them before or after a crop has run its course. Let the cover crop grow a while, then cut it, chop it up, and till it back into the ground (before it develops seeds). If you have the space, it's a good idea to set aside a portion of the garden each year for a cover crop, to give the soil a recess. Then, next year, use that section, and set aside another for a cover crop.

DOUBLE-DUTY CROPS. Many crops, especially beans and other legumes, can serve double duty after they are harvested. The remains can be plowed back into the soil as a cover crop.

ONE AFTER ANOTHER. If you live in a region with a long-enough growing season, crops can be planted successively, with early-varieties species followed by ones that grow late in the season. When doing this, choose crops from different families to follow in each planting, rather than similar ones.

PLANT GRADUALLY. Instead of planting a crop all at once, spread it out by planting some of the plants successively over a few weeks' period. This will help to spread out the harvest more gradually at the other end, supplying food over a longer period.

PHASING IN. You can plant a later crop while the earlier one is still working, by interspersing them in the garden. The early crop can be cut back or removed after it has been harvested to make room for the newer generation. Or you can start the later plantings as seedlings, and place them periodically in the garden when it becomes appropriate.

THINNING. As plants get bigger they are likely to begin crowding each other, so it's a good idea to thin them out periodically to allow the remaining ones to grow healthier.

THINNING APPROACHES. Different people take differing approaches to this. If you can pluck them out as they come up with no pangs of conscience—and don't mind the time it takes—that's fine. Or you can wait until they begin to bear small vegetables before you remove them, and consider it an early crop. You can take your chances, and put in fewer plants or seeds further apart in the beginning, and trust that they will survive.

PICK EARLY. Trust your taste buds when you decide to begin harvesting. When in doubt, begin to pick crops when they're young rather than wait.

VORACIOUS VEGGIES. Corn, tomatoes, and melons are among the vegetables that consume more nutrients from the soil, so take extra care to fertilize them.

NOURISHING WATER. Pour the water you use to rinse or boil vegetables back into the garden afterwards to return to the soil some of the nourishment the plant used. However, don't do this if you used soap or salt in the water.

TOO MUCH? One way to keep from wasting prolific zucchini and other crops is to grind them up and store them in the freezer. You can then add them to breads, cakes, and other foods gradually.

PERENNIAL VEGGIES. While you'll be starting fresh with most plants in the vegetable garden, mark the site of your perennial veggies like asparagus and rhubarb to avoid accidentally taking them out during preparation for next season. Also mark the sites of perennial herbs, fruit bushes, or flowers.

PART-TIME FARMER? If you are really bitten by the crop-growing bug, you may be able to make a little extra money by selling crops at a local farmer's markets or special events. These are often open to those who grow food as an avocation. Even if you don't make a lot of money, it can be fun and sociable.

The lawn

READ SEED LABELS. Read the legally required label listing specific contents for the true story. The promotional packaging on grass seed often gives a good basic idea of the type of lawn it will create, such as a rugged turf or a lush lawn, or if it's a shade or sun-loving lawn. But also read the specific ingredients for the type and diversity of grasses, the ratio of annual to perennial grasses, and the percentage of weed seeds listed.

AVOID ANNUAL GRASS. Unless you have to spruce up your lawn quickly for an impending visit from your in-laws, avoid predominantly annual grass-seed mixes. They grow quickly, while the perennials are still procrastinating. But they die out at the end of the season, so you'll have to reseed next year. Most mixes contain both, to provide a quick cover while more permanent grasses are establishing themselves. However, the annuals should be a small percentage of the total.

DON'T BE BAMBOOZLED. Annual seeds are less expensive. Reputable seed manufacturers make it clear when a mix is primarily annual, often calling it a "quick-grow" brand. But not all seed companies are that scrupulous. Some don't mention in their promotional packaging that a bargain brand is almost totally annual, and the only way to know is reading the content label.

VARY THE VARIETIES. A good general rule of thumb is to buy brands with a diverse mix of varieties. Different grasses have differing characteristics. For most general-purpose lawns, a varied mix allows the grasses most suited to specific sites to take over naturally. It will also make the lawn better able to withstand diseases or pests that may strike one variety of grass.

BUY A REGIONAL MIX. Make sure the seed you buy was mixed for your region, to get the grasses that do best in your soil and climate. Many national brands distribute seed regionally. You can also look for a house brand at your local garden center, which may have been created with your specific locale in mind.

BE IN CLOVER. Add clover to a lawn. Some people mix it in with grass seed, others establish separate sections exclusively for clover. It adds appealing diversity to your lawn, and color in the dry mid-summer.

MOVABLE TURF. If you're digging a garden bed in a healthy section of lawn, carefully cut the top layer of turf and remove it in blocks. You can then insert these in sections of your property where the lawn needs help. Also, consider moving sections of turf from lush, but seldom-seen sections of your property to more visible sections that need help.

ENCIRCLE TREES. Growing grass under trees is often a losing proposition: their leaves can block necessary sunlight and rain; it's difficult to get the mower flush against the tree, which creates a shaggy circle of taller grass; and you can damage the tree itself by nicking the bark with the mower.

Instead encircle the tree with a ring of myrtle, pachysandra, hosta, or other shade-loving ground cover. For sunnier spots, try day lilies or a small flower bed.

You can use the same approach for large rocks, walls, and other obstacles to your mower.

CUT TALL. Your grass will be healthier if you set the mower to medium height (at least 2 to 3 inches) and cut more regularly, rather than giving it an infrequent crewcut. The taller blades create a better environment at the base of the grass, and help minimize the possibility of disease and damage. It also helps keep it from drying out.

MOWING THE OLD-FASHIONED WAY. Consider buying one of the old-fashioned non-motorized push mowers. You'll reduce the aggravation of engine repairs, get a healthier workout (though a well-operating hand-powered mower is not that much harder to push) and you'll be doing your part to reduce pollution. And you'll save money too. New ones are less expensive, and you may find used ones at tag sales or second-hand shops.

WEEDS OR WILDFLOWERS? Many weeds are misunderstood wildflowers. While one person may be struggling to rid himself of a so-called weed, his neighbor may be at the garden store paying a hefty price for the same plants. Others are true terrors that will choke out everything in their path. Often the difference is simply a matter of location and the tastes of the property owner.

It's wise to know which uninvited plants you can happily co-exist with (and even encourage) and which you should get rid of. Also be aware of what you're buying: some innocent groundcovers or ornamental plants can get out of hand quickly.

FREE GROUNDCOVER. Among the weeds in your lawn are many great groundcovers. Ajuga can cover many sins. Wild thyme makes a comfortable carpet and has an appealing aroma when you walk on it. Ground ivy is another prolific covering.

WILDFLOWER MEADOWS. Wildflower meadows are an increasingly popular way to save mowing time and transform bland lawns into colorful natural gardens. To do it properly, it's advisable to dig the area up, plant appropriate grasses and wildflower seed mixes, and monitor closely.

SPOT SEEDING. If you're not up to that effort, you can create a similar effect by adding wildflower seeds—or transplanting them—to smaller sections of the lawn and allowing them to spread naturally.

INSTANT MEADOWS. There's an even easier method that may create an attractive instant meadow of flowing colors. Just wait a while before cutting the grass in the early season. Instead, allow the early blooming inhabitants of your lawn (violets, dandelions, ajuga, forget-me-nots, etc.) to flower before you break out the mower. If you want to keep them from spreading, cut the lawn before the flowers become seeds.

INSTANT ISLANDS. If you'd rather not have a shaggy lawn for that long, you can also create informal island gardens by mowing around clusters of wildflowers. When you see patches of forget-me-nots, ajuga, phlox, hyacinths, and other wildflowers, mow in a circle or other shape around them and see what happens. You can go back and mow over them later in the season.

MOVE WEEDS INTO GARDEN. Whether they are wildflowers or escapees from someone's garden, many weeds can be moved from the lawn for display in your garden. Yarrow, forget-me-nots, wild daisies, Queen Anne's lace, black-eyed Susans, and many other flowers found in lawns and fields make a great addition to the more formal part of the garden.

PEST CONTROL

Controlling weeds, insects, diseases, and animal pests is one of the most complex and controversial aspects of gardening. Our efforts to cultivate and reshape the landscape are both a part of nature and an aberration. Mother Nature doesn't instruct other creatures to stay away from the plants we are growing for our own use and enjoyment; in the larger scheme of things, they're just another food source.

It's hard to be philosophical when rabbits have consumed your lovingly tended vegetables. But accepting that what we call invasions by pests as part of the workings of the environment can at least give us a more realistic perspective.

It's a good idea to consult with experts and read up yourself before engaging in combat with the natural order. It's not always easy to differentiate between a beneficial member of a species and its more destructive relatives. Earthworms are a boon to the garden, but other members of the worm family are among its worst enemies. And a species that is your friend in one situation can turn on you and chomp away destructively at other crops.

Pest control is a combination of common sense, superstition, and science. For example, lore has it that marigolds planted near vegetables will ward off destructive insects. Perhaps it does, but it's often difficult to prove such theories. Who knows if it seemed to work only because a potential pest wasn't around to begin with?

Fortunately, science and folk wisdom are moving closer together, in the modern guise of integrated pest management, which studies natural controls in detail.

And ways to avoid the most hazardous impacts of chemicals are becoming better known, as are ways to use chemicals more carefully and wisely.

But again, you can often trust your instincts too. After all, even if a marigold in the vegetable garden doesn't ward off disease or harmful insects, it's still attractive.

BY THE ROOTS. Whether you're weeding out a true terror or simply keeping a more benevolent wildflower under control, be sure to pull the plant out by the roots, especially if it's a perennial. You may do more harm than good to simply cut them at the surface, because they may become even more prolific in revenge.

LOOK FOR THE SOURCE. With a long-established vine, it may be too late to get its roots out, because they are so deep and intractable. However, try to trace it back to the source stems, clip it from there, and periodically go back and remove the new shoots it will be sending out.

INVASIVE VINES. Wild grapes, bittersweet, and Virginia creeper are vines that can easily become rampant and will eventually smother whatever is in their path. Kudzu is a well known problem in the south.

WEED WHEN IT'S WET. Weed after a rain, when the ground is wet, because the plants will come out more easily.

WEEDING AIDS. If you don't have a weeding tool, try a fork, spoon, or pliers to help dig out and pluck weeds.

BOIL WEEDS AWAY. Pouring boiling water on a weed may scald it to death, especially if it's an annual. If you don't want to grow anything else there, use saltwater, because salt is fatal to many plants.

SPOT HERBICIDES. Commercial spot herbicides, which direct a narrow spray, allow you to take aim directly at individual weeds and prevent them from coming back. However, be careful where you use them: They can also eliminate nearby vegetation that you want to encourage.

BISHOP'S WEED. Bishop's weed is sometimes planted as a groundcover. But don't do it. And if you see it, get rid of it. Once it becomes established, there's no stopping it.

PURPLE LOOSESTRIFE. One of the most attractive menaces is purple loosestrife. Its purple flowers are lovely to behold. But it multiplies like crazy, and is threatening wetlands, prairies, and other habitats across the country.

CUTTING OUT BLIGHT. If you see a blighted branch on a tree, shrub, or other plant, removing it by pruning or sawing may help keep the blight from spreading. When you do that, keep the cutting tool disinfected with bleach to reduce the chances of transporting the problem blight to other plants.

ISOLATE DISEASED BRANCHES. Be sure to isolate, and eventually destroy, any branches and leaves you remove. Put them in a plastic trash bag. If regulations permit, burn them. If you can't do that at the time, either store them in the sealed bag until the next burning season or contact local authorities and ask where they can be disposed of legally.

CLEAN BUGS TO DEATH. Soap is toxic to many insects. Mix liquid detergent (one that's as pure as possible) with water in a weak solution and spray on plants for problems with mealy bugs, scale insects, and other pests. Commercial insecticide soaps are also available. Be careful because soap may damage the plant too. Try it out on a limited basis to see what happens before using it more widely.

STEWED SLUGS. A drink of beer placed in a container just above the ground can be fatally intoxicating to slugs. Or pour salt directly on them, but not while they're on plants or growing soil. You can also use copper edging around the garden to stop slugs.

RUB THEM OUT WITH ALCOHOL. A weak solution of rubbing alcohol and water can kill many pests on leaves. You can swab it on or make a spray. Use very carefully and test it because it can damage plants as well as pests. Best for tough, hardy leaves.

PICK AND FLICK. To control Japanese beetles non-toxically, mix dishwashing detergent and water in the bottom of a tall jar or can. Then wander out into the garden periodically, pick the beetles off, and drop them in. This method works with many other insects that are large enough to see and handle. Use thin kitchen gloves if you're not thrilled with the idea of handling the insects.

SHAKE THEM. You may be able to accomplish the same effect en masse. Place a bucket of soapy water beneath a stem or branch populated with beetles and other bugs. Shake the branch vigorously so they drop into the solution.

LET PLANTS BREATHE. You can reduce the chances of funguses and diseases on trees and plants by giving them air circulation. Leave room between plants and trim or prune them to open them up to light and air.

DON'T SMOKE. Curtail your nicotine habit when you're in the garden and near plants. Cigarette smoke can spread tobacco mosaic, a plant disease. Tomatoes are among the plants especially vulnerable. To be safe, smokers should wash their hands before handling plants, too.

CALL THE BEEKEEPER. One day in the spring you may wander outside and see a clustered swarm of bees so thick they cover entire branches in a scary-looking mass. They'll usually disperse after a few days. However, if the thought of living with that many bees makes your skin crawl, call a local beekeeper, who may be eager to take them off your hands. He might offer money, or at least a good supply of honey later on.

FIGHT BUGS WITH BUGS. Insects are not always malicious. Many species, including ladybugs, parasitic breeds of wasps, spiders, and certain flies, among others will help you ward off their damage-causing cousins. If you don't have a natural supply of these helpful insects, they can be purchased. Since it can be an exact art, a garden expert can advise you on the best beneficial predators to encourage.

BALANCE NEATNESS AND NATURE. To discourage disease and pesky insects, clean up rotting fruit or vegetables on the ground in the garden. At the same time, don't make your garden too neat, because that will keep away beneficial bugs. Allow some areas with flowers and hiding places they can use as a habitat around or in the garden.

COMPANIONSHIP. Planting certain plants together can reduce the population of pesky insects by providing homes for other insects that destroy them.

HELPFUL COMPANIONS. Goldenrod, catnip, yarrow, Queen Anne's lace, and sweet clover are among the plants that often encourage benevolent insects such as honeybees, parasite wasps, and ladybugs.

NECTAR WITH VEGGIES. Include nectar-producing flowers in the vegetable garden to entice beneficial insects.

ASTILBE. The beautiful flowers of the astilbe often act as a bug catcher.

FENCE ANIMALS OUT. Erecting a fence is the most common solution to discourage animal invaders from a vegetable garden. Make it deep enough to discourage burrowing animals too.

DISCOURAGING DEER. Wire spread flat on the ground for several feet out from the fence can discourage deer.

INDIVIDUAL FENCES. To protect especially vulnerable plants from animals, cover them with a small individual protective cover. Build a wooden frame. (If you plan to keep it on, make it slightly larger than you expect the plant to grow.) Attach wire mesh to the tops and sides, but leave the bottom open. Then securely place it over the plants.

BERRY BASKETS. For protection of small plants from weak creatures, place an upside-down berry basket (the kind with a pattern of open holes) over the plant.

DIVERT THEM. Put excess crops, or kitchen scraps on the ground a short distance away from the garden. Sometimes animals are satisfied by this easy-to-get food supply, and won't bother with less accessible bounty within the garden itself.

HUMAN SCENTS. Another potential weapon is human body odor. Place sweaty old clothes around or in the garden. If nature calls, you might also use ground near the garden to relieve yourself; some say human urine scares off animals.

DRIED BLOOD. It has a ghoulish name, and the scent may deter you from the garden too, but powdered dried blood repels many animals and enriches the soil. Use sparingly, and keep it off the top growth of plants. Dried blood can be purchased at stores.

FROST PROTECTION. Frost descends like a shroud, killing many annual flowers and vegetables. But it is not automatically a death sentence. If you know a frost is coming, a covering over the plants can provide protection. If they are movable, put them in the garage or under a porch roof.

Birds and other wildlife

C lean floors, safe electric wires, and reliable plumbing are, of course, all important. But the birds and bees are the spice of life.

Whether it is birds, butterflies, frogs, or rabbits, wildlife can add an intriguing element to your household. Attracting and observing wildlife can be fun for you or your children. Wildlife mitigates the dreariness of winter and helps you build a bridge to nature without even leaving home.

An estimated 65 million Americans watch or feed birds, according to the U.S. Wildlife Service, making it the second most popular household hobby after gardening.

You don't need a full-blown garden to offer a wildlife habitat. A bird feeder, box, and water bowl will attract its share of wildlife to enjoy. Even the most crowded of cities boast a wide variety of birds, many of which may perch on your window, given the right incentive.

Depending on your priorities, wildlife might prove to be more infuriating than exhilarating. If your preference is to see wildlife in the zoo, then you may want to skip this chapter.

GENERAL TIPS

THE BASIC GOAL. The best way to attract wildlife to your household is to offer an environment that includes food, water, cover, and areas in which to raise young. A wide variety of plants, foods, and habitats will attract the greatest number of birds and other animals.

FOOD. The ideal wildlife plan includes as much food supplies as possible through vegetation. Vegetation not only offers food in the form of acorns, berries, buds, nectar, nuts, and seeds, but also a natural cover area for wildlife to live and breed. With nature providing this foundation, you

178

can add seeds and other items to supplement a wildlife diet.

WATER. Water is essential for all wildlife. A birdbath, pool, dripping hose, or recirculating waterfall will give birds and animals a reliable source of water for drinking and bathing. The water source should be dependable all year long. In freezing temperatures, make sure there is open water. In the summer heat, be sure to replace the water regularly.

COVER. Whether it is protection from the weather or from predators, birds and animals need cover. This is especially true for animals that are reproducing and raising their young. Piles of brush, evergreens, stone walls, hollow logs, rock piles, tall grass, and trees (alive and dead) all provide habitat for a variety of wildlife. So do bird houses, poles, and manmade ponds. The more kinds of cover, the better to attract wildlife.

WILDLIFE ADVICE. Local nurseries are often stocked with wildlife accessories and staffed by at least one person with a passion for wildlife. They are usually a good source for information. The National Wildlife Federation Backyard Wildlife Habitat Program (1412 16th Street N.W., Washington D.C. 20036-2266) is also a tremendous resource. If you make a plan of your garden and send it to the federation, they will review it and make recommendations for a nominal fee.

BIRDS

BIRD DIETS. Different birds like different foods. Short of collecting bugs and flies, you can feed insect-eating birds such as swallows and woodpeckers suet (which can be bought packed as cakes or at the local supermarket) from a hanging metal feeder or packed into a metal can wedged between tree or bush branches. Above-the-ground seed eaters such as chickadees, titmice, nuthatches, and finches like sunflower seeds in hanging and standing feeders. Ground-feeding birds such as sparrows, blackbirds, bluejays, doves, starlings, and even pheasants enjoy cracked corn.

Other specific items that birds like follow:

- Blue jays: whole peanuts.

- Titmice and small woodpeckers: peanut kernels.

- Finches, goldfinches, pine siskins, and white-throated sparrow: niger thistle.

- Cardinals, doves, and white-throated sparrow: safflower seed.

- Orioles: sliced oranges.

HUMMINGBIRD GOODIES. Hummingbirds are among the most fascinating—not to mention tricky—birds to watch. Commercial feeders filled with sugar water (one part sugar to four parts water, changed weekly) will attract hummingbirds as will several types of flowering shrubs (flowering quince, weigela, lilacs, and azaleas) and vines (trumpet vines, honeysuckle, and morning glories). The following perennials and annuals will also lure hummingbirds:

Aquilegia	Larkspur
Bee balm	Lily
Cardinal flower	Lupine
Coral bells	Nasturtium
Delphinium	Nicotiana
Fuchsia	Penstemon
Globe thistle	Petunia
Hollyhocks	Phlox
Hosta	Salvia
Impatiens	Verbena
Iris	Virginia blue bells

PINE CONE TREAT. Cover a pine cone with bacon grease, honey, or peanut butter and roll it in birdseed or bread crumbs. Then tie the cone to a tree or place it in a bush.

CATS AND BIRDS. Cats may like birds, but birds definitely do not like cats. The best way to protect birds in winter and summer is to keep cats indoors, especially in the daytime during June when baby birds are leaving their nests. You may also be able to distract cats from the bird feeder by setting repeated ambushes, squirting the cat with water from a water gun or sprayer whenever it approaches the feeder.

SEED RECYCLING. Dried watermelon, pumpkin, squash, and cantaloupe seeds can be fed to birds. If you have a pet bird, leftover seeds can be placed in your bird feeder as well.

FATTY FEASTS. Excess fat can double as homemade suet. You can add bread crumbs or seed to the fat and let it harden in a cup or milk carton. The concoction can either be placed in a metal container, mesh bag, or in some cases, simply hung by a hook and put outside.

NESTING MATERIAL. Lint from your dryer, bits of string, extra yarn and hair from your brush all make excellent building material for bird nests. Clump it together very lightly and hang it from a tree branch.

BIRD-FEEDING LOCATIONS. The best location for a feeder is a sheltered southeastern exposure. Birds like to feed in the morning sun and out of the wind. Try to locate the feeder about 10 feet from a bush or bushes which offer welcome cover to feeding birds.

SQUIRREL FEEDERS. One way to prevent squirrels and other unwanted critters from getting to your bird feeder is to hang the feeder from a branch or pole with a wire coat hanger or heavy fishing line. For bird feeders in trees, you can circle the tree trunk with a wide metal band that the squirrel cannot climb over.

For bird feeders on posts, skirt the lower part of the feeder with a barrier such as Plexiglas that fences off the entrance into the feeder. Or cut a hole in an old plastic wastebasket or bucket and slide it upside down on the pole to the base of the feeder. Or smear petroleum jelly or grease on the pole. An active dog will also keep squirrels from your garden.

DIVERSIONARY FEEDERS. If none of the above tactics suits your fancy or doesn't work, you may want to throw in the towel and set up a diversionary feeder to keep the squirrels away from the bird feeders. Diversionary feeders can be bought commercially or you can buy field corn cobs and either hang them from trees or place them in special settings for your squirrels. Make sure to place the diversionary feeder a good distance from the bird feeder.

HAND TO MOUTH. Some birds will eat from your hand. Chickadees, titmice, and nuthatches can be trained to do so. Chickadees are the most fearless. It may take weeks of patience, but it can be done. Try standing motionless near the bird feeder during meal time and gradually inch closer over at each session. Eventually, you may be able place your hand filled with seed in an empty bird feeder until the chickadee eats from your hand. Once you've done this, the bird will be likely to return to your hand for more feedings.

WINTER BIRDBATHS. Several gadgets for heating water in birdbaths have recently hit the marketplace. Alternative ways to make sure the water stays open in freezing temperatures include placing a heating coil in the water or pouring hot water in the bath each morning and dumping the ice. If you make a daily practice of this, birds may line up and wait for you to prepare their baths each morning.

USING YOUR MARBLES. Drop some colorful marbles into your birdbath to attract birds.

BIRDCALLS. You can attract birds to your yard with squeaking noises by kissing the back of your hand or your spouse's hand. Another, less romantic tactic is to play tapes of bird calls.

BUTTERFLIES

BUTTERFLY FLOWER MAGNETS. Butterflies like sweet-scented, colorful flowers. The mere presence of nectar flowers in a garden will lure butterflies. Flowering vines such as trumpets and honeysuckle attract butterflies as do the herbs borage, catnip and hyssop. The following perennials and annuals will also lure butterflies into your garden:

Aster	Honesty
Alyssum sweet	Lantana
Bee balm	Loosestrife
Butterfly weed	Sage
Cimcafuga	Saponaria
Coneflower purple	Scabiosa
Coreopsis	Sedum
Dame's rocket	Thymus
Day lilies	Valarian
Gloriosa daisies	Veronica
Heliotrope	Violets

BUTTERFLY BUSHES. The following small shrubs will attract butterflies: buddleia, caryopteris, buddleia alternifolia, beauty bush, spice bush, lilacs, hydrangea, and summersweet.

CATERPILLAR FOOD. Before there are beautiful butterflies, there are less beautiful—and more voracious—caterpillars. Caterpillars are particularly fond of parsley, pearly everlasting and violet herbs, as well as birch, ash, and linden (tiger swallowtail butterflies); locust (silver spotted skippers); hackberry and linden (questions marks); currant and gooseberry (gray comma); and blueberry and dogwood (spring azure).

PESTICIDES WARNING. Butterflies like to eat a lot and they have a high metabolism, so pesticides rapidly build up in butterflies. It is not a good idea to use pesticides if you would like to attract and sustain butterflies.

BUTTERFLY BATHS. Butterflies need water. Birdbaths, dripping water, and saucers with water will do the trick.

WILDLIFE HABITATS

HOLLY DAYS THE YEAR ROUND. The American holly tree bears fruit throughout the winter, offering food for more than 40 different types of birds.

FLYING FOR COVER. Birds like bushes and trees as protective cover from hawks and other predators. If you have a birdfeeder, try to place it near a corridor of bushes or trees. The feeder should be about 10 feet away from the vegetation, close enough to hide from birds of prey but not close enough for a cat to pounce.

GIVE ME SHELTER. Rabbits, chipmunks and other animals that are active during the day will visit gardens if walls and dense shrubs are provided.

FROG HOMES. An overturned clay pot is an ideal home for a frog or toad. In addition to being fun to have around a garden, they will eat all types of insects including slugs that plague garden plants.

SWALLOW HOUSES. Swallows love to eat insects. If you have surface water nearby, it may be worth your while to erect a swallow bird house on your property. You will both get to enjoy the acrobatics of these fascinating birds and banish many insects from your property.

BIRD BOOT CAMP. Take an old boot outside and hang it upside down. Don't be surprised if a chickadee, swallow, or wren builds a nest in the toe area.

HOLIDAY HOME. Build a winter shelter for birds by piling the neighborhood's Christmas trees. The evergreen brush pile will provide excellent cover. If your tree is decorated with strings of cranberry or popcorn, birds will be especially appreciative.

WILDLIFE APPLIANCES

HOMEMADE FUNNELS. If you do not have a funnel to put bird seed in a feeder, cut off the top of a plastic jug or old milk carton for the task. Or pour the bird seed into an empty salt carton.

DISHPAN AND FRISBEE PONDS. Extra dishpans can double as excellent birdbaths placed either in or on the ground. Decorate the surrounding area with foliage and rocks. Frisbees can be converted into excellent hanging ponds by punching holes in three spots along the Frisbee's edge and stringing hanging wire through the holes to hang the saucer from a tree.

Hot tips

O n a cold winter day there is nothing quite as alluring as the prospect of a hot, sunny day on the beach. But as wonderful as the sun and the heat are when they arrive, they are also dangerous.

Heat exhaustion, skin cancer, sensitivity to the sun are all dangers that the sun poses. As those who live in the desert and very hot climates know, the sun is something you treat with respect. Too much exposure to the sun will accelerate the aging of your skin, giving it wrinkles and a leathery texture; it can cause skin cancer and may lead to cataracts in your eyes.

FIGHTING SUN RAYS

SUNSCREEN PROTECTION. Sunscreen offers very good protection against the sun's ultraviolet rays. Experts recommend using a sunscreen with a sun protection factor (SPF) of 15 or higher. The SPF is measured by determining how much longer you can remain in the sun before burning as opposed to not wearing any sunscreen. Dermatologists recommend using about an ounce of sunscreen and spreading it thoroughly.

COVERING UP. Cover exposed areas on your body from the sun by wearing loose-fitting clothes and a wide-brimmed hat to protect your head and face. Straw hats are the best to wear as they allow for ventilation.

LIP PROTECTION. Use a lip sunblock with an SPF of 15 or higher on and around your lips for sunbathing. Do not sunbathe if you have a cold sore.

STAY OUT OF THE SUN. For the best protection from the sun's rays, stay inside or in the shade as much as possible during midday. In desert climates, most of the work gets done in the early morning and late afternoon. During the heat of the day, desert dwellers prefer to rest in the shade or take a nap.

PROTECTING CHILDREN. Experts estimate that 80 percent of the average person's exposure to the sun occurs before turning 21. Doctors also say that research shows that one or more severe, blistering sunburns in childhood or adolescence may double the risk of melanoma—a particularly dangerous type of skin cancer—later in life.

CHILDREN'S SUNSCREEN APPLICATION. Apply sunscreen on children before they go outside. You should reapply it every 1 to 1 1/2 hours and after swimming. Because children swim so often, doctors recommend using a sunscreen lotion with waterproof qualities.

PRESCRIPTION DRUGS. The side effects of some drugs make a person more sensitive to the sun. Medications with side effects induced by the sun have a warning attached stating "You should avoid prolonged or excessive exposure to direct and/or artificial sunlight while taking this medication." Several relatively common pharmaceutical items such as dandruff shampoo, antihistamines, oral contraceptives containing estrogen, and water pills may cause photosensitivity. Some of the more common prescription drugs that this applies to include: Doxycycline (Vibramycin), Adapin, Sineguan, Doxepin, Elavil (Amitriptyline), Septrads (Sulfamethoxazde/TMP, Co-trimoxazole), Norpramin (Desipramine), Tetracycline, Dyazide, Maxzide, Pamelor (Nortriptyline), Pediazole, Tofranil (Imipramine). If you take any of these products, you should be especially careful about exposing yourself to the sun.

TANNING, NOT PROTECTION. Commercial products such as tanning pills or bronzers do not offer any protection for the skin. The federal Food and Drug Administration cautions that although these products may alter the color of your skin, the coloration may be inconsistent and (in the case of tanning pills) may turn your skin anything from pink to orange, depending on your skin type. Never use baby oil as a suntan lotion. It doesn't work.

INCOMPLETE PROTECTION. Beach umbrellas and materials that you can see through do not fully protect you against the sun's rays, so be careful.

SUNBURNS. If you do get a bad sunburn, apply any number of tropical analgesics with ingredients such as benzocaine, lidocaine, camphor, phenol, and menthol available commercially to soothe the pain. Use moisturizers like cocoa butter and petrolatum to relieve dryness when the skin starts to peel. If the burn is severe, see a doctor for medical treatment.

SUNBURN RELIEF. To reduce the inflammation and pain of a sunburn, take two tablets of aspirin every four hours. Do not apply heavy cream or oil that might trap the heat in your skin.

BURNED EYES. Place cold-water compresses over your eyelids for about 20 minutes if your eyelids are swollen or burned from the sun. You can also apply cold, wet teabags instead.

THE RIGHT SHADES. To qualify as a proper sunglass, according to federal voluntary standards, a pair of sunglasses must block out 99 percent of the ultraviolet B rays. This type of rating is good for moderate sunlight found in low altitudes and urban areas in temperate to northern latitudes. For intensely bright sunlight, you want sunglasses that block 99 percent of both ultraviolet A and B rays. These sunglasses block 60 to 90 percent of visible light. For prolonged daily use of sunglasses in very bright light such as beaches, deserts, and fields of snow, use side shields or goggles to prevent reflected light from affecting your eyes.

SUNGLASS LIMITATIONS. Never use sunglasses at night, in tunnels, or in dim environments. The only medical claims permitted on sunglasses are that they may prevent cataracts and photokeratitis, so don't trust the label if it claims more than that. All sunglasses must pass FDA's safety rules for breakage.

SUN RATING. The federal government has recently started giving a solar risk index (ranging from 0 to 15) measuring the relative potency of the sun's rays. The index is determined through a complicated formula measuring the ozone layer, pollution, and other factors. Any rating above 10 is very dangerous. Pay attention to the rating in the local weather report and act accordingly.

HEAT RELIEF

SPRINKLED CHILLS. There is no reason to just let children enjoy the cooling benefits of a run through the sprinkler on a hot day. Put on a bathing suit and let the wet spray cool you off. If there is no sprinkler available, take a cool glass of water and pour it over your head.

TAKE IT EASY. In very hot and humid weather, give yourself a break and take it easy. Overexerting yourself will only lead to heat exhaustion or heatstroke. This is especially true if you are not used to hot weather.

LIGHT CLOTHING. You may have noticed from the movies that Arabs do not travel through the desert shirtless and in shorts. They wear light robes to preserve body fluids. We are not suggesting that you wear a robe to the beach, but if you are working in the sun, wear a light, short-sleeve shirt. Wear lightly colored or white clothing in hot weather. The color will reflect the sun's rays. If your shirt gets very wet from perspiration, change shirts. The dried salt from your sweat may impede the ability of your skin to breath.

DRINK. It is important to drink often in hot weather. Heat exhaustion is caused by water depletion. You want to make sure to drink plenty of water, juices, Gatorade, and other non-alcoholic refreshments. Listen to your body. If you feel thirsty, take it as an indication that you are starting to dehydrate. Do not take salt tablets. Dehydration doesn't necessarily occur in a day. You may slowly lose your body fluids over the course of several days, so be sure to constantly drink fluids.

EATING SMART. Eat plenty of fruits and vegetables in hot weather. The water in them will help stave off dehydration.

PAY ATTENTION TO THE WEATHERMAN. Although the weatherman's reputation for poor forecasts is sometimes well earned, forecasters are usually pretty accurate in predicting hot summer weather. It is not as tricky as trying to determine whether a winter storm will result in frozen rain or a foot of snow. Pay attention to hot weather forecasts and plan your activities accordingly.

HEAT EXHAUSTION. Symptoms of heat exhaustion include dizziness, nausea, heavy perspiration, rapid breathing and pulse, faintness, dizziness, and cold clammy skin. If you have these symptoms or see someone with them, immediately sit or lie down in a cool spot. Loosen the clothes, fan the skin, and drink up to a quart of cold water.

USE TECHNOLOGY. If you start to feel the symptoms of heat exhaustion, use modern technology to fight it by going into an air conditioned room.

HEATSTROKE. If the symptoms of heat exhaustion are extreme or persist for 30 minutes or more despite the above measures, you may be suffering from heatstroke. Some of the symptoms are dilated pupils, unconsciousness, irregular breathing and pulse rates, convulsions, and hot and flushed skin. It is important to cool off as quickly as possible. Apply ice bags or towels soaked in cold water behind the neck, under the armpits, behind the knees, in the groin, and on the wrists and ankles. If you can, get in a cool or cold pool or bathtub of water. Call for emergency assistance. If you have put a person in a pool or bath, stay there to make sure he or she does not slip and drown.

Automobiles

While it may be true that you can live in your car but you can't drive your house, it is not something that we recommend. Nevertheless, for most people with a house, the automobile is their second largest household expense and it should be properly maintained for safety, comfort, and financial reasons.

The extent to which you devote yourself to your car depends on whether you view your car as a showpiece vehicle or as needed simply for personal transportation.

GENERAL TIPS

EMERGENCY KIT. Your car should include an emergency kit that contains a blanket, heavy chain, electrical tape, flares, first aid kit, fan belts, flashlight, fire extinguisher, ground cover, jack, money, rags and towels, sandpaper, solar blanket, snow shovel, traction mats, a white flag, and work gloves.

GOOD HABITS. Regular maintenance will sustain the life of your car for many years. Get in the habit of regularly changing the oil, checking the tires, and bringing the car to the mechanic for routine maintenance. This will save time, money, and aggravation.

BUYING A CAR

New cars

NEGOTIATE ON PRICE. Dealers may be willing to bargain on their profit margin, which is usually between 10 and 20 percent. This is typically the difference between the manufacturer's suggested retail price and the invoice price, which is what the manufacturer charges the dealer for the car.

ORDER A CAR OFF THE LOT. Consider ordering your new car if you do not see the car you want on the dealer's lot. This may involve a delay, but cars on lots often have options that you may not be interested in but will cost you money nonetheless.

RESEARCH. Check publications at a library or bookstore that discuss the cars you are interested in to get information on the dealer's costs. Shop around for different prices and lease arrangements. When considering the price and lease arrangement, keep in mind the total costs of the lease before making a decision.

CREDIT INSURANCE NOT REQUIRED. Some dealers and lenders may ask you to buy credit insurance, which pays off your loan if you die or become disabled. Before taking on this cost, consider the benefits from insurance policies you have. Buying credit insurance is not required for a loan.

Used cars

On average, new cars cost almost twice as much to operate than a used car on a per mile basis. But used cars are a more risky venture. Refer to Consumer Reports for information on the track record of cars you may be interested in and look them up in the NADA Used Car Guide for pricing information.

RAINY DAYS BAD. Try not to buy a used car on a rainy day. Rain tends to cover up the dullness and blemishes in a car.

RUST IS BAD. Check the underside, doors, and wheel wells for rust. When you look at the underside, also look for fluid leaks, new welding, or a broken frame. These are all bad telltale signs.

CHECK ODOMETER WITH STICKER. Check the odometer to see if its number corresponds with the figure on the service sticker on the door post.

UNDER THE HOOD. Check under the hood for: cracks and oil leaks in the engine block; repaired wiring that might indicate past electrical problems; problems with the belts, hoses, and cables. Rusty or strawberry colored radiator coolant indicates corrosion.

SHOCK CHECK. Press down hard on the car's fender and then let go. If it bounces excessively, the shocks may need to be replaced.

TEST DRIVE. When test driving make sure you go on a bumpy road, highway, parking lot, and city street. Check the brakes by applying the brakes hard; accelerate quickly to check the gears; make some sharp turns to test steering; check for shimmying, and excessive bumping on bumpy roads; and remove your hands from the steering wheel at about 20 miles per hour and brake slowly to test the front-end alignment. When the drive is over let the car idle for a few minutes and check the engine for leaks while the engine runs. Once you turn off the engine, check under the car for leaks.

BUYER'S GUIDE. The Federal Trade Commission's Used Car Rule requires used car dealers to display a Buyer's Guide that tells: whether a warranty is offered and specifically what the warranty is; that you should ask to have the car inspected by an independent mechanic before buying the vehicle; that you should get all promises in writing; and the major problems that may occur in any car. Pay attention to the guide and heed its content.

PROFESSIONAL CHECKUP. Before making an offer for a car, have an independent mechanic you trust or who has been referred to you check the car. The mechanic should test the car to make sure it meets your state's auto-emission standards, check for major repairs that may be needed and offer an estimate on the cost of those repairs, and perform a compression test and a cylinder power-balance test.

INSURANCE COST CUTTERS

COMPARISON SHOP. Prices for the same types of coverage can vary by the hundreds of dollars. It pays to shop around. Call your state insurance department and check your yellow pages for insurance company options. You can check with insurance companies and agents on prices and different types of service to get an idea of price ranges. When you have narrowed the field to three insurers, get price quotes.

HIGHER DEDUCTIONS. Deductibles represent the amount of money you pay before you make a claim. By requesting higher deductibles on collision and comprehensive (fire and theft) coverage, you can lower your costs substantially.

DROP COLLISION/COMPREHENSIVE FOR OLDER CARS. It may not be cost effective to have collision or comprehensive coverage on cars worth less than $1,000 because any claim you make would not substantially exceed annual cost and deductible amounts. Auto dealers and banks can tell you the worth of cars.

ELIMINATE DUPLICATE MEDICAL COVERAGE. If you have adequate health insurance, you may be paying for duplicate medical coverage in your auto policy. Eliminating this cost could lower the cost of your personal injury protection by up to 40 percent in some states.

BUY A LOW-PROFILE CAR. Before you buy a new or used car, check into insurance costs. Cars that are expensive to repair or are favorite targets for thieves have much higher insurance costs. Write to the Insurance Institute for Highway Safety, 1005 North Glebe Road, Arlington, VA 22201 and ask for the Highway Loss Data Chart.

TAKE ADVANTAGE OF LOW-MILEAGE DISCOUNTS. Some insurance companies offer discounts to motorists who drive fewer than a predetermined number of miles a year.

SEAT BELT AND AIR BAG DISCOUNTS. If you have automatic seat belts and/or air bags, you may be able to get discounts on some coverage.

INQUIRE ABOUT OTHER DISCOUNTS. Some insurers offer discounts for more than one car, no accidents in three years, drivers over 50 years old, driver training courses, anti-theft devices, anti-lock brakes, and good grades. Check with your insurance company.

FUEL SAVING

BUY THE RIGHT CAR. In deciding to buy a car, think about fuel efficiency. Air conditioning, automatic transmission, and power steering require gasoline for their energy. Power brakes, electric windows and seats, and radio antennas add to the vehicle weight, reducing fuel economy.

CARPOOLS. Carpools save time and money. Check with your employer, local government, or regional transportation agency to see if there are organized carpools that coincide with your needs. Watch for signs along the highway with a central carpooling number. If every commuter car carried one more passenger, the U.S. Department of Energy estimates that close to 1.5 billion gallons of gasoline would be saved a year.

CARPOOL RULES. Early decisions on carpool rules will save problems in the future. Smoking? Radio? Chronic lateness? Back-seat driving? Rules should be set on all of these issues by the carpool members before they become troublesome issues.

OBEY THE SPEED LIMIT. The U.S. Department of Energy estimates that as much as 1.5 billions of gasoline would be conserved a year if all motorists obeyed the speed limit. The ideal speed for fuel conservation is 55 miles per hour. Driving at 65 miles per hour uses 17 percent more fuel than driving at 55 mph.

COASTING CONSERVATION. If your car is truly on empty and you need to make those last few miles to the gas station and you have an automatic transmission, slowly accelerate to 30 miles per hour and place the car in neutral until it slows to 10 miles per hour. Then do it over again until you reach your destination. With a manual car, let the car coast down hills and don't let the vehicle slow down enough to require shifting into a lower gear.

GOOD TIRES. Radial tires, particularly steel-belted ones, improve gas mileage. Underinflated tires can lower your fuel efficiency 5 percent, so keep your tires well inflated. (See Tires section.)

RECYCLE MOTOR OIL. You can recycle motor oil by having a gas station that recycles the oil change your oil. If you do change your motor oil yourself, you can either bring the used oil to an establishment that recycles motor oil or you can get an oil recycling kit from an automotive store.

TUNE UP YOUR CAR. Have your car tuned as needed. Regular tune-ups prolong the life of your engine and improve fuel performance, paying for themselves in gasoline savings. A poorly tuned car uses up to 9 percent more gasoline than a well-tuned one.

LIGHTER MEANS BETTER. Remove unnecessary weight from the car. The lighter the car, the less fuel it uses. For every extra 100 pounds of weight, the typical car loses 1 percent of its fuel economy.

USE THE RIGHT GAS AND OIL. Use the gasoline octane and oil grade recommended in the car manual. Fuel with more octane than required for your car is inefficient and an unnecessary expense.

CAR WASHING

CAR WASH. Instead of using soap and water, wash your car with a gallon of water and a cup of kerosene. When you are done, wipe the car down with soft cloths. This will help prevent rust and make cleaning easier in the future. You also will not need to wax the car. Be careful: kerosene is flammable and poisonous.

BAKING SODA CLEANER. Use baking soda on a wet sponge or rag to wipe away grime from chrome, enamel, headlights, and windshields. Applying baking soda to the windshield wiper will also enhance its wiping ability.

VINEGAR CLEANSING. To wash the grime from your car windows, pour white vinegar on a wet rag and wipe. It pays to keep a bottle of white vinegar stored in the car for emergencies.

HOMEMADE WINDSHIELD WASHER. Instead of using the commercial products, make your own windshield washer by combining 1 quart rubbing alcohol, 1 cup of water, and 2 tablespoons of liquid detergent. This solution will not freeze unless temperatures drop below minus 35 degrees Fahrenheit.

ERASE THE FOG. Use blackboard erasers to remove fog from the windshield. To prevent fogging, rub the inside of the windshield with a cut onion.

BUMPER STICKER REMOVAL. Use vinegar, lighter fluid, or nail polish remover to soften bumper stickers and then scrape them away with a knife or razor blade. To remove rust stains on bumpers dip aluminum foil in cola and rub the spot.

CHROME CLEANING. Rub automobile chrome with dampened aluminum foil.

INTERIOR TIPS. Use a cloth dampened with floor-wax cleaner to wipe vinyl seats and dashboards. Or you can use a damp cloth dipped in baking soda, then wash with a mild solution of dishwashing liquid and water. Rinse thoroughly.

INSTANT INTERIOR CLEANING. For easy interior cleaning on the road, keep a detergent bottle filled with a little bit of detergent and a lot of water in your glove compartment.

SALT DEPOSIT PROTECTION. Wash your car regularly to prevent salt accumulation. Flush out the bottom by spraying between the bumper and the reinforcing bar.

ODOR BUSTERS. Clean all the upholstery and carpeting with a mixture of water and vinegar to remove car odors. Sponge the solution into the carpeting and use an old rag to blot it. For cigarette odors, you can leave a shallow pan of ammonia in the car overnight or all day, and then take the car for a spin with the windows wide open and the pan removed. Another anti-cigarette tactic is to place several containers of ground coffee in the car and let the wind blow through the car for several hours.

RUST PREVENTION I. At the end of the winter, rinse all of the salt from the bottom of your car by placing a sprinkler or lawn-soaker hose under the car and letting the water run for 20 to 30 minutes.

RUST PREVENTION II. Make sure all the drain holes under the car and at the bottom of the car doors are unplugged. These holes allow humidity and water to escape.

RUST PREVENTION III. Fix chips and scratches right away. Left alone, they will frequently grow into rust spots. Clean the area thoroughly and then apply either nail polish or a paint primer recommended for your car's model. After letting it dry, cover it with paint that matches your car's color. It does not have to be exactly the same color.

ONION NET BAGS. Use plastic onion net bags to clean the car windshield and headlights. Sprinkle baking soda on it to enhance its impact. Finish off the job by rubbing the windshield or headlight with newspaper or a soft cloth.

DESALTING CARPETS. Remove salt from carpets by letting the area dry and going over them with a stiff wire brush.

DEBUGGING. Spray the front of your car with cooking oil during the summer months before long trips. This will keep bugs from sticking to the grill. Any that do stick to the grill will wash off easily.

SHADY WASHES. To prevent streaking, wash your car in the shade on hot and sunny days.

PRICE SHEET REMOVAL. By applying hot vinegar, lemon extract, or salad oil to the sales price sheet and scraping it repeatedly, you can remove it.

CAR CARE

BATTERY CORROSION PROTECTION. Use baking soda and water to scrub the car battery terminals and holder. When you are done, cover the terminals with petroleum jelly. Another trick is to grease one side of a penny and place it in the middle of the battery, greased side down. The corrosion will tend to gather at the penny and not at the battery posts.

SCRATCH HIDER. To mask a light scratch on your car, find a crayon with a matching color and use it to cover the scratch.

RUST REMOVAL. You can remove rust spots with soapy steel wool, crumpled foil, or hot water.

STICKY DOORS. You can sometimes avoid costly problems of realigning your car door by spraying a penetrating solvent into the door's hinges. It is available at auto supply stores and will eliminate door squeaks.

DENT CORRECTOR. Light dents in cars can be repaired by popping them out with a wet bathroom plunger. This could save you the trouble—not to mention the money—of going to an auto body shop.

WINDSHIELD WIPER CORRECTION. If your windshield wiper is smearing your window, clean the windshield and wiper blade with rubbing alcohol. If this does not work, scrub the windshield with a low-abrasion scouring powder to remove buildup. Or replace the wiper's blades.

EASY LISTENING. To make the radio antenna slide more easily, either apply wax or rub it occasionally with wax paper.

INTERIOR HAZE. Sponge the inside of windows with vinegar to remove haze. Rinse the window with water and wipe it dry.

CARDBOARD SHADES. Cardboard shades in the windshield and side windows will both help keep the temperature down in a parked car in the summer and will prevent interior fabrics from fading. Temperatures in cars will soar when they are parked in the sun. Properly shaded, the car can be kept 30 degrees cooler.

TIRES

FROZEN AND RUSTED LUG NUTS. Use hot pepper sauce, lemon juice, penetrating oil, or vinegar to loosen frozen or rusted lug nuts. The next time you change the tires, apply an anti-freeze compound.

BETTER LEVERAGE. Cross-shaft lug wrenches give more leverage than the standard single-shaft wrenches. To get more power from the wrench, attach a piece of pipe over one of the wrench's arms. You usually get better leverage by pushing down on the wrench rather than pulling up. Use your foot if you can.

WHITEWALL TIRE BATH. Use undiluted liquid laundry detergent on wet tires with a rub brush to make your whitewall tires sparkle. Rinse thoroughly. Do not use laundry detergent to wash the main body of the car because it can damage the body.

COIN CHECK. To check out how much tread is left in your tire, stick a penny or dime into the tread head first. If you can see all of Lincoln's or FDR's head, it is time for a new tire.

USE THE CORRECT AIR PRESSURE. The proper air pressure can be found in your owner's manual or in a placard in the glove box or on the door-jamb of your car. The single greatest cause of tire damage is improper inflation. More than half the cars on the road in the United States are believed to have underinflated tires.

WINTER CONDITIONS

WINTER BLANKETS. Veteran winter car owners swear that placing a blanket over the engine of the car helps keep the engine warm by protecting it from howling winds. This makes it easier to start the car after frigid nights. Some people say that placing a lighted bulb in the car engine also helps keep the engine warm through the night.

WINTER EMERGENCIES. If you are stranded in your car in a winter storm, get whatever you need from the trunk—including an umbrella or jack handle to poke through the snow in the event that drifting snow covers your car—and then stick to the car. Signal your distress with a flare, reflective triangle or a brightly colored cloth attached to the car antenna. Keep warm by running the heater once an hour, or, in extreme cold, once every 30 minutes. If there are other stranded cars nearby, try to bundle in the same car; this will help keep the car warm. Never drink alcohol if you are stranded; it causes drowsiness and limits your ability to think clearly.

Warning: To avoid carbon monoxide poisoning, make sure the area around the exhaust pipe and outside heater vents is not obstructed by snow or anything else.

DEFREEZING FROZEN LOCKS. Heat your key with a match or cigarette lighter and turn the key gently in the lock. Do not force the key or you may break it—and then you will really be in trouble. You can also blow hot air from a hair dryer on the lock. If you spray some WD-40 in the car lock it is less likely to freeze.

PREVENTING FROZEN LOCKS. Place masking tape over the car's locks when you know a big snowstorm is coming. Also, use masking tape on the locks when you wash the car in the winter.

ELIMINATE ICE SCRAPING. If you know an ice storm or snowfall is on the way, cover your front window with the rubber mat from your car or a heavy plastic garbage bag. When it is time to drive, simply wipe away the snow and lift up the bag or rubber mat.

EMERGENCY KITTY LITTER. In case you get stuck in the snow or ice, put a bag of kitty litter in your trunk. Kitty litter provides excellent traction for cars and pedestrians. Or carry a pail or carton filled with sand.

FROZEN PREVENTION. To prevent the trunk and doors from freezing, wipe vegetable oil around their gaskets.

STRATEGIC PARKING. If you do not have a garage in which to park your car in the winter, park your car overnight in a position so that the sun will shine on the car hood in the morning. If you are parking the car for the whole day, position it for the afternoon sun. Warmth from the sun will make a difference when it comes time to start the car on a cold day.

TRACTION ENHANCEMENT. For extra traction in the snow and ice, place four 50-pound bags of sand or gravel in your car's trunk. The extra weight will improve the tires' grip on the road. And if you get stuck, you can use the sand to help get out of a jam. Or carry a shingle, plank of wood, or other material that you can place under the car's tires for better traction.

HOMEMADE SNOW SWEEPER. Cut the handle down from an old broom and use it as a snow sweeper for your car.

FROST PREVENTER. To avoid frost from building up on the inside of the windows, crack one window slightly open.

SALT SOLUTION. Table salt will melt the ice on your windshield. You can keep a carton in your glove compartment.

Home safety

A man's home may be his castle, but it can be a dangerous castle. And an increasingly hazardous one at that. It used to be that people knew they had to watch out for fire hazards and were careful about climbing ladders.

But every year as environmental awareness increases new discoveries are made about the invisible man-made and natural hazards that lurk in many homes. Radon. Asbestos. Lead paint. Formaldehyde. These are just some of the concerns that have risen to the forefront of home safety in recent years. Professional consulting or contractors are often required to reduce or eliminate many of these substances.

Fire remains the most serious household safety hazard. Each year, fire departments respond to about 500,000 residential fires resulting in the deaths of more than 4,000 people and $4 billion worth of damage.

It is virtually impossible to make a house completely safe. But relatively simple precautions can lower or even eliminate the level of risk within your own home. A homeowner must be especially aware of home safety if there are children in the house. Many of the tips offered in this chapter are directly pertinent to children, but refer to the chapter on childproofing your house for children for further information.

GENERAL SAFETY TIPS

SAFE WINDOWS. Install safety catches, bars, or stops for all upper-story windows.

GUN SAFETY. Do not keep a loaded gun in the house. If you have a gun, take gun safety and training courses. Keep guns and ammunition locked separately.

SAFE FLOORS. Use special non-skid polish for smooth hardwood and tiled floor surfaces. Replace cracked linoleum and vinyl flooring.

TAPED CORDS. Loose electrical and extension cords along the floor may trip people as they walk through the house. Keep them taped along the edges of the floor whenever possible.

DAMAGED PLUGS AND CORDS. Replace frayed cords and damaged plugs.

DOUBLE STAIR SUPPORT. Install a second handrail on the opposite side of the banister for climbing stairs, especially if there is an elderly person in the house.

THE RIGHT BOTTLES. Never put poisonous substances in bottles that were used for other substances. Someone may inadvertently drink the liquid thinking it is something else. Make sure all medicines and poisonous substances are tightly covered and clearly marked.

BATHROOM ELECTRIC CONCERNS. Keep all electric appliances, plugs, and outlets a safe distance from the bathtub to prevent anyone inadvertently touching them while in the bath.

BATH/SHOWER SAFETY. Use non-skid mats for the bath tub and shower. Shower doors should not be made of breakable glass. Install a grab bar in the bath to assist in getting out of the tub.

ELECTRIC BLANKETS. If you use an electric blanket, never turn it on if it is wet.

FIRE WARNING AND ESCAPE

Smoke detectors

SMOKE DETECTORS A MUST. Purchase a smoke detector if you do not have one. Smoke detectors provide an early warning that may mean the difference between survival and death in a fire. Smoke detectors are one of those things that are inexpensive and can save your life; they are required in many localities. Check local codes and regulations before you buy your smoke detectors. Some codes require specific types of detectors.

DETECTOR PLACEMENT. There should be at least one detector on every floor in a house and in every apartment. Detectors should be placed near bedrooms. Make sure detectors are placed either on the ceiling or 6 to 12 inches below the ceiling on the wall. Locate smoke detectors away from air vents or registers; high air flow or "dead" spots should be avoided. Read the instructions for ideal placement of specific detectors.

PROPER MAINTENANCE. Test the detector monthly and clean the detector regularly. Dust, grease, or other materials may cause the detector to malfunction. Vacuum the grill work of the detector. Follow the manufacturer's instructions for proper maintenance. The most expensive and sensitive detector in the world will not do any good if it does not work.

NEVER DISCONNECT. Avoid the temptation to disconnect the smoke detector if it has a tendency to go off while cooking. Instead, relocate the detector.

BATTERY REPLACEMENT. Replace the battery annually, or when a chirping sound is heard.

LOUD AND CLEAR. Make sure the detector has a distinct warning signal that can be heard whether you and the rest of the family are asleep or awake.

FIRE EXTINGUISHERS. Keep several fire extinguishers in the house to douse small fires before they get out of control. There should be at least one fire extinguisher on every floor. Make sure the extinguishers are properly maintained. For the kitchen, keep a container of baking soda in an accessible location to extinguish grease fires.

Escape plan

PLAN AHEAD. Establish in advance an escape plan and an alternate escape plan from the house for the entire family. Prepare a diagram of the house with all the rooms, doors, windows and porches that can serve as fire exits. The plan should include at least two exits from each part of the house and a place for the family to meet outside the house to make sure everyone escaped safely. Keep the diagram out as a reminder for everyone about the danger of fire and the different escape routes from the house.

REHEARSE ESCAPES. Hold periodic fire drills to rehearse the escape plan.

CHILD ESCAPEES. Make sure that children are part of the escape plan discussion and rehearsal. It is especially important that children understand that they must escape a fire and not hide from it under a bed, in a closet, or anywhere else in the house.

EMERGENCY NUMBERS. The fire department number—as well as other emergency numbers—should be posted on every telephone in the house.

EASY ESCAPES. Never block a potential escape route with heavy furniture.

BLOCKED ESCAPE. If you are trapped in a room, open a window slightly to let smoke escape, stay low to the ground and stuff wet towels or sheets around the door to block smoke from getting into the room.

MATERIALS THAT BURN

Upholstered furniture

THE DANGER OF SMOKING. About one half of all fires associated with upholstered furniture are caused by smoking materials. Always be extra careful with cigarettes and other smoking materials on furniture. Check the furniture where smokers have been sitting for improperly discarded smoking materials. Ashes and lighted cigarettes can fall unnoticed behind or between cushions or under furniture.

ERRANT ASHTRAYS. Do not place or leave ashtrays on the arms of chairs where they can be knocked off.

SAFE FURNITURE. Look for furniture designed to reduce the likelihood of furniture fire from cigarettes. Much of the furniture manufactured now has significantly greater resistance to ignition by cigarettes than upholstered furniture manufactured 15 years ago. This is particularly true of furniture manufactured to comply with the requirements of the Upholstered Furniture Action Council (UFAC) Voluntary Action Program. A gold colored tag on the furniture marks the item as meeting the program's requirements. The front of the tag states "Important Consumer Safety Information from UFAC."

SAFE FABRICS. Look for fabrics made predominantly from thermoplastic fibers (nylon, polyester, olefin) because they resist ignition from burning cigarettes better than cellulosic fabrics (rayon or cotton). In general, the higher the thermoplastic content, the greater the fire resistance.

Mattresses and bedding

NEVER SMOKE IN BED. The overwhelming majority of bed fires are caused by cigarettes, causing up to 700 deaths in the United States in a single year. Do not smoke in bed.

SAFE DISTANCE. Locate heaters and other fire sources at least 3 feet from the bed to prevent the bed from catching on fire.

NEW MATTRESS. If you have a mattress made before 1973, consider replacing it. Mattresses manufactured since 1973 are required to resist cigarette ignition.

Clothes

THE STATISTICS. About three-fourths of all clothing fires happen to people over 65, with the majority of those accidents being associated with nightwear such as pajamas and nightgowns. The most commonly worn garments associated with clothing ignition injuries are pajamas, nightgowns, robes, shirts/blouses, pants, and dresses.

FLAMMABLE CLOTHING. Some fibers burn faster than others. It is tougher to burn polyester, nylon, wool, and silk than cotton, cotton/polyester blends and rayon clothing, which ignite easily and burn rapidly.

FABRIC CONSTRUCTION. Fabric construction affects how easily clothes burn. Tight weaves or knits and fabrics without a fuzzy or napped surface are less likely to ignite and burn rapidly than open knits or weaves, or fabrics with brushed or piled surfaces.

EASY REMOVAL. Clothes that are easily removed can help prevent serious burns. Purchase garments that do not require being pulled over the head.

KEEP IT FLAME RESISTANT. If you have clothes marked "flame resistant" make sure that you follow cleaning instructions to preserve the flame-resistant properties.

Flammable liquids

TIGHT COVERS. Make sure that all flammable liquids—gasoline, acetone, benzene, lacquer thinner, alcohol, turpentine, contact cements, paint thinner, kerosene, and charcoal lighter fluid—are stored in non-glass containers that are tightly closed and properly labeled.

STORAGE LOCATION. The best place to store flammable liquids is outside. If this is not feasible, be sure that the products are stored away from heaters, furnaces, water heaters, ranges, and other gas appliances. Remember that flammable liquids produce invisible vapors that can ignite by a small spark at considerable distances from the flammable substance.

KEEP AWAY FROM CHILDREN. Make sure that the substances are stored and used well out of reach of children.

FIRE SAFETY

Cooking equipment

THE FACTS. The U.S. Product Safety Commission estimates that more than 100,000 fires are caused each year by cooking equipment and result in the deaths of close to 400 people and about 5,000 injuries. This sobering statistic is a reminder to be careful around the kitchen stove and oven, and to treat cooking equipment with respect.

PROPER PLACEMENTS. Never place or store pot holders, plastic utensils, towels, and other non-cooking equipment on or near the range because these items can be ignited.

TIGHT CLOTHING. Roll up or fasten long loose sleeves with pins or elastic bands while cooking. Do not reach across a range while cooking. Long loose sleeves are more likely to catch on fire than short sleeves, and are more apt to catch on pot handles, overturning pots and pans and causing scalds.

THINKING AHEAD. Do not place candy or cookies over ranges. This will reduce the attraction kids have for climbing on cooking equipment, and cut down on the chances of their clothing catching fire. Make sure the storage area above the stove is free of flammable and combustible items.

CONSTANT VIGILANCE. Keep constant vigilance on any cooking that requires more than the "warm" setting. It is very easy to inadvertently turn on the wrong burner or leave a burner on after removing a pot. Always make sure that part of your regular kitchen routine is to check the burners often. Never leave hot fat on the stove unattended. It can erupt into flames spontaneously.

Cigarette lighters and matches

CHILDREN AND MATCHES DON'T MIX. Of the 200 deaths associated each year with fires started by cigarette lighters, about two-thirds are the result of children playing with lighters. Keep lighters out of sight and out of reach of children. Children as young as two years old are capable of lighting cigarette lighters and matches.

CIGARETTE LIGHTERS ARE NOT TOYS. Never encourage or allow a child to play with a lighter or to think of it as a toy. Do not use it as a source of amusement for a child. Once their curiosity is aroused, children may seek out a lighter and try to light it.

EXTINGUISHED CIGARETTES. Always check to see that cigarettes are extinguished before emptying ashtrays. Stubs that are still burning will ignite the trash.

Wood stoves

PROPER INSTALLATION. Improper installation or operation of wood stoves is one of the more common sources of accidental fires. Do not use wood-burning stoves and fireplaces unless they are properly installed and meet building codes. Follow the label instructions on the stove, which recommends an inspection twice a month.

PROFESSIONAL SWEEPS. Have chimneys inspected and cleaned by a professional chimney sweep. Creosote is an unavoidable product of wood-burning stoves. Creosote builds up in chimney flues and can cause a chimney fire. Cut down on creosote buildup by avoiding smoldering fires.

FLOOR PROTECTION. Use a floor protector for wood stoves. The protector should extend 18 inches beyond the stove on all sides. This will cut down dramatically the chances of the floor being ignited.

BEWARE WALLS. Make sure you do not place the wood stove near a combustible wall. If the stove is placed near a wall, be sure to install proper protection for the wall as described in the instructions on installation.

ONLY WOOD. Wood stoves were not designed to incinerate trash; they are designed to generate heat by burning wood. Never burn trash in a stove. This could overheat the stove. Gasoline and other flammable liquids should never be used to start wood stove fires.

ASH REMOVAL. Use a metal container with a tight-fitting lid to remove ashes. Smoldering embers may be lying in the ashes, so be careful.

Kerosene heaters

NIX ON THE GASOLINE. Never use gasoline in a kerosene heater. Even a small amount of gasoline mixed with kerosene is dangerous. To avoid any confusion, always label containers to clearly describe the contents.

OUTDOOR STORAGE. Store the kerosene outside and out of reach of children. Keep the liquid in a tightly sealed, preferably blue, plastic or metal container.

HEATER PLACEMENT. Place the heater out of the path of traffic areas such as doorways and hallways. You do not want the heater to block or pose a hazard to an exit in case of fire.

1-K KEROSENE. Use 1-K kerosene. Other grades contain more sulfur and will increase sulfur dioxin emissions, posing a potential health hazard. When you buy kerosene from the gas station, be sure that the kerosene pump is used and not the gasoline pump.

FUELING SAFETY. Always refuel the heater outdoors to prevent spillage on floors and rugs which could later result in fire ignition. Never fill the heater while it is operating.

GOOD VENTILATION. Keep a door or window open for good ventilation when the heater is operating. This will prevent indoor air pollution and minimize health problems.

KEEPING ONE'S DISTANCE. Keep flammable liquids and fabrics away from an open flame.

EXTINGUISHING FIRES. Never try to move the heater or try to smother the flames with a rug or a blanket if a flare-up occurs. Activate the manual shutoff switch and call the fire department. Moving the heater may increase the height of the flames and cause leakage.

Gas-fired space heaters

PROPER PLACEMENT. Unvented gas heaters should not be used in small enclosed areas, especially bedrooms, because of the potential for carbon monoxide poisoning. Follow the manufacturer's instructions regarding where and how to use the gas space heater.

PROPER HEATER. Do not use a propane heater which has a gas cylinder stored in the body of the heater. Its use is prohibited in most states.

MATCH LIGHTING. Light matches, if needed for lighting the pilot, before turning on the gas to prevent gas buildup.

VENTILATION. Do not operate a vented style heater unvented. It could allow combustion products, including carbon monoxide, to reach dangerous levels. Use an unvented gas-fired room heater that has a label stating it has a "pilot safety system" which turns off the gas if not enough fresh air is available.

Portable electric heaters

THE 3-FEET RULE. Keep electric heaters at least 3 feet away from upholstered furniture, drapes, bedding, and other combustible materials. Also, never place a portable heater on a surface other than the floor.

BEWARE OTHER MATERIALS. When placing a heater, make sure that towels, clothes, or similar materials will not inadvertently fall on the appliance and trigger a fire. Never use heaters to dry clothes, shoes, or other materials. They are designed to heat, not dry.

EXTENSION CORDS. Avoid using extension cords unless absolutely necessary. If you must use an extension cord, make sure it is marked with a power rating at least as high as the heater itself. Keep the cord stretched out. Do not permit the cord to become buried under the carpeting or rugs. Do not place anything on the extension cord. The extension cord should be marked #12 or #14 American Wire Gauge (AWG).

HOUSEHOLD ENVIRONMENTAL HAZARDS

RIGHT TO KNOW. The federal government has established a hotline for information on hazardous materials and spills in homes and communities. That telephone number is 800-535-0202. In addition, most communities have health agents or boards of health that can provide information about household chemicals and hazardous materials.

Radon

RADON TESTS. Radon is an invisible, odorless gas that comes from the natural radioactive breakdown of uranium in soil, rock, and water. The Surgeon General has warned that radon is the second leading cause of lung cancer in the United States. The only way to determine whether radon is a problem in your house is by conducting one of two types of tests that can be bought in a local store or through the mail. Make sure the test package includes the words "Meets EPA Requirements." The EPA recommends that all houses have radon counts of no more than 4 picocuries per liter of air (pCi/L). If the test scores higher than this, take a second test for confirmation. The average outdoor radon level is 0.4 pCi/L.

RADON AND WATER. If your house tests positively for radon—the Environmental Protection Agency (EPA) estimates that one in 15 houses has radon levels greater than 4 pCi/L—and your home is served by well water, you should contact a certified lab to have the radiation level of the water tested. Or you can call your state radon office or the EPA Drinking Water Hotline (800-426-4791) for information.

RADON REDUCTION. In some cases, you can reduce the level of radon seeping into your house by sealing cracks in the floors and walls. In other cases, a simple system of pipes and fans can be used to cut down the level of radon. These systems are called sub-slab depressurization systems and are designed to remove radon gas from below the concrete floor and foundation before it enters the home. The cost of these systems usually ranges from about $500 to $2,500 depending on the circumstances at the house.

TEST FIRST. Before undertaking a major structural renovation such as converting an unfinished basement area into a living space, first test the area for radon. If the test shows a high level of radon, you can include radon-resistant renovations as part of the project.

RADON RENOVATION. Eliminating or reducing radon levels often requires technical expertise. Every state has a department that specializes in providing information and advice for radon concerns. Contact that office for information and lists of certified contractors that meet EPA and state criteria for radon reduction renovations. Always test for radon levels after the renovation to make sure the work has accomplished the task.

DON'T SMOKE. Smoking is one of the more hazardous things a person can do for their health. But it is particularly hazardous if there is radon in your house. The EPA estimates that the chances of getting lung cancer are close to 20 times greater for a smoker who lives in a house with radon than a non-smoker in the same house.

Asbestos

THE PROBLEM WITH ASBESTOS. The three things one can do with asbestos are leave it alone, contain it, or remove it professionally. Asbestos is a fibrous mineral used in home construction because of its qualities as a strong and durable fire retardant and efficient insulator. Unfortunately, it was identified as a carcinogenic long after it became a part of routine home construction. So long as asbestos is contained or covered it does not pose a health hazard. But when age, damage, cleaning, construction, or remodeling affect the asbestos, minute asbestos fibers are released into the air and can be inhaled by people and cling to clothing and flesh.

IDENTIFYING ASBESTOS. To get an accurate measure of the asbestos level in your house you should hire a qualified professional trained and experienced in working with asbestos. Generally speaking, houses built in the last 20 years do not have asbestos. Asbestos was primarily used around pipes and furnaces as insulating jackets and sheathing, in ceiling tiles, exterior roofing, shingles and siding, in some wallboards, mixed with other materials around pipes, ducts, and beams, and in door gaskets on stoves, furnaces, and ovens.

DON'T TOUCH. If asbestos material is in good condition and in an area that is not routinely used, you can leave the material in place without substantial risk.

PROFESSIONAL REMOVAL. If the asbestos needs to be cleaned or handled on a regular basis, the safest thing to do is hire a professional contractor to remove the material. This is especially true for remodeling projects.

VINYL FLOORS. Vinyl flooring products that contain asbestos can be cleaned in a conventional manner, but they can release asbestos fibers if they are vigorously sanded, ground, drilled, filed, or scraped.

Lead

LEAD ACCUMULATION. Lead can either be ingested in the air or swallowed. It can be present in the water, in paint used to decorate the interior or exterior of the house, in dust within a home, and soil around the home. Lead can cause permanent damage to the central nervous system, the brain, kidneys, and red blood cells. Even low levels of lead can increase blood pressure in adults. Exposure to lead can be particularly hazardous to pregnant women, infants, children, and fetuses because lead is more easily absorbed into growing bodies sensitive to the impacts of lead.

LEAD TESTS. Lead levels in water and paint can be determined by qualified laboratories. Contact your local or state health department for information about qualified testing laboratories.

LEAD IN WATER. You can cut down on the amount of lead in the tap water for drinking by letting the faucet run for about 15 seconds before drawing drinking water. The 1986 Safe Drinking Water Act banned any further use of materials containing lead in public water supplies and in residences connected to water supplies. Two years later, Congress banned the use of lead-based solder in plumbing applications. However, many houses built prior to 1988 contain lead-based solder in pipe connections, often leading to much higher levels of lead in the kitchen tap than those found in water at the treatment plant.

LEAD PAINT. If there is lead paint in your house and it is in good condition and there is little possibility that it will be eaten by children, you may leave the paint alone. If not, other options include covering the paint with wallpaper or some other material or completely replacing the painted surface. Pregnant women and women who plan to become pregnant should not do this work. The safest and best way to get rid of lead paint is to hire a professional lead paint remover.

OUTDOOR LEAD PAINT. If your house was built before 1950, there is a good chance that lead from the exterior surface paint has accumulated in surrounding soil. Keep the yard well vegetated to minimizes the chances of children being exposed to contaminated dust. Clean the floors, window sills, and other surfaces regularly with wet rags and mops.

Formaldehyde and other hazardous materials

THE PROBLEM WITH FORMALDEHYDE. Formaldehyde, a colorless, gaseous chemical, is a suspected carcinogen that also causes asthma attacks, skin rashes, burning sensations in the eyes, throat, and nose passages and breathing difficulties. The best way to avoid these problems is to not use materials that include formaldehyde. This, however, can be a difficult task because the chemical is often used in the adhesives that bond pressed-wood building materials and in plywood used for construction. Formaldehyde is also used as a preservative in some paints and coating products, and as an additive for clothing and draperies to enhance their permanent-press qualities.

FORMALDEHYDE REDUCTION. Consult with experienced builders to identify materials that emit high levels of formaldehyde. It may be difficult to identify the amount of formaldehyde in older buildings. This, however, is counterbalanced by the fact that formaldehyde emissions dramatically decrease after two or three years. If you are reacting to formaldehyde in your home, it may be worthwhile to replace the formaldehyde materials with new construction materials.

INCREASED CIRCULATION. Before removing formaldehyde materials, first try improving the ventilation and circulation of outside air into the home.

Pests

Ants

Ants enter houses in search of food, warmth, and shelter. When they find food, they establish a path that leads back to their nest outside. Follow the trail to the point of entry into the house and seal it off, if you can, with caulk.

Destroy and wipe up every ant you find. Locate nests and destroy them by pouring boiling water into the entrances. Then stir up the soil and repeat the process. Or, using a small hand duster, blow some boric acid powder into the entrances and into any cracks and wall openings where the ants are seen.

Some organic ant repellents may also be effective; scatter talcum powder, borax, cream of tartar, or oil of cloves at entry point. Or plant mint and tansy around the house foundations.

Aphids

Wash aphids off houseplants under a gentle flow of water. Spray a large group with a solution of mild detergent in water. Or dab the leaves with a cotton ball dipped in alcohol.

Cockroaches

Roaches lay their eggs in little brown satchel-shaped pouches that look like small seeds. Look for the egg cases in dark, damp, warm places: under sinks, behind stoves and refrigerators, inside drapery rods, and inside the folds of the drapery itself. Scrub them away or vacuum them up with the crevice nozzle of the vacuum cleaner and discard the bag!

Dust all cracks and crevices (especially under appliances, moldings and cupboards) with boric acid, diatomaceous earth, or silica aerogel dust.

The most effective commercial control has hydramethylnon as an active ingredient. Place several bait traps in the kitchen and wherever the roaches seem to be.

Fleas

Attack fleas in the house and on your pets.

Comb your pet regularly with a flea comb (finely spaced teeth) to remove adult fleas and eggs. Bathe the animal in a mixture of orange oil and shampoo. If you cannot find orange oil, buy a shampoo containing some citrus extract. Spray the animal's bedding with a non-toxic insect growth regulator, such as methoprene, which keeps flea larvae from developing into adults for up to 3 months.

Keep fleas out of the house by steam cleaning all rugs and pet bedding; wash pet bedding at a high temperature. Vacuum the furniture, rugs, and bedding and all baseboards.

Go to the vet and see if he/she stocks a product you can put on your lawn around the house. It is a type of larvae that just attack the flea larvae.

Lice

If you or the school nurse find head lice on your child's head, don't panic. Eradicate the lice with an over-the-counter shampoo that contains pyrethrin, a safe insecticide. Avoid self-medication with any product that contains lindane.

Wash, dry-clean, or spray everything in the house the child may have come in contact with: bedding, clothing, upholstery, etc. This is very important to stop the spread of the lice.

With a fine-toothed comb dipped in vinegar, check your child's hair, strand by strand, every night until you find neither lice nor their eggs, nor nits.

Make sure your child knows not to share combs, brushes, hats, or earphones.

Mice

If you have a mouse problem, move objects around to disorient the mice. They are easier to trap when they are trying to find their way around. If you use standard traps, don't fall for the cliché of baiting them with cheese. Use bits of peanut butter or cooked bacon. Mice seem to like these treats. To catch a mouse alive, when you see him running around the room try opening a black umbrella and holding it on the floor at an angle that allows the mouse to run in. Your prey, drawn to dark places, will head towards the umbrella. Then close it up, go outside, and let the fellow free.

Mosquitoes

Check each innocent indoor breeding place such as flower vases, the humidifier, and catch pan under the refrigerator. Change the water in them daily.

Moths

Substitutes for mothballs: Try cedar in your closets and chests. It is non-poisonous and comes in chips, blocks of wood, hangers, and drawer liners.

Use cheesecloth bags, clean baby socks, or nylon stockings to make moth-repellent sachets. Fill with any combination of the following: cedar chips, dried lavender, aromatic pipe tobacco, whole peppercorns, dried mint, and dried rosemary.

Rats

When you first try to catch rats, bait several traps but don't set them. Leave them out for a few days, replenishing the bait as needed. When the rats get accustomed to using them as a food source, you can set them.

Secure garbage cans so they don't leak or lose their lids when pushed over. Keep them raised about 1 to 2 feet above the ground and at least 2 feet away from any wall. (This is good for squirrel problems or raccoon problems, too.)

Plug all cracks and holes in the house (especially basement and attic) with steel wool. Then seal the holes with steel mesh or sheet metal.

Raccoons, squirrels

Place mothballs around holes and vents or in trash cans to discourage squirrels, raccoons, and other animal invaders.

Hang an electric bug zapper above the corn patch just as harvest time approaches. The sizzling and flashing will scare away raccoons for a while. But don't leave there too long; once raccoons get used to the sound, they might be attracted by the dead bugs!

Place a radio in the garden to deter animal visitors for a while.

Interplant the corn with pumpkins and squash. Raccoons don't like stepping on the prickly leaves.

Circle the garden with an 8-inch band of lime when the corn is just beginning to ripen; it can burn a raccoon's feet a little.

Use 1/2-inch chicken wire to fence raccoons out. Staple the mesh to 3-foot fence posts at ground level and let it project 12 to 15 inches above the tops of the posts. Or add a 12-to-15-inch overhang to your existing fence. When they try to scale it, they will pull the overhang down on top of themselves.

Homemade first aid

Homemade remedies for health problems great and small are part of American tradition and folklore, from Benjamin Franklin's advice to eat an apple a day to keep the doctor away to Julie Andrew's wisdom that a spoonful of sugar helps the medicine go down.

Some of the remedies actually work. Many herbal cures are just as effective as scientific medicines. Ginger root, teas, garlic, and other items you can find in your kitchen have medicinal powers. We're not recommending it, but there is even some medical basis for the use of leeches for blood problems.

Other traditional potions, however, are pure myth or even wrong. Milk, for example, does not help ulcers. Salt is not good for treating dehydration. Many of the cure-all remedies that were so popular in the 19th and early 20th centuries were heavily laced with opium and alcohol to make people think their ills were being cured, when in fact the symptoms were just being masked.

The best way to solve many common health problems is to take measures to avoid them in the first place through a healthy lifestyle that includes a balanced diet and a moderate amount of exercise.

Exercise does not have to include daily workouts on weightlifting machinery or aerobic routines. Good fitness could be as simple as taking the stairs instead of the elevator, walking or bicycling instead of driving for short trips, or taking a daily 15-minute walk. One of the more ironic aspects of late 20th century America is that people will spend hundreds of dollars a month for personal trainers, snazzy workout clothes, and exotic exercises but refuse to park more than 100 feet from a store because they do not want to walk that distance from the car.

A healthy lifestyle also means consuming only moderate amounts of alcohol and not smoking. Smoking is one of the most damaging things you can do for your health. It not only causes deadly diseases such as cancer, emphysema, and heart problems, but also contributes to a whole host of other, more minor ailments, such as ulcers, colds, fatigue, bronchitis, varicose veins, and laryngitis.

KITCHEN AND HERBAL CURES

THE REAL CHICKEN SOUP CURE. For instant relief from nagging colds, try this proven version of the chicken soup cure: Add 10 to 12 minced garlic cloves to a can of chicken broth and heat for 20 minutes. Then add juice from one lemon and cayenne pepper to taste.

HUNG OVER? A tablespoon of bicarbonate of soda in a glass of water combined with a cold shower might ease the pain from the previous night's pleasures. A glass of water just before going to sleep and right after waking up helps. Of course, the best cure for hangovers is not to drink too much the previous night.

SWEET RELIEF. Half a teaspoon of honey in the back of the throat will help ease a hacking cough.

CHERRIES FOR GOUT. Eating cherries is an old-fashioned remedy for relieving the pain that comes with gout. Many people attest to its curative powers. Herbal teas such as rose hip and peppermint are also said to be good for gout.

COOLING HEARTBURN. Two teaspoons of apple cider vinegar added to a cup of water is a traditional remedy for heartburn. A couple of capsules of ginger root is also a popular treatment of heartburn.

INSTANT HOT WATER BOTTLE. If you need a hot water bottle in a hurry, you can make a homemade one by pouring piping hot water into a soda bottle and wrapping it in a towel.

SUGAR SPRINKLES. Sprinkle some sugar on your tongue if it has been burned from hot soup, tea, or coffee.

RICE AND DIARRHEA. Rice is a great food to eat to treat diarrhea, including for children and pets. Foods that you do not want to eat when you have diarrhea include fruits, beans, pasta, and most dairy products.

COMBATING CHOLESTEROL. Some foods help keep cholesterol counts down. They include tea, fresh fruit, barley, oat bran, carrots, garlic, and all types of beans. Cut back on fats. If you smoke, stop. Exercise will help reduce cholesterol levels as will losing weight.

CANKER SORES SOURCES. Chocolate, strawberries, coffee, citrus fruits, and walnuts all cause or worsen canker sores. Yogurt helps heal and prevent them.

GINGER ROOT, BARLEY SUGAR, AND SYRUP. Three of the oldest treatments for motion sickness and nausea are nibbling on ginger root, sucking on barley sugar, and swallowing a spoonful of coke syrup. Sucking on a lemon is also good for stopping motion sickness.

OSTEOPOROSIS FOODS. Add vinegar to broth for soups to help fight osteoporosis and substitute parmesan cheese for butter.

BURNS AND SKIN PROBLEMS

UNCHAPPED HANDS. Scrub your hands in a solution of equal parts cider vinegar and pure glycerin to cure chapped hands. Also, avoid using soap and water as much as possible. Instead, use baby oil.

BICARBONATE RELIEF. For acid burns, remove the acid quickly by drenching it with water and then applying a solution of 2 teaspoons of bicarbonate of soda in a full glass of water or diluted ammonia water.

PASTE RELIEF. A solution of cornstarch, baby oil, and a little bit of water will make an effective paste that can be applied to a rash or chicken pox to relieve the itching.

THE NATURAL ANTIDOTE FOR POISON IVY. Break open a piece of jewelweed or impatiens and rub the herb's juices on to the poison ivy rash to treat it for itching. If you know you have been in contact with poison ivy or poison oak but the rash has not hit yet, scrub with ammonia or rubbing alcohol to head off the itch.

TAKING THE BITE OUT OF FROSTBITE. Keep in a cool place until affected parts have thawed to a red or normal color. You can help relieve the frostbite by wrapping it in cotton or treating as a first-degree burn. If the skin blisters, call a doctor.

ALOE HEALER. Keep an aloe plant in your kitchen to help mend minor burns and sunburns. When you burn yourself, break off a leaf and split it open and press the exposed part to the burned skin. Other treatments for minor burns include:

- Applying a thick paste of baking soda and water will ease the pain of a minor burn.
- Smearing a dab of toothpaste on the burn.
- Rubbing the cut surface of a raw potato against the burned part.

- Rubbing with vanilla extract for burns caused by splattered hot grease.

For major or first-degree burns, consult a doctor.

SUNBURN DOUSER. Drench a sponge in iced tea and apply it to a sunburn periodically to help ease the pain. Other kitchen remedies include smearing plain yogurt on the burn, rubbing a paste of cornstarch and water, or applying a slice of raw potato to the sunburned area.

BOILS. Warm compresses are the traditional way of treating boils, but other natural compresses can be used, including a slice of onion, cabbage leaves, or a hunk of tomato.

BLISTERING TIPS. The rule of thumb for treating blisters is to leave small blisters alone and to drain or cut large blisters. If you cut the blister, make sure you sterilize the pin or knife and leave the dead skin on top. If the skin falls off, cover the blister with an adhesive strip during the day and give it air at night.

CALLUS TREATMENTS. Soak a callus in warm water or light tea. Instead of using a knife to cut back a callus—which is a bad idea for you to do at home—rub the callus with a towel or brush to reduce it.

GOOD SHOES. One of the better ways to avoid blisters and calluses is to get properly fitted shoes. The length of the shoe should allow about enough space at the end of your longest toe for the width of your thumb and the width should allow enough room so that there is not pressure on the toes. When breaking in a new pair of shoes, some doctors recommend wearing a new pair of socks as well.

WAGING WAR ON WARTS. If you have a problem with warts, break open a fish oil capsule of vitamin A and smear the liquid on to the wart once a day until the wart vanishes. Or apply a couple of drops of castor oil on the wart every day and cover it with an adhesive tape.

BUMPS, BITES, AND CUTS

BAND-AIDS. Medically speaking, one may not always need to apply a Band-Aid or adhesive tape for cuts and bruises, but psychologically it is often a reassuring measure. While this is especially true for children, it also often applies to adults.

WITCH HAZEL. An alcoholic extract, this old-fashioned remedy is good for treating bee stings and other insect bites, cold sores, sunburns, and hemorrhoids.

BANDAGE REMOVAL. Fortunately there are ways to enjoy the gain of an adhesive bandage without suffering the pain of removing it. Instead of simply yanking the tape off, apply rubbing alcohol or baby oil to loosen the bandage. This will make removal less painful. If a scab is stuck to the bandage, soak it in a solution of salt water.

RAZOR CUTS. If you cut yourself shaving, apply a small piece of tissue paper or cotton to stimulate coagulation of the blood.

TRAVELING BRUISES. Black and blue marks often travel, so do not get alarmed if a mark starts by your elbow and then creeps down toward your wrist. What happens is that the blood in the bruise seeps down between the body's muscles. The same applies for black eyes sinking into the cheek area.

CHIGGER BITES. Apply a drop of kerosene or tincture of iodine to ease the pain from a chigger bite.

ICED BRUISES. Apply ice to bumps to stop them from becoming unsightly bruises. The purpose is to stop the blood flow by contracting the blood vessels. After 12 to 24 hours, you then want to apply heat to open the blood vessels for the natural absorption of the blood in the tissue.

BLOOD CLEANING. For cleaning scrapes and cuts use lukewarm or cold water. Hot water coagulates the blood, thus making it harder to remove.

UN-ITCHED BITES. Rub toothpaste into mosquito bites to cut down on the itching. Other recommendations include rubbing a paste of salt and water on the wound or applying a compress drenched in a solution of 1 teaspoon of baking soda mixed with a glass of water.

MOSQUITO BITE PREVENTION. The best way to stop itching mosquito bites is to discourage the bites in the first place. Some of the following methods have proven successful:

- Swallowing thiamine chloride pills, which are Vitamin B supplements.

- Applying bath oils such as Avon's Skin-So-Soft to your skin before going outside.

- Bathing in water with a couple of tablespoons of chlorine bleach. Be careful not to let the water get in your eyes.

ICE AND BEES. Apply ice to bee stings. Ice works as a local anesthetic that kills the pain. Smearing the sting with ammonia also helps.

BEE BANISHERS. Wear white or light clothes to discourage bees from coming your way. If bees are a persistent problem for you or you are allergic to their sting, add zinc to your diet.

MOTHERLY ADVICE

MORNING SICKNESS. Many veteran mothers recommend that nausea from morning sickness can be eased or eliminated by eating crackers in bed. Also, drink ginger ale or suck on barley sugar.

COOL TEETHING. Put your child's teething ring in the refrigerator to keep it cool. The colder the teething ring—within limits—the more effective it is.

CHILDREN'S MEDICINE. Crush the pills or open the capsules and mix in apple sauce or other food that the child likes to eat.

CHOKING OBJECTS. Swallowed peas, poker chips, or other small objects can be ejected from a child's mouth or throat by holding the youngster upside down and slapping him or her on the back to dislodge the item. If this does not work, call for emergency assistance immediately.

HELPING THE PILLS GO DOWN. Eat a banana after swallowing a pill that is having trouble going down. The fruit will help push the medication down your gullet.

DIAPER RASH. If your child has a diaper rash and you use cloth diapers, try adding vinegar to the water when it comes time to rinsing the diaper. Otherwise, give the baby's bottom plenty of exposure to fresh air.

INFANT EAR INFECTIONS. You can cut down the chances of your infant getting an ear infection by breastfeeding. Also, tobacco smoke and wood stoves increase the likelihood of ear infections, so stop using a wood stove if you can and put a stop to any smoking in the house.

FIGHTING PINK EYE. Use a warm compress applied about every 10 minutes to your eye to fight pink eye. If crusting forms, wipe it away with a piece of cotton drenched in clean water. When you are done with the washcloth or towel, wash it separately from the rest of the laundry to prevent the conjunctivitis from spreading.

COPING WITH HICCUPS. You can throw modern science out the window when it comes to hiccups. Doctors do not know why hiccups occur and have not found a cure for them. We are left to folklore and traditional wisdom to come up with cures for hiccups. We recommend either tolerating the hiccups until they go away or trying out your personal favorite cures until you come by a solution that works for you. Some of the remedies people swear by include:

- Drinking water upside down by leaning over the glass and swallowing the water from a bent-over position.
- Swallowing a spoon full of pure sugar.

- Holding your breath or breathing in deeply and then letting the air out very slowly but steadily in a very concentrated manner.

- Yanking your tongue.

- Gargling water.

- Getting spooked suddenly by someone else or being tickled by someone else, preferably a close friend or relative.

SMART TRAVELING. If you travel at night you will be less likely to get motion sickness. Fresh air is good for stopping motion sickness and the driver is usually the least likely person in a car to get car sick. Also, do not read in the car.

DODGING THE FLU. Not much here that your mother didn't tell you. Don't go out in cold or wet weather without proper clothing. Stay away from crowds if the flu seems to be going around and don't kiss people who may have the flu. For older people, in particular, it may be advisable to get a flu shot each fall before the traditional flu season begins.

TEETH AND MOUTH

CHAPPED LIPS. What you should not do for chapped lips is provide moisture by licking your lips. This makes the problem worse. Lip balm is the best way to go to cure chapped lips. If you do not have access to lip balm, lay your finger against the side of your nose to pick up some of your natural oils there and rub it into your lip. You can avoid the problem in the first place by drinking lots of liquids that provide moisture for your body.

TOOTHBRUSH REPLACEMENT. If you have persistent sore throats, try getting a new toothbrush. Toothbrushes often harbor the bacteria that cause these problems.

BRIGHT TEETH. Scrub your teeth with baking soda and hydrogen peroxide for an instant toothpaste and teeth cleaner.

TOOTHACHE RELIEF. Gargle salted water (1 teaspoon of salt for an 8-ounce glass of water) regularly to ease the pain of a toothache. Sucking on ice also helps.

COLDS AND OTHER RESPIRATORY PROBLEMS

ASTHMA PROTECTION. People with asthma should wear a scarf on very cold days.

CAFFEINE SUBSTITUTE FOR INHALER. If you are stuck without an inhaler, a couple of stiff black cups of coffee can serve as a temporary substitute. Do not make a practice of doing this, however.

CALMING HYPERVENTILATION. Breathe into a brown paper bag to calm down and restore a regular breathing pattern. This usually works best for people who have hyperventilated before and who understand the problem. Hyperventilation is often caused by tension, so try to find a way to relax or reduce the tension.

STEAM HEAT. Clear up the congestion in your nasal cavities from vicious colds, congestion in your sinus cavities, and bronchitis by applying some steam heat. Drape a towel over your head and lean over a boiling pot of water or sink with piping hot water. Keep your head face down in the steam tent for as long as you can stand it or 10 minutes. This should help drain your sinuses.

COLD RELIEF. Liquids and vitamin C may be the best natural remedies for the common cold. Garlic and licorice tea are also traditional homemade remedies. Warning: People may think they have a cold but in fact have something much worse. If your cold is accompanied by any sort of extreme pain, bloody sputum, unusually high fever, an unusual loss of appetite, shortness of breath or other unusual symptoms, consult a doctor.

DROWN A FEVER OR FLU. Almost any type of juice is an excellent combatant for high fevers. Chamomile tea with thyme is also good as is linden tea. Try sucking on an ice cube to fight the fever as well.

NO TALKING ALLOWED. The way to cure laryngitis is to rest your throat and restore its moisture. Stop talking, breathe through your nose, and hang your head over a bowl or pot of steaming water.

GARGLING SOLUTION. Gargle with salt water—about 1 teaspoon of salt with 1 pint of water—for sore throats and postnasal drip. You can also gargle chamomile tea, baking soda and water, or lemon juice with water for a sore throat.

SPICED SINUSES. Spicy food will clear up stuffed sinuses. Horseradish, garlic, and Cajun food are some of the best natural cures for a congested nose.

A GRAB BAG OF HEALTH HINTS

Muscle problems

EASING ARTHRITIS. Many doctors recommend applying a muscle ointment to muscles at night to ease arthritic stiffness in the morning and thus get the day off to a good start. Vegetable juice, which is rich in Vitamin C, is also a good way to ease the pain of arthritis. Many arthritis patients will go on sporadic vegetable juice fasts for a day or two.

CARPAL TUNNEL SYNDROME. The National Institute for Occupational Safety and Health reports that data processors, assembly line workers, cashiers, truck drivers, and other workers who must use their hands are the most susceptible victims of carpal tunnel syndrome. Ways to treat this problem include aspirin, hand exercises, raising your hands above your head, and applying ice.

BACK SWIMMING. Swimming is one of the most healthy ways to relieve back pains through exercise. Doctors also recommend a series of simple land exercises and riding stationary bikes.

BACK SLEEPING. Do not sleep on your stomach if you are suffering from back pains. Instead either sleep in the fetal position with a pillow between your knees or on your back with pillows under your head and knees.

Really annoying problems

DIMINISHED SNORES. If is very difficult to cure a heavy snorer. But two things that sometimes help are not using a pillow and sleeping on your side.

TONING DOWN MENSTRUAL CRAMPS. The best way to cut down on the problems that menstrual cramps bring is to eat a balanced diet and exercise regularly, but not too intensely. Cut down on coffee, coke, and other foods with caffeine and limit or eliminate the amount of alcohol you drink during your period.

LIQUID CURE FOR JET LAG. Drink lots of water and juice during the airplane ride to lessen the severity of jet lag.

FIGHTING FATIGUE. People are not like the Duracell bunny. We don't just keep going and going. At some point, fatigue sets in and there is really nothing you can do about it except getting a good old-fashioned rest. But there are some things that you can do to extend the amount of time it takes for fatigue to set in or avoid activities that bring on fatigue such as the following:

- Television is a drain. For some reason television is one of the more enervating recreational activities of contemporary society. Avoid watching too much television to keep your energy level high.

- Exercise. Ironically, exercise gives you more energy than it takes away. Regular and reasonable exercise routines will help sustain your energy level. This does not necessarily mean you have to have a regular exercise regimen. It can be as simple as going for a 5-minute walk during the middle of the day or using the stairs instead of an elevator.

■ Lots of liquids. Drink lots of liquids to keep feeling fit. This does not include alcohol and caffeine. Alcohol is a depressant and caffeine is an artificial stimulant. While the caffeine from a cup of coffee may give you a jolt of energy, too much of coffee will have the opposite affect.

■ Light lunches. A heavy lunch in the middle of the day will divert energy to the job of digesting food, so limit the size of your lunch.

INSOMNIA INSIGHTS. Get some sleep. Just kidding. Anyone who suffers from insomnia knows how frustrating a problem it can be. Some of the things you can do before bedtime, include taking a warm bath about four hours earlier, eating a light snack an hour or two before bedtime and doing some light exercise in the evening. Do not drink alcohol or anything with caffeine before going to bed or eat too much sugar. Instead, drink some warm milk. If you have chronic insomnia, see a doctor or sleep disorder specialist.

FIGHTING THE BLUES. Most people have their own ways of pulling themselves out of feeling down. Two of the more interesting ways that you may not have tried are exercise and drawing. There is no reason to start out too ambitiously on either of these activities. Just start slowly and let the activity take its course. Both activities help channel feelings or frustrations in a constructive manner. If you are truly depressed on a constant basis, you may be suffering from a neurochemical disorder which should be treated by a physician.

RESTLESS LEGS? If you have a sudden and fairly constant urge to move your legs in bed, you may be suffering from restless legs syndrome. Do not fight the urge. If you are driving a spouse crazy with it, try getting up and walking around.

Other problems

SWOLLEN LEGS. After sitting down or standing for many hours, your legs may get swollen. To eliminate this you should lie down and place your feet above the level of your heart. This is also a good way of preventing varicose veins.

DON'T BE DECEIVED. People often do not have allergic reactions to certain foods or other allergens with their initial exposure. It often takes time for you to develop antibodies that might cause the allergic reaction.

LESS HYPERTENSION. Lower your blood pressure by consuming less salt and alcohol but more fresh fruit and fish, which contain potassium. Also, get a pet. Studies have shown that people with pets are less likely to have high blood pressure. But the most important thing to do is to lose weight.

CONSTIPATION OBSERVATION. If you get constipated on a regular basis, it may be something you eat, such as milk. Different types of foods may cause constipation in some people but be perfectly fine for others, so you may have to be your own detective on this subject. Otherwise, gentle laxatives from the drug store may be the best solution.

IN SEARCH OF HIGHER BLOOD PRESSURE. Although high blood pressure is the more common problem, many people suffer from low blood pressure. By sleeping on a slant with your head about 1 foot higher than your feet, you can improve your well being.

EARACHE RELIEF. Many tactics can be employed to bring relief to an earache. They all involve ways of easing pressure on the ear. Techniques include:

- Sitting up. By sitting up you allow the fluids around your ear to drain.

- Swallow, chew gum, and yawn. Swallowing and chewing up brings movement to your Eustachian tubes and thus helps stimulate them to open. Yawning does the same thing.

- Warm air. Warmth helps relieve ear pains. A hair dryer blown toward your ear from a safe distance is a good source of warm air.

SLEEPING RED EYES OFF. Red eyes are often a symptom of a lack of sleep. Thus, one of the surest cures of solving the redness is to get a good night's sleep.

ALLERGIC ASSISTANCE. If you are suffering from pollen problems in your house, try running the air conditioner. It will help cleanse the room of mold and dust mites. Other preventative measures include getting rid of the carpet in favor of a hard floor with a throw rug and using a humidifier.

TENSION HEADACHES. Apply a heating pad to the neck to help the muscles relax.

DROWNING KIDNEY STONES. There is little one can do to stop the excruciating pain of passing a kidney stone, but there are ways to lower your chances of getting a kidney stone. The primary and best tactic is to drink lots and lots of liquids. If you have already had a kidney stone, it most likely consisted of calcium, so try to limit the amount of calcium you eat.

SHINGLES SOLUTION. To get some temporary relief from the almost unrelenting pain of shingles, try taking a long bath with 1/2 cup of cornstarch thrown in the water.

SORE FEET RELIEF. Two tips here. Elevate your feet to relieve the pressure of gravity on your feet or soak them in peppermint tea.

HEAT EXHAUSTION. For all of its curative and life-giving powers, the sun can also be a killer. Avoid heat exhaustion and sun stroke by staying out of the sun as much as possible by doing work in the early morning and late afternoon and wearing a hat. In addition, drink as much liquid as possible. Desert dwellers recommend that people drink a gallon of water, juice, or other healthy drink such as Gatorade on a daily basis. Salt tablets do not stave off dehydration or heat exhaustion.

YEAST DISINFECTING. For a yeast infection take a warm bath with either a 1/2 cup of salt or a 1/2 cup of vinegar added to the water.

You and the environment

We all want to be good global citizens, but how do we do it? Acting locally on improving the environment can be as simple as participating in the local recycling program or walking to the corner store instead of driving. Or it can be as complicated as founding a community group devoted to cleansing a river or making your entire house toxin-free.

Thirty years ago few people thought in terms of the environmental impact of their actions. Historically, the United States has had a slash and burn mentality toward its natural resources. For the first three centuries of the nation's life, settlers just kept heading west when they soiled their own land, rivers, and water sources.

Today life is not that simple. There are too many people and not enough land and water to perpetuate that lifestyle. Although it may seem to many as if raising environmental consciousness has been a slow process, when you look at it from the long term, the transformation in attitudes in a single generation has in some ways been rapid.

One of the reasons for this is that environmentalism makes sense. In most cases businesses and households can save money both in the long term and the short term by choosing the environmentally sensitive alternative.

This chapter offers a wide variety of environmental tips. Many of the hints suggested in other chapters overlap with the same theme. For example, the entire chapter on energy-saving tips falls under the category of environmentalism. However, we thought it would be appropriate to list in one chapter some of the more significant things you can do to be an environmentalist in your home, including innovative ways you can recycle old items for new household uses.

The following sections have information on several organic alternatives for cleaning and tips on how to read labels. Numerous books and pamphlets are available listing in great detail non-toxic alternatives to toxic substances including *Clean & Green: The Complete Guide to Nontoxic and Environmentally Safe Housekeeping* by Annie Berthold-Bond; *Non-Toxic and Natural and The Nontoxic Home,* both by Debra Lynn Dadd; and *The Guide to Hazardous Products Around the Home* by The Household Hazardous Waste Project.

THINKING ENVIRONMENTALLY

AUDIT YOURSELF. Think hard about the way you conduct yourself on a daily basis and run your household. There are almost certainly ways you can think of to cut down on energy consumption, water usage, trash disposal, and wasteful habits. By examining yourself and thinking creatively you will find many ways to adjust your behavior in an environmentally sensitive way.

ENVIRONMENTAL DIET. Highly processed foods take a considerable amount of energy and resources to produce compared to simpler foods. Think about the amount of resources that go into the manufacturing of junk food, for example, as compared to carrots grown in your backyard. Try to cut down on the amount of red meat you eat as well. The amount of grain and water needed to put one pound of steak on your dinner table is high.

COMPOSTING. Composting can be your way of using nature to recycle your yard or kitchen waste. It can be as simple as dumping the excess leaves, grass clippings, and weeds in a pile and letting the mixture rot. Composting bins can also be made for the collection of organic materials from the kitchen and the rest of the household. You will both save landfill space and create wonderful nutrients for your plants or your friends' gardens.

HAZARDOUS WASTE. Oil paints, lighter fluids, toxic detergents, pesticides, antifreeze, and other toxic materials are all considered hazardous waste, and with good reason. They are dangerous and should be disposed of properly. Many communities sponsor hazardous waste collections. Store these wastes in a safe place and in the original bottles and containers until the next collection date. If your community does not have these events, speak to someone in the local government about arranging one. Otherwise, find a commercial incinerator or a licensed contractor to handle the materials.

OFFICE APPLICATION. Don't just think about recycling in your home. Offices generate reams of waste. Apply your knowledge about recycling in your workplace as well as in your home. Set up paper recycling programs if one does not exist now. Encourage your company to use paper cups instead of Styrofoam cups. Find ways to recycle office materials such as manila envelopes internally.

PRECYCLING. You can reduce the amount of waste you generate by thinking about what you buy and how those items are packaged. Packaging is a major industry in the United States and it is a very wasteful one. There is no reason why you have to buy a small item wrapped in a large, glitzy box. Try to buy food in recyclable materials. Eggs in cardboard cartons, not Styrofoam. Sodas in glass bottles or aluminum cans. Purchase vegetables in loose form and not in plastic bags. Buy food and other goods in bulk whenever possible.

SIMPLE RECYCLING. Aluminum cans, glass bottles, newspapers, and even many forms of plastics can be recycled relatively easily. Many communities have recycling programs specifically for these materials. Participate in those programs. In the case of glass bottles and aluminum cans, you can often get money for returning the recyclables.

SOME DON'TS. Many seemingly simple things that we do in our daily lives seem harmless but can be very damaging. When people set off helium balloons for celebrations, those balloons have to land somewhere. They can be dangerous to the wildlife. Throwing things out the car window is one of the more irresponsible things a person can do. This may seem obvious, yet roadsides are littered with materials ejected from passing cars.

AVOID STYROFOAM CUPS. Styrofoam is made from a carcinogenic material called benzene and manufactured with a gas that uses CFCs. So Styrofoam is bad for the environment. There is no reason why you cannot use paper cups instead of Styrofoam. Or even better, use a mug. Some stores offer a 5-cent discount if you provide your own cup for coffee. If your local store or coffee shop does not have this policy, see if you can convince the owner to adopt it.

WATCH THOSE TOXINS. Find ways to cut down on toxic use. Air fresheners, permanent press clothes, mothballs, permanent ink pens, and many other seemingly harmless materials all have toxic compounds in them.

PAPER OR PLASTIC? How about cloth? Skip the debate over paper or plastic bags. Instead buy a few cloth bags with handles for all your grocery shopping. In most countries throughout the world this is the standard way to shop because grocery stores charge money for using their paper or plastic bags or they simply don't have bags for the customers.

RECHARGEABLE BATTERIES. Batteries are one of the more hazardous materials that can be put in a landfill because of the mercury, cadmium, and other heavy metals in them. Save money and the environment by using rechargeable batteries.

PAINTING SAFELY. Use water-based latex paints instead of oil-based paints. When cleaning brushes, do it inside to prevent spilling into the environment. If your house is served by a sewer system, it is safe to clean latex paint in a sink. If your community has a paint exchange program, join it. If not, try to help form one.

RAGS INSTEAD OF CLOTHS. The kitchen generates a disproportionate amount of waste. Look for ways to cut down on that waste. Use rags instead of paper cloths. Use reusable containers for holding food. Instead of going through dozens of coffee filters a month, get a coffee machine that does not require paper filters. If you must use coffee filters, get the unbleached filters.

CLIP THE SIX-PACK RINGS. Those plastic rings used to hold six-packs together pose a serious hazard to sea birds and other sea animals when they are dumped in the ocean. Clip all six rings with a scissors before dropping the plastic rings in the trash.

JUNK MAIL GALORE. By writing to Mail Preference Service, Direct Marketing Associates, 6 East 43rd St., New York, NY 10017, and asking to have your name removed from junk mail lists you will receive much less mail from direct marketers. In other cases, try sending notices to agencies or companies that keep sending you mail. The National Resources Defense Council estimates that 2 million tons of junk mail is delivered each year in the United States with close to half not opened.

YARD SALES. Rather than junking old furniture, toys, and books, why not hold a yard sale? This is a great way to avoid contributing to the landfill and adding to your pocketbook. Conversely, you should do some of your shopping at yard sales. You will find some very good bargains. If you want to really get into the yard sale scene, help organize a community yard sale in which many different people participate.

GLOBAL PURCHASES. Protection of the rainforests has become a major environmental priority. Several environmental groups have set up funds in which you can buy rainforest land to protect it. This is a great option both for yourself or as a gift to a child, friend, or relative. An excellent indirect way of helping to save the rainforests is to buy renewable materials that come from the rainforests. The idea is to make the rainforests pay for themselves through the development of renewable crops as an economic inducement for nations and companies to preserve the rainforests rather than cut them down for wood. Brazil nuts, straw hats made from tropical leaves, and skin and hair products made from tropical forest plants are all products that fall under this category.

COMMUNITY ACTIVISM. The best way for most people to contribute to a better environment is to find ways to improve their own neighborhoods, communities, towns, and cities. You can join an existing local environmental group or start a program yourself. The kinds of projects you can undertake are limitless, ranging from starting a local environmental newsletter to cleaning a river bank to establishing an environmental speaker's bureau or bulletin board.

THE NEXT GENERATION. With urbanization and suburbanization of America, many people have lost touch with nature and where most foods originate. It is startling how many urban children do not know where milk, eggs, and other natural foods come from. Instill a sense of nature and the environment in your children by taking them to a farm, farmer's market, or the woods. The impact can be profound in shaping their attitudes as they grow older.

THE NONTOXIC CLEANING CLOSET

Utensils

RAGS. There is little reason to stock up on paper towels or purchase commercial towels. Just take old socks and cotton shirts and use them as rags.

NATURAL SPONGES. Made from coral-like aquatic invertebrates, natural sponges are just as effective as commercially made plastic and synthetic sponges. If the sponge gets very dirty, wash it with white vinegar to restore its cleansing qualities.

TOOTHBRUSHES. Use old toothbrushes for cleaning small or difficult to reach spots.

CHEESECLOTH. Cheesecloth is an excellent all-purpose cleaning rag that can be used for polishing furniture, dusting, wiping windows, and many other purposes.

COTTON DISH TOWELS. Use cotton dish towels for drying the dishes. Just wash them when they get dirty and use them until they wear out.

LATEX GLOVES. Available in stores, natural latex work gloves are reusable and environmentally friendly.

Cleansers

BAKING SODA. It is difficult to exaggerate the handiness of baking soda. It can be used as a deodorizer, cleanser, and mild abrasive. It is a remarkable cleaning detergent that can be used for almost any scouring purpose. If you use it and it does not work, apply more.

WHITE VINEGAR. Next to baking soda, white vinegar is the second most handy non-toxic cleanser you can have in your house. Vinegar can be used for dusting, cleaning windows, cutting grease, polishing furniture, eliminating moldy growth, and many other purposes.

NATURAL SOAPS. Most health food stores carry all-natural soaps such as Dr. Bronner's that can be used for many household and personal cleaning purposes.

BEESWAX. This natural wax provides a hard surface and a pleasant aroma when used on furniture.

ALUM. A mineral that is good for cleaning porcelain stains, especially when mixed with lemon juice or vinegar.

CITRUS EXTRACTS. The peel from citrus fruits such as lemons, grapefruits, and oranges has many cleansing qualities. Adding lemon juice to other cleaners both increases the cleaning potency and adds to the air-freshening qualities. You can use lemon juice alone for washing windows. It also cuts grease and can be used for polishing furniture.

TOOTHPASTE. White toothpaste can be used as a household cleanser for porcelain pots.

HOUSE PLANTS. You can use house plants as air fresheners.

TABASCO SAUCE. Tabasco sauce can double as an all-purpose metal cleaner.

BORAX. Good for fighting mold, deodorizing, and disinfecting.

WASHING SODA. You can use washing soda for washing clothes. It is good at fighting grease and dirt.

Formulas

SPRAY CLEANING. For an all-purpose spray cleaning solution, mix 1/2 teaspoon of liquid soap with 2 tablespoons of lemon juice, 1/2 teaspoon of washing soda, and 1 teaspoon of borax. Add 2 cups of hot water and mix the solution until everything has dissolved.

ALL-PURPOSE CLEANER. For tough stains on countertops, woodwork, tiles, and other hard surfaces, try this all-purpose cleaning formula. Add 1/2 cup of ammonia and 1/2 cup of washing soda to 1/2 gallon of warm water.

BAKING POWDER SUPPLEMENTS. A 4-to-1 baking soda-borax solution is a good scouring powder for disinfecting. A 4-to-1 baking soda-washing soda creates a nontoxic scouring powder for cutting grease.

NATURAL FLOOR CLEANER. Add a cup of vinegar to a bucket of hot water for an all-purpose floor cleaner.

OIL CLEANSER. To remove oil from your hands, rub a mixture of 2 tablespoons of liquid soap with 3 tables of cornmeal and a teaspoon of glycerin.

CITRUS FRESHENING. For a natural air freshener, drop slices of a citrus fruit into a pot of hot water and let simmer with the top off.

CORNSTARCHED WINDOWS. You can clean glass with a solution of 1/2 cup of water combined with a couple of tablespoons of cornstarch.

ALL-NATURAL CLEANER FOR POTS AND PANS. Using a steel wool pad to scour, you can clean cookware with a combination of equal parts cream of tartar, baking soda, and vinegar and 1/2 part soap flakes.

CHALK + BAKING SODA. A solution of equal parts pulverized chalk and baking soda combined with enough water to make a paste can be used as a metal cleanser.

ALL-NATURAL GARDEN BUG REPELLENT. This is a sort of disgusting way to make a natural insect repellent but it works. Collect 1/4 cup of dead insects, pulverize the bugs into a juice, and then add a cup of water. Place the concoction in a sprayer and spray the plants with it.

GREEN ADVERTISING?

HEALTHY SKEPTICISM. With the increasing awareness of the environment, companies have learned the value of being perceived as good global citizens. While many businesses make genuine efforts on behalf of the environment, there is a tendency among some companies to exaggerate their role in improving the earth and marketing products that are good, or at least not bad, for the environment. As a consumer, you often have little to go on other than what is said on the label. If the item makes a broad comment about being "environmentally safe" or "ozone friendly," be especially careful to study the label's contents for confirmation of these often misleading descriptions.

POST-CONSUMER VS. PRE-CONSUMER. More and more labels on "recycled" products describe the origin of the recycled materials. "Post-consumer" materials come from previously used business or consumer products such as newspaper, plastic bottles, glass containers, or aluminum cans. "Pre-consumer" material is manufacturing waste. For example, an envelope manufacturer may recycle clippings left over when envelopes are cut from paper. The clippings can be turned into other paper products instead of being thrown away.

WHEN LESS MAY MEAN MORE. Products that state they "use less material" do not necessarily tell the whole story. Less than what? Look for a more specific claim such as "20 percent less packaging than our previous package."

RECYCLABLE QUESTION. Labels with "recyclable" claims mean that these products can be collected and made into useful products. While this is good, it can benefit you only if the material is collected for recycling in your community. Contact your local recycling office, trash hauler, or scrap dealer for this information.

WHICH RECYCLED CONTENT. Look for advertising claims that clearly state whether they apply to the product, its packaging, or both. The claim "recycled content" alone will not tell the full story and could be misleading.

ENVIRONMENTALLY SAFE DISPOSAL? Vague terms such as "safe in a landfill" or "safe in an incinerator" are not helpful in choosing an environmentally safe product. Most consumer products pose little environmental risk when disposed of in a properly designed and operated landfill or incinerator. Disposal safety depends more on how a waste facility is designed and managed than on the characteristics of any single material that is disposed.

BIODEGRADABILITY. Products that claim to be biodegradable are only environmentally beneficial if they are composted. Landfills are designed to minimize the sunlight, air, and moisture that break down a product. Thus, the rate of biodegradation even for food and paper is very slow. On the other hand, if your community has a large-scale composting facility, you would have access to a disposal system for products marked as biodegradable.

BOTTLED BIODEGRADABLE. With a few exceptions, most cleaning products such as detergents and shampoos degrade in wastewater systems and have done so for years. So a claim of being "biodegradable" on a cleaning product by itself may not be very meaningful.

CFC-FREE LABELS. CFCs are chemical substances called chlorofluorocarbons that can deplete the earth's protective ozone layer. They are used to provide coolant in air conditioners and refrigerators, to clean electronic parts, and to make certain plastic foam products. HCFCs are sometimes used as substitutes for CFCs and are less damaging to the ozone layer, but still cause some ozone depletion. Manufacturers are required to state the CFC and HCFC content on labels, so watch for that information when buying products that may contain the substances.

WATCH THE VOCS. VOCs—volatile organic compounds—contribute to ground-level ozone, which causes smog and breathing problems. Common VOC substances are alcohol, butane, propane, and isobutane. Although cars and factories are the major source of VOC releases, the compounds may also be found in household cleaning products, floor polishes, charcoal lighter fluid, windshield wiper fluid, and hair styling spray, gel, and mousse.

"ALL-NATURAL" SO WHAT? Just because something is "all-natural" does not necessarily mean it is good for you or the environment. There are plenty of things that are natural, such uranium or poisonous plants, that you do not want to consume or have in your home.

GOVERNMENT RESOURCE. If you have questions or concerns about environmental advertising claims, write Correspondence Branch, Federal Trade Commission, Washington DC 20580 or call 202-326-2222.

AIR POLLUTION REDUCTION

ENERGY SAVINGS. Pollution from power plants is one of the more significant sources of air pollution. Anything you can do to reduce the amount of energy consumed in your home will help keep air pollution down. See the Energy Savings chapter for tips on this subject.

ON THE ROAD AGAIN. Your driving habits and your car maintenance can either add to the problem of air pollution or help solve it. Any time you can avoid taking a car ride by walking or taking a bicycle for short trips or car pooling for long trips, you are helping to keep pollution down. Similarly, simple maintenance measures such as keeping the proper air pressure in the tires will cut down on air pollution. The Automobiles chapter has a section on ways to cut fuel consumption for further information.

AVOID SPILLING GAS. Take special care to avoid spills and the release of fumes into the air when refueling gasoline-powered lawn, garden, farm, and construction equipment and boats.

PROPER DISPOSAL. Do not pour household paints, solvents, and pesticides down the drain, into the ground, or put them in the garbage. Call your local environmental agency for information on proper disposal of these products.

SEAL CONTAINERS TIGHTLY. Make sure that containers of household cleaners, workshop chemicals and solvents, and garden chemicals are tightly sealed to prevent volatile chemicals from evaporating into the air. Don't leave containers standing open when not in use.

REDUCE WASTE. The less wasteful you are the fewer pollutants are created in the manufacturing of many different types of products and during the collection and processing of wastes for incineration or landfill disposal. When you make purchases, consider using products that are durable, reusable, or use less packaging. Repair broken items rather than buying new ones. Recycle and compost potential wastes before they become part of the waste stream.

BURNING WOOD. Use wood stoves and fireplaces wisely and sparingly. If you have a wood stove, learn how to burn cleanly and more efficiently. Burn dry, well-seasoned wood, and build efficient fires that burn hot and clean. Check your stack, clean your chimney, and inspect your catalyst annually. A well maintained and operated stove produces less pollution and is better for the environment.

REFRIGERATION DISPOSAL. Contact your local government or trash pick-up service to find out what procedures are being implemented in your area to ensure the safe disposal of cars and home appliances. In some areas, municipalities arrange for periodic pickups of home appliances that contain refrigerant.

RECYCLE REFRIGERANT. Individuals are prohibited from knowingly venting refrigerant into the atmosphere while maintaining, servicing, repairing, or disposing of air conditioning or refrigeration equipment. Make sure that the technician who services, repairs, or maintains your refrigerator or air conditioner has recovery equipment to capture any refrigerant that may be released. The refrigerant can later be recycled. Also, when possible, don't just refill leaky air conditioning or refrigeration systems; repair them.

WATER CONSERVATION

BATHROOM FIRST. Close to 75 percent of all water used by the family is used in the bathroom, so it is the best place to start in searching for ways to conserve household water.

ONLY FLUSH WHEN NEEDED. Do not use the toilet as a wastebasket. The average family flushes 40 percent of its water flow down the toilet.

BOTTLED ADDITION. Most toilets use more water than the 5 to 7 gallons that are really needed to do the job. To cut down on the amount of water used, fill a soda bottle with water and small rocks and place it in the toilet tank upright so it does not interfere with any moving parts. Do not use a brick because it may deteriorate and cause damage. Depending on the dimensions of the tank, you may want to use the bottom half of a gallon-sized plastic milk bottle weighted down with clean rocks or marbles.

CHECK FOR LEAKING FAUCETS AND TOILETS. Replace worn washers in leaking faucets and toilets. A small leak can waste many gallons of water daily.

234

To see if your toilet is leaking, listen after flushing to determine if the water stops running. To check if water leaks from the toilet tank into the toilet bowl, put a few drops of food coloring in the tank. If the colored water appears in the bowl, you have a leak that needs to be repaired.

SHORT SHOWERS. Bathing and showering consumes large amounts of water, 70 percent of which is hot water. The best way to save water is to take short showers or turn off the shower while you soap up. It is relatively simple and inexpensive to install a shower flow restrictor. In some areas, energy conservation agencies provide water-saving showerheads for free.

BUBBLE BATHS. If you take a bath, put the tub stopper in immediately and only put a few inches of water in the tub. Bubble baths are a great way of making it seem as if the water is higher than it actually is and help conserve the heat in the water.

WATCH THE FAUCET. The bathroom sink faucet does not need to run water continuously while you are washing, brushing teeth, or shaving. Use the drain stopper when washing. The same holds true for the kitchen sink: Plug up the drain for washing dishes or cleaning vegetables. Put an aerator in the faucet to reduce the flow and help purify the water.

BOTTLED WATER. Keep a bottle of drinking water in the refrigerator so that you don't let the water run when getting a cold drink.

FROZEN PIPE PREVENTION. If you let the water run to keep the pipes from freezing, only do so when necessary. Except for extreme circumstances, there is no reason to just let a very thin trickle of water run.

APPLIANCE TACTICS. Only use washing machines and dishwashers when there is a full load to maximize water usage.

CAR WASH BUCKETS. Use buckets of waters to wash cars instead of letting the hose run continuously.

INTELLIGENT FIXTURES. If you are having new plumbing fixtures installed, inquire about toilets, showerheads, and faucets that use less water and energy than conventional plumbing fixtures. Some communities require that water-saving fixtures be used if new plumbing is installed.

CREATIVE RECYCLING

General reuse

TRASH PICKING. Go on a walking excursion through your neighborhood or a relatively wealthy neighborhood on the lookout for useful items in roadside trash and dumpsters. Many people find useful items such as discarded bicycles, sleds, kitchen equipment, and partially damaged but easily repaired furniture.

AQUARIUM GARDEN. When you tire of fish but still have the aquarium, clean the tank and fill it with dirt for an indoor herb garden. Use the old gravel as drainage at the bottom of the tank after washing it. Add an inch-thick layer of charcoal chips and then half a foot of potting soil.

DONATING GLASSES. Discarded glass frames can be donated to a local service organization instead of thrown in the trash.

UPSIDE DOWN UMBRELLA. Give your broken umbrella a second life by removing the fabric and hanging the metal frame upside down in the laundry room and using it as drying rack.

BATTERY TRADES. When it comes time to get a new car battery, trade in the old one. In the future, try to get rechargeable batteries.

RECYCLED TOOTHBRUSH. Dentists recommend switching toothbrushes about every six months, but that does not mean you have to chuck them in the trash when your are done. Instead add them to the cleaning supplies or home workshop. The small brushes can be used to reach tight spaces for scrubbing and cleaning.

RETYPED RIBBON. Old typewriter ribbons can be given a new life by storing them in a dark bag with some ink for at least a month.

TENNIS BALLS BOUNCE BACK. Old tennis balls can come in handy in the home workshop. Cut them in half and slit a hole in them to slip onto a paint brush with open side pointing up. (You can use old plastic lids in the same way.) This way it will act as a drip catcher. Or you can use the tennis ball as protection from pointy and sharp tools by pushing onto the tips of the tools.

STYROFOAM CHIP STORAGE. Save Styrofoam chips you receive as packaging for when you need to pack something yourself. Ideally, you should use popcorn as a packing material.

TWO KEY RECYCLING TIPS. Old keys can be used as weights for fishing lines or for textiles if they are tucked inside hems or small pockets.

REUSED TUBES. Old toilet paper tubes can be used to hold electrical cords in a neat and organized fashion.

HOMEMADE PIGGY BANKS. Old cans or plastic containers are easily converted into new piggy banks with a coat of paint or decorative paper. Simply cut a slit in the lid to slip the coins through. Personalize the bank by writing a name of the bank owner or the purpose of the bank.

OLD DOORS. Old solid doors don't have to just sit against the garage wall or be tossed in a dumpster. Use the wood to make a table or bench.

COMB CONSERVATION. Don't throw away your old combs. Instead keep them in the cleaning closet to clean other brushes and vacuum attachments.

TOY SOCKS. Stuff your old socks and sew the ends to make a toy for your cat or dog.

PANTYHOSE STUFFING. Old pantyhose can be used as stuffing for pillows and quilts.

SPRAY BOTTLES. When you run out of liquid in a commercial spray bottle, wash the bottle out and use it as a mister for the plants, ironing, and cooler in hot weather.

SOCKING IT TO THEM. Old clothes and single socks make great rags.

CREATIVE KINDLING. Use old lint from the dryer as kindling for the fire. Cardboard egg cartons are excellent for starting fires.

TOWEL MOPS. Old towels can be used as mops for cleaning floors.

SHOEBOX REUSE. Save old shoe boxes as gift boxes.

ALTERNATIVE HANGER USES. Excess hangers do not need to be thrown in the trash. The wire can be reshaped for countless purposes, ranging from angel wings for Halloween costumes to plant hangers.

MOTOR OIL. If you cannot find a station that recycles motor oil, used motor oil can be used as a tool cleaner or as a rust protector for the bottom of your car; just spray the bottom of the car with the stuff.

BICYCLE RECYCLE. Rusting or discarded bicycle wheels can be used as overhead hangers in the closet or garage.

FILM CANISTER RECYCLING. Old film canisters can serve as handy storage compartments for very small items such as jewelry, stamps, pills, sewing kits, and other household objects.

Paper and other covers

WRAPPING PAPERS. Use old wallpaper, sheet music, the comics section of the newspaper, and maps as wrapping paper for gifts.

LEFTOVER WALLPAPER. Use leftover scraps of wallpaper as strips of cover paper for drawers and shelves. Or you can cut a piece out into an interesting shape, spray with acrylic, and use as a place mat.

DROPCLOTHS. Old sheets, blankets, and shower curtains can be used as dropcloths for painting projects.

BUBBLE TROUBLE. You know those sheets of plastic bubbles that are often used for packaging fragile items? Don't just throw them away. Instead save the sheets of bubbles and use them as a cushion for hard benches either in your home or for bleachers on trips to ball games.

Kids stuff

STUFFED SCARECROWS. Old stuffed animals can be placed in the garden on a pole to scare off birds.

STUFFED TIES. Convert an old tie into a stuffed snake by stuffing the inside of the tie and attaching buttons as eyes.

SOCK IT TO THEM. Use old socks with their ends cut out as protection for sleeves for your young children at mealtime.

ROLL-ON BRUSHES. Convert an old roll-on deodorant into an unusual paintbrush by removing the cap, rinsing it thoroughly with water, and adding tempera paint that has been thinned with water. Place the cap back on the top and it is ready to go.

WAYWARD FOOD. Use old sheets, blankets, and shower curtains to cover the floor when your young child is eating.

PUPPET PAINTBRUSHES. A little bit of creativity can turn old paintbrushes into new puppets. Just draw or paint a face on to the upright handle and the bristles instantly become a head of hair.

JUICE LID ARMOR. Make a medieval suit of armor for your child by saving the lids of frozen juice cans, punching holes in their sides and tying them together into a vest.

PUPPET GLOVES. Worn-out gloves can be converted into entertaining puppets with a sewing kit and some imagination by making faces on the finger tips.

MATTRESS PROTECTION. An old mattress makes for a very good trampoline for your children or as a safety mat under a jungle gym or on the garage wall behind the basketball net.

BOTTLED INNOVATION. Collect 10 old plastic soda bottles and use them as bowling pins.

CLOTH DIAPERS. Old cloth diapers can be used as household rags or window-washing cloths.

Kitchen reuse

STRETCHING SPONGE USAGE. If your sponge is past the point of usefulness as a cleanser, you can give it new life by either storing it for later use to apply paint on walls and other surfaces or you can put it in an old jar lid filled with water and use it to dampen stamps at your desk or office.

SQUEEZING NEW LIFE. Old mustard squeeze bottles can be used to hold liquid detergents.

CRUSHED SEA SHELLS. Instead of dumping discarded clam and oyster shells in the trash, use them as fill in the garden or crush them and use the pieces for drainage in the garden or in houseplants.

PLASTIC FOAM TRAYS. Plastic foam trays used for meats in the supermarket can be used to place between plates for storage or to pack lunches in.

REPOTTED. Old pots with handles can be used as scoops for all sorts of things ranging from gardening buckets to pet food dippers.

PLASTIC FOOD BAGS. Plastic bags used for holding breads, frozen foods, and other grocery items can be reused as sandwich bags or other household purposes. Do not use bags that have been used for storing meats.

BERRY BASKET USES. Those green plastic berry baskets can be reused as planters. Or place them upside down over seedlings to protect the young plants.

NEW JAR ROLES. It is extraordinary how many glass jars will pass through your kitchen. Rather than adding them to the pile of recycled glass or the trash, try some of the alternative uses for them after washing them out.

- Glass jars can serve as all-purpose containers for kitchen, office, and bathroom items. They have the advantage of being sturdy, attractive, and see-through.

- Jars are easily converted into homemade gifts by pouring candy, seeds, food mixes, nuts, or other items in the jar and tying on an attractive ribbon.

- Make a miniature terrarium by planting a tiny garden inside. There is no need to water regularly if you keep the lid closed. If it gets cloudy, remove the top.

- Place a small amount of sand in the jar and add a short candle to convert the jar into a candleholder.

DISHPAN PLANS. Worn out dishpans can serve as storage compartments for the closet, garage, or bedroom.

JUICE LIDS. Spray fluorescent paint onto frozen juice can lids and use them as reflectors for the driveway and mailbox.

CORK CUSHIONS. Used wine corks can serve as pincushions, floating devices for small items, or as raw material for small, floating toys in the bathtub.

EGG CARTON RECYCLING. Old egg cartons are natural organizational boxes for paper clips, stamps, thumb tacks, and other small items in your desk. Alternatively, the carton can be used as a seed starter or kindling to start fires.

SAVED RUBBER BANDS. There is no reason you cannot save the rubber bands used to hold spears of broccoli together. In some cases, the rubber bands are so fat you can cut them into two by splicing them lengthwise.

PLASTIC JUGS. The potential of discarded plastic gallon milk jugs is almost limitless. Cut the bottom off and use it as a scoop or bailer for a boat. Cut the top off and remove the cap and use it as a homemade funnel. Put the cap back on and string it through your belt and use it as a bucket attached to your hip for work in the garden. Fill it with water and use it as a weight for holding things down. Let your imagination run wild before you throw a plastic jug in the trash.

CEREAL BOX STORAGE. Convert old cereal boxes into magazine holders by cutting off the top third on a diagonal line.

CITRUS SMELL. Old orange and lemon peels can be clumped together and placed in drawers to serve as a deodorizer.

MESH BAGS. Those plastics mesh bags used for holding poultry and onions can be used as a hanging container or for scouring.

GROCERY BAG MAILER. If you have a pile of old paper grocery bags, cut some of them up and use the paper for wrapping things that need to be sent through the mail.

BOTTLE CAP SCRAPER. It is a relatively simple task to recycle glass bottles. Those metal bottle caps are another story. Save a whole bunch of the caps and then hammer them face up on to a piece of wood or plywood to make a homemade mud scraping door mat.

Outdoor innovation

GARDEN HOSE REUSE. Instead of throwing away an old and leaking garden hose, turn it into a soaker hose by drilling or punching more holes into it and sealing the end with a plastic end cap. Place the hose along the base of plants in the garden, turn the water on very low, and let the water seep out of the holes for 20 to 30 minutes.

METAL BED GATES. The head and foot boards of old metal beds can be used in your garden as gates or interesting outdoor ornaments.

RECYCLED LADDERS. An unsafe ladder may make for a perfectly adequate overhead hanger in the garage or even kitchen. Just attach the ladder to the ceiling and hang items from it.

PLANT CONTAINERS. Old buckets, barrels, and pots can be used as plant containers by simply punching holes in the bottom and filling them with dirt.

ICE CREAM STICK MARKERS. Used ice cream sticks make excellent identification markers for the garden.

BIRD BATHS. Use an old trash can lid or shallow cooking dish as a bird bath.

PUTTING TIRES TO NEW USE. The disposal of car tires is one of the more difficult problems facing the solid waste disposal industry. You can convert an old tire into a swing for the garden by attaching a chain and hanging it from a strong tree branch. Paint the tire white to prevent it from getting too hot in the sun and drill a hole in the bottom for water to escape

SEED STARTERS. Old egg cartons, film canisters, small jars, shoe boxes, and many other relatively shallow discarded containers can be used as seed starters for your garden. Be sure to punch small holes in the bottom of the containers for drainage.

LEAF COLLECTION. Give your old sheets or table cloths a new purpose in life in the great outdoors. When it comes time to gather leaves or light brush, pile it all on the sheet, which can then be used to carry the materials.

RUBBER GLOVE HANDLING. Extend the life of old rubber gloves by using them for outdoor work. You may want to cut the tips off the ends of the fingers to improve your dexterity. The gloves are especially good for picking berries or pruning in thorny bushes.

REFRIGERATOR RECYCLING. It often costs money to dispose of refrigerators. Rather than going to that expense, put your old refrigerator to use either as a storage area for the garage or, if you want to get elaborate, as a homemade root cellar in the garden. Dig a hole in the ground large enough to hold the refrigerator and line the bottom of the hole with rocks. Remove the refrigerator door and place the discarded appliance in the ground with the open side facing up. Place sand in the bottom of the refrigerator, then hay, and then the root vegetables within a layer of hay between each layer of vegetables. Cover the refrigerator with a large piece of wood.

NEWSPAPER MULCH. It's amazing how quickly newspapers accumulate if you have a subscription or are a regular reader. If you have a garden, save some newspapers to serve as mulch. Lay them out flat on the ground and drench the paper with water. The newspaper both blocks weeds from growing and serves as a nutrient when it breaks down.

HANGING AROUND. Old hammocks can be used for storage as a giant hanging basket from the garage roof.

REPOSTED MAIL BOX. Convert an old mail box into a garden tool box container either in the garage or in a strategically located spot in the garden.

LEAF RECYCLING. There are two ways of putting piles of leaves to work for you. One is to fill bags with leaves in the fall and then lining them along the base of your house to serve as insulation. The other is to use the leaves as compost material. Or you can do both. When winter is over, pour the bagged leaves onto the compost pile.

BROOM STAKES. Old broom handles work well as support stakes for large, heavy plants. Just sharpen one end of the broom into a point and plunge it into the ground.

STOOL STAKES. Upside down bar stools can be used as excellent stakes simply by removing the seat.

Saving energy

S aving energy is one of those activities in which greed and altruism intermingle. Energy conservation is not only good for the environment, it also cuts down on the fuel and electric bills.

Many homeowners spend thousands of dollars each year in home energy bills for heating, cooling, refrigeration, cooking, and other appliances. All told, household energy consumption totals close to $100 billion annually and represents about one-fifth of the energy consumed in the country, according to the U.S. Department of Energy. The breakdown of our household energy bills is as follows:

- 46 percent is used to heat and cool our homes.

- 15 percent for heating water.

- 15 percent for refrigerators and freezers.

- 24 percent for lighting, cooking, and appliances.

Experts agree that the total could be reduced if every home implemented simple and relatively inexpensive energy conservation measures, ranging from turning off the lights before going to sleep to getting a comprehensive energy audit and executing everything it suggests.

GENERAL TIPS

ENERGY AUDITS. If you are interested in taking a serious look at specific ideas for your home, many utilities offer low-cost or even free home energy audits to study and define where you could be wasting energy in your house. Contact your local utility to find out what services are provided.

PROFESSIONAL ADVICE. Professional servicemen may know ways to implement energy efficiencies. Seek their advice. This is especially true when you buy a new furnace, central air conditioning, or appliances. Contractors should have energy fact sheets for comparison shopping. Frequently, energy-efficient systems cost more initially but they will save in the long run. So buy smart.

243

READ THE LABELS. Companies are required to provide energy efficiency ratings on the labels of appliances. Read the labels carefully. For an energy label in dollars, the lower the number, the less it will cost to operate. For an energy label in Energy Efficiency Ratings, the higher the number, the less it will cost you to operate.

THINK AHEAD. By thinking ahead when you design, furnish, and equip your house, you can do a great deal to cut down on energy costs. While some methods are obvious, some are not. Water beds, for example, can be the largest electricity user in the house, so shy away from them. If you do have a water bed, use a comforter; it will save up to 30 percent of the costs of heating the water. Insulating the sides will save an extra 10 percent.

REGULAR MAINTENANCE. Routine maintenance on heating and cooling systems and appliances will keep your energy bills down. This includes replacing filters in energy systems on a regular basis.

SEALING THE HOUSE

SEEKING LEAKS. Check your windows and doors for air leaks. The best time to do this is on a windy day. Either feel around the windows and doors or make your own draft detector by attaching a piece of tissue paper to a coat hanger. Move the hanger around the window and door and in suspected cracks. If the tissue paper moves, you've found a leak.

PLUGGING LEAKS. Caulk and weather-strip doors and windows that leak air. The Department of Energy estimates you can cut down up to 10 percent of energy costs with a $40 to $50 investment in caulking and weather-stripping materials for an average house with 12 windows and two doors.

STORM WINDOWS. Storm windows stop air leaks and drafts from cold windows and reduce frost formation and water condensation. Windows can range from custom-made windows to clear plastic sheets attached with tape from the inside. Storm doors in very cold or very hot climates are often worth the investment as well.

GOOD WINDOWS. Use double-pane insulating glass throughout the house. Good window frames are just as important as the glass unit. Quality construction will hold the heat in and keep the cold out.

SNEAKY LEAKS. Don't forget to look for air leaks where plumbing or electrical wiring penetrate walls, floors and ceilings. White foam meat trays, washed of course, can be cut to fit under wall switches and other areas to cut down on drafts.

INSULATION. If your house is not insulated, you could cut your energy bill by up to 30 percent with a layer of properly installed insulation. Use a professional and reputable insulation dealer to do the job. The key to understanding insulation is learning about R-values which indicate the resistance of an insulation material to heat loss. The higher the R-value (listed on the package materials) the greater the insulation capability. Sources for R-value information include the Department of Energy, National Institute of Standards and Technology, American Society of Heating, Refrigeration and Air Conditioning Engineers, and the U.S. Department of Commerce.

SWEEPING INSULATION. Install door sweeps to reduce the air flow underneath doors.

INSULATING CURTAINS. Insulating curtains and shutters can stop the flow of warmth out the window. They can be made at home or bought commercially. Outside shutters also provide a layer of protection. Anything you can do to improve the insulating effectiveness of a window is a big plus. Experts estimate that the equivalent of all the oil pumped through the Alaska pipeline is lost from warm air escaping through windows and doors each year.

STARTING FROM THE TOP. Insulate your attic floor or top floor ceiling. Make sure the attic access door, in particular, is well insulated. If you have 3 inches or less of old insulation, it is likely that you need more insulation. Don't insulate over vents or on top of lighting fixtures or other heat-generating equipment. Keep insulation at least 3 inches from these types of fixtures.

CORNERED HEAT. To reduce heat loss to an unheated crawl space or basement, insulate between the floor joists. If pipes in the crawl space are candidates for freezing, insulate around their perimeters.

EXTERIOR WALLS. Insulating walls is expensive but may be worth it in very cold climates. Unless the construction material is made out of masonry, there should be enough space to accommodate blown-in insulation; insulation should be at least R-11 to R-13 to make it worthwhile. Have the job done by a professional.

INSULATING SNOW. In very cold areas, you can cut down on heat loss by shoveling snow against the side of the house to act as an insulator.

HEATING

THERMOSTAT CONTROL. The Department of Energy recommends keeping your thermostat at 65 degrees during the day and 60 degrees at night.

This should be considered a guideline and not a rule. The elderly, people with circulatory problems, and others may need to keep the temperature higher for medical reasons. On the other hand, if you are healthy and vigorous, there is no reason why you cannot set the thermostat lower and wear a heavy sweater inside and use an extra blanket at night.

WARM CLOTHING. Closely woven fabrics are the best type of clothing for maintaining body heat. A light, long-sleeved sweater equals about 2 degrees of added warmth, and a heavy sweater adds about 4 degrees. Two lightweight sweaters are the equivalent of 5 degrees. For women, slacks are at least a degree warmer than skirts.

WOOD HEAT. Especially in rural areas, wood heating can make a great deal of sense if you don't mind the work it takes to stack the wood and stoke the stove. If possible, provide a combustion air source for wood stoves.

SOLAR HEATING. Numerous solar heating options are offered commercially to take advantage of the heating power of the sun. The addition of a greenhouse or sunspace on the south side of house can be a good source of solar heat and add extra space for growing plants or as a play area. Check with a professional dealer for the options that might best suit your house.

FURNACE SPRAY. Furniture polish sprayed on the furnace filter will increase the amount of dust it picks up.

REGULAR SERVICE. Have your furnace serviced at least once a year. A slipping belt can reduce efficiency by as much as 50 percent. The summer is the best and least expensive time for routine servicing

TIGHT WINDOWS. Keep windows near the thermostat tightly closed. Drafts may keep your furnace working unnecessarily if the thermostat is being cooled while the rest of the room is comfortable.

DUCT LEAKS. Once a year, check the duct work for air leaks in a forced-air heating system while the fan is operating. Small leaks can be repaired or covered up with duct tape. Use caulking and tape for larger leaks.

CLEAN RADIATORS. Dust and grime impede the flow of heat, so be sure to dust or vacuum radiators on a regular basis. If you must paint the radiator, use flat paint. Black is the best color energywise.

ALUMINUM REFLECTORS. Aluminum foil laid shiny-side out behind radiators will reflect heat back into the room. This will prevent the wall from absorbing the heat.

UNBLOCKED HEAT. Keep baseboard heaters and radiators clean and unobstructed by furniture, carpets, or drapes. Air needs to freely circulate from underneath.

SEVERED ROOMS. Unless you have a heat pump system, close off unoccupied rooms and shut their heat off during the winter.

WATCH THOSE FANS. Ventilating fans definitely serve a beneficial purpose, but don't get carried away. In one hour fans can blow away a house full of warmed or cool air. When the fan has done its job, turn it off.

AUTOMATIC THERMAL CONTROL. Clock thermostats will monitor and adjust temperature controls automatically when you leave the house or go to bed. While you may be perfectly capable of adjusting the heat yourself, the convenience and reliability of a clock thermostat may be worth the $40 to $90 investment.

DRAPES AND BLINDS. Keep draperies and blinds closed at night, but open those on sunny windows during the day.

STUFFED INSULATION. Line the window in the children's room with stuffed animals to help insulate the room from the cold.

BOOK SMART. Place book shelves along the exterior walls. The reams of paper and cardboard will serve as an extra insulator to help keep the warmth inside.

CLOSED CLOSETS. When was the last time you needed to heat your closet? Keep the closets closed to save on heating costs.

FIREPLACE COVERUP. An open damper in a fireplace will let up to 8 percent of the heat in your house escape up the chimney. Be sure to close the damper when the fireplace is not in use.

FIREPLACES. A roaring fire may generate heat in a room it is in but there is a cost. The fire pulls in the warm air from the rest of the house and then sends that heat up the chimney. Several measures may be taken to lessen the loss of heated air:

- Lower the thermostat for the rest of the house to between 50 and 55 degrees.

- Close all the doors and warm-air ducts entering the room with the fireplace.

- Open a window near the fireplace about 1 inch or less. This will allow the fire to get its oxygen from outside the house, instead of drawing air from the rest of the house.

- For simple open masonry fireplaces, the loss of warm air through the chimney can be reduced by installing a glass screen, convective grate, radiant grate, or a combination convective grate with glass screen.

COOLING

NOT TOO COOL. Don't over do it when you cool your house; it gets expensive. The recommended temperature for an air conditioned home is 78 degrees.

BLOCKED SUN. Keep out the daytime sun with awnings or vertical louvers on the outside of the window or draw the blinds, shades, or draperies for inside.

COOL COOKING. Do your cooking and use other heat-generating appliances in the early morning or late evening hours on hot days.

LOW LIGHTS. Electric lights generate heat. Keeping your lights off or low will keep the heat down inside.

DON'T DO THIS. Setting your thermostat at a setting cooler than normal when you turn on your air conditioner will not cool the space faster. It will make the room or house cooler than you need.

COOL PLANTINGS. Plant trees or shrubs to shade air-conditioning units. You can increase their efficiency by up to 10 percent. If possible, locate air conditioners on the north side of the house.

PARTS ARE LESS THAN THE WHOLE. Consider using individual air conditioners rather than a central air conditioning unit. Select the lowest capacity and highest efficiency for the rooms you need to cool. This will cost less than a central system and use less energy.

WHOLE-HOUSE FAN. A whole-house ventilating fan installed in the attic or an upstairs window will help keep the house cool. The fan pulls cool air through the house and exhausts warm air through the attic or window.

FAN SPEEDS. When it is humid, set the air conditioner fan on low. You will get less cooling but more moisture will be removed from the air. Otherwise, keep the fan on high.

ADDED FAN. An extra fan by the air conditioner will spread the cooler air further without a drastic increase in power use.

PROPER PLACEMENT. Do not place lamps or television sets near the air-conditioning thermostat. Heat from the appliances will deceive the thermostat on the room's temperature and cause the air conditioner to run longer than necessary.

HOT WATER

EXTRA INSULATION. If your water heater is inadequately insulated, add insulation. But be sure not to block off air vents. You may also want to insulate piping.

SOME LIKE IT COOL. Most water heaters are set for 140 degrees, but you may not need it set that high, especially if you do not have a dishwasher. A setting of 120 degrees will offer adequate hot water for most families. This one measure can cut the energy bill for heating the water by 18 percent.

PLUGGED FAUCETS. Repair leaky faucets promptly.

COLD CLEANING. Do as much household cleaning as possible with cold water. Cold water should be used for food disposers and rinsing dishes before putting them in the dishwasher.

LOW FLOWS. Install aerators and low-flow shower heads to reduce water usage.

KITCHEN

PILOT LIGHTS. If you are buying a gas oven or range, get one with an automatic electronic ignition system rather than a pilot light. You will save considerably on gas use. If you already have a pilot light, make sure it is burning efficiently. If the flame is yellowish, it needs an adjustment.

FAST BOILING. Water boils faster in a kettle or covered pan. Boiling water for spaghetti without a cover on the top can consume as much as three times the energy. Also, once the water comes to a boil you do not need to keep the heat on high, so lower it a notch or two. The water will still boil. When the pasta is cooking, however, remove the cover.

ELECTRIC BURNERS. If you use an electric burner or stove, turn off the burner several minutes before the allotted time. The coils will stay hot long after you turn it off and will allow enough time to finish the cooking task.

NIX ON THE PREHEATING. Skip preheating the oven before cooking casseroles and meat dishes to save some energy.

TOASTER OVENS. Toaster ovens are wonderfully efficient for cooking small amounts of food. There is no need to bake one or two potatoes in an entire oven. In cases like this, use the toaster oven.

ONE-MEAL COOKING. Cook the entire meal in the oven to conserve energy.

TWO MEALS IN ONE. For meals that are good as leftovers, cook twice the amount that you want to eat for one meal and save the rest for later. This will save the energy of having to cook the meal twice.

CROCKPOT HEAT. Use a crockpot for soups and stews that require a great deal of time to cook.

249

UN-FOILED RACKS. Food cooks more rapidly if the air in the oven circulates freely. Do not lay down foil on the oven racks and try to stagger pans on the upper and lower racks.

CLEAN REFLECTORS. Keep reflectors under the range clean. The reflectivity affects the stovetop's efficiency by up to 38 percent.

CERAMIC AND COPPER COOKING. Ceramic and glass baking dishes retain heat better than other materials. You can lower the oven temperature by 25 degrees when you use these dishes. Copper-bottom pans heat up faster than regular pans.

USE A TIMER. Every time you open the oven door to check the food, massive amounts of heat escape. Use a timer or watch the clock to gauge the progress of the food.

MODERATE FLAMES. When cooking with a gas range-top burner, use moderate flame settings to conserve gas.

DISHWASHING IDEAL. Dishwashers should be full but not overloaded before you turn them on. When the wash cycle is complete, open the door and let the dishes air dry. If only a few of the dishes are soiled, don't use the "rinse hold." It uses 3 to 7 gallons of water each time.

COOL SPOTS. Locate the refrigerator in a cool spot. Do not place it in front of the window, especially if it is facing south.

ENERGY FOOD SENSE. Let hot foods cool off before placing them in the refrigerator. Cover food, particularly liquids, or they will release moisture into the refrigerator compartment. Mark food items that are not obvious so that you can quickly identify the food without keeping the door wide open.

ONE FRIDGE BETTER THAN TWO. If you have two refrigerators or freezers and one is almost empty, consolidate the food and shut one off.

REGULAR DEFROSTING. Frost buildup increases the amount of energy needed to keep the refrigerator engine running. Do not allow the frost to build up more than 1/4 inch. Also, make sure the refrigerator door seals airtight. You can test this by placing a piece of paper halfway in the refrigerator seal. If you can pull the paper out easily, the seal may need to be cleaned or replaced or the latch adjusted.

CLEANSED CONDENSERS COILS. The performance of refrigerators drops off as the condenser coils become caked with dust and dirt. The dust acts as an insulator, obstructing the heat transfer between the coils and the room air. Brush off or vacuum the coils—which are usually located on the back of the refrigerator or behind the front grill—when the dust begins to accumulate. Be sure to unplug the refrigerator first.

LAUNDRY AND BATHROOM

COOL WASHES. Wash most clothes in warm or cold water, and rinse in cold.

WASHING CAPACITY. Fill washers but do not overload them for maximum efficiency. The same principle holds true for drying.

WATCH THE DETERGENT. Do not use too much laundry detergent. Too many suds make the machine work harder and use more energy.

TOUGH SPOTS. Instead of washing a heavily soiled clothing item twice, pre-soak it.

LINT REMOVAL. Dirty lint screens impede the flow of air in the dryer. Clean the lint screen after each drying to maximize the air flow. Also, make sure the dryer's exhaust stays clean. A clogged exhaust lengthens the drying time.

CONSECUTIVE DRYING. Dry your clothes in consecutive loads without leaving too much time in between. It takes more energy to stop and start drying because a lot of energy goes into warming the dryer up to the desired temperature.

SEGREGATED DRYING. Separate drying loads into heavy and lightweight items. Because lighter items dry faster, there is no reason to intermingle them with heavier clothes that take longer to dry.

TOWEL DRYING. There is no need to dry towels completely in the dryer. Instead, partially dry them and then hang them to complete the job.

CLOTHESLINE. If you really want to cut down on the use of a dryer, use a clothesline and let the sun provide the energy. Clothes dried outside have the advantage of feeling fresher than mechanically dried clothes. Use the basement for drying space in the winter.

STEAMY IRONING. Hang your clothes in the bathroom while you're taking a shower to save on ironing needs. The steam often removes the wrinkles.

FLOW CONTROL. To keep the flow of water for a shower at about 3 gallons a minute, install a flow controller at the showerhead. The gadgets are inexpensive and easy to install.

SHOWERS OVER BATHS. It takes about 30 gallons of water to fill a bathtub. The flow of water from showers should average about 3 gallons a minute. Thus, a five-minute shower uses 15 gallons, or a remarkable savings of 2,000 gallons of hot water a year if you take five-minute showers instead of baths for the entire year.

LIGHTING

LIGHT DECORATING. You can save energy through decorating by using light colors for walls, rugs, draperies, and upholstery. The lighter the colors the more they reflect light and the less you need to provide artificial light.

NATURAL LIGHTING. Whenever possible, arrange your house to take maximum advantage of natural lighting from the sun. For example, place your favorite reading chair by a window on the south side of the house. Or build an extra skylight or window to increase the amount of natural light.

DUSTED LIGHTS. Keep all lamps, lighting fixtures and bulbs clean. Dirt and grime can impede up to 50 percent of the light emitting from a bulb.

SMART USAGE. Don't forget to turn off lights in rooms that are not being used and to turn off all the lights before going to sleep. Automatic sensory lights will turn off lights when you leave the room.

LIGHT ZONES. Concentrate lighting in reading and work areas. Reduce overall lighting in non-working areas by removing one bulb out of three in multiple light fixtures and replace it with a burned-out bulb for safety. Replace other bulbs with bulbs of the next lower wattage.

DIMMERS ARE GOOD. Install dimmers to reduce lighting intensity.

ONE INSTEAD OF MANY. Use one large bulb instead of several small ones in areas where bright light is needed.

CHRISTMAS LIGHTS. Use a Christmas tree lightbulb to replace the night light bulb.

COMPACT FLUORESCENT LIGHTS. Use compact fluorescent lights for much greater lighting efficiency. These lights can fit into many incandescent lamp sockets. They provide the same quality of light and are three to four times more efficient than conventional bulbs and last 10 times longer. Although the initial costs are higher, the savings in electricity costs more than make up for the difference in the long run.

FLUORESCENT LIGHTS. Fluorescent lighting for kitchen sinks, countertops, and makeup areas are a good choice for energy efficiency and attractive lighting.

TRIPLE LIGHTING. Use three-way lights and turn them down to the lowest lighting level whenever you can.

DIMMER FLOODS. 50-watt reflector flood bulbs in directional lamps provide the same amount of light as a standard 100-watt bulb. Similarly, 25-watt reflector flood bulbs in high-intensity portable lamps provide the same amount of light as a 40-watt lightbulb but uses less energy.

THE OUTDOORS

OUTDOOR GAS LAMPS. Unless they are essential, turn off decorative outdoor gas lamps. Eight lamps will consume as much natural gas as it takes to heat an average home for an entire winter. It costs up to $50 a year to light one gas lamp for the year

SOLAR-POWERED LAMPS. Install solar-powered outdoor pathway lamps or high-efficiency sodium lamps for outdoor security lighting.

GOOD PLANTINGS. Plant deciduous trees, shrubs, and vines on the south and west sides of the house to provide shade in the summer and sunshine in the winter. Air-conditioning energy use can be reduced by 40 percent by shading windows and walls. Position trees and shrubs to keep the sunshine off the building and nearby ground.

HAND TOOLS. Use hand tools, push lawn mowers, pruners, and clippers whenever possible, especially for small jobs.

SHARPEN. SHARPEN. SHARPEN. Sharp saws or bits cut much more quickly and thus use much less energy. So keep cutting edges sharp. Oil on bits and saws reduces friction.

Computers

It's a cliché but it's true: Computers are the future. Millions of homes are already equipped with personal computers. Personal computers are the vehicles of the much heralded information superhighway.

The range of what a personal computer can do and will be able to do in the future appears almost limitless. Game center, educational tool, word processor, information service, personal organizer, data center, legal aid, medical consultant, research center, desktop publisher, tax consultant. These are just a few of the things a computer can do now if properly programmed and operated.

There are basically two types of personal computers: Macintoshes and IBM-compatible PCs (personal computers). Which one is better is a matter of taste. The IBM-compatible PCs outsell the Macs, but those use who Macintoshes swear by them. Both are good and both will get the job done.

The four areas in your home where a computer can help you the most are in the kitchen, with the budget, as a communications means and as an educational/entertainment tool for you and your children.

One reassuring thing about computers is that they are only as smart as you make them. Before your computer can process or analyze anything, you have to give it the information either with a disk, through an on-line service, or manually. A personal computer, after all, is an electric appliance and only as useful as you make it.

GETTING STARTED

COMPUTERPHOBIA. Computerphobia is perhaps the biggest barrier to owning and operating a computer. Like entering a swimming pool, you can overcome it by either diving right in or testing the waters with computers owned by friends, colleagues, or family members. Children seem to have a natural ability to learn computers quickly and grasp their concepts, so if you have a child who is computer literate, he or she may be able to help you. Many high schools and colleges offer basic courses in computers if you want to get some formal training.

COMPUTER RESEARCH. If you know very little about computers, buy a couple of computer magazines and read the advertisements. They can be very instructive. Try reading some of the articles. They often do not make sense for the uninitiated but they can be helpful in identifying the pluses and minuses of different computers and computer software. Before buying a computer, thoroughly research the advantages and disadvantages of the different types of computers and capacities to make sure the computer matches your needs. For example, if you travel a lot you might want to consider buying a laptop. A laptop can serve as your primary computer, but you should take into account it is less expandable and sometimes more expensive than a desktop computer.

COMPUTER GAMES. The most accessible programs for computer novices are simple and entertaining games. Before delving into something more intimidating, try playing a computer game to overcome your fear of the computer.

MOUSE SOLITAIRE. Several word-processing programs have solitaire games as part of the program. To get used to the nuances of manipulating the mouse, play solitaire for about an hour. After 60 minutes, you'll feel like a pro.

MULTIPLE USES. Computers are such versatile machines that there is no reason to limit yourself to one function. Once you are comfortable with the computer, look into the different software options. You will be amazed at the possibilities.

SMART PURCHASES. As a rule you want to buy computers and computer programs from established companies, or at least companies that will provide services for their products, conduct training programs, and have a telephone service that answers your questions.

COMPUTER LOCATION. Do not set up the computer near a magnetic field and do not place the disks near a telephone. Keep the room well humidified to reduce computer static. Be sure to keep the computer covered and dusted as much as possible. Heat can damage disks, so make sure they are stored away from heat or light sources such as a heating vent, window sill, or hot desk lamp. The glare from the sun is sometimes a problem on a computer screen, so pay attention to the location of the window when placing the computer screen.

PROPER HEIGHT. The top of the computer screen should be at eye level for maximum comfort and ease of use.

CIRCUIT SHARING. Do not let the computer share the same electric circuit with an air conditioner, vacuum, refrigerator, or other heavy appliance with an on-off cycle.

THINKING ENERGY. Computers consume a fair amount of energy, particularly color monitors and laser printers, so keep that factor in mind when you buy a computer. Laptops use much less energy than standard computers.

DON'T FORGET TO REGISTER. When you buy a new computer or software program, the equipment or disks almost always come with a registration card or telephone number to register the purchase with the company. It is easy to put off registering. Don't. Usually when you register you become eligible for company services and discounts on future purchases. This is particularly important with software because new versions of old programs are constantly being released. There is no reason to pay full price for an updated version if you are already a legitimate owner of the old program.

COMPUTER MANAGEMENT

DIRECTORIES. Set up computer files, disks, and directories the same way you would for regular paper. Use codes in the file names to help identify the file. For example, save correspondence by using the first letter of the person's name followed by the first four letters of his or her last name and the calendar date. If you have a file of recipes, start each file name for baked goods with a B. Use a system that makes sense to you.

BACKUPS. Always save two copies of your files. One on the computer's hard drive; the other on a disk. If something happens to the computer or disk, you won't have to do the work all over again.

SURGE PROTECTION. Use a surge protector. You do not want to lose all of your work on the computer because of an electric malfunction or lightning strike. Surge protectors offer the added benefit of giving you more plug outlets and keeping the electric wires nice and tidy.

SHORTCUTS. Learn the shortcuts in your computer. Most programs have two or more ways to accomplish the same functions. Learn the quickest way to accomplish a task and you will save time and keystrokes.

OFF-ON. It is easier on the computer to leave it on all day rather than turning it off and on a few times even if you will not use it for an hour or two.

SAVING SCREENS. If you leave the computer screen on and untouched for a long time, the computer may burn impressions into the screen. Avoid this by either dimming the screen or installing a screen-saver program. Some of the programs being sold commercially are wonderful. They range from Disney cartoons to flying toasters to rotating impressionist paintings.

DATED FILES. Always date your files and provide brief descriptions. This can save time when you need to find the file quickly.

EASY VIEWING. Use a copyholder or clipboard to hold up a piece of paper you are working with so you can look straight at it while working on the computer. Good copyholders attach directly onto the monitor and can be adjusted in all directions.

FLOOR SPACE. You do not need to put all your computer equipment on the table and desk. Save room by placing some components on the floor. Most computer and office supply stores sell units designed specifically for computers. If you cannot find a way to set up your computer system comfortably and conveniently, it may be worthwhile to buy one of these units.

MARKED DISKS. Always label and identify your computer disks. Using a felt-tipped pen, describe the program used to create the document, whether it is high- or low-density, and the content of the disk. Keep floppy disks in a dust-free holder. If feasible, use different colored labels for different functions such as data bases, word-processing programs, or utilities. If you really want to be efficient, print out the directory of files for each disk and attach it to the disk folder.

CLEANING TIP. Do not clean the monitor with glass cleaner when the computer is turned on. You may get a shock. Instead, use a slightly damp cloth when the machine is turned off. Commercial anti-static cloths made specifically for screens are the best choice.

VIRUS PROTECTION. Make sure you install an anti-virus software program such as Norton Anti-virus or VirusScan. Be careful when you download programs or files from other people and scan every disk you put in the computer.

RECYCLED PRINTOUTS. You can use the reverse side of old computer printouts to save on the paper bill.

HOME MANAGEMENT

BILL RECORDER. There are a number of software packages available to manage and record bill payments and income. Income taxes can also be done on these programs. Some of the better programs for this include Quicken, and MacInTax. The trick with all of these is to stay up to date in your record-keeping. It is worth the effort.

RECIPE COLLECTOR. Store recipes on your computer with either your own program or a commercial one. You will always have a clean copy of the recipe available without the clutter of a recipe box. Programs such as

Cookbook Wizard and Cooking Companion are available to help you plan meals, scan recipes, convert measurements, and generate shopping lists with ease.

NUTRITIONAL COMPUTERS. You may not think of the kitchen as a place for the computer, but the computer may become as important an appliance as any in your kitchen. Not only can it be used for storing and accumulating recipes, but it is also an excellent resource for nutritional information. Software programs such as FoodWorks, Nutrition Pro, and Food Analyst Plus give valuable nutritional information on the food you are serving and offer alternative menus for nutritious meals. You can break down any recipe, meal or diet into its nutritional components with these programs.

HEALTHY HELPER. In addition to nutrition, computer software companies are creating more and more programs pertaining to health. Programs are available offering information on prescription drugs, clinical data, and home medical advice and reference materials.

HOUSEHOLD INVENTORY. Keep an inventory of household possessions for insurance purposes. When you keep this information in a computer it is easy to keep updated. Print a copy for your own files and another copy for the insurance company.

THAT'S ENTERTAINMENT. You can keep an entertainment file on meals that guests enjoyed or disliked, who was present at events, and recipe lists as a resource for planning future events.

PERSONAL ORGANIZER. Many new programs are being designed specifically to help you become better organized. Most of the personal organization programs include appointment calendars, notepads, memos, address books, appointment books, and other specialized features such as automatic speed dialers and built-in alarms.

CD-ROM. Some of the most interesting and educational software produced is being done on CD-ROMs, which have far greater storage capacity than standard disks.

SUBSTANCE OVER STYLE. It is very difficult to judge the quality of a software package from just the box or description in a catalog. The best way to determine quality before buying is to try it out either on someone else's computer or in the store on a demonstration computer. Short of that, use the following guidelines:

LOOK FOR HEFT. If the box feels empty and insubstantial, the computer software may be lacking in substance. The better the software, the more likely it will need accompanying materials to explain and amplify.

BEWARE GLITZ. Developing a great software program takes time. If you see a software program based on a recent television show or movie, it is unlikely that the program will have gone through the kind of rigorous and creative process needed in an innovative computer program.

FOOD OFF LIMITS. Do not mix eating with computing. Bits and pieces of food can easily fall into the cracks of the keyboard, liquids spill into the computer, and sticky stuff gets stuck on the keyboards. Any of these things can cause the computer to malfunction or make the computer less comfortable to work with.

THE RIGHT PROGRAMS. When you get a software program, double check to make sure it is compatible with your computer.

Children's tips

Parenting is like exploring an uncharted river. You never know what awaits you around the next bend and you are pretty much on your own in deciding how to handle each obstacle.

The best advice experienced parents give is to love and enjoy your child. With this as a broad guideline, there are a number of tips and hints that can help you navigate your way through parenthood.

The most important hints pertain to safety. One of the more horrifying facts provided by our federal government is that close to 400 children under four years old die each month because of household accidents. What this is means is you can never be too careful. Discretion and caution are not part of a toddler's vocabulary, so you have to make up for it by childproofing your house.

CHILDPROOFING

CRIB SAFETY. Cribs and playpens should meet the standards of the U.S. Consumer Product Safety Commission. Those standards state that crib slats cannot be more than 2 3/8 inches apart and that corner posts not stick out more than 5/8 of an inch in height. Sometimes babies want to climb out of the crib, so be sure to keep the crib's sides in the raised position. Also, remember that whatever you put in the crib will end up in the child's mouth. Never tie a toy attached to a string in a crib; your child can strangle on it.

CHILD'S EYE VIEW. To double check on all the things to eliminate as potentially hazardous situations for your child, crawl on all fours to get your child's perspective of the house. All precious, fragile, or dangerous items should be at least 4 feet above the ground. Be innovative in decorating. Use hanging plants instead of floor plants, mobiles instead of statues, and put things in baskets hanging from the ceiling.

LIFEGUARD DUTY. Never, ever leave your child alone in the bathtub. In addition to cleaning duty, you should think of bath time as lifeguard duty. Bath time is also a fun time for the child, so let him or her enjoy it with toys and plenty of time for playing. Keep the water level at about 3 inches for infants (you can raise the level of the water as the child grows older) and only use mild soap; perfumed soap will dry out the skin.

STAIR SAFETY. Don't let children play on the stairs. Install a sturdy gate to keep small children from the stairs.

PSEUDO BATHS. Children may view buckets of water, wading pools, and even toilet bowls as similar to bath tubs. Be careful to keep babies away from them and always keep the toilet cover down.

ELIMINATE TEMPTATION. Keep the child's favorite toys away from unsafe areas.

COVERED OUTLETS. Babies and young children will be tempted to poke small objects in the holes of a wall socket. Use outlet covers to make sure the child's exploration is kept safe. Whenever possible, place heavy furniture in front of outlets.

SHORTENED CORDS. Use cord shorteners to cut down on the amount of electric cords. Do not let the child chew or pull down on electric cords.

ANCHORED SHELVES. Anchor bookshelves to the floor to prevent a child from accidentally toppling them over.

ADHESIVE EDGE CUTTERS. Use weather stripping to pad sharp edges on furniture.

STYROFOAM BUMPERS. Instead of throwing away the Styrofoam casings that come with appliances and other packaged items, use them as bumpers for hard or sharp-edged furniture.

KNEE PADS. Tie sponges or athletic wristbands to your child's knees to act as knee pads.

WINDOW SAFETY. Install safety locks on windows and move any furniture near a window that your child might climb to gain access to a window.

OUT OF REACH. Babies and young children cannot distinguish substances which may be harmful, so pesticides, medicines, liquid cleaners, soaps, and other products should always be kept in locked cabinets or out of reach. Keep the washer and dryer area inaccessible to your child.

POISON. If you think your child has swallowed a poisonous substance, call the Poison Control Center or emergency dispatch immediately. Keep syrup of ipecac handy to induce vomiting, but only if you are instructed by a professional or emergency responder to use it.

CONTAINER CAPS. Babies are curious about containers. Use childproof caps and containers so your child cannot get the cap off and taste or spill the contents.

REVERSED SAUCEPANS. Saucepan handles are tempting for children to grab. When you are cooking, turn handles away from the child to prevent burning his or her hand and spilling the contents of the pan.

TABLECLOTH TUGS. Unaware of the dangers of lit candles and piping-hot meals and drinks, babies may tug on your tablecloth. If you must use a tablecloth with a baby around, be sure to secure it tightly to the table.

CAR SEATS. Get the safest car seat you can and secure it to the car backwards until the baby is 20 pounds. Then turn it around face forward. The safest spot in the car is the center of the back seat. Never leave a child alone in the car under any circumstances.

BELL WARNING. Attach a bell or bells to doors leading outside. When your child opens the door, the bell will warn you of his or her departure.

KITCHEN SAFETY. Remove the knobs from the stove when it is not in use. Unplug appliances and do not set them aside anywhere near the sink; electricity and water are a lethal combination. Make sure that plastic bags, cleaning products, knives, detergents, and other hazardous materials are either locked up or well out of reach. The kitchen is filled with extremely dangerous things, so be extra careful here.

PLASTIC KNOTS. Tie knots in plastic dry-cleaning bags before throwing them in the trash. These bags are an inviting but deadly toy for children, who could suffocate while playing with them.

HIGH CHAIR SECURITY. Be sure to use the safety straps in the high chair. For extra assurance, place a sink mat on the chair to prevent your child from sliding.

POISONOUS PLANTS. The following indoor plants are poisonous to children: autumn crocus, azalea, caladium, daffodil, elephant's ears, English ivy, false indigo, hyacinth, hydrangea, narcissus, philodendron, and poinsettia. Either remove them from the house or keep them out of your child's reach.

SWING IN SAFETY. Many swings made for the backyard have chains that will pinch a child's skin or hair. Prevent this from happening by removing the chain and slipping a piece of hose over the chain before hanging up the swing.

BATHROOM SAFETY. All medication should be stored in the bathroom; remember to keep cosmetics, deodorants, and perfumes our of reach. Use a night-light for the razor socket. Make sure that the door can be unlocked from the outside as well as the inside.

INFANTS AND TODDLERS

Babies

SCREENED VISION. Install a screen door to the nursery so you can see and hear the baby without opening the door.

HEATED CRIBS. Use a heating pad to warm up the baby's mattress while you feed or tend to his or her needs. When it comes time to return the baby to the mattress, it is nice and warm.

CLOTHESPIN ATTACHMENTS. Tie clothespins to the side of the crib as attachments to hold the blanket or quilt in place. This will help keep your child warmer.

MOBILE SLEEPER. If your baby is having trouble going to sleep, try taking him or her for a drive in the car—in a baby seat of course—or for a ride around the block in the carriage.

MIRRORED FUN. Place a small plastic mirror in the crib for your child to gaze at and keep occupied early in the morning.

FROZEN FOOD SUPPLY. Prepare baby food ahead of time and then freeze it in an ice cube tray. When the food is frozen, pop the cubes out and keep them in a plastic bag in the freezer. The portions will be about right and you will save yourself some time when you have to feed the baby.

STEADY MILK SUPPLY. Get as much rest and relaxation as you can to ensure a good supply of breast milk. This can be very difficult in the early days after a child's birth. Put up a Do Not Disturb sign to keep visitors away when you need a nap and take the telephone off the hook. Drink at least three quarts of fluid a day to assist milk production. Take a warm bath or go for a walk to release tension.

WARM MILK. Let bottled milk sit in hot water to warm it up for your child. Test it by spraying it on to your wrist. If it is too hot, place it in cold water.

SOUR MILK. Get rid of the sour smell in a plastic milk bottle by putting a teaspoon of baking soda in the bottle and filling it with warm water. Shake it up and let it sit overnight.

PICTURED PRESENTS. Instead of simply writing thank-you notes for baby gifts, take a picture of the gift in use. If the gift is a dress or outfit, photograph the child dressed in it.

Bathroom and kitchen

CRUNCHED TOILET PAPER. To cut down on the amount of toilet paper your child can pull out of the roll, crush the roll into an oval shape.

BATHING CAGE. Use one of those hard plastic laundry baskets to hold your child in when he or she takes a bath. No slipping or sliding. Or place a mat on the bottom of the tub.

CLEAN MEDICINE. If you can, give colored liquid medicine or vitamins at bath time. When it spills or you miss, the liquid won't stain your child's clothes.

JELLIED EYES. Rub a dab of petroleum jelly around the baby's eyes and eyebrows to prevent the soapy water from running into his or her eyes.

IMITATION JELLY. Instead of using petroleum jelly for your baby's bottom, Crisco vegetable shortening can do the job just as well.

CLOTH VS. DISPOSABLE DIAPERS. One could debate the merits and disadvantages of cloth versus disposable diapers for an entire book. Suffice it to say that environmentalists recommend cloth diapers because they can be reused, but many parents prefer disposable diapers because of their convenience. In the long run, it is less expensive to use cloth diapers. Don't be fooled by the fact that disposable diapers for the smallest babies seem inexpensive; the price goes up as the size increases.

EASY CLEANING. Save yourself some dishwashing by giving your child food in edible containers. An ice cream cone is the perfect vehicle for serving all sorts of soft foods such as tuna or egg salad.

RUBBER SUCTION. Get a bunch of rubber suctions cups to hold dishes, soap holders and other types of plates and containers to their place. This will be especially helpful when your child goes through the stage of tossing the dinnerware off the high chair.

BANDED CUPS. Wrap rubber bands around your child's drinking glasses to provide a better grip. This will reduce the number of spills and broken glasses.

Clothing

WET SHOELACES. Keep shoelaces tied by dampening them before tying.

RIGHT FROM LEFT. Mark the side of each shoe facing inward to identify which shoe goes on which foot. Teach the child that when the marks face each other, the shoes are on properly.

PROPER DRESSING. Mark the front of a shirt, dress, pants, or other garment so your child can tell the front from the back.

PINNED SOCKS. When your child takes off his or her socks make sure the child attaches the socks together with a rubber band, plastic clamp, or laundry pin to avoid splitting up the pairs and losing socks later.

STRINGED MITTENS. Put an end to lost single mittens by attaching the ends of a long piece a yarn to each mitten and running the yarn through the inside of the coat and sleeves.

MIRROR IMAGE. Babies love to watch themselves in the mirror. If you are having trouble dressing your child, try placing him or her in front of the mirror and doing the task there.

SLIPPERY SHOES. If you are having trouble taking off your child's shoes or boots, spray the insides with silicone. It will make the job easier.

FISTED DRESSING. If your child won't make a fist when you try to put his arm up a narrow sleeve, give him or her a small toy to hold on to so you can slip the sleeve over the grasped hand.

LAUNDRY INSTRUCTION. Having your child help you sort and fold the laundry is an excellent way to teach the different colors and clothing items.

EASY ZIPPING. It will be easier for your child to pull up his or her jacket zipper if you attach something large to the zipper such as a key ring and trinket. Run soap or a lead pencil over a zipper to help prevent it from sticking.

Fun, art, and more

BOXED MURALS. For fun and drawing practice, take a large cardboard box, cut off the top, and place your child in the box with a bunch of crayons to cover the walls of the box with his or her artwork.

CORNSTARCH CLEANSER. Use cornstarch to clean stuffed animals. Rub the dry cornstarch in, let it sit, and then brush it off.

CLEANING SOCKS. Use a sock to hold bits and pieces of soap and tie the open end. Now your child can wash without losing the slippery bar of soap.

KITCHEN FUN. Designate a kitchen drawer for crayons and construction paper. When it comes time to cook, just give your child the materials to free you up for the cooking.

RECYCLED CARTONS. Convert milk cartons into colorful containers by cutting off the tops and covering them with old wallpaper or construction paper. Or cut out the top and bottom of the carton and place the remaining box in a paper bag. The carton will strengthen the paper bag for packed lunches.

BEDTIME TACTIC. Let a toddler put several favorite toys to bed before it is his or her turn. This way the child will be the last one to go to bed.

CONSTRUCTIVE PAPER. Old dress boxes, cardboard sheets used for men's shirts, and the backs of cereal boxes and tissue boxes can be used for drawings and paintings.

PRESERVED ART. Spray your child's artwork with hair spray to prevent the colors from fading.

PUPPET FUN. Turn ordinary brown paper bags into puppets by drawing faces on them. You can also convert old socks into puppets by sewing features onto the sock.

SNEAKY PICKS. If you want to get your child into the habit of making decisions, but want to tip the scales a certain way, always mention your preference as the last choice. When given a choice, kids tend to select the last choice presented to them.

SOAKED BAND-AID. Use a piece of cotton drenched in baby oil to rub over the adhesive tape on a child's skin to loosen it. When the tape is removed, it will not hurt nearly as much.

SPLINTER DETECTOR. If you are having trouble locating a splinter, add a dab of iodine to the suspected area. The splinter will get much darker and thus more visible.

TASTY ICE PACKS. Instead of using an ice pack for a bruised lip or tongue, give your child a popsicle to suck on.

ALTERNATIVE ICE PACKS. Use old plastic bottles or self-sealing plastic bags as instant ice packs by filling them with water and placing them in the freezer.

HOMEMADE FINGER PAINT. Make your own fingerpaints by mixing two drops of food coloring for every one ounce of liquid starch. To make your job easier at cleanup time, add a dash of liquid detergent to the fingerpaint.

HOMEMADE PLAYDOUGH. Here is the recipe: Add a few drops of food coloring to two cups of boiling water. Add 1/2 cup salt, two tablespoons of alum, and two tablespoons of oil. Knead the mix well. When you are done, store it in the refrigerator.

HOMEMADE PASTE. Make your own nontoxic glue at home by mixing one part flour and two parts water with a teaspoon of salt. Place the salt and flour in a pan and stir the water into the flour slowly. Let it simmer for five minutes and allow it to cool. The paste is also good for papier maché.

CAR DOOR TIP. When children get in the car and fasten their safety belts, have them place their hands on or over their heads when they are ready. When you close the door you will know where everybody's hands are.

SHADES OF FUN. Hang a shoe bag over a car window. It can serve the dual purpose of blocking the sun and storing toys for your child to play with during the car ride.

GROWING UP

SOOTHING SIBLINGS. Encourage the older child to be actively involved in raising a new baby. Let the older sibling teach the baby how to smile by smiling at the baby. When the baby smiles back, the older child will feel that he or she is playing a role in the development of the baby. As a rule, after the first child try to make the baby fit into the household's routine rather than letting the household revolve around the new baby. This will soothe potential jealousy and make for a saner household overall.

CHILD LABOR. There is no reason why parents have to do all the work. Here are a few simple things you can have your children do to make your life easier:

- Put dirty dishes in the sink or the dishwasher.
- Wipe the bath tub, shower, or sink after using them.
- Replace the soap and toilet paper when they run out.
- Pre-sort dirty laundry into darks and lights in separate hampers.
- Put away their belongings when they are done with them.
- Set the table.

CALENDAR OF CHORES. Similar to an Advent calendar at Christmas, make a calendar of chores with a window for each day of the month. Behind each window is a chore that your child will do that day. To make sure that there is an element of fun in the calendar, give the child a day off, or even better, a fun trip or treat to enjoy.

LAUNDRY DEPARTMENTS. Instead of delivering the laundry to each family member's room when you are done cleaning it, set up a depot system in the laundry area. Put each person's laundry in designated areas marked by name. In this way the family members can pick up their own laundry.

LABELED ROOM. Label all drawers, cupboards, shelves, closet spaces, hooks, and laundry baskets to instruct your child on where all the clothes and toys should be when it comes time to clean up. Use words, pictures, or both on the labels, depending on how old the child is.

BREAD BOX STATION. Convert the bread box into a lunch station filled with sandwich bags, bread, healthy snacks, lunch tickets, and other items that might come in handy for boxed lunches. When it is time to make the lunches the night before or morning of school, line up the materials and start packing the lunches. The kids can help.

PREPPING FOR SCHOOL. To prepare for the first day of school, walk with your child to the school at least once before school starts. Make sure your child understands what will happen at school and what arrangements are in place for his return home. If the school has a cafeteria, take the child to the cafeteria or to a different one so that he or she understands how to get lunch. Try to arrange a meeting for your child with the teacher beforehand. Include a tag with the child's name, address, and telephone number in his lunch box.

HIGH VISIBILITY. If you are going to a crowded event or place such as the circus or carnival, dress your child in a brightly colored jacket. It will be far easier to keep track of him or her in a crowd this way.

UNHAPPY HUNGER. There are few things as annoying as going on a shopping excursion with a hungry child. Before leaving the house for a trip with your child, make sure that he or she has eaten. Eating out can be inconvenient and expensive.

CAR SNACKS. For long car rides be sure to bring a good supply of healthy snacks such as fruits, juices, and cheese cubes.

LOWERED RODS AND HOOKS. Lower the clothing rods and hooks in the closet to an appropriate height for your child.

REAL TOY BOXES. Improvised toy boxes can be dangerous, so make sure you get a toy box that was designed for that purpose. Safe ones have plastic hinges, light lids, air holes, and can be opened from the inside.

BIRTHDAY TREATS. Stuck over how to make a birthday special? How about going on a trip to the zoo, movies, or ice skating rink? To make the event more fun for your child, have him or her custom decorate cupcakes for each friend instead of having one large birthday cake.

PARENTAL DICTATION. Encourage your child to read and write by having him or her tell you a story and write it down as it is described. Leave room for drawings and pictures to be filled in by the child afterwards. Always praise the child's creativity.

SHARED HOMEWORK. If you have paperwork or office work that needs to be done at home, do it next to your child as he or she is doing homework. This will reinforce the importance of homework and make you readily accessible for any questions.

MUSICAL EAR. Expose your child to all kinds of music including classical by letting it play on the stereo as background. Or you can focus in on the music by asking the child what he or she thinks is happening with the music.

TALKING TELEVISION. When your child watches television, you should join in the viewing and discuss whatever is on. Rather than letting the child get into the habit of passively absorbing television, active discussions will encourage the child to think critically about what is on and even question the content of the television show.

CURSES. If your child curses at a young age, do not overreact. He or she may just be trying to get your attention. With older kids, they may be seeking a reaction from you as well. Some families make up substitute words for curses to vent their frustration in an acceptable manner.

BIRTHDAY GUIDELINE. The rule of thumb for birthday parties is one guest for each year that is being celebrated. In other words, if the child is three years old, invite three friends for the birthday party.

HANDLING MONEY. Money is a difficult concept for a child to understand, so get in the habit of letting your child watch you make small financial transactions with cash and not credit cards or checks.

BABYSITTER DATA. Keep a list of important telephone numbers and special instructions out in the open for babysitters to use in case of emergencies. You can write the information on a board in the kitchen or in a notebook; but wherever the list is, make sure the babysitter knows where to find it easily.

BABYSITTER NETWORKING. If you cannot find a babysitter, call some neighbors who you trust for recommendations or call a guidance counselor or teacher at the local high school.

HOME ALONE. If you cannot be there when your child arrives home from school, have him or her call you upon arriving home to reassure both of you. An alternative is for you to call home at an arranged time or have another adult stop by the house to make sure everything is fine. Some hotline services are available for children who are home alone.

SAFETY PRECAUTION. Teach your child what to do in case of an emergency. Make sure all important telephone numbers and names are posted in a prominent place and that your address and instructions on how to get there are posted. If there is an emergency, this information could be vital.

FAMILY BULLETIN. As your children get older they tend to lose touch with one another. Start a family bulletin early on with lots of pictures in which you describe what everyone in the family is doing. Make it fun. The bulletin will serve as a way of keeping everyone in touch with each other and will be a fabulous memento years later.

TWENTY-FIVE FUN ACTIVITIES

HOME THEATER. Rent a video from the video store or borrow one from the library and set up your own home movie theater. Make popcorn, invite friends, and give out tickets to make the event special.

FIREHOUSE VISIT. Visit your local fire department for a special treat. Call ahead and arrange the visit for a convenient time.

PUPPET SHOW. Using a sofa for cover and a bunch of handmade puppets, you, your children, and their friends can write and produce an enjoyable puppet show. Use a floor lamp for lighting.

INDOOR BOWLING. Stack a collection of toilet paper rolls as bowling pins and use a tennis ball or Nerf™ ball as the bowling ball.

EXCESSIVE DRAWING. Use a giant role of paper to do life-size and exotic drawings. For cheap paper use butcher paper or go to a local print shop and see if they have any excess rolls of newsprint.

TRACED CHILD. Get a giant piece of paper and trace your child, yourself and some friends onto the paper. When you are done tracing, fill in the faces and the rest of the body.

COOPERATIVE DRAWING. Take turns drawing different things on a piece of paper. After drawing each item, explain what it is and why it is part of the picture. You can do this with your children or your children can do it on their own.

HOME GALLERY. Draw or paint a series of artworks and select one for framing. You can make a gallery by selecting a drawing each month by your child and placing it in a collection of illustrations somewhere prominent in the house.

CRAYON MUFFINS. Break a bunch of crayons into little pieces and put them in a muffin tin that is lined with aluminum foil in each of the compartments. Place tin in a pre-heated oven at 300 degrees and let it sit for about 5 minutes. You do not want the crayons to melt completely, just blend together. When it is cooled off, remove the aluminum foil and admire the colorful muffins that can be used as art objects in themselves or as interesting large crayons.

FUN EXERCISE. Play a lively children's record, CD, or tape and dance to the music. You can turn the dance event into a regular aerobic exercise routine. You will get your exercise without leaving home, it will be fun, and your kids will get an enjoyable introduction to exercise.

LIVE THEATER. Convert your living room or garage into a theater and put on a show. Most libraries have plays written for children or you can have the children write a play themselves. Charge 10 cents admission to the show and invite some friends.

COLORED EGGS. Nobody ever said Easter was the only time you can color eggs. Make an event out of a rainy day by coloring hard-boiled eggs and decorating them with crayons.

HOME RESTAURANT. Let your child or children pretend they are managing their own gourmet restaurant with a menu of three or four different simple meals that they select. They present you with the menu, you pick the dinner, and they then prepare the meal and serve it in a restaurant-like setting.

OATMEAL BOX INVENTION. Turn an old round oatmeal box it into a mailbox for your child's room. The box can be made into all sorts of things such as a spaceship, tunnel, or peculiar looking truck. Cardboard boxes, shoe boxes, and tissue boxes can also be used as the basic material for other innovative ideas. Let your children's imaginations run wild.

MUSEUM TRIP. To make a trip to the museum more fun, scout out the museum and identify exhibits or pictures that will interest your child (do not pick more than 10, even for an older child). Then invent a series of games or questions to pique your child's interest in certain paintings. For example, go to a Picasso painting and ask your child to identify the shapes and describe what is going on. Discuss the exhibits with your child. Make the first visit short.

FROZEN TREATS. Make some healthy frozen homemade snacks by freezing grapes and banana slices by just putting them in the freezer. For a more elaborate treat, blend yogurt and fruit and pour the mix into a paper cup or popsicle mold. Insert a clean stick and freeze. When the yogurt is frozen, remove the mold or paper cup and eat.

PLANTINGS. Get some seeds and plant an indoor or outdoor garden. Or you can use seeds from an orange, lemon, or grapefruit in the refrigerator to plant a small citrus tree. Plant the seed 1/2 inch deep in some peat moss and keep it damp, but not soaked. Or plant some carrots by cutting off their tops, soaking the carrots in water, and planting them in the soil once roots start to form.

SPARKLING CANDY. Play mad scientist with a pack of Wint-O-Green Lifesavers and a pair of pliers. Go into the closet with the candy, pliers, and a small, clear plastic bag. After closing the door, squeeze the Lifesaver with the pliers inside the plastic bag until the candy breaks. A small flash of light will come out of the candy. Called triboluminescence, it occurs when certain types of crystals are crushed.

HOME NEWSPAPER. Convert your children into ace reporters and have them write a newspaper with articles, photographs, and cartoons about the family, friends, and neighbors. When it is completed, be sure to distribute the homemade publication to those same family, friends, and neighbors and others.

FAMILY FLAG. Have everyone get together to design a family flag. If anyone in the family is handy with a sewing needle, you can make the flag at home. If not, you may be able to have the flag done professionally at a store that specializes in selling flags. Or just make the flag using crayons and construction paper.

FUN MEMORIES. Gather a dozen or more objects and place them on a tray. Have the kids study the tray for two or three minutes and then remove the tray. Whoever can remember the most items wins. Change the items and their number for variety.

BIRD DECORATIONS. Decorate a nearby tree or bush with nuts, berries, and other goodies for the birds to eat. Strings of cranberries and pine cones spread with peanut butter are great treats for birds. When the decorating is done, stake out the tree to look for different kinds of birds and try to identify them.

NATURAL SCAVENGERS. Make a scavenger hunt with a list of different kinds of leaves, flowers, rocks, and other things that you can find around your yard and send the children out in search of them for a home safari. In addition to being fun, this is a great way to help teach your kids about different kinds of trees and flowers.

WATER MUSIC. Make your own musical instrument by getting six tall glasses and filling them with different amounts of water. Now take a metal spoon and tap the different glasses lightly to hear the different sounds they make. Play with the spoon and other utensils to make up some musical tunes; the sound they make is similar to a xylophone.

BALLOON BASKETBALL. Using a trash bin or laundry basket as the basket, have the children line up behind a line and toss the balloon into the basket. This game can be a big hit at parties and even can be done from bed when a child is sick.

ACTIVITY FILE. Write down any ideas that come to you and clip articles from newspapers and magazines, listing activities that may slip your mind later. The next time you are stuck for an idea, you will have a folder full of suggestions.

Clothes and textiles

BUYING CLOTHES

THRIFTY SHOPPING. There are few things more enjoyable for many people than shopping for new clothes. But it may not be the wisest way to shop. Fashion is a multibillion-dollar industry that devotes huge sums of money to marketing new styles and selling more clothes. As a result, there is a surplus of clothes at large for most practical purposes. You can take advantage of this surplus by seeking out used clothing in thrift shops, secondhand stores, and tag sales. Many people will wear an item just a few times or even only once before discarding the garment. Thus, much of the "used" clothing that is for sale is hardly used at all. In many cases, worthy organizations such as The Salvation Army run the thrift stores, so you can pat yourself on the back for assisting a good cause and getting a deal for yourself.

HELPFUL SHOPPING CLOTHES. Before going out to shop for clothes, think about what you are wearing for the excursion. You will want to wear clothes that are easy to take off and on, a small amount of jewelry and undergarments, and shoes that will match whatever type of clothes you are planning to purchase.

OFF THE BEATEN PATH. Seek out newly established and little-known stores for the best deals. Many thrift stores in high-priced districts charge very high prices. Similarly, stylish boutique-type secondhand stores will often charge significantly more than an out-of-the-way thrift shop in an obscure corner of the city or in a more rural town. Tag sales are the best way to find the cheapest clothing, but they usually offer the least variety.

INTELLIGENT SHOPPING. Instead of launching a search for a clothing item when you must have it, spend some time browsing around secondhand stores and flea markets to get a sense of what is available where and the kinds of prices to expect. When the time comes to buy a specific item, you will be in a much better position.

TIMELY SHOPPING. Try to time your shopping for new clothes to coincide with sales. Clothing stores will usually hold a sale at the end of each season. Thus, if you are patient you can buy next year's winter clothing as this year's winter comes to an end.

KEEP A NOTEBOOK. If you are shopping for a family, be sure to keep a notebook listing sizes, color and style preferences, and clothing needs for each family member. When you are out shopping, this information will come in very handy. Also, carry a tape measure when you are shopping, especially if you are shopping in a used clothing store.

YOU GOTTA BE YOU. Try not to bow to fashionable trends in picking clothes. You have a distinctive style and know best what types of clothes match your style.

IRREGULARS VS. SECONDS. Clothes in new clothing stores marked irregular may not be perfect but their flaws are usually slight. On the other hand, a clothing item described as a Second, or, even worse, Third may have a substantial problem with it.

CHILDREN'S CLOTHES. When you see a deal in a new or used clothing store for children's clothes, do not be tempted to buy the item if your child is more than two years away from being able to wear the garment. Two years is a long time. You may discover your clothing tastes have changed, you may find an even better deal, or the same or similar item may be given as a present. You can manipulate the clothing stores sales to your advantage by waiting for end-of-the season sales and then buying clothes for the next year one or two sizes larger than the child's current size.

REPETITIVE SOCKS. This tip may only be good for unfashionable boys and men, but solve the problem of matching socks and losing single socks by simply buying all of the same brand and color sock. In that way if you lose a sock, the pair does not go to waste. Plus it will be easy to match socks when it comes time to sort the laundry.

SIGNS OF QUALITY

GOOD CLOTH = GOOD CLOTHES. It should come as no surprise that most good clothing is made from high quality cloth. Good quality cloth feels good resting on your skin. Inspect the clothing by holding it up to the sunlight or a bright light. In general, cloth that smells good and has patterns woven in rather than printed on tends to be better in other ways as well.

WATCH THE WEAVES. If you hold the fabric up to the sunlight or a bright light you can see the weave pattern. You want cloth that is done on perpendicular angles rather than on diagonals. If the weaving is done on an angle, the fabric may eventually sag to one side.

WATCH THE SEAMS. When you buy blue jeans check to make sure the seams do not twist down the pants at all. The problem will worsen with wear.

THE CRUNCH TEST. Crush the fabric in your hand briefly. The fabric should bounce back to its original form with a minimum amount of wrinkles or no wrinkles at all.

GOOD CONDITIONING. Check the clothing for its overall condition. While this is important for new clothes, it is especially vital for used clothes. Check the seat of the pants for wear and shiny spots. Pull at the seams to see if they are still tightly sewn, particularly under the collar and sleeves. Run the zippers up and down. Check the pockets for holes. And give a good sniff. Some of the problems may be correctable. Some may be telltale signs of excessive wear and tear or poor overall workmanship.

THE QUALITIES OF CLOTH. Different types of fabric have different characteristics to suit your needs. The following list gives a quick rundown on some of the qualities of some of the more common fabrics.

- Cotton. Durable, easy to iron and wash, and simple to mend. It is a very comfortable cloth to wear. Cotton shrinks and wrinkles easily.

- Wool. One of the best types of clothing for insulating body warmth. It is often loosely woven into jerseys or flannels. A natural fiber, it is durable and holds stitches well. The downside of wool is that it shrinks drastically in hot water and often needs to be hand-washed or dry-cleaned.

- Nylon. The first drip-dry synthetic fabric to be popularized, nylon is mainly used as a supplement to cotton and other fabrics to add strength. Its main quality as a stand-alone fabric is that it dries rapidly; this advantage is limited by the fact that it is made of plastic and thus is shiny, non-absorbent, and feels clammy to wear.

- Acrylic fabrics. Fabrics such as orlon are man-made attempts to imitate wool. Like nylon, its main advantage is that it is easily washed and dried. On the other hand, the fabric tends to lose shape after several washings unless allowed to dry on a towel.

- Polyester. Fabrics such as dacron are often stiff and feel like plastic. They are often used as a supplement to cotton to add strength and wrinkle resistance.

- Linen. The fibers are crisp and thin, giving the fabric a coolness and crispness, both desirable qualities. It is a very elegant cloth, but it is also expensive, wrinkles easily, and requires careful washing or dry cleaning.

- Silk. A strong, crisp fabric. It is very absorbent and resists wrinkling and mildew well. But it easily gets water spots and is damaged by perspiration and chlorine bleach.

- Plastic. The only reason to wear plastic clothing is for protection from rain and water. Most plastic clothing is airtight and thus does not allow your skin to breathe or let moisture escape from your body. Superclose-woven cotton is a better alternative for water resistance.

SMOOTH LININGS AND MATCHUPS. Good clothes have smooth linings and seams, stripes and plaids that match. Stitching is smooth and straight.

RUGGED ATTACHMENTS. The buttons on new clothes should be securely sewn on, as should the trims and pockets. Zippers should work smoothly.

GLOVE TEST. Test the quality of gloves by putting on the glove and clenching your fist. Pay attention to how comfortable the glove feels on your hand and the quality of the stitching.

MODIFIED AND REINFORCED CLOTHES

PREVENTATIVE PATCHES. Add iron-on patches to the insides of knees in pants and the elbows of shirts and jackets for a preventative strike against wearing the garment out early. For a sweater, weave some extra yarn into the elbow area.

REINFORCED BUTTONS. Strengthen the bond on your buttons by dipping a bit of clear nail polish on the center of each button to seal the threads.

DENTAL BUTTONS. Use dental floss for extra sturdiness in sewing on buttons. It may not have a lot of fashion value but it is much stronger than normal sewing thread.

EXTRA STITCHING. When you bring home a new clothing item, check it again for loose stitching. If you see any loose threads, secure them. If the seams are loose or the stitching looks poorly done, sew a new row of stitching.

EASY JACKET ZIPPING. Attach a key ring to the zipper on children's clothing to facilitate the child's grasp of the zipper.

POCKET PROTECTION. Stitch a small triangle at the corner of each pocket to strengthen the pocket and prevent holes from forming.

STITCHED LACES. Strengthen your or your children's shoelaces by stitching the laces with the sewing machine.

DYEING TO CHANGE. If you like everything about a piece of clothing except its color, consider dyeing. Dyeing really only works well with natural fibers, but light colors or clothes with light patterns can be transformed into new, deep colors to your liking. It is worth investing in more expensive professional dyes than in cheap dyes available in discount stores to make the clothes look especially good. However, remember that it is difficult to obliterate a very dark or brightly colored pattern and virtually impossible to dye old army clothes.

HOMEMADE STONEWASHED JEANS. Stonewash your jeans at home and without stones by drenching some towels in a solution of half water and half bleach and dumping them in the dryer with the dry jeans. Let the dryer run for 15 to 30 minutes, depending on your personal taste on how "washed" you would like the jeans to appear. Or you can add bleach to the water in the washing machine and throw the blue jeans in after you have drenched them with water from the sink.

STRETCHED PREVENTION. Add elastic to the cuffs of mittens and sweater sleeves to prevent stretching.

REPAIRING AND MAINTAINING CLOTHES

MENDING KIT. A good mending kit for clothes should include scissors, extra buttons, glue stick for basting and pinning, a tape measure, hand needles of all sizes, a magnet, pins, a bar of soap, threads of many different colors (including black, brown, grey and white), and hooks, eyes, and snaps.

UNSHRINKING WOOLENS. Mix a small amount of hot water with an ounce of Borax and then add the solution to a gallon of warm water. Place the shrunken woolen garment in the water and gently tug it back into the desired shape. Rinse the fabric in warm water with a splash of vinegar mixed in.

LOOSE CUFFS? If the cuffs of your woolen sweater have gotten too loose for your taste, dip the end of the sleeve in hot water and quickly dry it with a blow dryer.

CLEAN ZIPPING. If the zipper is running hard from dry cleaning, apply some soap on the teeth to lubricate it.

LEAD ZIPPING. A sticky zipper can be cured by rubbing it with a lead pencil.

SMOOTH ZIPS. To keep your zipper running smoothly, apply beeswax to the inside and outside. This will also help with the dust and dirt.

ZIPPER REPLACEMENT. Replacing zippers is not as difficult as you may think. The trick is to find a new zipper that is the same length as the one being replaced. When replacing the zipper, carefully snip off the threads and pin the new zipper on as you go along. In this way when the old zipper is removed, the new one is in place to be easily attached.

VELCRO SUBSTITUTE. Instead of a new zipper, consider attaching a velcro strip. It is a very useful substitute.

TAPED HEMS. Clear adhesive tape can be used to hold up a hemline in a pinch. You may have to skip appearances and use duct tape if the material is denim or another heavy fabric.

MEASURING TROUSER HEMS. The bottom of a pants leg should touch the top of the shoe in front and then taper down slightly to the back. Once you have measured the first leg, measure the second leg at the same length.

SIMPLER MEASURING. It may be easier in some cases when you mark a hemline to slip a rubber band around the appropriate spot on your ruler for measuring. In this way you do not have to strain your eyes each time to find the exact spot on the ruler to make your mark.

PATCHWORK REPAIRS. When adding a patch sew both the outer edge of the patch—with its ends turned under—to the garment and the area around the hole or rip. This will ensure that the patch is firmly attached.

PATCH SELECTION. Use strong cloth for patches. It is very difficult to conceal a patch so rather than even attempt it, go for a color that matches your style. Be bold.

POCKET PATCHES. In some cases you may want to use a patch as a pocket. Just leave the top portion of the patch unstitched. For light tears or decorative patches, the addition can serve as a useful pocket. You may also want to consider making knee patches like this to insert foam rubber or knee pads for gardening or other work that requires you to crawl on the ground.

SEWING BUTTONS. When sewing four-hole buttons, don't do all four button holes at once. Instead do two holes and then break the thread. The buttons will hold better this way.

CUTTING BUTTONHOLES. Using a razor blade, cut a buttonhole in the fabric with a bar of soap underneath.

LINGERIE REPAIRS. Place a piece of paper behind nylon lingerie or jackets when repairing seams. Simply stitch through the paper and the fabric. This will make it easier to sew the material. When you are done, rip off the paper.

BURR SLICING. Use a disposable razor to cut away burrs stuck in your sweater or pants.

PLASTIC PANTS PROLONGER. Prolong the life of your plastic pants by placing them in the dryer with a bunch of towels. This will also soften the pants if they have gone stiff.

DE-CREASING TIP. To eliminate a deep crease from an old hemline, press out the crease with an iron and then dampen the crease with soapy water and press it again with the iron on steam.

RECYCLED CLOTHES AND OTHER TEXTILES

TIES AS BELTS. Old neckties can be used as women's belts by simply braiding the ties together. Or you can sew a whole collection of old ties into a bold-looking skirt.

TIGHT SWEATERS AS CARDIGANS. Resuscitate a tight sweater by cutting it down the middle, stitching both sides, and adding buttons and corresponding button holes. Now your uncomfortable sweater is an elegant cardigan.

SWEATERS AS MITTENS. Just because your sweater is falling apart does not mean the whole thing has to go to waste. Mark out a pattern from your hand on the sweater with the cuffs of the sweater becoming the cuffs of the mittens. Sew the patterns together into new mittens.

SHIRTS AS APRONS. Old cotton shirts can be easily converted into aprons by cutting the sleeves and collar.

SHEETS INTO PILLOWCASES. Old sheets can be refashioned into pillowcases with relative ease.

DRESS PIECES. The parts may be greater than the whole when it comes to dresses. Instead of getting rid of an old dress, convert the top into a blouse and the bottom into a skirt.

STORING CLOTHES AND TEXTILES

STORE CLEAN AND DRY CLOTHES. Before storing clothes make sure they are well cleaned and thoroughly dry. Dampness will encourage mildew. Similarly, you do not want to store clothes in plastic bags that will trap moisture.

AIR CIRCULATION. Do not pack your clothes in the closet or bureau too tightly. You want air to circulate to keep your clothes dry and fresh.

MILDEW STOPPERS. Make sure closets are dry and well ventilated. Mothballs will help absorb moisture in the closet or drawers. An alternative to mothballs for absorbing moisture is several pieces of chalk.

MOTHBALLS. Mothballs will both absorb dampness and keep moths from your clothes. There are natural mothballs and many alternatives to the chemical mothballs that are as effective as the old-fashioned mothballs and safer. Mothballs are poisonous for pets and children. Keep them out of reach of children by hanging them in an old sock or stocking from the top of the closet. Mothball vapors are heavier than air, so you want to keep them high in any case.

KITTY LITTER DEODORANT. Leave a pot of kitty litter deodorant in a closet for a day or so to absorb the smell of mothballs.

ALTERNATIVES TO MOTHBALLS. Add crushed black pepper to your clothes as an alternative way of discouraging moths. A bag of cedar shavings added to the closet or clothes box will also do the trick. A few bars of soap tossed in the storage box will fend off the moths. Or hang cloves or rosehips in the closet with the clothes.

CEDAR CHESTS. There is no need to worry about moths if you use a cedar chest, which naturally repels the insects. Be sure to line cedar wood with acid-free paper to protect the clothes from resins.

SAVING CHILDREN'S CLOTHES FOR ANOTHER DAY. Develop a storage system for saving used children's clothing by using boxes marked according to the appropriate age and sex for the clothing. This system can be as complicated or as simple as you like. It establishes a way to store children's clothing for future use by your younger children.

PILLOWCASES AS STORAGE COMPARTMENTS. Use pillowcases to store different categories of clothing such as socks, underwear, informal clothing, and other articles that do not require careful folding.

ALTERNATIVE CHILDREN'S COAT HANGERS. For extra strength in hanging children's clothes, sew a key chain into the collar of shirts, blouses, or dresses to hang them from hooks.

TIGHT TOPS. When hanging clothes, be sure to button the top button. Clothes are designed to be hung in that manner.

WOOD OR PLASTIC OVER WIRE. Avoid using wire hangers. They rust and may misshape clothes.

RUBBER BAND ADDITION. If straps are slipping off the hanger, place rubber bands at strategic points on the hanger.

AROMATIC CLOTHING. Keep your clothes smelling fresh by sticking an open box of baking soda in the closet or hanging some potpourri. For the drawer, place a scented bar of soap in with the clothes. Mothballs will also counter the smell of the vapors.

CLOSET OR DRAWER? The rule of thumb on whether to hang a clothing item or fold it in the drawer is that looser fabrics such as knitted items and fine fabrics such as silks are folded instead of hung in closets. When storing folded items, place the lighter, more fragile clothing on top to avoid unnecessary creasing. Insert tissue paper to cut down on creases in folded items.

ROLLED LINENS. Try not to fold linens because they crease easily. Instead roll them for mid- to long-term storage.

SOCK RINGS. Use the plastic rings from milk bottles to hold matching pairs of socks together. You can even use the ring to hold the socks together in the washer and dryer.

ROLLED T-SHIRTS. Instead of folding T-shirts, roll them. This will save space and (if done carefully) can make it easy to identify the shirts without opening them.

TEXTILE TIPS

WAX REMOVAL. Remove candlewax that has melted on a tablecloth by rubbing ice on it and then scraping the wax off. Use rubbing alcohol or a solution of bleach and water to remove the wax dye. Or place paper towels above and below the wax and iron it.

RED WINE CLEANSING. If red wine is spilled on a tablecloth, first clean up much of the liquid with a disposable towel, moisten the spot, and then liberally cover the stain with salt. Let the salt absorb the wine for several minutes and scrape it off. Finally, clean the cloth as you normally would.

INKED UPHOLSTERY. Clean ballpoint ink marks from upholstery and clothing with rubbing alcohol.

SHEET SPLICING. Extend the life of your sheets by cutting them down the middle and then reattaching them at the opposite ends. The worn parts in the middle will now be on the edge and the fresh parts on the edge will now be in the middle.

SEWING AND OTHER NEEDLEWORK TIPS

BUTTON CONTAINERS. Use small glass jars to store different buttons. You can see through the glass to instantly identify the buttons.

BUTTON COLLECTIONS. When you discard an old shirt or other piece of clothing be sure to remove the buttons for future use. Save all the buttons by sewing them together. You will always be able to match them.

PILLOW SUPPORT. To lessen the strain on your back when hand sewing, place a pillow on your lap so you do not have to reach over to do your work.

THIMBLE ADJUSTMENTS. Dip your finger in water before putting on a sewing thimble. Suction will help secure the gadget to your finger. If your thimble is too loose, try placing thin pieces of adhesive tape on the inside until the thimble fits comfortably.

TOUGH THREAD. Strengthen your thread by pulling it through beeswax.

MARBLE DARNING. When sewing the ends of fingers in gloves, use a glass marble as a darning egg.

THREADING THE NEEDLE. Always cut a thread at an angle to simplify matters when you thread the needle. Do not break or bite the thread to break it. If you have difficulty threading the needle, try blasting the end with a bit of hair spray to stiffen the thread.

COOL SYNTHETIC THREADS. Store synthetic threads in the refrigerator to prevent them from attracting static electricity and collecting humidity, both of which make the thread difficult to manipulate. However, synthetic threads are not nearly as good as natural-fiber threads. Do not use them for sewing machines because they will jam.

HANDY SCISSORS. For easy access, string a ribbon through a small pair of good scissors and place the ribbon over your neck.

EASY MEASURING. Attach a tape measure to the base of your sewing machine for a handy ruler that you can use to easily measure thread.

MARKING SOAP. Use white soap as an alternative to marking chalk for marking clothes that you can wash.

CLEAN PUNCTURES. Rub soap over a piece of heavy fabric to soften it up for the needle to penetrate.

PINNED SOAP. Use a bar of soap instead of a pin cushion to stick needles into. The soap will both hold the needles and lubricate them at the same time.

NEEDLE SHARPENING. Stitch the sewing machine needle through a piece of fine sandpaper to sharpen it.

MARKED NEEDLES. Mark the end of a needle with a touch of paint or colored nail polish to easily distinguish the pointy end from the dull end.

COLLECTION TIME. Attach a magnet to the side of the sewing machine to hold needles in place while working. Use the magnet to pick up needles on the ground and a damp sponge to attract threads from the floor. Place a small bag on the edge of your sewing table to collect scraps.

DROPPED STITCH. When knitting, use a smaller needle to pick up a dropped stitch. This will create a stitch tighter than the loose one that would be made if you used the same needle.

MARKED CROCHET. Mark the spot where you are when you leave your crocheting with a clothespin to keep the last stitch in place.

SHOES, BELTS AND OTHER ACCESSORIES

TRY SANDALS. If you can, try wearing sandals. They are designed to let your feet breath and allow your feet to serve the purpose they were designed to serve. The best reason not to wear sandals is if you are working on a construction project or elsewhere that requires protection of your feet.

STARCHED SNEAKERS. Buy some spray starch with your sneakers. Spray it inside the sneaker to keep it clean and fresh longer. Spray starch on clean shoes will help prevent dirt from building up in the cloth.

NEW LACE TIPS. If the plastic tips have fallen off your shoelaces, dip the stringy ends in nail polish to seal them up.

PROTECTED HEELS. Apply clear nail polish to the heels of your shoes to help prevent scuffing.

SOLE PLUGGING. Plug a hole in the bottom of your shoe's soles by sticking a piece of cardboard or newspaper over the hole. For a more permanent solution apply a double layer of cloth tape over the hole. This will extend the life of the shoe by at least a couple of months if you do not wear it when it is wet outside.

WATERPROOFED SHOES. Enhance the water-resisting qualities of your shoes by spraying them with silicone.

TIRED HEELS. A sharp knife, a piece of rubber tire and wood, several short nails, and some expert cutting are all the ingredients you need to make a new heel for an old shoe. Remove the old heel before it is too worn down, carefully carve out the shape of a new heel from the rubber, and then hammer the rubber onto the piece of wood. Nail the wood into the shoe from the inside and then replace the inner sole.

ROUGHED UP HEELS. If your new shoes are slippery, rough the bottoms up quickly by rubbing them with sandpaper.

SHINY HEELS. Make your wooden heels shine by applying lemon oil.

SALT STAIN REMOVAL. Get rid of salt stains on your boots or shoes by wiping them with a heavy solution of water and white vinegar.

BUFFED WHITE SHOES. Use a crumpled piece of wax paper to buff white shoes after they have been polished.

SCUFFED WHITE SHOES. Rub white shoes with polish, dressmaker's chalk, or typewriter correction fluid to cover up scuff marks.

SCUFFED DARK SHOES. Cover up scuff marks in dark shoes with a crayon or magic marker that matches the color of the shoe.

"NEW" SUEDE SHOES. Dump a sponge in cold black coffee and wipe your suede shoes to restore the footwear's new look. You can also steam clean suede shoes by holding them over a pot of boiling water and letting the steam ooze into the suede. Use a soft brush or cloth to brush the steam. Always make the strokes go in the same direction. Be sure to let the shoes dry completely before wearing them again.

PATENT LEATHER SHINE. Make patent leather shoes shine by rubbing them with a bit of petroleum jelly.

LEMON FRESH SHINE. Add a couple of drops of lemon juice to the shoeshine polish to add some zest to the shine.

THE RAW POTATO RUB. Rub a raw potato on white shoes before applying white shoe polish to make the polish go on smoothly and evenly.

KEROSENE SOFTENING. Rub kerosene into boots and shoes that have been hardened by water. The kerosene will soften them.

SHOE STRETCHERS. If your shoes are too tight, try applying rubbing alcohol to the tight spots and sticking a shoe stretcher or block of wood in the appropriate place for several days.

NEWSPAPER BOOTS. Stuff crumpled newspapers inside of boots and shoes to absorb the smell. If the boots are wet, stick some wire mesh to hold the boots up for drying before placing the newspaper inside the boots.

BEST BELTS. The longest lasting belts are made of a solid strap of leather instead of laminated layers of leather. Body moisture and warmth tend to rot the threads that hold the leather together.

BELT STORAGE. Place some hooks along the bottom of a wooden hanger for an instant belt hanger.

STEAMED REFRESHMENT. Apply some steam heat to old ties and hats to refresh their appearance. Simply hold the item over a boiling kettle of water or hang it in the bathroom while taking a hot shower.

RESHAPING STRAW HATS. Soak a straw hat in salt water before trying to reshape it and then stuff the hat with newspaper to hold the new shape in place.

Pets

Pets can be a wonderful addition to any home. Medical evidence suggests that elderly people with pets live longer because of the companionship a dog or cat offers. People with pets tend to have lower blood pressure and cholesterol levels than people without pets, and they are less likely to suffer from heart disease. Pet fish and birds are proven to relieve stress for their owners.

It is important to bear in mind, however, that certain pets may not be appropriate for certain households. If you live in a one-room studio apartment, for example, you do not want to own an Irish wolfhound. If you are allergic to cat hair, don't get a cat. If you travel a lot and nobody is home for great stretches of time, you probably should not have a pet—it would not be fair to the animal.

Be aware that pets require time, money, and work. Dogs, cats, and even rabbits live up to 15 years, and some birds live past 50. Veterinarian bills, shots, and food all cost money. Even low-maintenance pets like fish require regular feedings and care. Be prepared to make a long-term commitment to your animal.

In selecting a pet, make sure that the needs and habits of the animal match your own situation. Do some homework before picking a pet, so you know what you are getting yourself in for.

GENERAL TIPS FOR PETS

GET THEE TO A LIBRARY. Go to the library to learn about the pet you want to acquire before you make the commitment. This will save time and money in the long run.

DOG AND CAT SHOWS. If you are not sure what kind of dog or cat to get, go to a dog or cat show and look around. When a particular breed strikes your fancy, ask an owner about the pet. Is it high strung? Does it like children?

Is it easy to take care of? How often does it need to be groomed? Pet owners are often the best people to give advice and usually happy to give it.

CAGES. Cages are good. Many dog owners swear by cages, using them to transport or even house dogs. Remember that wild dogs and their relatives live in dens, so it is not cruel to put your dog in a cage. A good cage is crucial for the transportation of any animal, except of course fish.

CARS AND SUMMER. Never keep an animal in the car during hot summer days. It is extremely dangerous to your pet.

IDENTIFICATION. Always make sure your pets are properly tagged, identified by a name, address, and telephone number.

WATER. Keep your pets supplied with a steady supply of clean water. This is especially true for pets that eat dry food. In the summer, you can keep the water cool by putting ice cubes in it.

HEALTH. Make sure your pet has all of the appropriate vaccinations. Keep written records of its medical history.

POISONS. Many household items are poisonous to pets. Unfortunately, they may also be attractive to pets. Car antifreeze tastes good to dogs and cats but can be fatal, as are pellets that kill slugs, and pesticides for ants, roaches, and other pests. Certain houseplants such as oleanders, caladium, English ivy, elephant's ears, philodendrons, and monsteras are poisonous to cats. Always keep these items out of reach of pets.

RADIO SALVATION. Leave the radio on when you are gone to keep your pets company.

POSITIVE REINFORCEMENT. Pets have feelings too. Just like people, they want to be loved—even cats. The best way to ensure having a friendly and cooperative pet as a companion is to display affection and positive reinforcement to your pets. Experienced dog owners say you can often tell the characteristics of a person by the behavior of their dogs. Always praise good behavior. A well-treated dog is eager to please.

REPRODUCTION. If you do not want your pets to reproduce, have your pet spayed or neutered. Animal shelters are overflowing with unwanted cats and dogs. Don't add to the problem.

PET DIPLOMACY. If you already have a pet at home and are adding a new pet to the household, let the animals get used to each other slowly. For example, section off an area for the new cat or dog with a gate or other obstacle that allows the old pet to see and become familiar with the newcomer before they start to interact directly.

DOGS

Selecting a dog and bringing him home

SELLERS. Buy dogs from breeders or animal shelters. Do not get them from pet stores. Dogs at pet stores are usually raised in dog farms where they often are not properly treated.

PUPPY PARENTS. If you can see a puppy's parents, do so. Puppies, like children, often grow up with temperaments similar to their parents.

AGE. The best time to get a puppy is when it is six to ten weeks old.

VETERINARIANS. Have a veterinarian look at any animal you are thinking of acquiring. It is best to have a professional examine the dog for some of the telltale signs of poor health. In general, you want a puppy or dog to have the following characteristics:

- The eyes should be bright and alert.
- The body should be well proportioned.
- The skin and ears should be clear and smell clean.
- The coat should be smooth.
- The dog should seem happy and not too boisterous.

PEDIGREES VS. MIXED BREEDS. Mixed breeds are usually more stable and less fragile than pedigree breeds, which tend to be more high strung.

BIG DOGS, LITTLE DOGS. Big dogs tend to be more expensive to care for, small dogs tend to bark a lot more. Male dogs are more likely to roam than female dogs, who usually prefer to stay home.

COMFORT CLOTHS. To make the puppy feel comfortable when it is brought home, take a piece of clothing or cloth with its mother's scent on it and place it in the new puppy's own area.

Feeding

RECYCLED WATER. Reuse water from cooking vegetables to mix with your dog's dry food. This will provide vitamins and extra flavor.

DOG DISHES. A rubber suction cup at the bottom of the dog dish will help prevent your dog from pushing the dish all over the kitchen floor.

DOG DISHES II. If your dog has tendency to knock over his dish, place it outside and drive a stake through the middle of it. For the water dish you can use an old upside down bunt cake pan with a stake holding the center in place.

BONES. Never give your dog real bones to chew. Splinters from the bones can choke or even kill the dog. Instead use rawhide bones. A constant supply of rawhide bones may discourage him from taking an interest in chewing other items such shoes or the furniture.

RAW EGGS. Giving your dog raw eggs on an occasional basis will help make its coat shine.

General care

STRESS. Some problems with dogs such as vomiting, skin allergies, and diarrhea may be caused by stress and boredom. If this is the case, try to change the dog's environment to relieve the cause. Consult your veterinarian to both make sure the problem is not caused by something else and for advice on how to change the conditions that may be creating the stress or boredom.

BARK PREVENTION. There are several tactics to stop your dog from barking. One is to sharply reprimand him either verbally or by yanking his collar when he barks, and reward him with hugs and praise when he obeys commands not to bark. If your dog barks when he is left alone, try leaving a radio on with him. With puppies you may want to leave an old clock in their blanket. The tick-tocks offer reassurance. Finally, you may want to fake leaving the house. When your dog barks, return and reprimand him. When he does not bark, hug him. Do this repeatedly.

YES, BARK. If you do want your dog to bark on command, say to your dog "Bark" or "Speak" or another word and then do something to make it bark such as banging on the table. As soon as the dog barks, give it a lot of praise. Practice this repeatedly until your dog responds on a reliable basis. To stop him from barking, select another term such as "Stop" and use it firmly. Once the dog stops barking, again give the dog a lot of praise.

INJURIES. If a dog is injured, approach him carefully. Carefully wrap a cloth around his muzzle to prevent him from biting. Do not do this if the dog is vomiting or bleeding from the mouth. Use a blanket to transport the dog by placing it under the dog and using it as a stretcher. With the help of others you can then move him without disturbing his injury.

Housetraining and odors

THE NEWSPAPER TACTIC. There are several ways to housetrain a puppy. One is to fill the puppy's room with newspapers and let the puppy select his or her own site for relieving himself. Once that location is picked, remove the newspapers from the rest of the room. Then gradually move the newspaper toward the door. Eventually, remove the newspaper entirely. The dog will know that he can relieve himself only outside the door.

THE CAGE TACTIC. By placing your dog in an open-sided cage when he is not playing, eating, or exercising, you are giving your dog its own territory. If the cage is fairly small, the dog will not soil its home. This approach, like the newspaper strategy, is predicated on you the owner bringing the dog outside regularly so he can relieve himself properly. If the dog is whining, barking, or appears to be uncomfortable, it is likely that he has to relieve itself. Bring the dog outside as quickly as possible when this happens.

REMOVAL. If the dog relieves itself in an unwanted place, remove the material with an old dust pan and sponge. Apply vinegar or lemon juice, then scrub with warm, soapy water. Sponge, dry, and repeat.

ODOR REDUCTION. Sprinkle baking soda or cornmeal on accident sites to cut down on the smell. Leave it there for a couple of hours and brush off the excess, then vacuum. If this does not work, there are special solutions available at pet stores.

SCOLDING. Only scold your dog when you catch him in the act. A dog's memory is short and he may not know what he is being scolded for later. Do not rub your dog's nose in its own feces. The dog's interpretation of this may be to eat the feces.

POSITIVE REINFORCEMENT. Teaching a dog to be housetrained is not just about punishing him. It is just as important, if not more so, to offer the dog positive encouragement when he relieves himself outside.

HITTING. Do not hit your dog, or any other pet, for any reason. It is unnecessary and cruel. It only makes the animal nasty and stressed.

HOMEMADE POOPER SCOOPER. To scoop the poop more easily from your lawn, sidewalks, and streets, make a pooper scooper by attaching plastic painter trays cut in half to the bottom of two broom handles.

Grooming and baths

BETTER EARLY THAN LATE. The earlier you get your dog used to regular brushing, baths, and grooming, the better. Start as early as possible. Make brushing a pleasure for both you and your dog by playing, talking, and reassuring him while you brush his hair.

VACUUM. Believe it or not, many dogs do not mind being vacuumed. A vacuum cleaner can not only be used to help get fleas and molting hair, but also helps clean the dog's coat. You may have to train your dog to tolerate the vacuum. Try gradually introducing the vacuum to the dog first without turning it on, then with it on but not placing it on the dog, and finally vacuuming the dog. Offer constant reassurance while you are doing this.

OATMEAL AND BAKING SODA. Oatmeal and baking soda can be used to help groom your dog's coat. Dry oatmeal rubbed into a dog's hair will help bring grease and dirt out when you brush it. Baking soda will help deodorize his coat. Do not use baking soda on dogs that must restrict their intake of sodium.

BURRS. You can remove burrs from your dog's hair by either carefully crushing the burr with a pair of pliers and then removing it or applying a dab of shampoo or light oil, waiting a little bit and then combing the burr out.

GUM. Let gum harden and then cut off the hair that it is stuck in.

BATHS. Before giving your dog a bath, make sure he has relieved himself, is in a good mood, and well brushed. Once you have finished lathering the dog with shampoo in a warm environment, make sure you rinse him thoroughly and then dry him. To help make his coat shine, add lemon or vinegar with a little baking soda to his coat while your washing him. Add baking soda to the dog's bathwater to add luster and softener to the dog's coat when you are shampooing.

DRAINS. If you wash your dog in a bathtub, place a steel-wool pad in the drain to catch the hairs.

SHAKE, SHAKE, SHAKE. To prevent your dog from shaking water and soap all over the place, wash his head last. A wet head leads the dog to want to shake himself dry. To prevent soap from seeping into his eyes, put down a thin layer of petroleum jelly over the eyebrows.

Fleas

FLEAS AND THEIR ENVIRONMENT. Fleas don't just live on dogs and cats. They also reside in homes. Just treating fleas on your pet or your home separately will not work. You have to banish fleas from both your pet and your home to do the job properly.

OUNCE OF PREVENTION. To help prevent fleas, rub brewer's yeast on the dog's coat. Many people suggest adding brewer's yeast to your dog's food to keep fleas from developing. Fennel, rosemary, or rue also work.

FLEA BATHS. Mixing orange oil and shampoo for weekly dog baths will help remove fleas.

CHEMICAL FLEA COLLARS. Recent evidence shows that flea collars laced with chemicals may be bad not only for the fleas, but also for the dogs. Try other alternatives before taking this route.

FLEA TRAP. To catch fleas in your house, make your own homemade flea trap. Take a low dish or shallow pan and fill it with dishwashing detergent mixed with water. Place it in the middle of the room. At night turn off all the lights with the exception of one lamp that is focused over the pan. The fleas will go for the light and fall into the dish. Keep the trap and lighting system in place for at least two weeks to make sure you get all of the fleas, as well any fleas that had not hatched when the trap was set.

SALT. To cut down on fleas in your house, sprinkle salt in areas where your pet lounges and vacuum it 10 to 15 minutes later.

Transporting

TOWELS. Place a damp towel over a pet's travel cage to keep it cool during the summer and cut down on static electricity.

SAFETY. Never, ever leave a dog or any pet in a car with all the windows closed. If you have to leave your pet in the car, leave it in the shade with the windows slightly open.

FOOD AND WATER. On trips, bring food and water from home to feed your dog. This will help the dog adjust to the disruption. In the case of water, the dog will not have to adjust to unusual microbes.

WALKS. Before going on an extended trip, give your dog a good, long walk. During the trip, whenever possible, stop every two to three hours so the dog can stretch its legs, relieve itself, and drink.

KENNELS. If you are traveling and cannot take your dog along with you, see if a friend or relative will take care of the dog. If not, you can use a kennel. But visit the kennel first to make sure it is clean and the people who work there are reasonable. When you drop off your dog leave a toy, towel, or rag from home with him so he will have a scent from home for reassurance.

Miscellaneous

CHILDREN'S WANTS. If your children are dying to have a dog and you're not, do your neighbors a favor and have your children walk their dog for a month. If the kids still want a dog, at least they've proven themselves.

DOG BOOTS. If your dog is bothered by salt and ice on its pads when it goes for walks, you can make dog boots out of baby booties, small socks, or golf-club covers. Socks may also be used to secure bandages to a dog or cat's leg.

CHEWED WOOD. To protect wood from dogs that chew, sprinkle the wooden object with cayenne pepper, red pepper, or oil of cloves.

ALLERGY-FREE. Some dog breeds (including poodles, miniature schnauzers, and Kerry blue terriers) do not shed and may not affect people with allergies.

DOG TRACKS. To cut down on dog tracks in your home, carry a small towel with you when you go for walks with your dog on rainy or snowy days. When you return home, immediately wipe the dog's feet with the towel. This will save time and aggravation later.

OLD SHOES. Do not give your dog an old shoe to chew. This may lead him to believe that it is acceptable to chew any and all shoes.

DIGGING. If your dog persists in digging up a spot, you may want to bury some crushed toilet freshener cake there. Dogs do not like the smell.

SHEDDING. To remove dog or cat hair from furniture or clothes, either roll some masking tape around your hand and use it to pick up the hairs or use a damp sponge. For baseboards and wooden furniture, use a dampened paper towel.

THUNDER. Many dogs go berserk in thunderstorms. To relieve thunder induced anxiety, try the following approach. First, get your dog comfortable by having him sit or lie down and give him a treat. Next, turn on a tape recording of thunder very softly. Give the dog another treat. Gradually increase the volume of the thunder, praising the dog and rewarding him with a treat with each increase in the volume. Then reduce the volume. Repeat this exercise several times.

DOGFIGHTS. Do not dive into a fight between dogs to break it up. Dogs have been known to inadvertently bite their owners quite badly. Instead, try the following tactics. (1) Make a very loud noise to distract the dogs—don't shout, this may make it worse. (2) Throw a blanket on top of quarreling dogs. (3) Grab their rear legs and yank the animals away from each other.

SKUNKS. Dogs sometimes like to play with skunks even if skunks don't like to play with dogs. If your dog has been sprayed by a skunk, there are several options on how to remove the odor. You may:

- Give the dog a bath with tomato juice.
- Bathe the animal with a combination of equal parts vinegar and water.
- Bathe the dog with a solution of two packets of Massengil Douche Powder available at drugstores and grocery stores.

CATS

Selecting

NEW KITTENS. Look for kittens that appear healthy and happy. Look for clean and dry ears, a pink mouth with white teeth, a smooth coat, and a damp nose. They should be lively and inquisitive.

PROVISIONS. You should give your new cat a bed, litter box, and its own water and food bowls. If you get a grown cat, one tactic to make him comfortable in his new home is to place a dab of butter on his paws.

VACCINATIONS. The arrival of a new cat or kitten should correspond with a trip to the veterinarian to make sure the cat has all the appropriate vaccinations and is given a thorough checkup.

Feeding

DIET. Cats need protein and they like variety. Bear these two thoughts in mind when you shop for cat food.

CARNIVORES. Cats, like their brethren in the wild, are carnivorous, so do not try to impose any vegetarian habits on them.

SARDINES. To help prevent your cat's fur from balling and ease constipation, give your cat a sardine about once a month.

MILK. If your cat has diarrhea, its digestive system may not accept milk. Most cats prefer water to milk.

WATER. If you feed your cat dry food, give it plenty of water. Dry food may cause bladder and kidney problems. Make sure that you give your male cat pure water. Water with salt or chemicals can cause urinary tract disease leading to fatal kidney failure.

Housetraining, kitty litter, and odors

INSTRUCTION. It is generally far easier to housetrain a cat than a dog. Usually you can just show the cat the kitty litter, take its paw, and run it through the kitty litter.

ORANGE PEELS. To prevent your cat from relieving itself in undesirable areas in your garden, scatter orange peels in those locations. Cats don't like the smell and will stay away.

LEMON EXTRACT AND AMMONIA. If your cat urinates in the same spot in the house, you can discourage it by dipping a cotton ball in lemon extract and hanging the ball in an aluminum tea ball at the location. Keep the lemon fresh on a weekly basis until the problem is solved. Or you can rub the spot with ammonia. The cat won't do it there again.

ALUMINUM FOIL. To stop a cat from repeating its offenses, cover the area with aluminum foil. Gradually cut back on the size of the foil for about a month until there is only a small piece left.

ALTERNATIVE KITTY LITTER. Sand, wood shavings and peat can be used as an alternative to kitty litter. For long-haired cats, do not use peat because it will stick to their coats.

DEODORIZED LITTER. Baking soda on the bottom of the kitty litter pan will help keep down the odor. Adding one part borax to six parts litter will also remove the smell.

EASY CLEANING. For easy cleaning of the kitty litter, use a plastic lining or garbage bag as the lining for the kitty litter pan. When it is time to remove the kitty litter, all you need to do is lift out the plastic. Clean the kitty litter often. Cats are clean animals. They don't like dirty kitty litter either, so if the kitty litter is dirty they may seek other more desirable places for them but less desirable places for you.

KITTY LITTER USES. Kitty litter doesn't just have to be for cats. You can use it to absorb oil, fill dolls, toys, and beanbags, deodorize garbage cans, and preserve flowers in airtight containers.

FLEAS. Cats get fleas just like dogs. For information on removing fleas, see the Fleas section under Dogs. Warning: Do not use dog flea spray for cats; it could be poisonous to them.

Grooming

BATHS. Cats generally keep themselves pretty clean. They usually need a bath only if grease or grime gets on them and they cannot cleanse themselves.

MANICURES. When trimming cat's claws do not cut the vein of the cat's nail. The vein runs about two-thirds to three-fourths the length of the nail. File the nail after cutting. By pinching the cat's toe between your fingers, you can force the claw to extend.

MATTED HAIR. Use a seam ripper to pry apart badly matted hair before regular brushing.

LONG-HAIR TIPS. Brush talcum power or fuller's earth into the coats of long-haired cats to prevent matting. Brush it off immediately. Frequent grooming will keep the hair handsome and tangle-free.

SHORT-HAIRED TIP. Use a piece of silk, velvet, or chamois leather cloth to polish a coat of short hair. This will make the coat appear glossy.

WHISKERS. Do not cut or trim a cat's whiskers for any reason.

Transporting

CARRIERS. It is best to transport cats in cat carriers. If one is not available, you can use two laundry baskets laced together. You do not want your cat running about free in your car while you are driving. He poses a hazard to the driver.

PLACING THE CAT IN THE CARRIER. Try not to wait until the last minute to put the cat in the carrier and don't chase the cat around the house. Prepare the carrier early by having it open in a convenient location. At a quiet moment, lift your cat up with one hand and comfort it with the other. Then, place it in the carrier with its rear going in first.

COMFORT CLOTHS. To lessen the discomfort of being cooped up in a carrier for your cat, place a familiar blanket or piece of clothing in the carrier.

COOLING OFF. In hot weather, cover the carrier with a wet towel.

LEAVING A CAT BEHIND. If you cannot take your cat with you, you may want to leave him behind and have a neighbor or friend feed him on a daily basis. Cats can take care of themselves for up to 48 hours at a time as long as there is food available. When you are packing, however, keep the cat locked up. It may panic and bolt from the house.

Miscellaneous

SCRATCHING. Rub wooden furniture legs with chili sauce to prevent cats from scratching them.

TREETOP RESCUES. Is your cat stuck in a tree? Leave it. The rule of thumb is that if your cat can climb up a tree, it can—and will—also climb down.

SCRATCHING POSTS. A scratching post will discourage a cat from scratching upholstered furniture. You can make the post yourself; it should be about 2 feet high on an 18-inch base. Or you can buy one.

CAT TOYS. Cats like open paper bags laying on the ground to play with, ping pong balls to knock about, and crumpled paper hung by a piece of string to bat around.

CAT JUMPING. To stop a cat from jumping onto the kitchen counter or furniture, either place several aluminum baking pans near the edge so they will fall and make a racket when the cat lands or tie some inflated balloons that will pop. Cats hate loud noises.

SQUIRT GUNS. Cats are not dumb. They generally do not need to be punished severely for any type of training. If you would like to keep a cat from a certain area, shoot water from a squirt gun or mist sprayer at the cat when he enters the area. He will eventually give up.

VOMIT. The best way to remove cat vomit is to let it dry first—gross as this may be —and then scrape it with a knife or flat edge.

POTTED PLANTS. To keep cats from digging in your houseplants you can cover the plants with a nylon net, chicken mesh, marbles, or almost anything else that blocks the soil.

WINDOWS. As horrid as it may sound, many cats are injured or killed from falling out of open windows. If your cat lives in a high-rise apartment, make sure that all the windows are screened.

FISH

SELECTING FISH. In picking out fish for your aquarium you want to make sure your fish appear healthy and are compatible with each other. Some fish are more aggressive than others, and some combinations of fish should be avoided. Consult a pet store owner or experienced fish owners for advice on the behavior of different species.

ADDING FISH. Fish tend to be territorial. When you add a new fish to an aquarium you may want to rearrange the tank decorations to disrupt the territories and thus make conflicts between new and old fish less likely. To ease a new fish's adjustment to the tank's water temperature, do not simply dump the fish in the aquarium. Instead, place the plastic bag in which you carried the fish home in the water for 15 to 20 minutes before releasing the fish.

DECORATIONS. Do not place sea shells that have not been properly treated in the fish tank. Dirty decorations can contaminate the water. Buy tank decorations that have been varnished. To clean decorations, soak them in a solution of water and bleach (16 parts water to one part bleach) for a week and then rinse the decorations very thoroughly.

CHANGING THE WATER. Fish tank water should be changed regularly. By replacing about a third of the water on a weekly basis, the tank will be kept fresh. The easiest way to remove water is to siphon it out with plastic tubing or a hose. Fill the tube with water from a faucet and pinch both ends. Place one end of the tube in the tank and put the other in a pail below the fish tank. The water will flow from the tank to the pail. After removing enough water, refill the tank with fresh water.

FERTILIZER. Used water from *fresh* water fish tanks is a good fertilizer for your plants. Rather than simply discarding the water when you are finished with it, use it to water your plants. Do *not* use salt water on your plants.

BIRDS

RAISED AS PETS. Only buy birds that have been bred and raised in captivity. Many wild birds, including endangered species birds, are captured for commercial use. In addition to often being illegal, this is also cruel.

TWO'S A JOY. Birds like company. If you do not plan to be a constant companion to your bird, get more than one. If you have only one bird, make sure he has bells and activities to occupy himself. Keep the radio on when nobody is at home.

BIRD IN THE HAND. To pick up a bird, hold it in the center of its body and place your fingers on either side of its neck.

CAGES. Cages should be appropriate for the size of the bird. They should include a birdbath, perches, and swings. Line the cage with layers of newspapers. In this way, you can clean the cage by simply removing one layer at a time. You should clean the cage on a regular basis, as often as once a week depending on the number of birds.

SUNLIGHT. Birds like both the sun and the shade. Try to find a spot for the cage that has partial sunlight to allow it to bask in the sun and cool off in the shade.

DIET. Birds like green vegetables, seeds, fruit, mineral blocks, egg, cat chow, and dry dog food. Water should be changed daily.

CAT ATTACKS. If your cat likes to stalk or attack your bird, place the cage on a pedestal or hang it from a ceiling. If it persists, spray the cat with a squirt gun or plant mister when it is on the prowl.

CUTTLEBONE. Birds like to sharpen their beaks and claws on pieces of cuttlebone, which can be wedged into the side of the bird cage.

PARAKEET BEAKS. Parakeets need their beaks and claws trimmed by a veterinarian if they appear to be getting too long. If its claws get too long, the bird may not be able to perch properly. When the beak gets too long, it curls around to the point where the bird can no longer eat.

TRAVEL. Despite their wings, birds do not like to travel. It is very unsettling. Whenever possible try to have somebody tend to your birds when you are away.

RODENTS

PLASTIC DISHES. Do not use plastic dishes to hold food for rodents. They may eat the dish.

PREGNANT? When you buy a female rodent, find out how long it has been with other rodents in the store. The longer it has been cooped up with its peers, the more likely it is to be pregnant.

CONTAINERS. Do not use cardboard boxes to transport rodents except for very short trips. The animals can eat their way out of the box.

SOLITARY HAMSTERS. Hamsters are solitary animals and will often fight if you place more than one in a cage. Other rodents are more sociable and prefer company. Unless you want to multiply your stock of rodents, do not mix males and females in the same cage.

ESCAPEES. If your mouse, gerbil, guinea pig, or rabbit escapes and you do not have time to chase him down, place the animal's favorite food in its container near the area where you think he is hiding to try to lure him back.

BATH REFUGE. When cleaning a small rodent's cage, put him in the bath-tub. He can't climb the tub's slick walls.

Gerbils and hamsters

LIFTING. Do not pick up gerbils by their tails. Instead, put something on your hand for the gerbil to eat and let him come to you.

DIET. Pellets, nuts, fruit, or vegetables may be given to gerbils. Don't be alarmed if your gerbil eats its own feces. Gerbils need some green food such as grass, dandelion, or clover every day. Do not feed them carrots because it will stain their fur, and avoid cabbage because it make their urine smell.

PLAYGROUND. A gerbil likes to be active so install a wheel for it to play on and put in lots of wood chips or sawdust for it to dig tunnels through.

Mice

FEMALES. Try to pick female mice as pets. They tend to be less smelly and more alert, sleek, active, and curious.

ESCAPEES. To catch an escaped mouse, herd it into an open shoe box.

CAGES. Do not use newspaper to line cages, which should be at least two cubic feet. The ink from newspapers is bad for mice. Instead, use sawdust, sand, or hay.

MOUSE PLAYGROUND. Mice like to keep active. Install an exercise wheel and use toilet roll centers, wooden branches, and other items to make a jungle gym.

DIET. Mice like variety in their diet. Seeds, nuts, mice pellets, brown bread, and dried dog food all can be given to mice. If you have access to an oak tree, you may want to gather acorns for your mice. You can preserve the acorns by putting them in the freezer.

Rabbits

LIFTING RABBITS. Never pick a rabbit up by its ears. Instead, grab the rabbit's loose skin by its shoulders with one hand and place the other hand under the animal.

DIET. Feed rabbits pellets from the pet store as well as a limited diet of greens, carrots, grass, and lettuce. Too many greens will give the rabbit diarrhea.

HOUSEBREAKING. To housebreak a rabbit, put it in an enclosed area. When the rabbit relieves itself, place a kitty litter tray at that location. The rabbit will return to the spot. Clean the tray on a daily basis.

Getting organized

When it comes to household organizations, genetics seems to prevail. Some people are so well organized that they have files on their magazine subscriptions and have a written schedule of meals for the month. Others literally do not plan more than 10 minutes into the future and are lucky to find a pair of socks that match in the morning. And there doesn't seem to be much you can do to alter the behavior of either group.

No matter how many tips are offered to the poorly organized person, he or she will never implement the tools of a structured household. And for the truly well organized person, there is no reason to read a bunch of tips on a subject he or she already knows.

Nevertheless, most of us fall somewhere in between these two categories. We have some organizational abilities and would like to be better organized. The good news is that there are many simple ways to better organize your household that do not require a significant change in lifestyle. The bad news is that a well organized person is usually well disciplined and will follow a routine on a regular basis. If you do not have these two qualities or cannot nurture them, then you may be destined to start from scratch constantly to organize yourself or your household.

Well organized people write things down, don't let things pile up, keep their homes constantly stored with basics, finish what they start, and are persistent in completing a task. If you have all or most these traits, then you are well on the way to having an organized household.

STARTING FROM SCRATCH

DEPERSONALIZING A MESS. It is almost inevitable that in a household with more than one person, there will be a difference of opinion over how the house should be organized and what constitutes a, serious mess. The reason why the play, movie, and television series "The Odd Couple" did so well was that so many people identified with the conflicts of Felix the neatness fanatic and Oscar the hopeless slob. If you are in such a house- hold, try always to respect the perspective of the other person and at the same time appreciate other points of view on your own behavior. Do not let these differences become personal issues. It is very rare indeed that a person likes to tidy things up—or make a mess—just to irk his or her spouse or children.

ORGANIZATIONAL TOOLS. Some of the tools you will need for an organized home are a highlighter, labels, color-coded stickers, files, folders, a retractable knife, a Swiss Army knife, hooks, a tape measure, a spiral note- book, a loose-leaf notebook, a Rolodex, and pens and pads for lists.

STARTING FROM SCRATCH. When you tackle a major project (whether it's a filing cabinet, the attic, or an overflowing closet), the best strategy is usu- ally to start from scratch. Take everything out, spread the items on the floor, and start organizing.

FAIR WARNING. Before attacking a major pile or cleaning out the attic, give fair warning to all family members that you are about to embark on this project. Many collections of valued comic books, baseball cards, and childhood toys have ended up in a dumpster to the horror of their owners because of the unilateral decisions of the cleanser.

UNILATERAL DECISION MAKING. With the above as a caveat, when it comes time to clean out the attic, basement, or overflowing closet, it is often best to make the decisions by yourself as to what goes and what stays. Some tough decisions may have to be made, so you do not want messy senti- mentalism and overly tender feelings to get in the way.

THIS STAYS, THAT GOES. As you plow through the mess, separate items into three categories: things that you want to keep, things to give away, and things to throw away. Have several large trash bags on hand as well as boxes to place the items in the different categories. Once you have deter- mined what to keep, break that category down into other groupings according to where they should go in the house. These groupings could include items that need to be repaired, returned to the owner, belong in different rooms, and should be included in a future tag sale. You may want to create a pile of items you are not sure how to handle and save tak- ing action on it until you are done with everything else.

HARDEN YOUR HEART. In deciding what goes in the trash, try not to let sentiment get the best of you. This does not mean you have to throw away your first letters to your spouse, but do think hard about whether you really want to keep old shirts that no longer fit or are badly tattered, some ratty plates from your younger days, or other items of marginal nostalgic value and little practical use.

CLOTHING CRITERIA. The rule of thumb for clothes is that if you have not worn the item in at least a year, you should seriously consider discarding or giving the item to family, friend, or a charity.

CRITERIA FOR FURNITURE. When deciding whether to keep furniture—which is generally large and bulky—think hard about whether you or your children will ever have cause to use it again for storage, a college dorm, or an informal recreational room. If not, get rid of it.

CATEGORIZE AS YOU GO. Although you may be able to think of categories to place items you want to keep as you organize the clutter of a closet, cabinet, attic, or basement, there is no reason why you should not establish new or different categories as you go. You will not be able to think of every category at the outset and you will often think of better ways to categorize as you progress.

CLEAN AS YOU GO. So long as you are in the straightening-up mode, it is a short and easy step to clean up as you reorganize a portion of your house. As you clean out shelves, wipe them as you go with a rag, dust obscure corners, and clean wherever it is needed. You may not have the opportunity to clean these areas again for a long time, so take advantage of the fact that you have already removed the clutter to clean what is underneath or behind.

DON'T STOP. Once you have started a major reorganization project, do not stop until you are finished other than for short breaks. You may not get back to the project for a long time.

THE IMPORTANCE OF LABELING. If you think that labeling a box is a chore, just think about how much of a chore it will be to find that one item in the 15 boxes in your attic that you have not labeled. It is difficult to be too specific in the labeling of any box that you place in storage.

STORAGE TOOLS. When it comes time to sort and store all of the items you have decided to keep, make sure you have the appropriate storage spaces and tools. There is only so much you can do with a bare floor in the attic or a single rod for hanging clothes in the closet. Filing cabinets, kitchen cabinets, boxes, old book shelves, and even custom-made organizational units should be acquired for efficient storage space.

EVERY ITEM IN ITS APPROPRIATE PLACE. A good rule to follow when decided where and how to store things is to place items in containers that are the appropriate size. In other words, keep small items such as jewelry in small boxes and on narrower shelves. It makes things more manageable as well as efficient.

DESIGNATED WORK CENTERS. Designate an area or areas for routine tasks such as paying bills, sorting the mail, making breakfast, or doing the laundry, and equip and design those areas for maximum efficiency.

THE FAMILY BULLETIN BOARD. To improve communication in a family with two or more children, place a bulletin board in a centrally located spot to leave messages and reminders for family members to pass on to each other. You can expand the board to include stations for leaving lost items, mail, and messages.

CALLING IN A PRO. There are professional organizers who will visit your home, scrutinize the mess, and come up with a system to meet your needs. You should only consider seeking professional help if you intend to be serious about executing the suggestions. Otherwise, the professional organizer's visit will merely be an organized interlude in the ongoing chaos known as your home.

CLUTTER CONTROL

OLD CABINETS. Old kitchen cabinets are wonderful vehicles for holding items in attics, basements, large closets, or the garage. The mixture of drawers, shelves, and cabinet space offers natural storage space for many different types of household items.

HOMEMADE MAGAZINE HOLDER. To make your own magazine holder, take the top off a detergent box and cut the box at an angle from the top of one side to the bottom third or half of the other side.

ROLLING STORAGE. Use the space under a bed as storage space by placing wheels on an old drawer. You can place all sorts of items in the drawer and gain access to it easily in this out-of-the-way spot..

LUGGAGE. Save space when you store your luggage by placing smaller pieces of luggage inside larger pieces.

QUICK DECLUTTERING. If you want to quickly straighten up a room, first remove all the items that do not belong, then stack all the magazines, put misplaced items in the room back in their place, and quickly vacuum all the open spaces.

MARKING THE SPOT. If you are cleaning or reorganizing a shelf filled with various items that you would like to put back in place when you are done, mark the spots that items belong with a small piece of tape.

FAMILY MEMENTOS. Consider two things when storing family mementos. One is to use some discretion in saving items. There is no reason to keep every drawing and painting done by your child as a three-year-old. Instead, keep the ones with special meaning. The second important issue is the durability of the item in the setting that you are keeping it. Newspaper deteriorates quickly, so you may want to copy the article onto acid-free paper. Photographs may not wear well in an attic or garage where the temperatures change quickly.

ALPHABETICAL MAPS. Keep maps in alphabetical order.

ADJUSTABLE SHELVING. For maximum flexibility, get adjustable shelves. You can position the shelves according to the needs of the items being stored or displayed.

POSSESSIVE BOOKS. If you are the sort of person who frequently lends books to friends, family, and colleagues, then you may want to get stickers or a stamp that states that the book belongs to you. This may save trouble down the line.

JEWELRY STORAGE. A custom-made drawer may be the best way to store your jewelry in the most efficient manner. Otherwise, you can use ice tray cubes to keep earrings paired, strips of cardboard to wrap necklace chains around, and cushions for pins. It may not be the safest place to put them, but you may also want to consider hanging some of your jewelry in the dressing room. If it is good looking enough to wear, it is sure to be an attractive addition to the room.

LESS CLEANING CLUTTER. If you want to keep down the clutter in your cleaning closet, get one type of all-purpose cleaner instead of several different types of specialized cleaners. Keep the cleaners at eye level for easy access.

CLUSTERED GROUPINGS. When you put away seasonal items such as skis and winterwear or summer clothing, be sure to keep all related items together. When it comes time to collect them again, they will all be together.

DRAWER ORGANIZERS. Install dividers and organizers in drawers to keep things in order. Otherwise, items will inevitably get mixed up because they will constantly shift around as you open and close the drawer.

EXTENSION LEAVES. Store table extension leaves in the back of a closet.

HIDDEN WIRES. Stray wires look bad and can be dangerous if someone trips over one. Make your house look less cluttered by hiding wires behind furniture, running them along walls or under rugs wherever possible.

UNDERCOVER BLANKETS. Store your extra blankets between the mattress and the bedspring.

CAMERAS AND VIDEO CAMERAS. Always keep your camera and/or video camera loaded with film and stored in the same location. There is nothing more frustrating than trying to preserve a precious moment only to discover the batteries are dead and there is no film or, even worse, that you can't find the camera.

VELCRO TELEVISION REMOTE. Attach a strip of Velcro to the television and a corresponding strip to the back of the television remote.

PHOTO ROUTINES. If you are keeping a photo album—it is a very good idea to do so— be sure to put the photographs in the album as quickly as possible. If you do not, it will not take long to discover that your pile of photographs has become not only daunting but also jumbled and you cannot remember what event came when. Also, be sure to date and write a short description behind each photograph with a pen that does not leave a mark on the photo side.

POSITIVE TIP ON NEGATIVES. Always save and label negatives for photographs.

GOING TO THE VIDEOTAPE. Always label your videotapes and stand them upright in a temperature controlled environment.

BATHROOM ORGANIZER. Place a plastic-covered wire shelf in the shower or bathtub to hold soaps, razors, shampoos, conditioners, and other items you may want to have immediately at hand.

BATHROOM RACK. Place a standing coat rack in your bathroom to hold robes and large towels. It is a very efficient and handsome way to keep things in order in the bathroom.

THE MEDICINE CABINET. Keep the clutter down in the medicine cabinet by purging it regularly of prescription bottles that have gone past the expiration date and other items that are not used any longer such as old fragrance bottles. When you dispose of an old prescription bottle, record the date, name and dose, doctor, and pharmacy number for possible future reference.

ORGANIZED PLAGIARISM. If you cannot figure out a system or set to organize your items, try going to a store that sells the items you are having trouble putting in order. The store may have a system that you can copy or adapt for your own home.

AN ANNUAL PURGE. Once a year, make a thorough inspection of your house, its furniture, and the decorations and look for ways to trim out the extraneous items. This will help you keep a lid on the clutter that may accumulate.

DUPLICATION. This tip may seem contrarian for a chapter on clutter control, but there are many instances when you will want more than one item in a house. An upstairs and downstairs vacuum will save you the inconvenience of schlepping the vacuum all over the house. There is no reason to cut down on the number of clocks in a house, so long as you do not go overboard. Cleaning materials can be stored in the bathroom, kitchen, and laundry room. A pair of scissors is one of those utensils you cannot have too many of for the kitchen, desk, and bathroom.

THE ORGANIZED CLOSET

SIGNS OF AN ORGANIZED CLOSET. In a well organized closet, all items are clearly visible and accessible. There are few, if any, extraneous items. If your closet does not already have these characteristics, than these are your goals.

CLOSET SENSE. As much as possible, try to group related items in closets. Typical categories include clothes, linens, food groups, toys, and other groupings.

SHARED CLOSET. If a closet is being shared for clothing, make sure that each person has his or her own shelf and hanging space or there may be some confusion.

MEASURING A CLOSET UP. Get out a measuring tape and measure the dimensions of the closet. Then carefully think about ways you can make the closet more efficient. If you lower the hanging pole by a few inches, can you build a new shelf above it for extra storage space? Would it make more sense to have one hanging pole for coats, dresses, and other long items or two hanging poles for shirts, blouses, and other shorter hanging items?

MODULAR ORGANIZERS. Many home centers have do-it-yourself organizational tools and kits to maximize storage space in closets. One of these may come in handy for your purposes. If you are ambitious and handy with a hammer, you may try building a customized storage unit yourself.

CLOSET BOXES. Stackable vented plastic storage boxes or open basket drawers are useful storage compartments in closets for clothes, shoes, and knick-knacks. You may also be able to place a small chest under the area where clothes are hung.

CLOSET LIGHTS. A light in almost all closets is a must. It will make life easier for organizing the closet, cleaning it, and finding items in it.

CLOSET PLACEMENT. Place the most frequently used items in a closet at eye level.

STORING UNDER SHELVES. Undershelf storage baskets are sold commercially. They hang from a shelf and hold light items. They can be very handy for adding to your closet or shelf storage capacity.

CLOSETS WITH CLOTHES. Try to categorize your clothing according to the type of garment and color. In the process of doing this you may discover duplications. You may also want to install a mirror in your clothes closet as a way to check out how your clothes fit once you put them on.

LABELED CLOSETS. Labeling where items go in closets and clipboards will prevent the storage area from becoming a jumbled mess.

CLOTHING PURGES. Once a year, go through your clothing closet with an eye toward discarding old clothes. You might want to try some of the clothes you haven't tried on for a while to see if they still fit. It's amazing how some things shrink over the years.

LINEN CLOSETS. When you fold and stack towels and sheets, it is wisest to stack bed sheets in sets, towels and/or sheets according to family members, and to place them on the shelf with the folded sides facing out so you can more easily count the number of sheets or towels you have on hand.

HOOKS ARE GREAT. Place as many hooks as you can reasonably expect to fit in a closet. Hooks are wonderful tools to hang items in what would normally be unused space. Don't forget the back of the door. It is often an ideal spot for a hook or two.

STAIR STORAGE. In addition to closets, see if there is space under your stairs for storing things. You may want to add a shelf to expand its storage capacity.

THE PAPER BLIZZARD

OH, YOU WONDERFUL ROLODEX. Is it a coincidence that many successful business people have fat Rolodexes? Probably not. By keeping up to date on friends, family members, and associates' telephone numbers and addresses on a Rolodex, you can save yourself the trouble of keeping pieces of paper with telephone numbers scratched on them and constantly referring to the telephone book for pertinent information. Also, don't just use the index cards for names and numbers. Jot down pertinent information such as personal notes or the time-zone difference. Use a pencil for easy corrections and address changes.

PERSONAL ORGANIZERS. Several organizers are available commercially. They include sections for addresses, notes, schedules, appointments, maps, and many other categories. You may find them helpful in organizing your life. The key is sticking to a system and being consistent about it. Otherwise, you many not even want to bother.

GET A FILING CABINET. Between the daily influx of mail, taxes, personal and financial records, most people have little choice but to find a way to properly store and sort their written records. A filing cabinet is a must. They range in size from small plastic filing boxes to five-deck metal cabinets. How large a filing cabinet you use depends on how substantial your needs are.

SUSPENDED FILES. The great advantage of suspension filing system—where the folders hang from two rods running along the filing drawer—is that the folders do not collapse like dominoes. If you have a hanging file, it is often convenient to place one or more manila folders in the file to hold different groupings. When you need to pull out the information, all you have to do is lift the folder.

LATERAL FILES. Although most people prefer standard vertical filing cabinets, you may want to consider a lateral filing cabinet. These cabinets are very wide with the files running from side to side within the cabinet. If you have enough space in your office, lateral files offer the advantage of your being able to see all the files at once when you open the drawer.

A FILING SYSTEM. Many people like to color code their filing systems and then alphabetize the files under each color. Others, however, find this overly complicated. The key is to figure out a system that works for you and then stick with it. If the files are used by more than one person, there should probably be some sort of index explaining what goes under each category. For example, does a child's college tuition information go under the child's name, finance, or education? Only you can decide that.

WHAT TO FILE. File information that is important to you, your creditors, and the government. Although there is quite a bit of latitude in what can be filed, there are a few musts or near-musts. Always file documentation for the following subjects: tax records, warranties, bank records, important car records, insurance policies and documents, housing records, education records, and investment information. Optional subjects to file include church information, articles and information on potential holidays, pet records, hobby information, lists of gifts, information on entertaining, and non-essential but interesting or informative newspaper and magazine articles.

MORE THAN A LETTER. For filing systems that are done alphabetically, if a category starts to take over the folder for a certain letter, it is time to create a file just for that category.

STARTING A FILING SYSTEM. When you start a filing system, create the categories as you go along. If you go through a pile of materials and cannot think of an appropriate category, set it aside for the end and decide then what to do with it.

SECURITY BOXES. Some records are so important that you should not subject them to the potential dangers of damage, destruction, or misplacement in your home. You should put them in a safe-deposit box. Documents that fall under this category include birth certificates, wills, your marriage license, and vitally important names and telephone numbers of pertinent accountants and lawyers.

ACTIVE VS. INACTIVE FILES. As your files start to build up you may want to start an "inactive file" for tax, financial, and educational records you still want or need to keep, but really do not use very often. The advantage of an inactive file is that you can place it in a storage area and thus make room in your active filing system.

FILE PURGES. Purge your files of unnecessary documents every year or so. If the documents are no longer needed—such as the warranty on an appliance you no longer have —then toss it. You may be able to place other documents in the inactive file.

REMIND YOURSELF. If you have to take out a file or part of a file for more than several days, place a note in the filing cabinet to remind yourself where the documents were located. Do not trust your memory.

STAPLE, DON'T PAPER CLIP. Paper clips have a way of attaching themselves to the wrong pieces of paper, falling off, or jamming things together. Whenever you want to attach pieces of paper together for the filing cabinet, use a staple.

DOUBLE DOCUMENTATION. If an important record could or should fall into two different filing categories, there is no reason why you cannot make a copy of it and place it in both. The alternative solution is to place a note in the file where you decided not to place the record, cross-referencing the document's location.

DRAFT COPIES. If you have several drafts of a manuscript or document, be sure to properly mark it. It is far easier than you think to mix up which draft is which for even the simplest of documents.

MAKE FILING A HABIT. It is easy to let the "To file" stack pile up before filing the records. Try not to let this happen; it only weakens the filing system. The best way to handle the files is to file the information as soon as you are done with it.

DESKTOP FILES. The best desktop organizers include vertical files that allow you to separate things according to urgency. Stackable letter trays are also versatile. You can make stacks of up to 10 or 12 trays or you can just have one.

RECORD THE DATE. Always, always make sure there is a date on the papers you are filing. You may remember now when it was filed, but in two years it will be a total mystery.

TICKLER FILES. Some people like to create "tickler files" in which information for the future is stored in different files. The standard way to create these files is to get 13 folders— one for each month and one for the present week—and place invitations, reminders, appointments, bills, insurance matters in the appropriate folder. As each month arrives, you pull out the pertinent tickler file to remind yourself of what needs to be done. There are many alterations to this type of system. Newspaper editors often have daily tickler files to remind themselves of important meetings, deadlines, and events.

EXTRA FILES. Always keep a few extra file folders in the back of your file so you can easily expand the file if necessary.

STARTING THE NEW YEAR. Enter all important recurring dates in your calendar at the start of the new year and mark them with a bright color. When it comes time to do the chore next year, it will be easy to find the repeat dates.

MAIL SORTING. When you get the mail, immediately throw away the items that you have no interest in. They will only clutter up things later. These should include catalogs you are not interested in, solicitation requests from organizations you have no intention of assisting, bogus contest letters, and junk mail that does not appeal to you. Respond to invitations right away as well as to correspondence that requires a response for an appointment or other sort of answer. The one exception is when you get a letter from a real person. You may want to wait for a more relaxed moment to write back. But do not wait too long.

ENVELOPE PREPARATION. You can save time by getting a stamp with your name and address on it and using it to press a return address on blank envelopes. You may also want to place stamps on the envelopes ahead of time while you are watching television or speaking on the telephone.

BILL PAYING. When you receive bills, place them in a bill paying pile. Twice a month go through that pile and pay the bills. Place the receipts either directly in the filing system or in a special household file for bills you have paid during the year. The file can come in handy at the end of the year when you do your taxes if you constantly keep it updated. You should include solicitation letters that you intend to respond to in the bill pile.

CALCULATING TIP. Get a good calculator to work on bills and keep track of your finances. Try to get one of those that disgorge a paper output.

CATALOGING CATALOG PURCHASES. If you order a product through the mail or by telephone, be sure to write down on the catalog or a piece of paper what you ordered, the price, and the date. Place the information in a file folder until the item arrives. You may need the information if the item is never delivered or if there is a mix-up on what was ordered.

CATALOG STORAGE. Keep catalogs separate from magazines and keep them in alphabetical order if your pile starts to get unwieldy.

MAGAZINES. The rule of thumb among professional organizers is that if you have not read a magazine by the time the next issue arrives, throw away the old magazine and consider canceling the subscription when the time comes for a renewal. This is not a hard and fast rule, but something you should consider if you get in the habit of not reading magazines that once held your interest. If there is an article in an old magazine that you wanted to read but never had an opportunity to do so, cut the article out and throw the rest of the magazine in the recycling bin.

THE HOUSEHOLD NOTEBOOK. Start and keep a household notebook filled with information about the house and its appliances. The notebook, which should be a loose-leaf notebook, would include information on how to operate machinery, a household maintenance schedule on when to check, clean, or do routine maintenance on different parts of the house, directions on what to do if something disastrous or inconvenient happens, and other projects or topics pertinent to the maintenance and preservation of your house. A well kept notebook can be a very helpful and convenient resource for your home.

SERIAL NUMBERS. Keep a file in the household notebook or in your filing system just on serial numbers and receipts for appliances.

STORAGE JOURNAL. As your storage increases, consider writing a storage journal to keep track of where you have placed everything.

REPAIR CHECK. When you are organizing your house or a room, keep an eye out for repairs or projects that need to be done. Write down your thoughts and put them in the household notebook. You may want to periodically go through the house to update the list.

REFRIGERATOR REMINDERS. Use the refrigerator door to post important reminders and lists. Just get some magnetic pads to hold the paper to the door.

HOW LONG? Use the following guidelines for when you can dispose of these records: mortgage papers: three years; insurance policies and investment records: four years past expiration; bank records, canceled checks, credit-card records, and tax records: six years; contracts: seven years past expiration. If you did not file taxes or submitted false returns, you should never throw away your financial records for the year in question. The IRS may catch up to you and you will need those records badly.

TIME MANAGEMENT

ACT PROMPTLY. Prompt action saves time in the long run for a whole host of household chores. Make the bed as soon as you get up. Wipe up a spill as soon as it occurs. Wash dishes as soon as you are done with the meal. Remember, procrastination is the mother of clutter.

CLUSTERED HOMES. Try to store items near to where they will be used to save time. Keep all the laundry materials in the laundry room, the television remote near the television, and office supplies near or in your desk.

KEY IDEA. If you constantly misplace your keys, try placing a spare key in your wallet for emergencies. Or give a copy of the car keys to a trusted neighbor, more responsible family member or a nearby relative.

KEY PLACEMENT. Hang a wooden box near the entrance door with several pegs to hold keys. Whenever you come in or out of the house, place your keys in the box. You will always remember where you left them.

MARKED-UP TELEPHONE BOOK. There is no reason to try to maintain the pristine quality of a new telephone book. Feel free to mark up the telephone book to make things easier for you. Circle personal and business numbers that you are likely to seek out again, jot down comments by stores and restaurants with your views on them.

PREPARING FOR GUESTS. To save time when guests are visiting, try to get as much accomplished before their arrival as possible. Do the dishes, set the table, pre-prepare as much of the meal as possible and clean out the trash.

WAITING FOR APPOINTMENTS. There is perhaps nothing more frustrating than sitting in a doctor's office waiting for your turn when you know you have a million and one things to do. You can cut down on your anxiety by always bringing a project that you can work on in the waiting room while you are waiting.

ALWAYS PREPARED. You can be like one of those people you know who always seem to be prepared to make a meal for eight at a moment's notice by simply keeping your kitchen stocked with homemade fast foods and some essential ingredients including bread mixes, chicken and beef stock, canned tomatoes and tomato paste, frozen pie crust, and a variety of meals you made that you can keep in the freezer. The rule of thumb when you cook a meal such as spaghetti sauce, soups, or quiches is to cook twice as much as you plan to eat and freeze half.

THE TO-DO SHELF. Designate a shelf, small room, or closet as the household "to-do" spot where you place items that require some action, whether it be wrapping a gift, returning a library book, or dropping off a radio that needs to be prepared.

LISTS. Lists can be helpful, but do not get carried away with them. There are two basic types of lists, the macro and micro. The macro list is a master list of all the general things that need to get done in the long and short run. A micro list is a list of the tasks that need to be accomplished in the immediate future or for a specific project. It is good to have a macro list to keep track of the big projects and issues you need to confront, and micro lists help you narrow down and focus in on the activities or work that has to be done right away. You may want to use a spiral notebook with the master list in the front and the various smaller lists in the main body of the notebook. Do not hesitate to mark down comments or next-steps on the lists to remind yourself of certain things.

SHOP ON ONE DAY. You can save a lot of time by saving your grocery shopping for a designated day each week. Be sure to have a complete list, a file of coupons on hand if you use them (and we recommend you do), and shop alone and on a full stomach. When you buy the groceries, help pack the bags with an eye toward packing similar or grouped products in the same bags. For example, try to get all the items that go in the refrigerator in the same bags. This will save time when you unpack the bags.

THE STAIRWAY BASKET. Place a large basket at the foot and the top of the stairs to place items that need to go to the next floor. When you are heading up or down the stairs, bring the basket with you and place the items in the appropriate places. This will save time and energy.

USE A COMPUTER... INTELLIGENTLY. Personal computers can save enormous amounts of time with several of the programs now available. Refer to the chapter on computers for further information on working with computers. However, a computer may do you no good at all if you are the type who refuses to use it. Also, computers are such intriguing appliances that many people have, become totally absorbed by the wonders they offer and will spend many hours just playing with the computer. So if you are interested in a computer for time management purposes, you may have to impose some self-discipline.

MAKING LIFE EASIER ON YOURSELF. There are many things you can do to cut down on the routine maintenance of keeping a house. Instead of a sheet, cover, and blanket, use a comforter for your bed. Keep cleaning materials within easy access for the kitchen and bathroom. Cluster closets with items that go together. If you have a telephone that programs frequently dialed numbers, use it. Group the forks, spoons, and knives together when you place them in the dishwasher. By thinking creatively you will come up with ways to cut down on the number of steps it takes to do a task.

ODE TO THE VCR. Use the VCR to save time. It is a wonderful way of accomplishing two things at once. As soon as you figure out how to record programs while you are doing something else, you can watch the programs at your convenience. Plus you can save time by fast-forwarding through the commercials.

USING MODERN TECHNOLOGY. Electronic banking, on-line computers, and other aspects of modern technology can simplify your life and save you time if properly done. Many companies will directly deposit your paychecks or automatically withdraw from your banking account for routine payments such as insurance or mortgage payments. This can save you a considerable amount of time and paperwork; just be careful to keep close tabs on the accounts to make sure everything is being done properly and no errors are made.

CALL ME. If you have an important task that has to be accomplished or you want to remind yourself of something while you are away from home, try calling home and leaving a message on the answering machine for yourself.

CLEVER REMINDERS. Other ways to remind yourself of important things to do include placing a note on the bathroom sink to remind you first thing in the morning or on the inside of the door as you walk out of the house. If you have a package that needs to be mailed or box that needs special handling, place it somewhere that you will literally trip over to remind yourself to tend to the matter.

SEEKING CONFIRMATION. You may be well organized, but the person or business you are meeting with may not be. You may save yourself some time and frustration by always calling ahead of time for appointments to confirm the time and place of a meeting.

Christmas and the holiday crunch

F or many Americans, Christmas is either the most enjoyable or most stressful time of the year. The key to enjoying Christmas is to not drive yourself crazy with extravagant preparations or unrealistic expectations.

Different temperaments call for different tactics. Some people thrive on last-minute shopping. Others go to great lengths to find the perfect gift and will prepare months ahead of time. If you have great expectations for Christmas celebrations and hate disorder, then you better get organized well in advance.

It is easy to get wrapped up in the glitz and chaos of contemporary Christmas. Bear in mind that Christmas is about good will, family, and children. Make these your priorities and you have taken the most important steps toward enjoying Christmas.

GENERAL TIPS

PRIORITIES. This may sound silly, but with all the hoopla surrounding Christmas you may want to devote some time to thinking about what you want to accomplish at Christmas time. You may not be able to fit everything into one Christmas season, so decide what your priorities are and then plan your Christmas around them. Is it to draw your family together? Fun for your kids? Spiritual enjoyment? Survival? Whatever the answer is, that should be the guiding force in planning your Christmas.

SHOPPING TACTICS. Shop early in the morning when salespeople are alert and friendly. You also tend to avoid the larger crowds in the early morning.

Before Thanksgiving, take a shopping trip to buy Christmas staples such as batteries, film, paper products, and stamps.

INCLUDING CHILDREN. Make your life easier by assigning certain tasks to children who want to participate in the excitement of Christmas. Have your children decorate the tree, seal envelopes and lick stamps, make gifts, display the cards, hang lights along the banister, sing songs, or write poems. Do not expect perfection.

CHILDREN'S ROUTINE. Christmas is a very exciting time for children, who are therefore prone to getting overtired and irritable. Try to maintain a reasonable routine for children that includes regular bedtimes, naps, and sit-down nutritious meals.

BIG FAMILIES?!?! If you have several brothers, sisters, cousins, close friends, and family members on your shopping list and can no longer keep up with shopping for a crowd, you may want to consider giving gifts only to children. This can be done by mutual arrangement. To cut your list even more drastically, you may decide among your own family to select only one family member each to give presents to. Do this by putting all your family members' names in a hat and having each family member pull out a name to give a present to that Christmas.

GIFTS, CARDS, AND WRAPPING

RECYCLED CARDS. It is easy to make colorful Christmas baskets for your tree out of old or discarded Christmas cards. Cut the cards into one 11x1/2 inch strip and nine 8x1/2 inch strips. Use eight of the 8-inch strips to make an eight-pointed star that is glued together in the center, similar to the hub in a spiked wheel. Lift up the eight points to make a basket and glue them to the remaining 8-inch strip. Take the 11-inch strip and glue each end to the edge of the basket to act as a handle. The basket can be used to hold Christmas candies, little flowers, holly, or other decorations.

RESTORING USED WRAPPING PAPER AND RIBBON. To remove wrinkles from used wrapping paper, lightly spray the back side with starch, then press it with an iron. To restore wrinkled ribbon, run the ribbon through a warm curling iron.

STRAIGHT CUTS. To cut a straight edge, place the wrapping paper on a table with leaves over the crack and cut the paper with a sharp knife.

PAPER STORAGE. Use a narrow wastebasket to store rolls of wrapping paper. For added convenience, add scissors, ribbon, tape, and tags to the basket.

ALTERNATIVE WRAPS. Use your imagination when wrapping a gift. Sheet music, the Sunday newspaper comics section, old maps, large-sized magazine paper, wallpaper, and other types of paper can be used to wrap almost any type of gift. They add a little interest to the gift and are often more attractive than commercial wrapping paper.

HOMEMADE WRAPS. Wrap your gift in plain paper and draw your own illustrations on the gift, or have your children do the illustrating. Or you can take the excess scraps of wrapping paper and glue them together into a collage wrapping paper.

ADVENT CALENDARS. Do not torment children by placing the gifts under the tree way ahead of time. They may not understand how long a week or two weeks is and will be very eager to open the presents. Instead, start a tradition of Advent calendars to count down the days to Christmas. You can buy Advent calendars in stores or make your own. Some Advent calendars include small gifts offered every day, others open windows to colorful holiday scenes.

CREATIVE CULINARY GIFTS. Make your own innovative food baskets by selecting a culinary theme and collecting food items and accessories around that theme. For a tea drinker, you could get an antique cup and saucer and some fancy teas and place them creatively in a basket. Other themes could be coffee, martinis, wine and bread, and pasta. Or buy a cookbook with appropriate kitchen tools.

NATURE'S BOUNTY. If you're in a pinch on what to get the person who has everything, turn to Mother Nature. Put together a natural Christmas present with an old clay pot filled with seasonal bulbs. The easiest bulbs to force are paperwhite narcissus and amaryllis. Place a handful of bulbs in a container with some potting soil or gravel and water. Decorate the gift with pinecones and sheet moss.

NON-TREE PRESENTS. Not all Christmas presents have to be wrapped or placed under a tree. Give your loved one roses delivered to his or her office every Monday morning, or croissants and coffee delivered from the local bakery every Saturday for breakfast. City dwellers may want a year's supply of wood for the fireplace. A gift of long-distance phone service for someone with family far away is always appreciated.

MEANINGFUL CALENDAR. Take a wall calendar given to you by a bank, insurance company, or other business and place photographs of family members over the illustrations using rubber cement.

SAVING MONEY. You have to think ahead, but you can save a lot of money on Christmas wrapping paper and cards by buying them on Dec. 26. Almost all stores will slash prices to free up shelf space for other merchandise.

LISTS. Keep a list of gifts you have received. When it comes time to writing thank you notes, you won't have to stretch your memory or guess to figure out who gave you what. This may save some embarrassment.

TREES

TREE FARMS PREFERRED. When you buy a Christmas tree, check to make sure it comes from a tree farm and not from the wild. You don't want to contribute to the denuding of American forests.

BUYING TIPS. Try to buy fresh trees. Needles are an excellent indicator. If the needles are brittle or fall off, the tree is not freshly cut. The more pliable the needle, the fresher the tree. The brightness of the green needles is another guideline for freshness.

Balsam, Douglas and Fraser fir, and Scotch pine trees tend to keep their needles longer than most. Spruce trees retain needles the shortest length of time.

CHRISTMAS TREE PRESERVATION TECHNIQUES. When you first get a Christmas tree, make sure the bottom has been freshly cut. If not, cut off the bottom an inch or two from the trunk to help it absorb moisture. Some people take a step further and drill a hole from the bottom up and stuff strips of sponge or cotton balls that help the tree absorb the water.

Trees tend to absorb warm water better than cold water. Add aspirin, sugar, or Pinesol to the water to make your Christmas tree last longer. Keep the tree in the coolest part of the room and away from fireplaces, heaters, and radiators.

ALTERNATIVE TREE STAND. Fill a bucket with wet sand or gravel and place the tree trunk in it. This eliminates the frequent hassles and complications of inserting the tree just right into a tree stand.

TREE PITCH REMOVAL. To wash the sticky tree pitch off your hands, use salad oil and wipe it off with a paper towel.

FIREPROOFING. Christmas trees are fire hazards, especially dried-out ones.

The longer you can keep the tree outside in the cold, the longer it will stay fresh. You can fireproof a tree by making a solution of 1/2 gallon of warm water, 1 cup alum, 2 tablespoons of borax, and 4 ounces of boric acid and spraying it on to the branches. Pour the remainder into the tree stand.

CHILD/PET ALARM. If want an early-warning detection device for wayward children or pets playing with the tree, place a few small bells near the bottom of the tree.

TREE REMOVAL. You can avoid dropping tree needles all over your house by wrapping your tree in a large bedsheet when it comes time to remove the tree. It may take more than one person to do this task.

VACUUMING NEEDLES. Use a pantyhose leg to vacuum Christmas tree needles. Place the pantyhose on the nozzle and the vacuum will suck in both the hose and the needles. Make sure you hold the pantyhose to the nozzle. When you are done vacuuming, just pull out the pantyhose away and throw it away, needles and all. This avoids the problem of plugging up the vacuum hose.

RECYCLED TREES. Some communities compost trees. You may want to find out if yours does. Or you can chop up the tree yourself and use the branches for other purposes. Christmas tree boughs placed vertically along tree trunks have been known to discourage neighborhood dogs from leaving their mark. Other innovative uses of evergreen branches include hanging clusters of boughs in the bathroom as an air freshener, using them as kindling, or as mulch. A denuded tree trunk can be used in the spring as a bean pole or for supporting ivy.

DECORATING AND ENTERTAINING

OUTSIDE LIGHTS. Save yourself the annual headache of securing outside lights by screwing in small hooks along the eaves of your house, banister, or porch.

SEASONAL AROMAS. Use potpourri and pomander balls to bring a holiday scent to your Christmas celebration. You can also add to the holiday aroma by placing orange rinds, cinnamon sticks, cloves, and fresh ginger in a pan covered with water that is brought to a boil and then simmers on low heat.

Or sprinkle cinnamon on a cookie sheet and put it in a warmed oven. Or throw orange rinds and pine cones into a fireplace, or use fragrant woods for burning.

TREE LIGHT DETANGLERS. To prevent tangled tree lights, wrap the lights around old wrapping paper tubes. Place the end of the cord in the inside of the tube and then wrap the lights around the tube. Use a rubber band to secure the lights.

CANDLELIGHT. There is nothing like candlelight to illuminate your Christmas. Place candles in front of mirrors to double the impact of the lights. Freeze the candles first and they will burn slower. Beeswax candles do not drip. Core several fresh artichokes and spray them with gold paint to serve as holiday candleholders.

PAPER HEARTS. Make colorful paper hearts for your Christmas tree by cutting heart patterns shown above and weaving them together. Depending on the size of the hearts, you can use them to store candy, decorations, or small gifts. Use different colors for variety and use heavy paper for strength.

KIDS ORNAMENTS. Use cookie cutters for children to outline Christmas figures on pieces of cardboard and then cut out the figures. Cover them with white glue and sprinkle glitter over the glue. String a ribbon through a punched hole to hang them from the tree.

POPCORN HINT. It is easier to string one-week-old stale popcorn than fresh popcorn, which has a tendency to fall apart.

DECORATION STORAGE. Egg cartons can be used to store smaller decorations throughout the year. Cardboard liquor cartons complete with dividers make excellent storage space for larger tree decorations. Make sure to wrap fragile ornaments in paper.

DECORATION HANGERS. A wide array of items can be used to hang decorations from a tree. Try using bent paper clips, bobby pins, twist ties, or green pipe cleaners.

WINDOW DECORATIONS. Use toothpaste to decorate your windows with festive scenes or holiday messages. When the Yule season is over, use the paste to wash the window. This is fun for the kids and practical for the household. A rare combination.

WHITE BROWS. Short of rapidly aging, the best way to whiten your brows as Santa Claus is to smear a little bit of petroleum jelly on your eyebrows and sprinkle it with flour or cornstarch.

POINSETTIA PRESERVATION. To preserve your poinsettia's color, keep it well watered and in bright—but not hot—light. When the plant fades naturally in January or February, cut off the stalks, leaving three joints at the base of each stem. Keep the plant dry and cool for the next six weeks and then start to water. When new shoots start to appear, apply all-purpose fertilizer. When it gets warm, place the plant outside in a sunny but sheltered spot. Pinch back new shoots in July to one or two shoots and keep the plant well watered and fed through the summer. Take the plant indoors in late September and place it under bright light for no more than 10 hours a day. It should be in a cool, dark place (closet or cellar) at night. By December it will be ready for display.

Fun and entertainment

Fun can be work, as you already know if you've ever thrown a party, entertained out-of-town guests, or even tried to organize the family for an outing.

But that doesn't mean it has to be a chore. The goal is to minimize the work and emphasize the fun. The key is to know what you want to get out of your entertainment activities, and plan in a way that allows you to focus on that.

If your main goal for a gathering is to get together with people you like, you'll probably want to keep the trappings simple. But you may be one of those people who find that planning and preparing a lavish and creative party is as enjoyable as the event itself.

The purpose of a party will also determine how you prepare for it. Having friends over for dinner and a video is a pretty straightforward proposition. But if it's an event to celebrate a special occasion, more planning is necessary. And if you are holding a business soiree for a client, actual enjoyment is probably low on your priority list.

Whatever the case, it's always a good idea to balance spontaneity and planning when you're looking for fun and expecting guests.

GENERAL TIPS

SIGN IN PLEASE. Begin a tradition of keeping a social scrapbook, with brief descriptions and impressions of parties and smaller gatherings. Include a guest book for your visitors to sign and to write comments in. In addition to preserving memories, this can also help you plan guest lists for future entertaining.

A LIBRARY OF FUN. "What are we going to do today?" You'll spend less time pondering that question if you organize a little reference library of regional attractions that you can pull out whenever you're planning a short outing, day-trip, or weekend getaway with family or visitors. It should include guidebooks, maps, and any other information helpful for planning fun. Keep the material together in a drawer, folder, shelf, or other holder.

PICK UP THOSE FREEBIES. You can get a lot of information at no cost if you make it a habit to pick up those freebie regional tourist guides and promotional brochures found in stores and restaurants. And keep the seasonal fun guides that local newspapers and magazines regularly publish. Also clip and save articles about places of interest.

PROGRAM FOR FUN. If you're a computer nerd, create a program listing potential recreational activities that you can categorize and update as necessary. (If you're really a computer nerd, that's probably your idea of fun anyway.)

AROMA CONTROL. When expecting company, fill a pan with apple cider and cinnamon and let it simmer on the stove for an hour or two before guests arrive. This will give your house a natural, cozy aroma. (Keep the heat low and remember it's there, so it doesn't boil away and burn.)

OLD STANDBYS. Perhaps you don't like to cook, and are usually happy to eat TV dinners or other simple fare. If so, learn at least two or three more festive—but simple, tasty and safe—standby meals that you can prepare when you have company for dinner. That will make it easier for you, and your guests won't have to politely compliment you on the meal while secretly wishing they had some Pepto-Bismol handy.

OUT-OF-TOWN GUESTS

WHAT WOULD THEY LIKE? Before they arrive, ask your visitors what kind of activities they want to do while they're with you. Do some research, so you'll have a list of suggestions ready. If they're outdoors types, have ideas for suggested hikes or other activities. If they're looking for culture or entertainment, find out what concerts, exhibits, etc. will take place while they're here.

ADVANCED ARRANGEMENTS. Restaurants are often full and shows are often sold out. So it's a good idea to make dinner reservations at a restaurant you think your guests will enjoy or reserve tickets to events. Ideally, of course, it's best to ask your friends first. If you're not able to, take your chances as a standby. You can change plans if necessary. (Out of courtesy, be sure to cancel the reservations far enough in advance to free up the table or seats for other people.)

PLAN FOR RELAXATION. You and your guests are probably not always going to be chatting or running around during their visit, so be prepared for quieter relaxation time.

■ Buy a selection of magazines and light reading matter that your guests would enjoy thumbing through. For game-loving guests, have some crosswords or other game books, or a pack of cards. If you have a computer in the main living area, have a stock of easy-to-learn, entertaining computer games.

■ For guests who are arriving on a weekend, be prepared for possible couch-potato time and rent a good, new video or two. You're more likely to find new ones in stock on a weeknight, so bite the bullet and pay for an extra night or two by going to the video store on Thursday.

■ Set up your badminton net, croquet set, and other yard games before your guests arrive, so they can play at their leisure.

PREMAKE MEALS. Prepare meals and freeze or store them away before your guests arrive, so that you can spend more time visiting and less in the kitchen during their visit.

SOCIAL COOKING. For some people, mealmaking with their guests is a social occasion. If so, have the ingredients purchased and ready to go, to make the actual work with guests smoother.

LUGGAGE AWARENESS. Make sure there is a luggage rack or other suitable holder for guests' bags in their room. A clothing rack is also helpful.

LIGHT AT NIGHT. Either leave on hall lights or have nightlights on the route from the guest room to the bathroom or other areas they may be wandering in at night.

NICE TOUCHES. In addition to the prerequisite clean sheets, provide some additional welcoming touches for your guests' room when they arrive. You might leave a selection of information about possible activities in the room for them to peruse at their leisure. Or buy some sample sizes of shampoo and other toiletry items, and place them in a basket on the bed. Magazines or light books in the room also are appreciated.

HAVE COMPANY. If your guests will be staying long enough, plan a small get-together with friends while they're here. Your visitors are likely to appreciate the chance to meet other people from the area. If your visitors are former residents of your hometown, invite some of their old acquaintances.

WHEN KIDS ARRIVE

THINK LIKE A PARENT. If you're childless (or your own are grown) and are expecting out-of-town visitors with young ones, think like a parent before they arrive. Parents cannot be as spontaneous as those who don't have the constant demands of children to think about.

LOOK FOR ACTIVITIES. Look around for activities that children their age would enjoy. If you plan to visit museums or other attractions, find out if they have features of interest to kids. Also look for events or attractions specifically for kids, like puppet shows, children's museums, playgrounds, etc.

STOCK UP ON AMUSEMENTS. Quiet relaxation is not in the vocabulary of most kids, so buy, borrow, or rent some toys and games that will help keep them amused at your home. Children's videos are often inexpensive.

THE VALUE OF FRIENDSHIP. Friends are important, for kids and adults. If you have friends who are parents of children the same age as your young visitors, ask if they would be willing to invite them over for a day or afternoon. This can provide the young visitors with playmates, and give you and your adult guests some time alone. Assuming the kids get along, you can return the favor by inviting your friends' children over to your house, to give their parents a break.

ADULTS-ONLY TIME. If you and your guests want some adults-only time, ask around for reliable babysitters or day-care centers that take children on a daily basis. Also check with museums, girls or boys clubs, or other organizations to see if they sponsor one-day camps, classes, or other supervised activities for children. Call to find out if you'll need to make arrangements in advance, and plan accordingly.

PREPARE YOUR CAR. If your guests will be carless while visiting, get a child's safety seat to use in your auto while they're here.

BATTEN DOWN THE HATCHES. Kids can wreak havoc in ways that non-parents can't even imagine, so it's wise to childproof your home before they arrive. Make sure any loose, valuable objects are safely out of reach. Also look around your home for any potential hazards, such as holes in the yard, steep drop offs, loose sharp objects, protruding nails or loose boards, etc. Correct what you can and warn the parents when they arrive. A friend who is a parent may be able to help you inspect your home.

AVOID AWKWARD MOMENTS. Childless adults don't usually worry about whether the books, videos, or records around the house are suitable for young eyes. To avoid awkward moments, take a quick look around and store away anything that may be too violent or racy or scary for impressionable young minds. That way you'll avoid the embarrassment of having a young child innocently come into the room holding your copy of, say, Madonna's book, "Sex," and asking, "Mommy, what is that woman doing?"

PARTY PLANNING

The possibilities for parties are endless, from spur-of-the-moment get-togethers with a few friends to more elaborate and formal affairs. Your entertaining style will reflect your own personality. In addition, you may have different parties for different purposes.

Whatever the case, your entertaining will be more entertaining for you, and for your guests, if you have a clear picture of why you are hosting an event, how to create the effect you want, and getting as many details taken care of early.

To make the preparation easy, and to give you time to be creative, plan ahead and pace yourself rather than rush around at the last minute.

SCHEDULING. Even if it's an informal gathering, set a time schedule for the specific pace of the party so you can organize your preparations around that. For example, you might allow an hour for pre-dinner socializing and then a certain amount of time for dinner. This can obviously be flexible, but it will help you plan elements like cooking time, cleanup, and other duties.

PETS. Make arrangements for your pet when you have a party. Keep it in a spare room with lots of food, water, and a litter box, or place it outside. If your pet is especially skittish or overly friendly, it may be best to take it to a friend's or the vet for the night.

THE NEIGHBORS. If your party will be large and/or noisy enough to be noticeable, be a good neighbor. The easiest way to avoid potential conflicts is to invite the neighbors. In any case, at least inform those neighbors who are likely to be affected by your party, and ask them to let you know if they are having problems with noise or other aspects of the party.

CLEAR INVITES. While the way you deliver your invitations will depend on the nature of the party, they should answer the questions your guests will have, either verbally or in written form. Include whether the party has specific hours or is open-ended; if dinner is served and what time; whether it's BYOB and/or a potluck; the type of dress expected; and any special activities.

HOW MANY? You'll also want a general idea of how many people will show up. If your attitude is "the more the merrier" let your guests know they are welcome to bring family and friends. If you want to control or limit the number, ask for an RSVP.

FAMILY AFFAIR? Let your guests know whether it is a family party or an adults-only gathering. If kids are invited, plan how they will be included. Have a play area with games and decide whether you should have a separate meal for them. If you're expecting a large number of kids, considering hiring an entertaining babysitter, to make the party easier for you and your adult guests.

PARKING AT PARTIES. Prepare a parking plan before the party. Figure out how many vehicles your property can hold, and how to place them to get the most efficient use of that space. If you are expecting more cars than your property or adjacent streets can hold, find alternatives, such as nearby public parking or neighbors who would be willing to allow people to park on their property. Let your guests know in the invitation where to park. If it's really tight, suggest that they carpool or use public transportation.

TO SMOKE OR NOT TO SMOKE? That is the question each host must answer individually. It's easier to discourage smoking at parties today, because most people assume that smoking is not allowed. If you don't want puffing in your main party area, do your best to accommodate the nicotine addicts, and make them feel welcome despite their bad habit.

SMOKING SPACE. Smokers will feel more welcome if you provide a comfortable smoking area, rather than make them feel that they have to sneak a smoke in the driveway. Weather permitting, set up a smoking area outside with a couple of chairs and ashtrays. If you have the space in your house, a smoking room is appreciated in cold weather.

SUBTLE SIGNS. One of those subtle No Smoking graphics (a circle with a line through it over a cigarette) at the door is a diplomatic way to get the message across. If you are providing a designated smoking area, rather than saying "No smoking," give the message more positively, such as "Smoking lounge in the side yard."

MOOD LIGHTING. Experiment by being a lighting designer before the party. A bright cheery room is fine, but avoid harsh overhead lighting. If you want a more intimate mood, put lower-wattage bulbs in your lamps or try colored lights. Candles can do a lot to enhance the atmosphere of a room.

MUSIC. Music can help you choreograph your party. Choose your selections of albums beforehand, so you don't have to rummage through your collection during the party. Or make tapes that reflect specific moods. If your selection of music is limited, ask a music-loving friend to make you some tapes. Or find and tune in a suitable radio station beforehand.

MUSICAL VARIETY. Have a diversity of musical selections so you can have more flexibility in setting or reflecting the tone of the party. You may want quieter music for talking and eating time and more raucous music for dancing later.

KEEP MUSIC IN ITS PLACE. Have you ever been to a party where the music is so loud you can't talk without shouting? Find a volume level for your music that doesn't overwhelm, so the background music doesn't become the foreground for your guests. (You can crank it up later if it's time for dancing.) Also, remember that instrumental music is less distracting than music with prominent vocals.

LIVE MUSIC. If you have friends who are musically inclined, ask them to bring along their guitars or other instruments. Be clear, though, on the role of music, and have a specific area set aside for it. There's nothing more fun for participants and listeners than a spontaneous music-making session. But there's nothing more deadly than a party where everyone is gritting their teeth waiting for overzealous (or undertalented) musicians to finish demanding their attention.

THEME PARTIES. Themes can make a party more memorable. Nostalgia parties often go over big. Or something incongruous, like a beach party in January, with summer music, posters, and cookout food (even if you have to cook it indoors). When planning, have fun trying to tie all of the elements into the concept, including the invitations, decorations, food, music, activities, and costumes.

COMFORTABLY COSTUMING. If you're throwing a theme costume party, take the different comfort zones of guests into account. Some people love dressing up in flamboyant garb and makeup, while others feel awkward in anything other than street clothes. You'll want both types to enjoy themselves, so make clear in your invitations that people can be as outrageous or conservative as they want.

BACK TO THE 80'S. The 1980's are now nostalgia. For a new twist , throw a 1980's theme party. Ask people to wear the clothes that reflect the decade to them. Break out those old New Wave dance records, Rambo posters, and other memorabilia of the 80's. Serve nouvelle cuisine.

GEOGRAPHIC GOING-AWAY PARTY. If you're giving a going-away party for friends who are moving to a very different region, consider a geographic theme party. It can either be the characteristics of the region they are leaving or the place they're moving to—like a California party if they are moving to Los Angeles from New England.

MOVIE THEMES. While a video party can be simple, you can also go all-out by giving a movie party. Pick a film and structure the decorations, food, etc. around its ambiance. For example, rent a copy of "Casablanca" and then decorate your home like Rick's Cafe, with potted palms, bamboo screens, and rattan chairs. You might even set up a roulette table and serve middle eastern food, and play torch songs from the 1940's. The host could don a white tuxedo just like Bogey.

TOURNEY PARTY. One idea is to center a party around a specific game or activity, such as a volleyball, badminton, or croquet tournament. Indoor parties might include a monopoly tournament or card game.

ITEM PARTIES. Set a theme around specific items, such as balloons. In addition to designing creative balloon decorations, look in party-game books for a selection of activities that involve balloons. (On a hot day, for example, have a balloon toss. The guests stand close to each other and pitch a water balloon back and forth, taking a step backward after each throw. You can guess what eventually happens.) Or think of other objects that can be used as themes. If a mess is involved, be sure to let your guests know so they can dress accordingly.

FOOD AND SERVICE

SERVICE STYLES. You have a choice between several basic traditional ways to serve a meal to guests.

- In English service, the empty plates are placed on the table along with the serving dishes by the host, who serves the meal and passes the plates to each guest.

- In Russian service, food is brought to the table already on the plates from the kitchen.

- Country or family service. The serving dishes are passed around the table and guests serve their own portions as they pass them.

- Buffet. The food is laid out on a large table, and guests serve themselves before sitting down.

MENU PLANNING. Your party planning will go more smoothly if your food planning starts with a menu. Choose specific dishes, snacks, refreshments, and desserts. Also calculate the amount of food for the number of guests you are expecting. Then you can base your shopping list on that.

KEEP THE HOMESTRETCH EASY. The simpler the actual final preparations have to be, the better. If you get too ambitious, you may find yourself in the awkward position of having to stall for time while waiting for the roast to finish cooking or the sauces in a delicate meal to simmer just right.

SIMPLE IDEAS. For the least amount of hassle, use salads, cheeses, coldcuts, and other simple foods that don't require preparation. For hot dishes, rely on recipes such as casseroles and pizzas that you can prepare in advance and don't require anything more than heating before they are served. Cook what you can freeze or store as many days in advance as you can.

LEFTOVERS? Don't overload on perishable food or dishes that won't last. If you feel like you need to overstock your pantry to be safe, emphasize foods that you can store and reuse if you have a surplus.

WHAT THEY ENJOY. When you're entertaining a small number of guests, ask about the type of food they enjoy beforehand. Some people might like light meals, others love heavy pasta or meat and potatoes. Others will eat anything put in front of them.

DIVERSITY OF FOODS. For larger gatherings, plan for a diversity of items that accommodate different tastes and individual considerations. Even if you have a central theme for your food—such as a pizza party—make sure you include alternatives for guests who don't have pizza-loving palates.

FOODS TO AVOID. In this health-conscious era, it's important to know what foods not to serve. Sometimes it seems that everyone is a vegetarian or has a food allergy. Also, if you know a guest is a recovering alcoholic, don't serve foods with alcohol in the sauces. For larger gatherings, provide a variety of dishes that will offer alternatives for vegetarians and recovering alcoholics. It's a good idea to have at least one dish that's extremely simple and obvious, to be safe.

MAKE-YOUR-OWN BUFFETS. One way to please differing palates and stimulate your guests' creativity is a make-your-own buffet. Have one or two base foods, such as pasta, rice, pancakes, or waffles, and surround them with a selection of as many sauces and toppings as your imagination and budget allow.

ICE CREAM BUFFET. Take a similar approach with dessert. Put out ice cream and a selection of toppings: fresh fruit slices, crumbled cookies, hot fudge sauce, fresh coffee grounds, maple and other syrup, marshmallow sauce, heavy liqueurs, nuts, cinnamon, etc. Also put out brownies and bananas. It's also a good idea to include frozen yogurt for those who can't indulge in ice cream.

TAG-SALE SUPPLIES. Check out tag sales for items that can provide inexpensive party decorations and supplies. You can often find serving dishes, plates, glasses, etc., that will enliven your display of food. Also, look at items that can be altered from their original purpose, such as old pails or boxes for decorations.

COLOR FOR THE HOLIDAY. You can add to the spirit of a holiday event by coordinating the color and display of food for the season. Examples: for July 4, line up three white punch bowls—one with a red raspberry or cherry colored punch, another with clear white grape juice punch, and a third with dark grape or blueberry. For a Christmas party, emphasize the red tomatoes and green lettuce in the salad display. Or garnish desserts with a display of green grapes and cherries or strawberries. The possibilities are endless.

FLOWERFUL FOOD. Brighten your salads and other dishes by garnishing them with nasturtiums, pansies, and other edible flowers. (Obviously, make sure you choose edible ones.)

SEE-THROUGH DESSERTS. To add visual appeal to desserts like ice cream, puddings, gelatin, or similar desserts, place them in clear glass containers rather than opaque ones.

SUITABLE SIZES. Centerpieces and other decorations add a lot to a party and the dinner table. Make sure, though, that you don't overdo it. A table with too many non-essentials can quickly become crowded and difficult to serve and eat at. The centerpiece shouldn't be so large that guests have to crane their necks to see guests on the other side of the table.

PLACEMAT SIZES. If you're buying or making placemats, measure your table surface and divide it into the number of people you plan to seat, plus enough elbow room between them for comfort. Placemats that are too large may reduce the number of seatings at a table or crowd your guests.

MEASURING BUFFET. Do a dry run of your buffet-table setup as part of the early party planning. Design its layout by actually placing the serving dishes you will be using on it. That way you can see how many dishes and decorations will fit on the table, and the most efficient and appealing setup.

MESSY SPOONS. To keep spoons from being left in casseroles and other dishes and becoming messy, place a small dish to hold them next to the larger serving dishes.

BUFFET-TABLE TRAFFIC. For easier maneuvering when it's time to serve the buffet, gently encourage your guests to form a line down (or to circulate around) the table in one direction, rather than a free-for-all. The direction should keep their right side facing the table. (Sorry, lefties.)

KEEPING HANDS FREE. Put the eating utensils and drinks at the end of the buffet table that guests will reach last, so their hands will be free while loading their plates.

CHARCOAL TIP. Use a moderate amount of charcoal when cooking out. Too much charcoal will cause more heat than you want for grilling.

FROM THE LEFT. Place plates to seated guests from their left side. In addition to its being traditional, it minimizes the possibility of a plate's getting struck by a wayward gesture from the guest's right hand.

KEEP COFFEE ON TABLE. Pour coffee for seated guests only when their cup is sitting in the saucer on the table. Don't pour while the guest is holding it.

NO STEAKS ON LAPS. If your guests will be holding their plates or using trays, use food that doesn't have to be cut with a knife or require other maneuvers.

STRONG PLATES. To reduce the possibility of sloppy accidents when guests will be holding their meals, make sure you use plates that will not bend or get soggy.

A COLD GLASS OF ... To make cold drinks more inviting, chill the glasses in the refrigerator or freezer just before bringing them out. You can also fill them with crushed ice to chill them before serving.

DON'T SCOOP WITH GLASSES. Use a separate metal or plastic scoop to place crushed ice or cubes in a glass. Don't scoop the ice using the glass itself because it may chip or break. Also, don't chill glasses by embedding them in crushed ice, for the same reason. Instead, place the ice in the glass, and then dump it out when you serve the drink.

LARGER CUBES. Remember, the larger the ice cube, the slower it will melt. Use plastic cups or other larger containers to make ice for punch bowls.

JUICE CUBES. When making your punch, set aside some of the juice, put it in ice trays, freeze it, and use those cubes in the punch. As they melt, they'll add juice to the punch instead of water.

SERVE YOURSELF FIRST. Traditionally, hosts fill their own glass first when serving a new bottle of wine, to make sure there is no cork or other sediment in the wine of guests. (You can, of course, pour yourself another glass if there is an excess of cork in your glass.)

BOOZE CONTROL

EAT AND BE MERRY. "Eat, drink, and be merry" used to be the motto for partygoers and partygivers. Now people have become more wary about the "drink" portion of that phrase, for social, legal, and personal reasons.

So when you're planning a party, include provisions to monitor and control your guests' alcohol intake—especially their condition when leaving.

COCKTAIL ALTERNATIVES. Have a large supply of soft drinks, juices and other non-alcoholic beverages. Also offer festive boozeless drinks, like truly virgin Marys and non-alcoholic punches.

MAKE BAR VISIBLE. To help keep alcohol consumption under control, place the bar in the kitchen or another spot that is away from the main areas where people congregate. That way you'll be better able to keep an eye on the drinkmaking activity.

DON'T MAKE IT TOO EASY. If you make the bar area somewhat hard to get to, you can also reduce the temptation of guests to replenish their glasses continually. Or you can make the booze totally inaccessible, and serve drinks yourself or have a bartender.

HIDE THE EXTRAS. While you probably want enough alcohol to satisfy your guests, you don't have to put it all out at once at self-service bars. Keep your backup bottles hidden away, and only bring them out when necessary, so the supply will look smaller.

PREPARE FOR AFTERWARD. Plan to handle guests who are not in a condition to drive home. Try to arrange for another guest to give them a lift. Also have the number of a cab company available and a supply of extra cash on hand to pay the fare if necessary. Have a bed or cot and sheets ready, in case it's better for them to sleep over.

AN ASSERTIVE FRIEND. Controlling the consumption of alcohol and the departure of inebriated guests can occasionally be awkward, and requires a combination of tact and forcefulness. If you're not the type of person who can comfortably handle the role—or if you're too busy—ask an assertive and diplomatic friend beforehand to help as bartender and to keep track of the condition of guests as they leave.

THIRST-INDUCING FOODS. You can reduce the urge to imbibe by avoiding thirst-inducing hors d'oeuvres and munchies, such as salted peanuts.

HOME ENTERTAINMENT EQUIPMENT

You don't want to end up trying to drive the Information Superhighway with a Model T, so it's especially important to shop carefully for electronic equipment today.

Technology is changing so quickly that experts can't keep up, let alone the average homeowner who simply wants to make wise purchases for enjoyment and information.

Often the different versions of new technologies are not compatible with each other. This creates numerous dilemmas. Should you replace your outdated equipment now or wait until the equipment you are considering becomes more widely accepted? How do you choose between one format and another, if the selection of material you can play on them is different?

For example, the battle between different video-tape formats of the 1980's has settled down enough to make the purchase of a VCR a fairly safe bet today. But laser discs are also becoming more popular and often offer special features and programming not available on video.

While there are no easy answers, your chances of making the right choice will be increased if you keep one eye on the present and the other on the future. Read up in consumer publications and general-interest newspapers and magazines to find out what's the safest bet this week, and what will be most compatible with next week's changes. Is that television equipped to handle the explosion of cable channels? Can you eventually hook it up to a computer as interactive services become more widespread?

EQUIPMENT TIPS

LET OTHERS PIONEER. It's best to wait a while before buying the latest gizmo on the market. Let others be the pioneers. That way, you'll know it will be useful in the long run, rather than becoming obsolete soon after it has been introduced. It also gives the manufacturers more time to work the bugs out, and prices generally are lowered as a product becomes established.

HARDWARE AND SOFTWARE. Those are buzzwords to remember when you're shopping around for equipment. In plain English, hardware is the equipment and software is the material that is played or recorded on that equipment. A VCR machine is the hardware, the tapes of movies and programming available to play on it is the software.

WHAT SOFTWARE IS OFFERED? Before you choose one format, look at the catalog of albums, movies, and other material available for it. Is there already a good selection of software for it? And is the choice likely to grow over time, or will the format be abandoned by its makers? (Remember 8-track tape players?)

COST OF THE SOFTWARE. Also consider the cost of the software. You don't want to buy sexy new equipment and then not be able to afford to buy material that plays on it.

THE SHAPE OF TV. The movement to change the shape of television is underway—literally. Television's visual quality is being improved by altering the traditional box-shaped image to wider screens proportioned like those in movie theaters. But the exact technology is still being fought over in the marketplace. If you are considering an expensive television for the longterm, make sure you know the prospects for the type of system and screen you're buying.

TOO COMPLICATED? Make sure you and your family can actually figure out how to use the equipment you're considering. If you want a lot of bells and whistles, make sure that the equipment is designed so that the most technologically klutzy member of the family can at least figure out the basic controls.

CABLE CHOICES. Before deciding on a package of channels when ordering cable TV service, peruse a few weeks' worth of TV Guides or newspaper television listings and visualize yourself sitting down on the couch with remote control in hand. How often do the channels on more expensive packagers offer something you're really likely watch? Are there at least specific channels in the higher-priced selection that appeal to you enough to justify paying for channels you're never likely to visit?

CABLE COSTS: NOW OR LATER? If you're considering saving money on your cable bill by temporarily ordering a lower-priced package of channels, make sure it is economically worthwhile. Some cable companies may charge a hefty service fee to change subscription packages. If yours does, figure out the monthly savings between the lower- and higher-priced packages. Divide that amount into the changeover cost. This will tell you how many months you'll have to postpone the upgrade to actually save money. You may find that it's more economical to keep or start with the higher-priced service, rather than pay the extra service charge to upgrade a few months from now.

TUNE IN THE WORLD. For a fascinating alternative to the usual radio fare, buy a receiver that has shortwave (or world-band), as well as AM and FM. Shortwave listening is not just for technical nerds. On world-band radio you'll find news, music, documentaries, drama, sports, and many other programs in English and other languages from the BBC and hundreds of other broadcasters throughout the world. And shortwave receivers today are almost as inexpensive, portable, and easy to use as your basic AM/FM radio.

ANTENNA TIP. For the best and most versatile reception of FM, buy a directional antenna with controls that allow you to adjust its position for different stations. A stationary antenna that can't be adjusted means that you'll have to choose one position that may be good for one station, but does not receive another as well.

LONGER ISN'T BETTER. If you're having trouble getting a clear signal on a station, try shortening the antenna. Sometimes stations fail to come in clearly because their signal is overloaded or the antenna is picking up interference from other sources.

FINE-TUNING. Look for radios or tuners that allow you to fine-tune the station. Some only go from the center of one frequency to the center of the next, which doesn't allow you to make the tiny adjustments that can reduce interference and find the sharpest signal.

SURROUNDING SOUND. Even the humblest of TVs and VCRs can often make your home sound like a movie theater when hooked up to your home stereo system. Look in the rear panel for the audio output jacks. Buy connection cables with plugs that match the design of the jacks on the TV or VCR on one end and the stereo on the other. Some VCRs will give you stereo sound, others may be mono, but still give a dramatic aural effect. (If you're buying a new VCR or TV, look for one that can pump stereo into your stereo.)

KEEP THE ORIGINALS. If you've decided to cull your records to save space, look up their value before disposing of them. With the emergence of CDs, the value of record albums is rising among record-loving audiophiles and collectors.

SPEED FOR QUALITY. To save money and get more time from your videotapes, use the slowest recording speed when you're taping a program. If you want the best recording and playback quality (and are willing to use up significantly more tape), use the fastest speed.

A TAPING TAPE. How often has a program come on that you want to tape at the last minute, but you don't have a fresh tape ready? (Or you're not sure what is on the tapes you have on hand?) One way around this dilemma is to buy two tapes specifically earmarked for last-minute taping-one for shows you are just taping to watch once at a later time, the other for movies or programs you want to keep for posterity. Keep them handy and clearly marked.

KEEP TAPES REWOUND. Video tapes should always be rewound to the beginning when they aren't in use. Don't leave tapes in the middle when you remove them and put them away. If you want to add new material on a partially-recorded tape, don't leave it at the point where you want to start taping. Instead, note the tape counter reading where you can start taping new material or make a small mark by the tape window on the cassette. Then fast-forward to that point when recording.

NO MAGNETS. Keep your video and cassette tapes away from speakers or other devices that have magnets in them. Magnetic fields will erase or degrade the tapes.

CLEANING CDS. When you clean compact discs, gently move the cleaning cloth in a straight line form the center of the disc out to the edge (or vice versa), instead of using a circular motion. Scratches that are semi-circular are more likely to affect the sound quality of CDs than lines across them.

STORING ALBUMS. Your record albums should be stored vertically, and with enough pressure to support the entire albums evenly from both sides. If the pressure is not even, the jacket and record can be bent out of shape, especially those towards the ends of the row.

BASS BOOST. For the most balanced sound, place speakers off the floor on stands, and away from walls or corners. Placing speakers against walls, directly on the floor, or in corners will increase the bass levels, often at the expense of the middle and higher frequencies. (However, a tinny speaker might benefit from such a bass boost.)

EAR LEVEL. The upper half of the speakers should be close to the height of your ears in the position you are most likely to be listening, to make higher frequencies more audible.

TRIANGLE OF SOUND. To create the best stereo effect with two speakers, pick the spot you are most often listening from. Then place the speakers so that they and you are all an equal distance apart. While there are many variables in the size and shape of rooms, the closer you can get to this arrangement the better.

Bibliography

Clutter Control by Jeff Campbell. New York: Dell Publishing, 1992

500 Terrific Ideas for Organizing Everything by Sheree Bykofsky. New York: Simon & Schuster, 1992.

500 Terrific Ideas for Cleaning Everything by Don Aslett. New York: Simon & Schuster, 1991

The Handbook of Do-It-Yourself Materials by Max Alth. New York: Crown Publisher, 1982.

The Prevention How-To Dictionary of Healing Remedies and Techniques edited by John Feltman. Emmaus, PA: Rodale Press, 1992.

The Doctors Book of Home Remedies by the editors of Prevention Magazine Health Books. New York: Bantam Books, 1991.

Henley's Formulas for Home and Workshop edited by Gardner D. Hiscox. New York: Crown Publishers, revised edition 1979. Originally published in 1907.

Mary Ellen's Best of Helpful Hints by Mary Ellen Pinkham and Pearl Higginbotham. New York: Warner Books, 1979.

Mary Ellen's Best of Helpful Hints Book II by Mary Ellen Pinkham. New York: Warner Books, 1981.

Ideas That Really Work by Mary Ellen Pinkham. Minneapolis: Mary Ellen Pinkham, 1992.

Hints from Heloise by Heloise. New York: Avon Books, 1980.

All-New Hints from Heloise: A Household Guide for the '90s. New York: Perigee Books, 1989.

Heloise Household Hints for Singles by Heloise. New York: Perigee Books, 1993.

The Smart Kitchen by David Goldbeck. Woodstock, NY: Ceres Press, 1994.

Organize Your Home by Ronni Eisenberg with Kate Kelly. New York, Hyperion, 1994.

Clean & Green: The Complete Guide to Non Toxic and Environmentally Safe Housekeeping by Annie Berthold-Bond. Woodstock, NY: Ceres Press, 1994.

Consumer Guide to Home Energy Savings by Alex Wilson and John Morrill. American Council for an Energy-Efficient Economy, 1991.

Fifty Simple Things You Can Do to Save the Earth by The Earth Works Group. Berkeley, CA: Earthworks Press, 1989.

The Next Step: Fifty More Things You Can Do to Save the Earth by The Earth Works Group. Earth Works Press, 1991.

1,001 Helpful Tips, Facts and Hints from Consumer Reports by the editors of Consumer Reports Books. Mount Vernon, NY: Consumers Union, 1989.

How to Clean Practically Anything by the editors of Consumer Reports Books. Yonkers, NY: Consumers Union, 1992.

Living Poor With Style by Ernest Callenbach. New York: Bantam Books, 1972.

Getting Organized! by Arline Bleecker. Boca Raton, FL: Globe Communications, 1994.

The Indoor Kitchen Garden by Joy O.I. Spoczynska. New York: Harper & Row Publishers, 1989.

Child's Play by Leslie Hamilton. New York: Crown Publishers, 1989.

Household Hints and Tips by Better Homes and Gardens. London: Dorling Kindersley Ltd., 1989.

365 Ways to Prepare for Christmas by David E. Monn. New York: Harper Collins Publishers, 1993.

76 Ways to Get Organized for Christmas by Bonnie McCullough and Bev Cooper. New York: St. Martin's Press, 1982.

Family Circle Hints, Tips & Smart Advice, edited by Carol Guasti. New York: The Family Circle Inc., 1988.

The American Frugal Housewife. Boston: Applewood Books, 1832.

Once-A-Month Cooking by Mimi Wilson and Mary Beth Lagerborg. Colorado Spring, CO: Focus on the Family Publishing, 1992.

The Fuel Savers by Bruce Anderson. Lafayette, CA: Morning Sun Press, 1991.

Too Busy to Clean? by Patti Barrett. Pownal, VT: Storey Publishing, 1990.

Better House and Planet by Marjorie Harris. Toronto: Key Porter Books, 1991.

The Tightwad Gazette by Amy Dacyczyn. New York: Villard Books, 1993.

Money and Time-Saving Household Hints. The Leader-Post Carrier Foundation, Inc., 1992.

The Home-Owner's Survival Manual by Alex Markovich. New York: Crescent Books, 1992.

Sunset Home Repair Handbook. Menlo Park, CA: Sunset Publishing Corp., 1992.

Reader's Digest Practical Problem Solver. Pleasantville, NY: The Reader's Digest Association, 1991.

Reader's Digest Household Hints and Handy Tips. Pleasantville, NY: The Reader's Digest Association, 1988.

Kitchen Wisdom by Frieda Arkin. New York: Holt, Rinehart and Winston, 1977.

The Expert's Guide to Backyard Bird Feeding by Bill Adler Jr. and Heidi Hughes. New York: Crown Publisher's Inc., 1990.

The Complete Home Improvement and Renovation Manual by the editors of the Time-Life Home Repair and Improvement Series. New York: Prentice Hall Press, 1991.

Government Publications

A Home Buyer's Guide to Environmental Hazards, U.S. Environmental Protection Agency.

A Citizen's Guide to Radon, U.S. Environmental Protection Agency

What You Can Do to Reduce Air Pollution, U.S. Environmental Protection Agency.

Green Advertising Claims, U.S. Environmental Protection Agency.

Tips for Energy Savers, U.S. Department of Energy.

Growing Vegetables in the Home Garden, U.S. Department of Agriculture.
Heating with Wood, U.S. Department of Agriculture.
Eating for Life, U.S. Department of Health and Human Services.
Your Money's Worth in Foods, U.S. Department of Agriculture.
Eating Better When Eating Out, U.S. Department of Agriculture.
Making Bag Lunches, Snacks and Desserts, U.S. Department of Agriculture
How to Read the New Food Label, U.S. Food and Drug Administration
Home Wiring Hazards, U.S. Consumer Product Safety Commission.
Illustrated Guidelines for Rehabilitating Historic Buildings, U.S. Department of Interior.
Asbestos in the Home, U.S. Consumer Product Safety Commission
Biological Pollutants in Your Home, U.S. Consumer Product Safety Commission.
Your Home Fire Safety Checklist, U.S. Consumer Product Safety Commission.
Simple Home Repairs: Outside, U.S. Department of Agriculture.
Simple Home Repairs: Inside, U.S. Department of Agriculture.
Cool Tips for a Hot Season, U.S. Department of Health and Human Services.
We the Americans...Our Homes, U.S. Department of Commerce.
Backyard Bird Problems, U.S. Department of Interior.
Buying a Used Car, Federal Trade Commission.
Recycling Used Oil, U.S. Environmental Protection Agency.

Index